Successful
Pension Design
For Small- to Medium-Sized Businesses

second edition

Robert F. Slimmon

Prentice-Hall, Inc.
Englewood Cliffs, New Jersey 07632

Library of Congress Cataloging-in-Publication Data

Slimmon, Robert F. (date)
  Successful pension design for small-to medium-sized
businesses.

  Includes index.
  1. Pension trusts. 2. Small business—Personal
management. 3. Profit-sharing. I. Title.
HD7105.4.S56   1987   658.3.253   87-2489
ISBN 0-13-860255-7

Editorial/production supervision: Lisa Schulz Garboski
Interior design: Meridee Mucciarone
Manufacturing buyer: Margaret Rizzi

The publisher offers discounts on this book when ordered
in bulk quantities. For more information, write:
  Special Sales/College Marketing
  Prentice-Hall, Inc.
  College Technical and Reference Division
  Englewood Cliffs, NJ 07632

Printed in the United States of America

10 9 8 7 6 5 4

ISBN 0-13-860255-7
ISBN 0-13-864620-1   {SPECIAL ED.}   025

Prentice-Hall International (UK) Limited, *London*
Prentice-Hall of Australia Pty. Limited, *Sydney*
Prentice-Hall Canada Inc., *Toronto*
Prentice-Hall Hispanoamericana, S.A., *Mexico*
Prentice-Hall of India Private Limited, *New Delhi*
Prentice-Hall of Japan, Inc., *Tokyo*
Prentice-Hall of Southeast Asia Pte. Ltd., *Singapore*
Editora Prentice-Hall do Brasil, Ltda., *Rio de Janeiro*

For Rebecca, Sarah, Bissie, and Mr. Potato Head,
who provide the incentive to get projects like this done.

Contents

Chapter 3 Effective Use of Integration: The Key to Pension Design 37

Chapter 4 How Defined Contribution Plans Should Be Set Up for Maximum Results 51

✓ Chapter 5 Setting Up Effective Profit Sharing Plans to Compensate Employees for Inflation 69

Chapter 8   How Defined Benefit Pension Plans Can Boost Plan Efficiency   147

Chapter 13   Special Considerations in Plan Design   237

Preface: What This Book Will Do for You

Pension and profit sharing plans provide one of the most comprehensive planning tools available for small businesses attempting to accumulate, manage, and efficiently dispose of an estate. No other single medium can provide a complete income tax deduction for contributions, totally tax-deferred investment return, and favorable taxation on ultimate distributions. All of this is available from a pension plan, without the risks generally associated with other tax shelters. And yet many small businessmen do not have qualified plans. Why?

Everyone can agree on the positive nature of these advantages. Unfortunately, putting them into practice is very difficult. Complicated actuarial methods, the maze of government rules and burdensome regulations surrounding such key topics as integration, and the cost of covering non-key employees in a poorly designed plan have all discouraged practitioners from recommending plans for their clients. *Successful Pension Design for Small- to Medium-Sized Businesses* can help.

This book will unlock the mysteries of pension design for you and your clients. It will simplify the concepts of actuarial methodology so that you can effectively use those concepts to your advantage. It will explain the critical element of plan design—integration—so that pension contributions can be slanted toward higher-paid participants. It will show you how to measure your clients' objectives, to identify the right plan for a situation, and to control the ongoing efficient administration of that plan. Most importantly, you will learn the *secrets* of pension design.

Most small businesses have a limited budget for their pension plans. Before they adopt a plan they must be shown that it will benefit primarily their key employees. You will see how different parameters such as age and service can affect the budget chosen by a particular businessperson. Also, they must be shown that the tax advantages of a qualified plan will not be offset by administrative and employee costs. These are the subjects of pension design.

Successful Pension Design for Small- to Medium-Sized Businesses explores in depth the myriad alternative types of pension plans. To ensure an "apples-to-apples" comparison, as well as to keep the design process within the constraints of a budget, the book analyzes most alternative plan formats with reference to consistent employee census information and contributions. Therefore you can see the effect of changing actuarial assumptions, plan design, integration, or other factors that control pension costs and contribution allocations. When not otherwise stated, all interest for pre- and post-retirement discounting is at 7%.

This book sets forth numerous tables, charts, forms, checklists, and over 40 planning tips to aid you. Where illustrations are included, you will see why certain techniques were used to accomplish a positive result for your client. You will be able to see what situation would be most suitable to a particular plan. Several sophisticated plan documents appear for reference in the Appendix. You will see how to provide nonshareholder employees with maximum benefits at the least cost to the company. You will see the advantages and disadvantages of choosing a fiduciary as well as the steps for terminating a plan.

The following questions indicate just a few of the situations for which this book offers practical answers:

- What happens when your client's financial situation changes? How do you make changes in midstream?

- Games Company's President and key person, Ms. Parker, wants to know what the comparative costs would be in terms of initial contributions of utilizing an aggressive versus a conservative set of actuarial assumptions. What do you tell her?

- How do you plan around the Limitation on Annual Additions to get the greatest benefit for your client?

- As sole stockholder and key employee of DEF Corporation, John wants to set up a two-tiered defined contribution plan that will provide him with the maximum annual addition. What would be the contribution rate for generating John's maximum annual addition?

- What happens when a business owner who is contemplating setting up a defined benefit plan providing retirement income equal to 50 percent of pay has two employees, each earning $75,000 annually, and one is 20 years older than the other?

- Compare Incorporated is considering a defined contribution or a defined benefit plan and has $20,000 to spend. What are the choices offered by these two alternatives?

With this book you will be able to show your clients their alternatives. You will be able to explain the long-term advantages and disadvantages of those alternatives. You will gain in-depth knowledge of the jargon and special rules that have previously made pension plans an attractive but excessively complicated subject. With this knowledge, you can provide your client with guidance in what is probably the most efficient capital accumulation and transfer vehicle available in our economy.

The book is updated for TEFRA, REA, ODRA and TRA '86, and Social Security benefits as of October 1986. It therefore can be used as a guide to design in the post-TRA '86 era. However, the book **does not** deal with TRA '86's transitional rules, a subject of significant import but so complex as to require a volume of similar size. Therefore practitioners dealing with pre-TRA '86 plans should seek specific guidance about the applicability of transitional rules and safe harbors. Some, but not all, are pointed out in the text. Finally, the book goes to press without the guidance of IRS Regulations with respect to TRA '86 and represents the author's best (conservative) estimate of how things will shape up. Any pension practitioner should check updates in his or her pension service.

There are entirely different motivations for a small- and medium-sized businessman's implementation of a qualified plan from those of his counterpart in a large organization. These different motivations spring simultaneously from a lack of extensive capital resources and the entrepreneurial instinct of smaller business owners. *Successful Pension Design for Small- to Medium-Sized Businesses* has been written to address the objectives of these entrepreneurs and smaller business owners and operators.

Robert F. Slimmon

1

Why Your Small Business Clients Need Qualified Plans

In this Chapter we will discuss the benefits inherent in well-designed qualified plans as well as provide the facts you need to whet and maintain your clients' interest.

¶100 *HOW YOUR CLIENTS WILL BENEFIT FROM QUALIFIED PLANS*

Most practitioners perceive qualified plans as powerful tax planning tools. However, they also discover that these plans have a complicated web of reporting and disclosure requirements that can bog down the planning process. It is important to generate sufficient enthusiasm with the positive aspects of qualified plans to "carry" your client through the planning process. The positive aspects are quite compelling and include the following:

1. Income tax deductions for contributions, the bulk of which should go to key employees, without current income tax consequences;

2. Postponement of, and increased options for, taxation of benefits ultimately received;

3. A "carrot and stick" motivational tool to attract and retain key employees; and

4. Tax-deferred return on invested assets.

1

The combination of these factors provides compelling reasons to consider qualified plans. With the 1986 Tax Bill's elimination of many traditional tax shelters, qualified plans now, more than ever, represent the ''best show in town.''

¶101 *HOW TO IDENTIFY THE RIGHT TYPE OF CLIENT*

Small businesses confront monumental challenges. They are generally undercapitalized, they must compete with the broad advertising capacity of larger competitors, and they usually lack the manpower to develop a structured and sophisticated business organization. For those few small businesses that overcome these obstacles, the most vexing problem of all awaits—taxation. Income, gift, and estate taxation lurk behind every transaction. It is little wonder that most small businessmen value the relationship with their tax accountant or attorney highest among their relationships with professional advisors.

The first step in identifying whether your client is a good prospect is a thorough analysis of his or her personal and business status to determine whether problems exist that qualified plans can solve. The answer isn't always self-evident. The following three tests will help.

¶101.1 *The Psychological Test—Has Your Client's Lifestyle Matured?*

The self-sacrifice and self-discipline that are prerequisites for a small business's success create an interesting psychological dilemma. When a small businessman achieves financial success, he is often torn between spending his new-found wealth to make up for past abstinence and continuing the frugal instincts that contributed to his success. Frequently these clients develop a ''you can't take it with you'' attitude, which leads to a substantially more expensive lifestyle—larger home, larger cars, more vacations, and so on.

The problem is commonly compounded by high educational expenses that seem to mature at the same time as the business. These factors tend to create cash flow problems at a time heavy taxation creates the greatest incentive for plan implementation.

Your client will not be a good prospect for *any* sort of qualified retirement plan unless he or she:

1. wants to save money;

2. can afford to save money;

3. needs to save money; and/or

4. wants to protect his employees.

In other words, his personal financial goals must largely have been fulfilled. He must have reasonably satisfied his material needs and still have disposable cash flow. If this hasn't occurred, then no matter how cleverly you design a retirement program, your time and effort will have been wasted. The primary prerequisite for setting up a pension or profit sharing plan for a small businessman is that he makes the long-term *personal* commitment to "stick with" his plan.

¶101.2   *How Mature Is Your Client's Business?*

Just as important as the business owner's personal need for cash is the business's cash flow demand. If there is going to be a plan, the company must have disposable income. Often there is no disposable income for one of the following reasons:

1. To achieve success the business owner has continually reinvested company earnings;

2. The business is capital intensive and requires substantial disposable cash for current operations;

3. The owner, to satisfy his own personal financial goals, "zeroes out" the business's income by paying himself year-end bonuses, leaving no cash in the company; or

4. The business is in a period of growth so excess cash is committed to plant capacity and personnel expansion.

If some or all of the above factors are present, your client may be better off without a qualified plan even though his being without one will result in higher taxes. Sometimes it is more important to have accessible after-tax dollars than to have pre-tax dollars tied up in a plan.

¶101.3   *How to Apply the Corporate and Personal Tax Test to Your Client*

The single most important reason to implement a qualified retirement program in a small business is to avoid corporate and personal income taxes. Generally a qualified plan's effectiveness will be proportional to your client's personal marginal income tax rate. The tax rate applicable to your client's business is of lesser importance, at least in the small plan domain. This is so because he's unlikely to leave much taxable income in the corporation, preferring to take bonuses instead, or electing Subchapter S status to avoid the problem altogether.

Example

Many small businessmen are impressed with the low 22% effective tax rate applicable to their first $100,000 of corporate earnings. They argue in favor of paying the tax and leaving the balance in the business. If Savit Company earns $50,000 of corporate income, it pays a total tax of only $7,500. Compared to confiscatory personal rates, that seems fairly mild. And, perhaps, the $42,500 left in the business can earn a higher rate of return than alternative investment media. However, consider the option presented by a qualified plan assuming a comparable investment return.

Year	Corporate Income Available	After-Tax Corporate Income	Cumulative Invested @ 10% Gross*	Potential Pension Contribution	Cumulative Invested @ 10%
1	$50,000	$42,500	$ 46,113	$50,000	$ 55,000
2	50,000	42,500	96,145	50,000	115,500
3	50,000	42,500	150,430	50,000	182,050
4	50,000	42,500	209,329	50,000	255,255
5	50,000	42,500	273,234	50,000	335,781
6	50,000	42,500	342,571	50,000	424,359
7	50,000	42,500	417,802	50,000	521,794
8	50,000	42,500	499,428	50,000	628,974
9	50,000	42,500	587,992	50,000	746,871
10	50,000	42,500	689,004	50,000	876,558
20	50,000	42,500	2,230,786	50,000	3,150,125
30	50,000	42,500	5,727,852	50,000	9,047,171

*The 10% yield assumed would also be subject to tax, assumed here to be 22%. This example pointedly illustrates the potential power of a Qualified Plan . . . the 20-year projected pension balance of $3,150,125 is 141% of the amount that would be accumulated within the Company.

ADDITIONAL PROBLEMS MAY FOIL YOUR CLIENT'S ATTEMPT TO USE HIS CORPORATION AS A TAX SHELTER

Apart from the attractiveness of pension plans as accumulation vehicles for surplus funds, these plans offer your client protection from two additional pitfalls:

1. **Accumulated earnings tax penalties** can be applied to businesses that retain earnings beyond their reasonable needs. The "trigger mechanism" for most small businesses comes at $250,000 of accumulated earnings. The penalty for retained earnings is dire—27½% of the first $100,000 and 38½% of the excess—in addition to regular corporate taxes; and

2. **The earnings may trigger a higher tax** when the owner tries to get them out of the business. Suppose your client accumulates $100,000 in his business after paying the low corporate tax rate. What does he do with the $100,000 if he doesn't need it for the operation of his business? Paying it out as salary or bonus will trigger more taxes at the personal tax rate. Collapsing the corporation through liquidation to obtain long-term capital gains has lost its viability in light of the Tax Reform Act of 1986—capital gain rates will be the same as ordinary income. Thus, the short-term use of the corporate shelter may lead to long-term problems.

In short, the key income tax test for small businesses should be applied to the owner and his key employees, since sooner or later business earnings will be paid out to employees. If your client's corporate or personal tax bracket is 30% or higher, he should at least consider how a well-designed plan could retrieve lost tax dollars.

A Word About Tax Rates. As this book goes to press, Congress has just enacted the Tax Reform Act of 1986 (TRA '86) with much ballyhoo about "lower" tax rates. However, with a massive federal budget deficit, the ink was barely dry on TRA '86 before talk of raising the "Reformed" rates began. Planners may be well advised to present plan illustrations to their clients showing future results not only based on today's "low" rates, but also on higher rates that may be required in the future.

¶101.4   *A Checklist for Profiling the Ideal Prospect*

Your client is a good candidate for a qualified plan if he

- is taking enough salary to satisfy his personal needs comfortably;
- doesn't have any major "cash crunch" on the horizon such as college expenses for which no funds have been set aside;
- is subject to a high personal tax rate;
- is conscious enough of his goals to establish a reasonably long-term "game plan" and has the self-discipline to stick with it;

and if his business

- generates cash in excess of operational requirements;
- has adequate reserves to weather periodic economic slowdowns; and/or
- doesn't anticipate major structural, operational, or personnel changes that cash reserves or bank financing wouldn't adequately cover.

If your client passes this simple ''screening test,'' you ought to tell him what a qualified plan can do. Better that you can explain the pros and cons and have him reject the idea than risk his finding out about the opportunities from someone else.

¶102   USING PENSION PLANS TO ACHIEVE YOUR CLIENT'S GOALS—A COMPARISON OF TWO ALTERNATIVES

The tax advantages of qualified plans are generally well known and understood. However, because they are so important they warrant repetition. For comparative purposes let's assume your client has a pre-tax sum of $10,000 per year for investment and is in the 30% income tax bracket. He considers the following options:

1. a pension plan invested in long-term stocks and bonds expected to provide a total return of 12%;

2. a portfolio of tax-free municipal bonds yielding 7%; or

3. a personal portfolio of stocks and bonds with an aggregate yield of 12%.

Your client asks you to evaluate these alternatives, primarily from the tax perspective.

¶102.1   *How Pension Plans Can Multiply Your Client's Investable Dollars*

If your client wants to personally buy municipal bonds or a stock/bond portfolio, his first check will be to the IRS. These purchases can only be made from after-tax dollars. Thus the $10,000 will be whittled down to $7,000 before any investment can be made. On the other hand, contributions to qualified plans are deductible; therefore no tax need be paid on the $10,000 deposit.

Here is a simple comparative illustration:

Item	Municipal Bonds	Stock/Bond Portfolio	Pension Plan
Pre-tax Dollars to Invest	$10,000	$10,000	$10,000
Less: Income Taxes Payable	(3,000)	(3,000)	(00)
Net Available for Investment	$ 7,000	$ 7,000	$10,000

With the pension alternative your client will have 43% more dollars to invest. Over a 20-year period he will have invested $200,000, as opposed to $140,000 under either the municipal bond or stock/bond portfolio alternatives. That type of leverage may command his interest.

¶102.2   *How To Multiply Your Client's Yield*

Tax-exempt bonds appeal to high-bracket taxpayers because their yield is exempt from federal income tax. High-bracket taxpayers accept a slightly lower rate of return, or "spread," since after taxes, they represent a better net yield than that available under higher return but taxable investments. A portfolio of stocks and bonds used to be attractive because some of the appreciation would be taxed at the long-term capital gains rate, substantially lower than that used for ordinary income. Under TRA '86, this advantage is lost. However, investments in qualified pension trusts are exempt from current taxation. Thus, pension plans may offer the best of both worlds—high rates of return with deferred taxation. Over a long period of time tax-free compounding is the most significant aspect of pension plans.

Following through with the simple analysis in 102.1, let's see how your client fares under the three alternatives compared:

Item	Municipal Bond	Stock/Bond Portfolio	Pension Plan
Amount Invested (see 102.1)	$7,000	$7,000	$10,000
Rate of Return	× 7%	× 12%	× 12%
First Year Earnings	490	840	1,200
Less: Income Taxes	0	(252)	(0)
Net Income	$ 490	$ 588	$ 1,200

The long-term effect of this tax-free compounding, combined with larger amounts available for investment because of tax deductibility of pension contributions, really adds up. Consider the cumulative effects of our analysis after 10, 20, or 30 years:

Time Period	Municipal Bond	Stock/Bond Portfolio	Pension Plan
10 Years	$ 73,918	$ 80,024	$ 196,546
20 Years	219,323	259,298	806,987
30 Years	505,365	660,911	2,702,926

Pointing out to your client how he can double or triple his accumulated assets simply by using the tax-deductible medium afforded by pension plans will probably enhance your professional position. However, a logical question from your client might be, "If this is true, is there a devastating tax when I take the money out?"

¶103   WHAT ARE THE TAX EFFECTS WHEN TAKING MONEY OUT OF PENSION PLANS?

Your client will receive the benefits he has accumulated in the plan in most cases either at his retirement or his death. Thus, it is important to consider the ultimate tax effects at distribution time. Surprisingly these results continue the trend of favorable taxation for qualified retirement plans. The following discussion will show you the alternative distribution methods available and how they work.

¶103.1   *Ten-Year Income Averaging and Its Tax Effect*

If your client was a plan participant and had attained age 50 by January 1, 1986, 10-year income averaging may prove to be the most favorable of all distribution methods. Ten-year income averaging is really very simple. Merely compute the tax on one tenth of the total distribution (plus $2,480) as if no other income were received. Then multiply that tax by 10. The product becomes the total tax on the distribution. Ten-year income averaging can yield very favorable results.

Consider the following taxes applicable to lump-sum distributions under 10-year income averaging:

Amount of Distribution	Total Tax	Net Distribution	Effective Tax Rate
$100,000	$ 15,420	$ 84,580	15%
300,000	73,050	226,950	24%
500,000	157,730	342,270	32%

The above table should answer your client's well-conceived question about taxes at distribution time. The pension plan is at least 50% more efficient than its closest competitor. However, TRA '86 phases out 10-year income averaging (except as indicated above), and replaces it with 5-year income averaging. Effectively, that means most larger plan distributions will be taxed at approximately 28%.

For your interest, here's a chart (based on 1988 Tax Rates) showing income taxes for various-sized distributions if they're eligible for 5-year income averaging:

Amount of Distribution	Tax Under 5-Year Rule
$ 50,000	6,900 (13.8%)
100,000	16,450 (16.4%)
250,000	60,110 (24%)
500,000	142,610 (28.5%)
1,000,000	282,270 (28.2%)

Important Note.   TRA '86 also added a significant trap: an excise tax of 15% on annual benefit payments in excess of $112,500 (unless the benefits were accrued prior to August 1, 1986). For purposes of lump sums, the $112,500 becomes $562,500. Note that on lump sum distributions larger than about $400,000, 5-year income averaging actually is preferable.

¶103.2 *Periodic Payments Provide One Alternative*

Rather than a lump-sum distribution, a retiring participant may elect a series of periodic payments over a time frame not exceeding the joint life expectancy of himself and his spouse. If periodic payments are elected as the distribution method, the payments are simply added to the retired participant's other income as they are received. Since most of your clients, as small businessmen, will have accumulated substantial other assets prior to their retirement, they are likely to have additional income. If that's the case, then the periodic payments will probably be thrown into the 28% bracket.

Let's suppose we *are* subjected to the top rate of 28%. Consider the ultimate bottom line of our example and paragraph 102.2:

	Municipal Bond	Stock/Bond Portfolio	Pension Plan
Amount Accumulated, 30 years	$505,365	$660,911	$2,702,926
Income Tax Liability	N/A	N/A	(756,819)
Net Distribution	$505,365	$660,911	$1,946,107

Caution.   Never assume that the results of comparisons like the ones above can be generalized. Most of your clients will be well worth the time it takes to analyze the alternatives thoroughly. Frequently, unusual personal circumstances affect the decision about what distribution method to use. Also, remember to beware of the 15% excise tax on benefit payments exceeding $112,500 under TRA '86.

¶104   WHAT ARE THE TRADITIONAL PROBLEMS WITH QUALIFIED PLANS?

Clients and practitioners frequently raise several common issues, thus blocking or forestalling implementation of qualified plans. These include:

1. communication limitations imposed by the special jargon applicable to qualified plans;

2. the financial and legal liability associated with qualification and administration of the plan; and

3. the cost of covering non-key employees.

Let's examine each of the three common complaints separately.

¶104.1   *How to Overcome the Problem of Pension Jargon*

The pension business, like many other professional services, involves words or terms uniquely applicable to the pension field. Phrases such as "actuarial equivalency," "funding standard account," and "limitation on annual additions'' make plans seem overly complicated and, therefore, undesirable. To some extent that's true, since many pension functions can't be explained in simple layman's language.

The fact is that many clients will not ''buy'' what they cannot understand, and the time involved in explaining these terms often does not justify the reward. However, the opportunities illustrated in this chapter are clearly worth pursuing. The easiest solution is to present plans to your client with numeric illustrations rather than verbal explanations. Attract your client's attention with the tax advantages before introducing him to the jargon.

¶104.2 *How to Solve the Legal and Financial Burden of Qualification, Reporting, and Disclosure*

Pension plans require constant attention. The design process can take several months. Preparation of documents for submission to the IRS to obtain a Letter of Determination involves substantial clerical and supervisory time. Dealing with the IRS to make the amendments necessary to obtain such a letter is an unpredictable time burden. Ongoing reporting and disclosure are very time consuming, and constant monitoring is required because the government frequently revises its procedures and regulations. Retirement plans have been a major focal point of legislation for the last decade. Further, even if your firm provides only part of the services required and some other ''link in the chain'' breaks down, your client may look to you as the responsible party.

These are legitimate concerns, both from the client's perspective (he must understand the ongoing services and charges that will be associated with maintenance of his plan), and also from your perspective (you may not feel qualified or want to make the time commitment involved in proper handling of plans).

The Solutions. If you feel strongly that the opportunities inherent in well-designed pension plans are too great to ignore, you must do one of two things:

1. Make an affirmative commitment to be in the pension business, meaning that you or a member of your firm must devote most of his or her energies to the qualification and administrative problems associated with your plans; or

2. Develop a qualified plan ''team'' of advisors who, among them, can provide sufficient
   a. expertise;
   b. continuity; and
   c. sound financial structure

to handle your client's needs. The "team" may well involve an attorney, an accountant, an investment advisor, and others. Critical to the success of any team, however, is the orderly and effective delegation of responsibilities, objectives, timetables, and monitoring systems.

¶104.3 *Who Should Do What on the Pension Team?*

A typical planning team involves an attorney, an accountant, a plan administrator, and an investment advisor. Their respective tasks are detailed below:

1. **Attorney:** Ultimate responsibility for drafting initial plan documents, including
    a. Plan and Trust;
    b. IRS Submission Forms;
    c. Summary Plan Description;
    d. Notice to Interested Parties; and
    e. Notice of Participation.
    The attorney should also be responsible for overseeing the qualification process with the IRS, including proposed and finalized amendments. Finally, the attorney should be involved in the initial planning process, such as helping to decide what form of plan best fits the client's unique circumstances.

2. **Accountant:** Best qualified to comment on and illustrate the effects of the tax aspects and cash flow demands of a qualified plan. The accountant should also have input into all documents and submission materials prepared by the attorney and should be closely involved in budgeting and monitoring the cash flow required by the plan within the client's business.

3. **Plan Administrator:** Responsible for employer and employee record-keeping, calculation of accrued benefits and distribution amounts, and timely preparation of annual administrative forms for the government, the employer and the plan's participants. The plan administrator should be involved in every phase of plan design and document preparation, to insure that plan provisions are clear and easy to administrate. In most small companies, the plan administrator is either the company itself or one of its key employees, though the work and responsibilities are typically delegated either to the accountant or an outside firm specializing in plan administration.

4. **Investment Advisor:** Ultimate responsibility for selecting the investment or combination of investments best suited to fulfilling the corporate objectives contained in the plan. The investment advisor or

trustee has considerable ongoing responsibility to keep abreast of changing economic conditions and ensure that the goal can be met most efficiently by the funding policy utilized.

More important than any other aspect of delegation is the appointment of a team "captain." By far the largest source of dissatisfaction relative to qualified plans happens when one team member thinks that the other has been assigned a particular task, and the task goes unfinished. Constant communication among the team members, together with a clear understanding of who is the "captain," will make the pension planning process simple, profitable, and effective.

¶104.4 *The Cost of Covering Non-Key Employees—Major Obstacle to Implementation*

Most small businessmen, given the examples presented earlier in this chapter, would opt to put $10,000 a year into a qualified plan if the entire $10,000 went into their account. Unfortunately, even after applying exclusions for age, service, and coverage tests, there will still be employees left over who must be participants. Many small businessmen balk at providing pension coverage for employees they feel are overpaid and probably have no use for pension benefits anyway. Therefore a primary object of pension design in small closely held businesses is to minimize the cost of including non-key employees in qualified plans. This job has become very difficult in recent years as Congress has focused on tax-oriented pension plans as a source of revenue.

Obviously, if your client must put $3 in the plan for employees for every $10 he puts in for himself, he has achieved little in terms of his own personal financial statement. He will merely have "paid" employees money that he would otherwise have paid in taxes to the government. While he may prefer that, it usually does not provide sufficient incentive to establish a plan and endure the administrative burdens that follow. However, if he can put $9,000 into his own account and $1,000 in other employees' accounts, he can take the position that the $1,000 paid for regular employees was simply a "cost of doing business" to obtain $9,000 worth of tax advantages for himself. In fact, this is the essence of Plan Design in most small- to medium-sized companies.

This book will show you how you can help your client minimize that "cost of doing business." Most of your clients will tolerate or even appreciate a modicum of benefit/contribution for regular employees who have been with the firm for a certain period of time. Your job as a pension planner is to use aggressively the opportunities available to help your client fulfill that goal.

¶105   *SPECIAL CONSIDERATIONS FOR UNINCORPORATED BUSINESSES*

One of the most important changes to be wrought by TEFRA was to introduce the concept of "parity" between corporate and noncorporate entities in terms of retirement benefits and opportunities. In the past, sole proprietorship and partnership plans and, to a limited extent, plans of "Sub-S" businesses were required to use a completely different set of rules, assumptions, and reporting mechanisms in order to enjoy the privilege of a qualified plan. As of 1984, these unincorporated businesses have the same choices as their corporate cousins. Thus, the following material makes no distinction between corporate and unincorporated business entities. The practitioner should keep in mind two lingering unique aspects of unincorporated plans, however, since they do have some impact on planning.

¶105.1   *Special Compensation Taken Into Account*

In a conventional corporate retirement plan, compensation is simply the salary and/or the bonus of each employee (not exceeding $200,000). Since unincorporated businesses compute compensation as simply the "bottom line" after paying all business operating costs, including employee compensation, there needs to be a slight adjustment to the definition of compensation used in computing retirement plan benefits for these businesses. Very simply, the technique is to "back into" the compensation that an unincorporated businessman would have had after plan contributions if he had been incorporated. The result of this technique is that an unincorporated businessman can, using his regular "bottom-line income" as the benchmark, provide for plan benefits/contributions that are 80% of those of his corporate counterparts.

Example ———————————————————————
ABC is a corporation whose key employee earns a salary of $120,000. The company contributes 25% of that amount, or $30,000, to the key employee's retirement account. DEF, an unincorporated businessman, has net income, after figuring all employee compensation and operating costs, of $150,000. DEF can contribute 80% of 25%, or a total of 20%, to his retirement account. Note that 20% of $150,000 is $30,000, the same as the contribution made for the key man in ABC.

¶105.2   *No Loans*

In corporate plans, participants may make loans from their individual accounts equal to the lesser of

1. $50,000; or

2. 50% of their vested account balance.

No such privilege is extended to unincorporated businesses. Since the opportunity to borrow one's own (untaxed) money is extremely attractive, practitioners will want to point out that this limitation applies to noncorporate plans.

¶106 *WHAT ARE THE CONCEPTS THAT MAKE PENSIONS WORK AND HOW DO THEY AFFECT YOUR CLIENT?*

To protect yourself from the jargon associated with the pension industry, you need to understand it and use it to the advantage of your clients. Furthermore, you must understand and use the various assumptions and factors that affect the choice of a pension design. For instance, you must understand why an older key employee would probably prefer a defined benefit plan over a profit sharing plan. This book will discuss in great detail how various factors such as age, service, interest rates, and actuarial assumptions can predetermine what type of plan will serve your client's needs.

¶106.1 *How You Can Use Creative Design to Multiply Plan Effectiveness*

Since the most common and significant objection raised by clients is the cost of covering non-key employees, it stands to reason that a thorough knowledge and understanding of alternate pension forms, designs, and assumptions will help you minimize that cost, and be of greater service to your client. The job of the pension designer is to:

1. **Identify** the client's philosophical and budgetary objectives;

2. **Review** census information to minimize coverage of non-key employees by discovering which employees might be excludable;

3. **Test** various alternative plans to find the one that conforms most closely to the objectives identified; and

4. **Explain** how that design will affect your client, both personally and within his business.

This book provides a significant number of detailed comparative analyses of alternative plan formats and requirements that should help you to carry out the planner's job.

¶106.2 *How to Control Office Procedures to Simplify Qualification and Administrative Burdens*

If you are going to design qualified plans, you need to be able to implement and administer them. Without well-conceived procedural routines, all of your "profit" from designing a clever plan will be absorbed by overhead. This book includes, wherever possible, checklists and actual examples of time- and money-saving procedures that will allow you to effectively monitor the ongoing administrative process without an unnecessarily large commitment of your time and energy. However, as noted earlier, success of a pension operation is primarily dependent on a personal commitment to be involved in a large number of plans. Since qualification and administrative services are largely repetitive in nature, no matter how efficient and clever your office procedures may be in theory, they will not work in practice unless there is a constant flow of new and old plans through the cycle.

¶107   *SUMMARIZING YOUR OPPORTUNITIES*

Qualified retirement programs present one of the most creative and demanding opportunities available for your clients. They combine uniquely attractive income tax advantages with potentially burdensome reporting and disclosure costs. They offer income tax-free appreciation of assets as long as very complicated and ever-changing rules are followed. They offer exceptional business planning opportunities, although, at the same time they may require expensive coverage of certain non-key employees. All of this leads to the conclusion that pension plans are great if you can survive the regulatory and semantic maze that has developed over the last 20 years, particularly since the 1974 enactment of ERISA and, more recently, TEFRA, DEFRA, REA, and TRA '86.

More and more practitioners are dropping out of the pension field, creating an exceptional opportunity for individuals willing to make the necessary personal commitment. Those who do fill these openings will have an opportunity to provide one of the most attractive and socially worthwhile financial management vehicles available to a client who, as a result, can only be deeply appreciative.

2

Key Ingredients
for Effectively Structured
Pension Plans
for Your Small Business Clients

The alternative plans we will discuss in Chapters 4 through 13 present a broad and dramatic range of planning opportunities. However, all of these plans can be affected by variables in your client's census information. Furthermore, costs and/or benefits for virtually all types of plans can be significantly affected by the implicit and explicit actuarial assumptions applied in various projections.

The purpose of this Chapter is to show you how these internal plan variables can affect the design process. You must be aware of the planning potential inherent in these variables so that you can use them to the advantage of your client. Furthermore, TRA '86 has placed considerable constraints on the flexibility plan designers have traditionally enjoyed. Because of the number of variables involved in a plan, some unscrupulous planners have played the "figures lie and liars figure" game once too often. Now we are all subject to close scrutiny for our individual assumptions.

¶200 GOAL-ORIENTED DESIGNS START WITH YOUR CLIENT'S CENSUS INFORMATION

Most closely held corporations have relatively few "key" individuals. Generally, the group is conspicuous for some attribute relative to other employees. For instance, the "key" group may be younger, older, have more past service, or have consistently higher income than average. These are some of the factors that affect pension design.

The single most important function, and your first step in pension design, is meticulous review of your client's census data to determine what attributes separate the "key" individuals from the rest of the employees. Once you identify these attributes, you can select a pension plan formula that will work in favor of employees in that key group. The process of census analysis significantly narrows the search for an appropriate plan and comprises the bulk of the pension planner's design work.

Some of the most significant variables are age, past service, and actuarial assumptions. It is important that you understand how these individual parameters may affect the ultimate design of a qualified plan in terms of relative contributions—our objective in pension design. Once you understand the operation of these variables, you can predict their effect and use them for your client's gain.

The following discussion isolates each variable to show its effect upon plan funding. Throughout this chapter you will find staggering opportunities for your client, depending on your choice of plan parameters and assumptions. Keep our caveat about TRA '86 in mind, though, and be prepared to justify your selection of parameters.

¶201   *HOW TO LIMIT PLAN PARTICIPATION THROUGH AGE, SERVICE, AND OTHER ELIGIBILITY REQUIREMENTS*

ERISA recognizes the cost to employers of including "higher turnover" employees in a pension plan and allows that a plan will qualify if employees are in the plan within six months after

- the attainment of age 21; or

- the completion of a year of service.

Thus, many employees can be excluded from your calculations.

PLANNING TIP ────────────────────────────────
You should eliminate all ineligible employees. This is the first step in the process of census review. Otherwise, you may design a plan for the wrong group.

Example ────────────────────────────────
Let's say Turnover Company has 10 employees. It operates on a calendar year. The objective you have been given is to maximize the older employ-

ees' share of a $25,000 contribution. Without proper exclusions, you could design the wrong plan.

CENSUS PARAMETERS

Situation 1— Forgot to Exclude	Employee	Age	Date of Employment	Situation 2— After Exclusions
Eligible	A	55	01/01/50	Eligible
Eligible	B	55	03/01/79	Ineligible—Service
Eligible	C	50	01/01/70	Eligible
Eligible	D	60	06/01/79	Ineligible—Service
Eligible	E	24	01/01/75	Ineligible—Age
Eligible	F	19	01/01/78	Ineligible—Age
Eligible	G	35	01/01/77	Eligible
Eligible	H	40	04/01/79	Ineligible—Service
Eligible	I	30	02/01/79	Ineligible—Service
Eligible	J	45	01/01/70	Eligible
41 years	Average Age			46 years
6 years	Average Service			10 years
$2,500	Average Contribution			$6,250

The significance of a five-year age differential or a four-years-of-service differential, plus the fact that under "Situation 2" the $25,000 contribution will be shared by only four as opposed to 10 employees, cannot be overlooked.

¶201.1 *How Employees Are Further Excluded*

You should use age and service requirements concurrently with a requirement that eligible employees be employed on the last day of the plan year to share in the contributions. This will further reduce the pool of covered employees and help you

1. maximize benefits for nonexcluded groups; and

2. minimize reporting and disclosure obligations for the high turnover group.

Caution.   A defined benefit plan cannot use this technique. (See Chapters 8 through 11.) Also, a plan cannot exclude more than a certain number (see discussion below) of otherwise eligible employees on this basis, or it will run afoul of the new coverage requirements of TRA '86.

¶201.2 *Combining Age and Service Requirements for Effective Plan Language*

The following language may provide one of the simplest methods for using age and service requirements to your advantage:

> "Employees will become participants in the plan on the first day of the plan year nearest, forward or backward, to the later of the following events:
>
> a. Completion of a year of service; or
> b. Attainment of age 21."

The allocation section of a Defined Contribution plan may further require that a participant be employed on the last day of the plan year to be an active participant (as long as the plan meets TRA '86 coverage requirements). Only active participants need to receive contributions for a particular plan year. An "active participant" is generally one who works more than 1000 hours during the year.

Example ——————————————————————————

Benson is employed on April 1, 1986, by a calendar year company that allocates profit-sharing contributions on December 31. He completes his year of service on March 31, 1987. The first day of the plan year (January 1) nearest, forward or backward, to March 31 is January 1, 1987. Therefore, Benson is a participant in the plan on January 1, 1987.

Example ——————————————————————————

Use the same facts as in the first example, except Benson is employed on August 1, 1986. He completes his year of service on July 31, 1987. The January 1 nearest that date is January 1, 1988. Benson becomes a participant on January 1, 1988.

Example ——————————————————————————

Use the same facts as the second example, but Benson quits on December 28, 1988. Although he became a participant on January 1, he will not receive an allocation of the 1988 profit sharing allocation, since he was not employed on the last day of the plan year.

The eligibility provisions discussed above substantially eliminate short-service employees and allow your client to spend his limited budget most efficiently. Be certain you take full advantage of the opportunity. Be careful not to forget the requirement that a certain percentage of eligible employees must be covered (as discussed in Section 202).

¶201.3 *Alternative Approach Using Eligibility for Special Circumstances*

There is an alternative to bringing employees into the plan after a year of service. Your client can require two years of service prior to participation, if he's willing to have 100% vesting on all contributions. That may seem attractive, but watch out because:

1. In small corporations, it may result in operational discrimination in favor of the "prohibited group" of highly paid employees; or

2. If the shorter eligibility requirements are used, vesting can possibly be deferred for as long as five years under TRA '86. Usually, it is better to control the plan funds through vesting; after all, if participants do not "own" employer contributions, what has the employer lost? Note that if a plan becomes "topheavy" (more than 60% of its benefits accrue to "highly compensated" employees) then the five-year vesting must be replaced by a graded schedule (discussed later in this Chapter).

Caution. The two-year option is not available for 401(k) plans.

¶202 *BEYOND STATUTORY EXCLUSIONS*

After you finish eliminating potential participants on the basis of age and service, consider applying one or more "class" exclusions. Under TRA '86, plans will need to meet at least one of the following tests after December 31, 1988.

1. 70% of nonhighly compensated employees must be covered;

2. The percentage of nonhighly compensated, covered employees must be at least 70% of the percentage of *highly* compensated covered; or

3. The group of covered employees satisfies a subjective "fair cross section" test *and* average benefits provided to nonhighly compensated employees (as a percentage of compensation) are at least 70% of average benefits to highly compensated. This test considers the economic value of *all* fringe benefit plans (not just pensions), and therefore requires such a high level of sophistication to apply that it is not likely to be used by small businesses.

In addition to meeting one of these coverage tests, a new "minimum participation rule" will be applied. This rule requires *each plan* to cover the lesser of

1. 50 employees; or

2. 40% of all employees.

For purposes of the above tests, you need to know who is a "highly compensated employee." These are up to 100 employees of a company who:

1. are 5% owners;

2. earn more than $75,000 per year;

3. earn more than $50,000 per year and are in the top 20% of employees; or

4. are officers earning at least 150% of the dollar limit on annual contributions to defined contribution plans (currently $30,000, making $45,000 the compensation threshold).

If no employees fall into one of the above definitions, then the top paid company officer is considered highly compensated.

Example

Cover Co. has 100 eligible employees. Let's look at the top ten to see who's highly compensated.

Employee	Stock Ownership	Officer ?	Comp.	Status	Reason (see above)
A	25%	yes	$40,000	Highly	1
B	0%	no	$80,000	Highly	2
C	0%	no	$51,000	Highly	3
D	0%	yes	$46,000	Highly	4
E	75%	yes	$100,000	Highly	1,2,3,4
F	0%	no	$70,000	Not Highly	N/A
G	0%	yes	$40,000	Not Highly	N/A
H	0%	yes	$44,000	Not Highly	N/A
I	0%	no	$80,000	Highly	2
J	0%	yes	$46,000	Highly	4

Thus, out of 100 eligible employees, seven are highly compensated. That means, as a practical matter, our plan must cover either

a. 65 nonhighly compensated employees (70% of 93); or

b.   more than 70% of the percentage of highly compensated covered (e.g., if five highly paids were covered, we'd have to cover 47 nonhighly paid - $\frac{5}{7} \times 70\% \times 93$).

Note.   Until 1989, pre-TRA coverage requirements remain in effect, under which at least 70% of all employees must be *eligible*, and 80% of those eligible must be participating.

¶202.1   *How to Use Coverage Requirements to Your Client's Advantage*

Assuming you design a plan in which 100% of the highly compensated employees are participants, 70% of the nonhighly paids must be covered. That gives you **30% that could be excluded** from the plan, and therefore a 30% *saving* in your client's expense. Consider excluding a specific "class" of employees, such as those paid on an hourly basis or those assigned to a different plant location.

Warning.   Do not exclude employees on the basis of any socially based discrimination (such as age). Use only exclusions generic to the workplace.

¶202.2   *How Maximum Age Requirements Can Be Effective*

Under certain conditions, your client can eliminate employees hired within five years of the plan's normal retirement date. Defined benefit and target benefit plans can impose maximum-age requirements for participation. Congress recognized that the expense of forcing employers to fully fund retirement benefits for employees hired at an advanced age would discourage their being hired. As an alternative to reduce funding pressure, these plans may define retirement date as the later of normal retirement age (usually 65) or completion of 10 years of plan participation. Often the choice is difficult.

Example

XYZ Company has hired 10 employees between ages 55 and 65. Its retirement plan specifies 65 as the normal retirement date. All participants receive a $5,000 per year retirement benefit. Your job is to determine which of the following would be more expensive:

1.   Giving full benefits at age 65 but excluding employees hired within five years of age 65; or

2.   Giving full benefits to all participants at the later of age 65 or 10 years of plan participation.

I. NRD* @ 65, Exclude Within 5 Yrs.		Census		II. NRD @ Later of 65 or 10 Yrs.	
Retire. Age	Annual Contribution	Employee/Hire. Age		Retire. Age	Annual Contribution
65	$ 3,728	A	55	65	$ 3,728
65	4,276	B	56	66	3,682
65	4,964	C	57	67	3,637
65	5,854	D	58	68	3,520
65	7,044	E	59	69	3,520
Excluded	N/A	F	60	70	3,509
Excluded	N/A	G	61	71	3,468
Excluded	N/A	H	62	72	3,428
Excluded	N/A	I	63	73	3,389
Excluded	N/A	J	64	74	3,351
N/A	$25,866	TOTAL	N/AS	N/A	$35,232

* Normal Retirement Date

At first, the exclusion for employees hired within five years of retirement date appears preferable. But it wouldn't take too much of a shift in the above illustration to change your decision. *Always* test the two alternatives.

Caution. Employees excluded because they were hired within five years of normal retirement date are not part of the "age" or "length of service" group eliminated prior to application of the coverage tests. Therefore, if you apply the rule without being careful, you may inadvertently fail to meet ERISA's participation standards. Also, late 1986 amendments to the Age Discrimination in Employment Act specifically preclude certain (larger, interstate) employers from using this provision.

Example
Careless Corporation excludes from coverage four nonhighly paid employees within five years of retirement date(s). On its IRS audit, the plan is disqualified because

of the nonexcluded employee group 10

some were excluded—hired at age 61 4

The remaining eligible employees 6

fail to meet the requirement for 70% coverage 60%

¶203 *HOW YOUR PLAN'S VESTING SCHEDULE CAN PERFORM FURTHER HOUSECLEANING*

Even after your employees become participants by escaping the swath of eligibility or class exclusions, they still are not entitled to receive benefits. For that they must become ''vested.'' Vesting means the degree to which an employee-participant **owns** the benefits which have been accrued on his or her behalf. TRA '86 specifically authorizes several acceptable vesting schedules, among which are:

1. ''cliff'' vesting, under which a participant's accrued benefits must be 100% vested only upon completion of five years of service;

2. ''graded'' vesting, with 20% after three years, and 20% per year thereafter (full vesting after seven years); or

3. if a plan requires two years of service for eligibility, then all employer accrued benefits must be *immediately* 100% vested.

Note that if a plan is ''topheavy'' (more than 60% of the value of accrued benefits belong to key employees), then the graded vesting schedule described above must be accelerated by one year, and the 5-year ''cliff'' option is not available. At the time this manuscript was being updated for TRA '86, it was unclear whether a topheavy plan could utilize a three-year eligibility waiting period with 100% vesting, or whether TRA's more stringent (2 years/100%) requirement will supersede.

Any employee who terminates prior to the time vesting begins forfeits all accrued benefits. A participant who terminates when partially vested takes part of his benefits and forfeits the balance. Note that all the vesting options listed above allow your client some additional time to weed out employees who for one reason or another won't become longstanding participants. Don't feel guilty; a plan is for people who stay, not those who leave.

The recovery of these forfeited funds will be used in one of two ways, depending on the type of plan adopted:

- to reduce future employer contributions; or

- to provide an extra allocation for those employees who remain behind.

Thus, to the extent your client has a continual turnover of employees with one to five years of service, he may recover a portion of his contributions and be in a position to apply those to the benefit of long-term employees.

¶204   HOW TO USE EMPLOYEE AND PLAN VARIABLES TO YOUR ADVANTAGE

After excluding as many employees as possible from your client's census information, it is important to scan the remaining participating employees to find some attribute of the key employees toward which you can orient the plan. Such factors as average age, length of service, and interest or actuarial assumptions significantly affect your choices. To make intelligent choices you need to know what effect the various parameters will have.

¶204.1   *How the Age of Participants Determines Your Choice of Plans*

Some pension formulas favor older employees in terms of relative contributions. Some favor younger participants. This is because certain plans (defined benefit and target benefit) are predicated on providing specific benefits at a specific age for all participants. For instance, a plan might promise each participant income of $5,000 per year at age 65. Depending on how old a particular participant is at entry, his funding costs can differ dramatically, since the number of years to retirement obviously affects employer deposits.

Participation Age	Lump-Sum at 65 to Pay $5,000/Yr. Retirement Income	Annual Deposit Required Assuming 6% Interest
25	$52,083	$ 317
35	52,083	622
45	52,083	1,336
55	52,083	3,728

In these plans, the funding goal ($52,803) never changes: time to accumulate the goal is the only variable. Depending on the amount of time, compound interest may do more or less of the work.

Other plans guarantee only that specific contributions will be made. These plans tend to favor younger participants, since deposits generally relate primarily to salary. Age is irrelevant. Benefits are simply the sum of employer contributions and fund earnings (or losses). Using the average deposit determined under the illustration above, look what happens to participant lump-sums at age 65:

Participation Age	Annual Deposit	Lump-Sum at 65 if Deposit Is Invested at 6%
25	$1,500	$246,195
35	1,500	125,765
45	1,500	58,518
55	1,500	20,957

In these defined contribution plans, benefits are the variable, deposits the constant. It is clear that employers with limited budgets should be aware of the different results generated by benefit- or contribution-oriented plans.

Example

Real-life situations provide even more graphic illustrations of the effect of your choice. The following example demonstrates the application of two different plan formulas, one of which relates primarily to relative *salary,* the second to relative *age.*

Employee	Age	Average Compensation	% of Total	Plan I—5% Interest Deposit	Plan I—5% Interest % of Total	Plan II—8% Interest Deposit	Plan II—8% Interest % of Total
A	50	$ 75,000	41	$17,593	70	$19,194	77
B	30	75,000	41	4,203	17	3,024	12
C	40	12,000	7	1,426	6	1,278	5
D	40	12,000	7	1,426	6	1,278	5
E	25	7,500	4	352	1	226	1
TOTAL		$181,500	100	$25,000	100	$25,000	100

Plan I results in a deposit allocation exactly proportioned to salaries, notwithstanding significant age differentials. A simple change to Plan II dramatically orients the same deposit toward older employees. This example offers dramatic proof of the necessity for clients with limited budgets to carefully define their objectives. Then you can select the plan which most' closely fulfills those objectives.

In many closely held corporations, the age of key individuals is higher than the average age of employees in general. Assuming your client's corporate objective is to reward those key employees, you should design a formula yielding deposits similar to those in Plan II.

¶204.2   *Identifying Opportunities to Use Past Service*

In addition to age, key employees in closely held corporations will tend to have more past service with the employer than most employees. For instance, many such businesses have an owner who has worked in the business for 30 or 40 years, but whose employees, because of turnover and lack of opportunity for advancement, have relatively little past service.

Example ————————————————————————————————

The following schedule of deposits illustrates two divergent plan formulas. Plan I, as in our previous example, emphasizes relative salary as the key element in determining contributions. Plan II, on the other hand, is heavily weighted toward years of service with the employer.

Employee	Age	Years Past Service	Average Compensation	% of Total	Plan I— Salary		Plan II— Past Service	
					Deposit	% of Total	Deposit	% of Total
A	50	10	$ 75,000	41	$10,331	41	$15,439	62
B	30	10	75,000	41	10,331	41	5,804	23
C	40	1	12,000	7	1,653	7	1,219	5
D	40	20	12,000	7	1,653	7	2,112	8
E	25	1	7,500	4	1,033	4	426	2
TOTAL			$181,500	100	$25,000	100	$25,000	100

Notice that employee D, who in all previous illustrations had contributions identical to those of her equal-pay, equal-age counterpart, employee C, receives almost twice the deposit under this "past service" plan. Many plans emphasize service in their benefit formulas. Sometimes your client's key employees will not have unusually large salaries. Alternatively, your client may feel that the budget should be oriented toward employees who have shown longstanding loyalty to the company. In either case he would clearly prefer the past service formula utilized in Plan II. This illustration, too, underscores the opportunities that are available for the minimal effort involved in thorough census review.

¶204.3   *Short-Term Planning with Interest Rates*

In certain types of pension plans, your client or his actuary must specify an assumed rate of interest for the accumulation of plan assets. In effect, an actuary's job is to build a hypothetical model of plan performance and then monitor actual experience. To the extent actual investment experience fulfills the actuary's expectations, the choice of high versus low interest rates can lead to dramatic variations in the Plan's funding costs.

¶204.4   *How to Use Interest Rate Assumptions to Benefit Your Client*

In general, an employer whose key employees are older than the group average will derive the greatest benefit from higher interest rate assumptions. Younger employees have substantially more time than their older peers to accumulate a fund sufficient to pay their retirement benefits. The longer the funding period, the greater the effect of compound interest. As an illustration, consider the following example:

Employee	Age	Average Compensation	% of Total	Plan I—5% Interest		Plan II—8% Interest	
				Deposit	% of Total	Deposit	% of Total
A	50	$ 75,000	41	$17,593	70	$19,194	77
B	30	75,000	41	4,203	17	3,024	12
C	40	12,000	7	1,426	6	1,278	5
D	40	12,000	7	1,426	6	1,278	5
E	25	7,500	4	352	1	226	1
TOTAL		$181,500	100	$25,000	100	$25,000	100

Although the above alternatives must eventually provide identical retirement benefits, the deposits for the older key person are increased 10% by a simple change in interest assumptions. However, since pension plans generally require the employer to use overfunding occasioned by excess interest to reduce future deposits, this relative increase could be short-lived if too unreasonable an interest rate is used. Also, TRA '86 adds specific sanctions (in the form of excise taxes) against employers who deliberately overfund their plans by making unreasonable assumptions.

This can create a "Catch-22," in which your client may have to trade off relative contributions against tax deductions. However, by selecting moderately aggressive or conservative investments, your client may control to a considerable extent the degree to which his assumed rate of interest parallels actual investment experience. Further, certain pension plans simply use the assumed rate of interest as a target, with actual investment experience reflected in individual participant accounts.

¶204.5   *Creative Planning Using Actuarial Methods and Assumptions*

Many qualified plans require the selection of an ***actuarial method*** for calculating plan deposits. An actuarial method simply provides the structured environment to measure the relationship between plan assumptions and actual experience. Depending upon the actuarial method used, you can also generate significant divergence in funding patterns. It is important to consider all the options.

¶204.6   *How "Salary Scales" Can Shift Your Client's Deposit*

Because of periodic bouts of rapid inflation that have dramatically affected payroll costs over the last decade, many plans assume a degree of "wage inflation" in their funding. In other words, your client may decide to "prefund" part of his anticipated future costs. Obviously, to the extent we prefund future benefits instead of spending for currently earned benefits, more of our budget will be used for these anticipated costs. In many small plans, your client will be able to choose between using or not using salary scales. The difference can be significant.

Example ─────────────────────────
XYZ Incorporated cannot decide whether or not to use a 4% salary increase assumption and asks you to calculate the financial effect of the options.

			Option I: 4% Salary Increase		Option II: No Salary Increase	
Employee	Age	Pay	Estimated Benefits @ 65	Annual Deposit	Estimated Benefits @ 65	Annual Deposit
A	50	$ 75,000	$50,088/Yr.	$16,337/Yr.	$43,908/Yr.	$18,262/Yr.
B	30	75,000	98,100/Yr.	4,822/Yr.	43,908/Yr.	3,560/Yr.
C	40	12,000	11,856/Yr.	1,656/Yr.	7,020/Yr.	1,439/Yr.
D	40	12,000	11,856/Yr.	1,656/Yr.	7,020/Yr.	1,439/Yr.
E	25	7,500	13,356/Yr.	529/Yr.	4,392/Yr.	300/Yr.
TOTAL		$181,500	N/A	$25,000	N/A	$25,000

The difference is quite remarkable for such a small change in assumptions.

Caution.   Do not forget that in the long run your actuarial model will be replaced by actual experience. Therefore, if your actuarial model is not reasonable, in the long run you will pay the price.

¶204.7 *How Much Will Retirement Benefits Cost?*

Central to employer costs is the funding target. For example, how much does your client need to have at age 65 to provide a $5,000 per year retirement benefit for a plan participant? That depends on a couple of assumptions:

1. The form in which the benefit will be paid, such as a "life only" or a "joint and 100% survivor" annuity; and

2. The assumed cost of whatever benefit form is chosen, such as might be determined by application of the 1971 GAM or UP 1984 actuarial tables.

Example ───────────────────────────────

XYZ Incorporated wants to know the funding costs associated with providing a $5,000 per year retirement income to plan participants under some different assumptions. They are quite surprised by the differences:

Retirement Income	Assumed Form of Benefit	Settlement Option	Lump-Sum Required @ 65	Annual Deposit for 45-Year-Old
$5,000/yr.	Joint & 100% Survivor	Ins. Co. Rate	$75,758	$1,943/yr.
5,000/yr.	Life only	Ins. Co. Rate	60,582	1,554/yr.
5,000/yr.	Life only	'71 GAM Table	52,083	1,336/yr.

There is a 40% difference in funding costs without any change in benefits.

PLANNING TIP ───────────────────────────────

If your client has older key employees and a limited budget, he may prefer using conservative (expensive) benefit-cost assumptions. That way the limited budget will be necessarily skewed toward the key employees.

Example ───────────────────────────────

Games Company's president and key employee, Ms. Parker, wants to know the effect, in terms of initial contributions, of using an aggressive versus a conservative benefit-cost assumption. The results are worth thinking about.

Employee	Age	Pay	Option A: Conservative Costs*		Option A: Aggressive Costs**	
			Annual Ret. Benefit	Annual Deposit	Annual Ret. Benefit	Annual Deposit
Mr. Parker	50	$ 50,000	$18,290	$ 9,561	$18,290	$ 7,217
B	40	35,000	12,803	2,749	12,803	2,075
C	40	20,000	7,316	1,571	7,316	1,186
D	30	20,000	7,316	746	7,316	563
E	30	10,000	3,658	373	3,658	282
TOTAL		$135,000	N/A	$15,000	N/A	$11,323

  * Male age 65 receives $6.19 per $1,000 principal.
 ** Male age 65 receives $8.20 per $1,000 principal.

Note that making the simple change from a conservative estimate of the cost of providing future benefits to one more in keeping with current costs, reduces Games Company's funding cost for identical benefits by almost 25%. Alternatively, 30% more benefits could theoretically have been provided if the contribution ($15,000), rather than the benefits, were held constant. Integrated defined benefit plans with limited budgets can exaggerate planning opportunities even further (see Chapter 8).

¶204.8   *How Actuarial Methods Can Affect Employer Flexibility*

Apart from assumptions and parameters affecting cost, the actuarial methods themselves hold substantial opportunity for creative planners. For the time being, let's consider two significantly different actuarial methods that might be used in small plans, the Individual Level Premium Method and the Entry Age Normal with Frozen Initial Past Service Liability Method.*

THE INDIVIDUAL LEVEL PREMIUM METHOD— INFLEXIBLE BUT ACCURATE

Under this actuarial method, the actuary determines a level funding cost for each participant from date of participation to date of retirement. Once the level premium is established for a particular "block" of compensation, it never changes. As salary changes generate benefit increases or de-

---

*See Appendix for a case history showing the actuarial methods commonly used in small plans of a major pension software firm.

creases, the incremental level premium for those benefits is added to the prior level cost. In effect, your client uses a "building block" approach to funding retirement benefits. However, because of the level premium nature of the system, your client may be apprehensive—after all, he's seen a lot of ups and downs in his business. Sometimes a small business can't budget effectively for substantial, inflexible payments.

ENTRY AGE NORMAL WITH FROZEN INITIAL PAST SERVICE LIABILITY (FIPSL) CAN PROVIDE A SAFETY VALVE FOR YOUR CLIENT

In this method, the actuary pretends that a business has always had a pension plan and asks the question, "If we had had this plan from the beginning, how much money would we have accumulated at this point?" Entry age normal plans effectively divide a participant's service into two components—one for past and one for future employment. Future costs are funded basically on a level premium approach. But the planning opportunity derives from the past service element. Participants have a "past service liability" (the amount determined by the actuary's question). This past service liability can be amortized by your client over anywhere from 10 to 30 years. For clients whose employee census reveals a lot of past service, the amortization provides very substantial flexibility.

Example

Simplicity Corporation learns from its actuary that its future cost level funding will be $10,000 per year, and that its past service liability is $100,000. Further analysis shows the following flexibility:

Future Cost Funding	30-Year Past Service Amortization	10-Year Past Service Amortization	Minimum Deposit (1 + 2)	Maximum Deposit (1 + 3)
$10,000/yr.	$6,854/yr.	$12,818/yr.	$16,854/yr.	$22,818/yr.

Since your client has discretion over his deposit (e.g., minimum, maximum, or in between) there is a lot of budgetary flexibility inherent in this example to accommodate periodic fluctuation in business conditions. You may ask why anyone would choose not to use it.

Caution. Entry age with FIPSL does not *reduce* funding, it only spreads it out. Sooner or later, all costs have to be paid. If your client has some older participating employees and consistently funds only the minimum required deposit, he may not have enough money on hand to pay off these older participating employees, particularly if lump-sum distributions are desired. An "Emerging Liability Report" is a good investment: it shows cash flow requirements of the Trust Fund over time, given variables such as level of deposit, interest, etc.

Possible Solution. Be careful about offering retiring employees in small plans the option to take lump-sum distributions if you're using entry age normal with FIPSL. This will preclude the cash flow problems that might otherwise occur.

¶204.9   *Comparing the Cost of Both Actuarial Methods*

Ms. Jacobs, of XYZ Incorporated, asks you to show the funding requirements associated with the two actuarial methods we've discussed. She wants to spend between $20,000 and $30,000. Here is your answer:

Employee	Age	Years Past Service	Pay	Level Premium Annual Deposit	Entry Age Normal with FIPSL Minimum Deposit	Entry Age Normal with FIPSL Maximum Deposit
A	50	10	$ 75,000	$17,773	$14,861	$21,029
B	30	10	75,000	3,703	3,553	5,028
C	40	1	12,000	1,547	1,398	1,480
D	40	20	12,000	1,547	1,335	2,150
E	25	1	17,500	430	296	313
TOTAL			$181,500	$25,000	$21,443	$30,000

¶205   COMBINING FACTORS TO YIELD SPECTACULAR RESULTS

Clearly the various design parameters discussed in this chapter provide a tremendous opportunity for pension practitioners by themselves; when applied in combination, the results are even more spectacular. Older employees tend to be favored by formulas "making up for lost time." These involve high interest rates, emphasis on past service, and actuarial methods based on current rather than prospective income. Consider the following example, which compares two alternative plan formulas over our standard group. The goal is to benefit employee A, who is relatively old and has a medium amount of past service. Plan I uses a simple nonspecific formula. Plan II, on the other hand, orients all parameters to emphasize the unique attributes of employee A.

Employee	Age	Years Past Service	Avg. Comp.	% of Total	Plan I— Nonspecific		Plan II— Orient to "A"	
					Deposit	% of Total	Deposit	% of Total
A	50	10	$ 75,000	41	$10,331	41	$19,194	77
B	30	10	75,000	41	10,331	41	3,025	12
C	40	1	12,000	7	1,653	7	1,278	5
D	40	20	12,000	7	1,653	7	1,278	5
E	25	1	7,500	4	1,033	4	225	1
TOTAL			$181,500	100	$25,000	100	$25,000	100

These relatively simple concepts, when applied in conjunction with the concepts integration discussed in the following chapters, are the pension practitioner's tool. The process must begin with a thorough analytical review of your client's census data to discover some unique characteristics of the key employee group. That done, you can compare the unique parameters discovered to select an appropriate benefit formula.

The purpose of this discussion of parameters affecting pension design has not been to learn the formulas underlying different plans. Rather, the intent was to generate awareness of significant design opportunities available, even at the most simple level. Any of the factors considered above could be used in conjunction with actual plan formulas to tip the balance of contributions toward our key employee group. Although it is important to remember that "figures lie and liars figure," there are certain ranges of acceptable plan variables. Over a period of time and with employee turnover, these variables may in the long run significantly affect pension design for the closely held corporation. The bottom line is an opportunity to save you time and provide the most efficient plan design opportunities for your clients.

3

Effective Use of Integration:
The Key to Pension Design

Integration of qualified pension plans is of paramount importance. It is a tool that your client can use to give highly paid employees a larger percentage of plan benefits or contributions without fear of discrimination. Integration has historically been considered a monster, difficult to tame. However, conceptually it is nothing more than a pension plan's recognition of employee retirement income provided by the Social Security system. Proper integration merely allows your client to offset his own plan's benefits with those provided under the Social Security system.

In this Chapter, we will explore the concepts of integration and how they can benefit your client. Later Chapters will show how to apply integration rules to specific alternative plan formulas. You will learn how integration can boost any type of pension plan's efficiency for key employees and, as a corollary, learn to control pension plan costs for lower-paid employees—costs that most discourage clients from adopting qualified plans.

¶300   HOW SOCIAL SECURITY FAVORS LOWER-PAID EMPLOYEES

Every employer provides a pension plan whether he likes it or not—Social Security. Benefits are paid for with a component of Social Security taxes with matching employer-employee contributions—each currently 7.15%—

that are applied to the taxable wage base, which is $42,000 in 1986. Both the taxable wage base and contribution rates are slated to rise in future years. The contributions fund a combination of death, disability, survivor, and retirement benefits. In 1986, the component of total Social Security Taxes paid by the employer *for retirement benefits* is 5.7% of the taxable wage base, or a maximum of $2,394. Ultimate retirement benefits are determined by a complex formula that roughly compares the taxable wage bases to which an employee has been subject during his working life. The secret of plan integration is to effectively offset those benefits provided by a qualified retirement plan with those provided by Social Security.

¶301 HOW INTEGRATION SOLVES THE PROBLEM OF DISCRIMINATION IN CONTRIBUTIONS AGAINST KEY EMPLOYEES

Social Security contributions primarily benefit lower-paid employees since there are no contributions payable on account of employee compensation above $42,000. For example, if your client adopted a simple pension plan and contributed 13.774% of all participants' income, he would substantially skew plan deposits toward lower-paid employees.

Example

Consider the effects of such a plan on a typical employee group:

Employee	Age	Pay	% of Total	5.7% Social Security Deposit	13.774% + Plan Deposit	Total = Deposit	% of Pay
A	50	$ 75,000	41	$2,394	$10,331	$12,725	17%
B	30	75,000	41	2,394	10,331	12,725	17
C	40	12,000	7	684	1,653	2,337	19
D	40	12,000	7	684	1,653	2,337	19
E	25	7,500	4	427	1,033	1,460	19
TOTAL		$181,500	100%	$6,583	$25,000	$31,584	N/A

Employees C, D, and E, between Social Security and the employer's private pension plan, receive a total allocation equal to 19% of their pay, while the two highly paid employees receive contributions totaling just 17% of their salaries. The rationale for integration is that employers should be able to provide uniform retirement benefits or contributions over all compensation. Since Social Security is designed primarily to provide a "floor," employers can build their retirement plans with that floor in mind.

¶301.1 *How Social Security Affects Contribution-Oriented Retirement Plans*

There are two ways of looking at the Social Security System:

1. in terms of the current *contributions* it mandates; and

2. in terms of the *retirement* benefits it ultimately provides.

Figure 3.1 graphically depicts the 1986 relationship between employer deposits and income level.

The relationship between employer contributions and income is linear up to $42,000. Employees earning more than $42,000 (the 1986 taxable wage base) receive no contribution for their excess pay.

¶301.2 *How Integration Provides Nonshareholder Employees Maximum Benefits at Least Cost to the Company*

Integration merely allows your client to extend his contributions to compensation above the taxable wage base in order to provide uniform deposits for all employees, regardless of pay level. Figure 3.2 illustrates this. As long as this continuum between Social Security and employer-paid contributions remains linear, a pension plan is properly integrated.

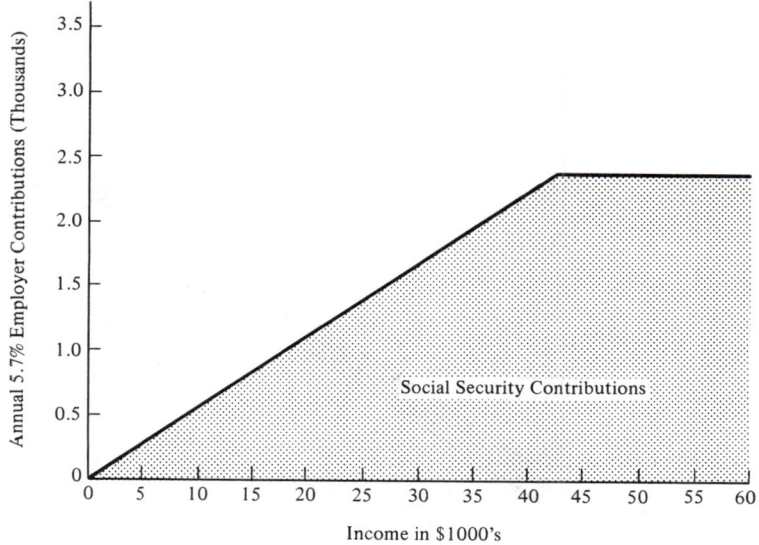

FIGURE 3.1

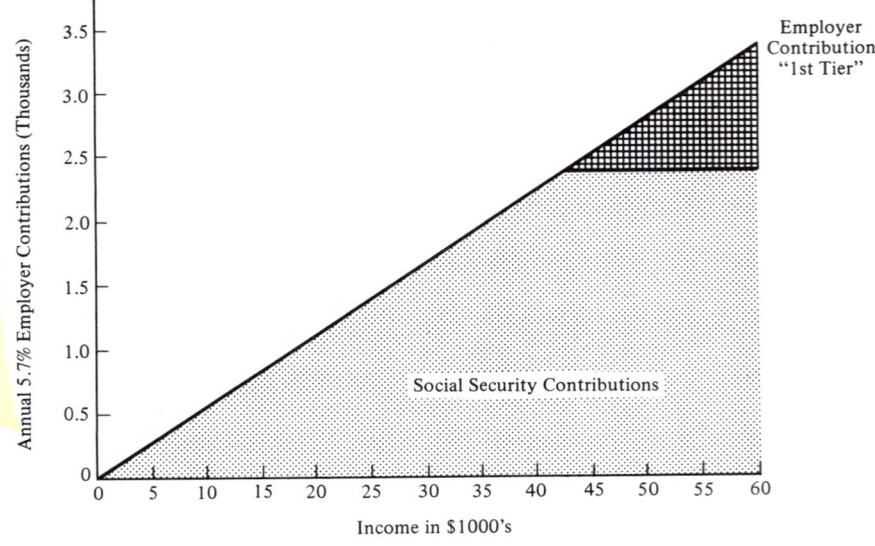

FIGURE 3.2

To extend the concept further, an employer may provide a "two-tiered" pension plan as shown in Figure 3.3. The first tier of the plan makes up for compensation not covered by Social Security. The second tier provides uniform contributions above and beyond the first tier. The combination generates a properly integrated plan.

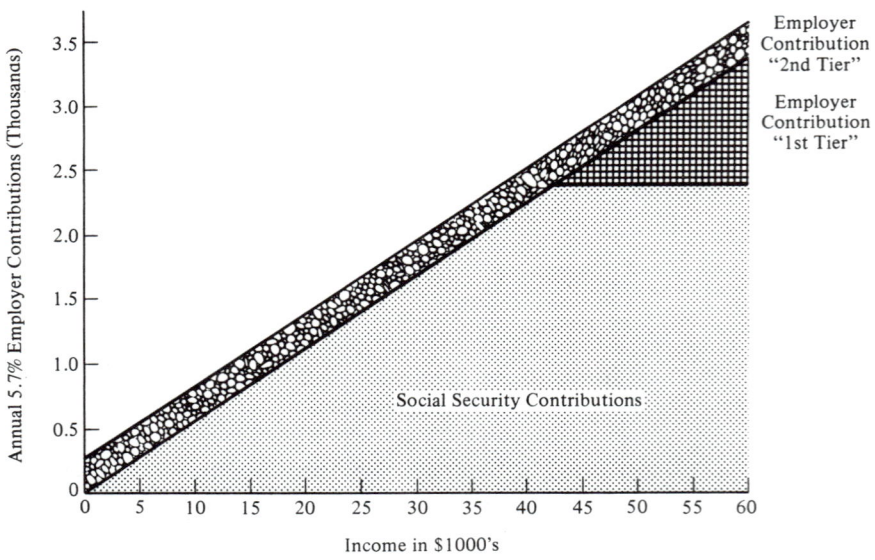

FIGURE 3.3

Example ──

Continuity Corporation sets up a defined-contribution plan, to which it contributes 10% of a participant's compensation **plus** 5.7% of compensation in excess of $42,000. (The 5.7% figure represents the maximum "catch-up" contribution rate, deemed to create uniformity between government and employer-sponsored plan deposits.) Compare the results to those illustrated in Section 301.

CONTINUITY CORPORATION
COMPARING INTEGRATED AND NONINTEGRATED ALTERNATIVES

Employee	Pay	Social Security +	10% Basic Deposit +	5.7% Excess Deposit =	Total Allocation	% of Pay
A	$ 75,000	$2,394	$ 7,500	$1,881	$11,775	16%
B	75,000	2,394	7,500	1,881	11,775	16
C	12,000	684	1,200	0	1,884	16
D	12,000	684	1,200	0	1,884	16
E	7,500	428	750	0	1,178	16
TOTAL	$181,500	$6,584	$18,150	$3,762	$28,496	N/A

"Integrated" Plan Contributions

Employee	Pay	Total Deposit	% of Pay
A	$ 75,000	$12,725	17%
B	75,000	12,725	17
C	12,000	2,337	19
D	12,000	2,337	19
E	7,500	1,460	19
TOTAL	$181,500	$31,584	N/A

Nonintegrated Alternative

If your client has a limited budget, make certain he is aware of the possibilities offered by integration.

Important Note. The Tax Reform Act of 1986 (TRA '86) added a new wrinkle to integration rules, designed to prevent "Excess Only" Plans—those that provide contributions only for compensation above the integration level. Specifics of the new rules are discussed in the following relevant material.

¶302   HOW INTEGRATION SOLVES THE PROBLEM OF DISCRIMINATION IN RETIREMENT BENEFITS AGAINST KEY EMPLOYEES

Similarly, discrimination in *retirement benefits* would occur if your client overlapped his own nonintegrated qualified plan with Social Security. This is because Social Security benefits are based only on compensation that has been subject to Social Security tax during an employee's working life. For instance, if an employer adopts a defined benefit pension plan that promises participants retirement pay equal to 50% of their salaries, the higher paid employees receive proportionately reduced benefits, since Social Security benefits relate only to "covered compensation," a figure as low as $9,000.

Example

LMN Company establishes a 50%-of-pay defined benefit plan with no "off-set" for Social Security. Its key employees later observe that their overall benefits provide relatively less retirement income than their lower-paid counterparts.

Employee	Age	Pay	% of Total	Social Security Benefits @ 65	Plan Benefits @ 65	Total Benefit	% of Salary
A	50	$75,000	41	$ 9,072/yr.	$37,500	$46,572	62%
B	30	75,000	41	10,241	37,500	47,741	64
C	40	12,000	7	5,628	6,000	11,628	97
D	40	12,000	7	5,628	6,000	11,628	97
E	25	7,500	4	4,169	3,750	7,919	106

The lower-paid employees under this approach receive substantially higher overall benefits. Assuming your client's goal is to maximize the allocation of his limited budget to those key employees, he will much prefer to utilize an integrated pension plan.

¶302.1   *Understanding Integration of Benefit-Oriented Pension Plans*

The concept of integration is that your client should, if he voluntarily adopts his own qualified retirement plan, be able to recognize benefits provided by the mandatory Social Security program when computing benefits under his own plan. In other words, the government will allow your client to establish a plan which, when combined with Social Security, provides continuity of benefits to all participating employees at all income levels. In effect, your client picks up where Social Security leaves off.

¶302.2   *How To Integrate Benefit-Oriented Retirement Plans*

An employee's Social Security retirement benefits are computed by a weighted formula that considers length of employment and level of compensation. The results of this computation are expressed as an employee's "Covered Compensation." Integration under Benefit-Oriented Retirement Plans may be achieved by using Covered Compensation.

Covered Compensation is, therefore, simply a level of pay up to which an individual participant's Social Security benefits are presumed to be provided. The government publishes Covered Compensation tables periodically in two forms:

- Table I, which provides Covered Compensation amounts for bracketed (average) ages; and

- Table II, which provides Covered Compensation amounts for individual ages.

Any year's table can be used to form a plan's integration level. The author, as of late 1986, uses primarily the 1978 or 1979 tables, since more current ones, due to inflation, create unnecessarily high integration levels. Covered Compensation Tables I and II (published for 1978) are reproduced here:

TABLE I.   COVERED COMPENSATION 1978

Calendar Year of 65th Birthday	Amount	Calendar Year of 65th Birthday	Amount
1978	$ 8,400	1997–1998	$13,800
1979–1980	9,000	1999	14,400
1981	9,600	2000–2001	15,500
1982–1983	10,200	2002–2003	15,600
1984–1986	10,800	2004–2005	16,200
1987–1988	11,400	2006–2007	16,800
1989–1992	12,000	2008–2012	17,400
1993–1994	12,600	2013 and later	17,700
1995–1996	13,200		

TABLE II. COVERED COMPENSATION 1978

Calendar Year of 65th Birthday	Amount	Calendar Year of 65th Birthday	Amount
1978	$ 8,256	1996	$13,308
1979	8,724	1997	13,680
1980	9,156	1998	14,040
1981	9,540	1999	14,412
1982	9,900	2000	14,784
1983	10,224	2001	15,144
1984	10,524	2002	15,468
1985	10,800	2003	15,780
1986	11,052	2004	16,068
1987	11,292	2005	16,344
1988	11,508	2006	16,632
1989	11,712	2007	16,920
1990	11,904	2008	17,160
1991	12,084	2009	17,364
1992	12,252	2010	17,484
1993	12,420	2011	17,592
1994	12,564	2012	17,664
1995	12,936	2013 and later	17,700

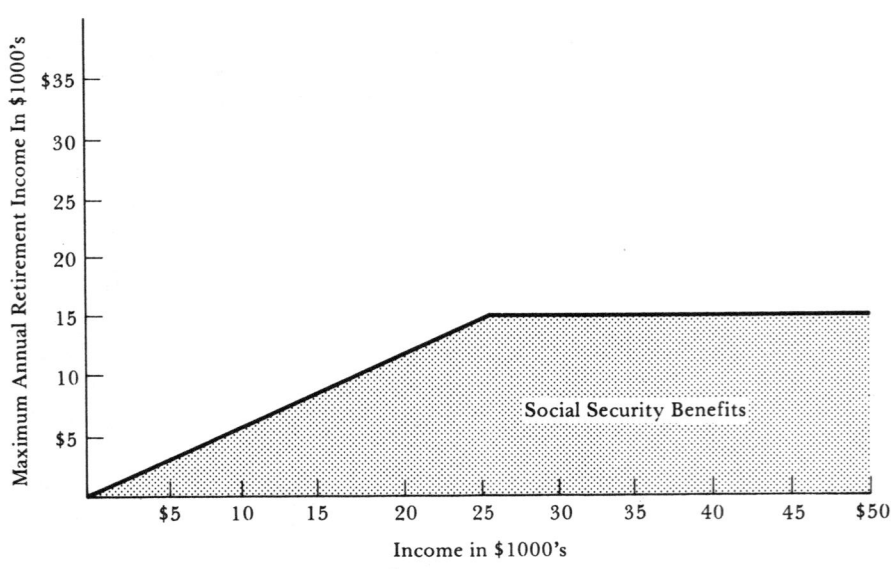

FIGURE 3.4

Figure 3.4 graphically illustrates the relationship between Social Security Retirement Benefits and employment compensation.

¶302.3   *How To Develop A One-Tiered Plan For Further Exclusion*

As with our consideration of contributions to Social Security, note that benefits, too, are provided only for limited levels of compensation. This is in keeping with the purpose of the system, namely to provide basic security. Integration as it applies to pension plans which recognize Social Security benefits simply provides employees with benefits for compensation not covered by the government system.

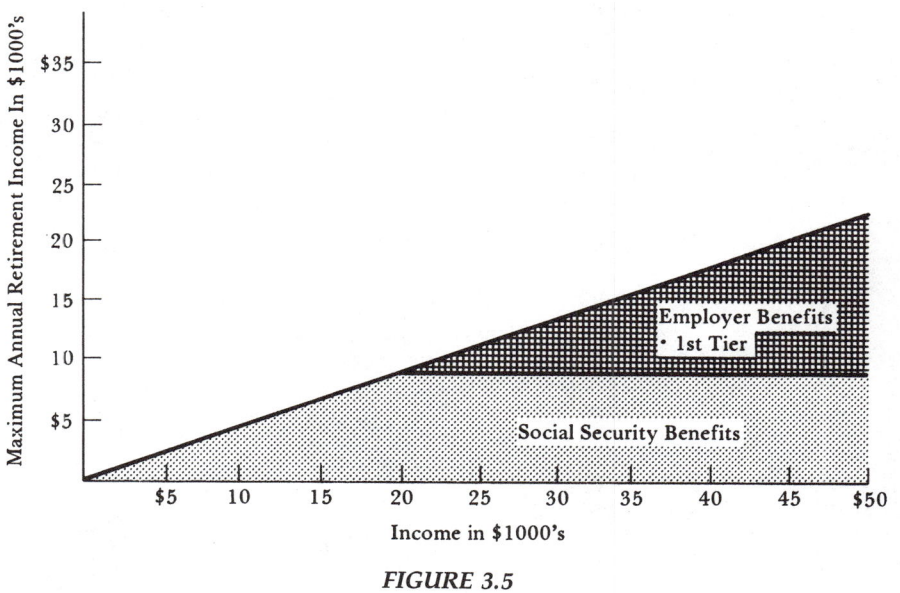

FIGURE 3.5

Example

There are several different integration methods for defined-benefit plans. One is called the "step rate" method. This allows your client to provide a benefit equal to approximately 26% of compensation in excess of the integration level. Assuming a $9,000 integration level, consider the benefits which can be provided at age 65 to employees of Simplicity Corporation:

Employee	Age	Pay	Excess Pay	26% of Pay Excess Benefit
A	50	$ 75,000	$ 66,000	$17,160
B	30	75,000	66,000	17,160
C	40	12,000	3,000	780
D	40	12,000	3,000	780
E	25	7,500	0	0
TOTAL		$181,500	$138,000	N/A

As with defined contribution plans, it is possible to reduce coverage for some lower-paid employees, as long as *TRA's* coverage requirements and the top heavy rules (discussed later) are observed.

¶302.4   *How To Develop Two-Tiered Plans Within A Budget*

As with plans integrated by reference to Social Security contributions, the alternative benefit approach can generate two-tiered pension plans providing a "catch-up tier" of benefits for all participants. Figure 3.6 illustrates the concept of two-tiered benefit oriented integrated plans.

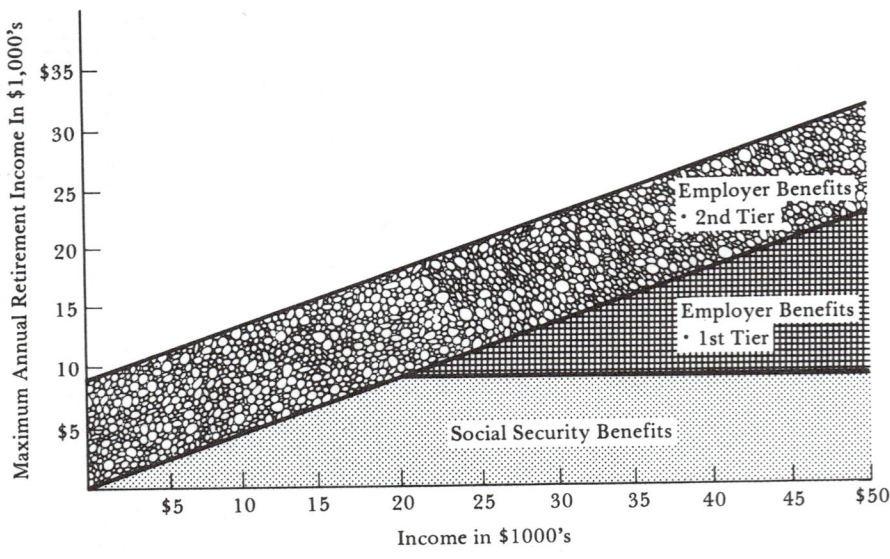

FIGURE 3.6

PLAN I. 50% OF PAY

Employee/Pay	50% of Pay Benefit	+	Social Security	=	Total Ret. Income	% Income Replaced	Annual Contribution	% of Total
John $18,000	$ 9,000	+	$8,000	=	$17,000	94%	$ 5,850	23%
Jim $60,000	$30,000	+	$8,000	=	$38,000	63%	$19,150	77%
							$25,000	100%

PLAN II. 60% OF PAY REDUCED BY 50% OF SOCIAL SECURITY

Employee/Pay	60% of Pay	–	Less: 50% of Soc. Sec.	=	Net Plan Benefit	+	Social Security	=	Total Ret. Income	% Income Replaced	Annual Contribution	% of Total
John $18,000	$10,800	–	($4,000)	=	$ 6,800	+	$8,000	=	$14,800	82%	$ 4,460	18%
Jim $60,000	$36,000	–	($4,000)	=	$32,000	+	$8,000	=	$40,000	67%	$20,540	82%
											$25,000	100%

Example ───

John and Jim work for Level Ltd., earning $18,000 and $60,000 respectively. Each will be receiving approximately $8,000 per year from Social Security when they retire. Level Ltd., considers two alternative pension plans. The first promises retirement income equal to 50% of pay. The second, recognizing Social Security, is a two-tiered plan promising 60% of pay, reduced by 50% of the estimated Social Security payments.

Observation. **Proper integration is *not* discriminating. In fact, without integration your plan *will* discriminate against the key employees.** (Note under Plan I that the lower-paid employee receives substantially more retirement income as a percentage of his compensation.) **If your client has a limited budget and wants it to reward key employees to the maximum, a two-tiered plan is a must.**

¶303 CONTRIBUTION VERSUS BENEFIT APPROACH: PREVIEWING THE OPPORTUNITIES INHERENT IN INTEGRATION

Social Security integration is of paramount importance for designing pension plans geared toward highly paid employees. Later chapters will show you how to apply specific integration rules to alternative plan formulas. Naturally, the combination of Social Security integration and the parameters discussed in Chapter 2 can yield spectacular results. **Consider the following two examples of integrated plans in which the employer's** stated objective was to maximize the deposit for participants A and B. Plan I uses a "contribution" approach, Plan II, a "benefits" approach.

PLAN I. CONTRIBUTION APPROACH

Employee	Age	Years Past Service	Average Compensation	% of Total	Nonintegrated Plan Deposit	% of Total	Plan Integrated @ 12,000 Deposit	% of Total
A	50	10	$ 75,000	41	$10,331	41	$11,587	46
B	30	10	75,000	41	10,331	41	11,587	46
C	40	1	12,000	7	1,653	7	695	3
D	40	20	12,000	7	1,653	7	695	3
E	25	1	7,500	4	1,032	4	436	2
TOTAL			$181,500	100	$25,000	100	$25,000	100

PLAN II.   BENEFIT APPROACH

Employee	Age	Years Past Service	Average Compensation	% of Total	Nonintegrated Plan		Plan Integrated @ 12,000	
					Deposit	% of Total	Deposit	% of Total
A	50	10	$ 75,000	41	$17,591	70	$19,197	77
B	30	10	75,000	41	4,203	17	3,878	16
C	40	1	12,000	7	1,427	6	866	3
D	40	20	12,000	7	1,427	6	866	3
E	25	1	7,500	4	352	1	193	1
TOTAL			$181,500	100	$25,000	100	$25,000	100

Observation.   Apart from the general opportunities provided highly paid employees with integration, Plans I and II predict further creative challenges. Consider employees A and B. A and B differ only in terms of age (and therefore future service). Under Plan I, integrated by reference to contributions to Social Security, A and B receive *equal* shares, totaling almost 90% of the total company deposit. Under Plan II, integrated by reference to Social Security benefits, A and B still receive about 90% of the company deposit, but their relative shares are dramatically altered. The distinction between Plans I and II therefore is more than an exercise in Social Security integration. It foreshadows two totally different approaches to pension design.

Caution.   Top heavy rules and TRA's coverage rules may impose minimum benefit or contribution requirements. Make sure you consider their impact.

Social Security integration and the variables discussed in Chapter 2 are powerful tools that will help you build a plan consistent with your client's objectives. While complex, they are so essential that they must be used aggressively. And their complexity is not conceptual, but rather mechanical. With an awareness of the effects of integration and other basic plan variables, you can always check the specific rules as they apply to a particular client. The result—powerful design capacity—is well worth the effort.

Caution.   TRA '86 mandates IRS to reformulate its integration rules, presently expressed primarily in Revenue Ruling 71-446. These rules had not been updated as of late 1986, and practitioners are urged to keep abreast of IRS's latest pronouncements.

4

How Defined Contribution Plans Should Be Set Up for Maximum Results

In Chapters 1 through 3 we discussed general variables applicable to all types of qualified plans. With that background, it is time we consider more specific programs.

There are two major families of qualified retirement programs—the defined contribution family and the defined benefit family. Defined contribution plans, as the name implies, are tied to specific rates of contribution that are defined in the plan instrument. This family includes profit sharing and money purchase programs.

In Chapters 4 through 6 we'll detail the operations of defined contribution plans.

Chapter 4 sets the groundwork by

- explaining what defined contribution plans are;

- examining how they operate;

- considering their pros and cons;

- establishing whom they benefit most or least; and

- emphasizing which employers should adopt them.

This information applies to all defined contribution plans.

¶400   WHAT IS A DEFINED CONTRIBUTION PLAN AND HOW DOES IT WORK?

The Internal Revenue Service requires that pension plans have "definitely determinable benefits." Normally, one would construe "definitely determinable benefits" to mean a specific promise for some dollar amount of future benefits. In fact one family of pension plans, the "defined benefit" group, meets that construction. In "defined benefit" plans, participants know exactly what their retirement income will be. For example, Guaranteed, Incorporated, establishes a defined benefit plan providing participants with a 50% of pay retirement benefit. Joe Safeway, earning $10,000, knows that, barring changes in his compensation, he will get $5,000 per year when he retires.

There is, however, a second way to meet the criterion of "definitely determinable benefits." Under this alternative approach, the employer specifies the rate or allocation method that will govern contributions. The contribution system must relate all employees on some nondiscriminatory basis, most commonly their current level of compensation. Plans that use allocations of contributions to meet the "definitely determinable benefits" requirement are called "defined contribution plans." Defined contribution plans define the contribution rate or allocation method that an employer applies to current employee compensation to determine deposits.

¶400.1   *How Allocations to Participants Are Determined*

In general, the allocation of the defined contribution deposits is made by comparing each participant's compensation or service to that of all participants' compensation or service. Whatever percentage each participant represents of the total will generally be the percentage of contribution he receives.

Example ————————————————————————————————

Simplicity Corporation sets up a defined contribution plan to which it was to contribute $25,000 to be shared equally by participants according to relative salaries.

Under Simplicity Corporation's simple defined contribution plan, contributions are simply shared according to relative salaries. The plan provides "definitely determinable benefits" since the allocation method is consistently applied.

SIMPLICITY CORPORATION SALARY RATIO
DEFINED-CONTRIBUTION PLAN

Employee	Age	Pay	% of Total	Share of Contribution	% of Total
A	50	$ 75,000	41	$10,331	41
B	30	75,000	41	10,331	41
C	40	12,000	7	1,653	7
D	40	12,000	7	1,653	7
E	25	7,500	4	1,032	4
TOTAL		$181,500	100	$25,000	100

¶400.2　*Definitely Determinable Does Not Imply Guaranteed Future Benefits*

While participants in a defined contribution plan can easily compute their share of contributions, there is no way for them to determine what their benefits will ultimately be. Note that defined contribution plans cannot guarantee even estimated benefits. Our best effort at benefit prediction is simply a guess based on reasonable interest and compensation assumptions. The age of the various participants can dramatically affect benefits, as well.

Example

Simplicity Corporation wants to tell plan participants what they should expect at age 65 from their defined contribution plan. While it is easy to calculate contributions, benefits are estimates until retirement actually occurs. Consider what happens to cumulative participant accounts in the following circumstances. The plan earns an average rate of return of 6%, 0%, and −6% (loss):

Participant	Age	Pay	Contribution	Account Balances at Age 65 If Fund Earns:		
				6%	0%	−6%
A	50	$ 75,000	$10,331	$ 240,564	$154,965	$ 97,873
B	30	75,000	10,331	1,151,233	361,585	143,292
C	40	12,000	1,653	90,691	41,325	20,383
D	40	12,000	1,653	90,691	41,325	20,383
E	25	7,500	1,032	159,714	41,280	14,807
TOTAL		$181,500	$25,000			

The difference in ultimate benefits occasioned by a change in interest assumptions is quite dramatic.

Caution. Never let your client promise benefits under a defined contribution plan. Participants are entitled only to periodic employer contributions allocated by a definitely determinable formula.

¶400.3   *How Age Makes a Difference*

Apart from the dramatic effect of interest rates on plan benefits, participants should focus on age as a critical variable in defined contribution plans. Since contributions will generally be the same for all participants earning the same salary, regardless of age, it is obvious that young employees will ultimately derive the greatest benefit from the plans. That's because they receive

- more employer contributions over their longer working lives;
- more compound interest; and
- in the case of profit sharing or money purchase plans, more reallocated forfeitures.

The result is a substantial skewing of estimated benefits toward younger participants.

Example ───────────────────────────────────

Look at the relative estimated benefits for participants C and E of Simplicity Corporation. Even though C earns 60% more than E, E, assuming 6% interest, will end up with 70% more benefit at retirement age. Many employers balk at this orientation, even though they like the concept of equal allocations.

PLANNING TIP ───────────────────────────────

If your client has a specific budget for his plan, make certain you ask him the following question: Which is more important—that the key employees get most of the contribution, or that the allocation formula is simple. If your client is most inclined to orient his deposits toward older key employees, expose him to defined benefit as well as defined contribution plans.

¶401   *HOW TO COMPUTE PARTICIPANT ACCOUNT BALANCES*

Defined contribution plans use individual "account balances" for measurement of participant benefits. The Plan Administrator or his delegate must maintain a separate recordkeeping account for each participant. The account is composed of:

1. employer contributions;

2. investment earnings (or losses); and

3. forfeitures occasioned by termination of nonvested participants.

Since all three of the components of account balances are variable, it is easy to see why benefits cannot be guaranteed in defined contribution plans. What *isn't* subject to variability is what the Administrator does with contributions, gains or losses, and forfeitures. To comply with the "definitely determinable benefits" requirement, each must be governed by the defined contribution allocation method. Usually:

1. contributions are allocated by relative salary, relative service, or a combination thereof;

2. forfeitures are shared according to the same ratio as contributions; or

3. earnings or losses are distributed by ratio of account balances.

Example
Simplicity Corporation contributes $25,000 to its profit sharing plan in Year One, and $15,000 in Year Two. The plan's assets earn $2,500 in Year One and lose $1,000 in Year Two. Forfeitures are $2,000 in Year One and $0 in Year Two. Compensation remains constant. See Figure 4.1.

Observation.   It may be instructive to track participants A and B through the above sequence. A's salary represents 41% of total payroll. Therefore, he receives 41% of Year One's contributions (41% of $25,000 = $10,250). Also, he receives 41% of the $2,000 of forfeitures (41% of $2,000 = $820). However, his beginning account balance ($10,000) represents only 33% of the $30,000 of total participant account balances. Therefore, he receives 33% of Year One's earnings (33% of $2,500 = $825). Observe that participant A's ending balance at the end of Year One ($21,895) has increased to 37% of total participant account balances. In Year Two participant A's sal-

FIGURE 4.1. SIMPLICITY CORPORATION—TRACKING ACCOUNT BALANCES

Participant	Assumed Salary	% of Total	Assumed Beginning Balance	% of Total
A	$ 75,000	41%	$10,000	33%
B	75,000	41%	8,000	27%
C	12,000	7%	6,000	20%
D	12,000	7%	4,000	13%
E	7,500	4%	2,000	7%
TOTAL	$181,500	100%	$30,000	100%

Participant	Contribution, Year One	% of Total	Forfeitures, Year One	% of Total	Earnings, Year One	% of Total	Ending Balance, Year One	% of Total
A	$10,250	41%	$ 820	41%	$ 825	33%	$21,895	37%
B	10,250	41%	820	41%	675	27%	19,745	33%
C	1,750	7%	140	7%	500	20%	8,390	14%
D	1,750	7%	140	7%	325	13%	6,215	10%
E	1,000	4%	80	4%	175	7%	3,255	6%
TOTAL	$25,000	100%	$2,000	100%	$2,500	100%	$59,500	100%

Participant	Contribution, Year Two	% of Total	Forfeitures, Year Two	% of Total	Earnings, Year Two	% of Total	Ending Balance, Year Two	% of Total
A	$ 6,150	41%	00	41%	($ 370)	37%	$27,675	37%
B	6,150	41%	00	41%	(330)	33%	25,565	35%
C	1,050	7%	00	7%	(140)	14%	9,300	13%
D	1,050	7%	00	7%	(100)	10%	7,165	10%
E	600	4%	00	4%	(60)	6%	3,795	5%
TOTAL	$15,000	100%	00	100%	($1,000)	100%	$73,500	100%

ary is assumed to remain constant at 41% of total payroll; therefore, he receives 41% of the total contributions (41% of $15,000 = $6,150). However, he receives 37% of the fund's second year earnings (in this case, a loss). Thus, his account balance is debited by $370, which represents 37% of the $1,000 loss. Participant B follows the same "track" except that the employee's share of both payroll and initial account balances differ.

PLANNING TIP _____

Recordkeeping in large defined contribution plans can be quite time consuming. Make sure your client has the capacity, either through a service agency or his asset manager, to keep track of account balances. Also, be careful to limit the number of reports participants will receive during each plan year. Most professional administration firms provide one annual report which combines all contributions, gains or losses, and forfeitures occurring during the year. Exception: plans with employee contributions generally provide statements at least quarterly, increasing the need for professional administration.

Example _____

Here is a typical format for a participant's statement/annual report in a defined contribution plan.

JOHN J. DOE
ANNUAL STATEMENT OF ACCOUNT IN THE
SIMPLICITY CORP. PROFIT-SHARING PLAN

I.	Information We Used to Calculate Your Contributions and Status		
	Your Date of Birth	05/06/25	
	Your Date of Employment..................	03/27/77	
	Your Compensation for the Fiscal Year...	$75,000	
II.	Your Account Reconciliation		
	Balance at 12/31/86.............................		$10,250
	1987 Employer Contribution..............	$10,25	
	Your Share of Forfeitures	820	
	Your Share of Investment Results	825	
	Total Additions.............................	$11,895	
	ENDING BALANCE, 12/31/87		$21,895
III.	Vesting Information		
	Your Completed Years of Service	3	
	Your Vested Percent Earned	20%	
	Your Vested Account Balance, 12/31/87		$4,379

¶402   HOW TO USE ANNUAL ADDITIONS TO YOUR CLIENT'S ADVANTAGE

Of critical importance to defined contribution plans is the concept of "maximum annual additions." ERISA limits the amount allocated to participants during a particular limitation year (generally a 12-month period, usually the employer's fiscal year, during which participant records are computed and maintained). Without the limitation, employers would be able to make contributions, subsidized by taxpayers, far in excess of what Congress intended.

¶402.1   What are the Components of the Annual Addition?

The maximum annual addition for any participant is computed by adding to the following:

1. Employer contributions allocated to the participant during the plan year;

2. Employee contributions (deductible or nondeductible); and

3. Reallocated forfeitures.

Annual additions are computed on a participant-by-participant basis. It isn't always possible, referring to the plan formula, to tell what each participant's addition will be. Because of the limitations described below, it is important to test employee allocations carefully.

Example

Maxin and Maxout have compensation of $20,000 and $30,000, respectively. Because of integration and various other plan parameters, they receive employer contributions of $3,000 and $6,000, respectively. Forfeitures are $500 and $1,000 respectively. Each employee makes a $1,500 voluntary contribution. Each participant's annual addition is computed as follows:

	Maxin	Maxout
Employer Contribution	$3,000	$6,000
plus forfeitures reallocated........	500	1,000
plus voluntary contributions	1,500	1,500
Total annual addition	$5,000	$8,500

¶402.2   How Much Is the Maximum Annual Addition?

ERISA set the limitation on annual additions at the **lesser of**

- $30,000; or

- 25% of compensation.

The $30,000 limit is slated to increase in the future when maximum allowable defined benefit limits reach $120,000 under indexing slated to begin in 1988 (maximum defined benefit limit is presently $90,000 so it will be a long time before the $30,000 defined contribution limit increases). That means your clients cannot have defined contribution plans in which the sum of any participant's

*   employer contributions;

*   employee contributions; and

*   reallocated forfeitures

exceed those overall 25%/$30,000 limits.

Example _____

Maxin and Maxout (see example in ¶ 402.1) each meet the $30,000 limitation. Furthermore, Maxin's annual addition represents 25% of his compensation, so he also meets the percentage test. Maxout, on the other hand, fails to meet the percentage test since his annual addition represents 28⅓% of his compensation. ¶402.4 will discuss how this overage is resolved.

¶402.3   *How Is the Maximum Annual Addition Adjusted?*

Starting in 1988, the government will provide new maximums in accordance with cost-of-living statistics. Under TRA '86, indexing for defined contribution plans is slated to start when the $30,000 limit is equal to 25% of the defined benefit limit (presently $90,000). Don't hold your breath!

PLANNING TIP _____

Defined contribution plans may include language allowing automatic increases in the maximum annual addition when and as they are granted. This language can preclude time consuming annual amendments. Make sure it is included in your client's plan.

Caution.   Automatic cost-of-living adjustments may be included in defined benefit plans, but for *contribution* purposes, the plan's actuary may not assume future increases.

¶402.4   *How the Maximum Annual Addition Affects Your Clients*

Let's consider the application of this limitation on annual additions with an employee earning $50,000 per year, who makes a voluntary contribution of $3,800 and receives forfeitures from terminating nonvested employees totaling $700 as well as an employer contribution of $7,500.

Calculation of Limitation on Annual Additions

A. ASSUMPTIONS:	Employee Earns		$50,000
	Employer Contribution		7,500
	Forfeiture Allocation		700
	Voluntary Contributions		3,800
B. CALCULATION:	Maximum Annual Addition = The Lesser of		
	(a) 25% of pay	12,500	
	(b) dollar limit	30,000	$12,500
	Composed of		
	(a) employer deposit		7,500
	(b) forfeitures allocated		700
	(c) employee contributions		3,800
	SUBTOTAL: ACTUAL ANNUAL ADD		$12,000
	SAFETY MARGIN ($12,500–$12,000)		$ 500

The employee has underutilized his maximum annual addition by $500; therefore, he has not exceeded ERISA's limits. If, in our example, forfeitures allocated to his account had been $1,500 rather than $700, then our subtotal of actual annual additions would have been $12,800, $300 in excess of 25% of his pay. The $300 excess would have to be held in a suspense account until the next limitation year.

Since the object of most defined contribution plan design involves maximization of annual additions for key employees without exceeding the 25%/$30,000 limitation imposed by Congress, this "suspense account" procedure can be counterproductive. When integration of the defined contribution plan is contemplated, the situation can be substantially complicated. Furthermore, under TRA '86, overcontributions may well be subject to the excise tax.

¶402.5 How to Plan Around the Annual Addition To Get the Greatest Benefit for Your Client

Since, as discussed at 402.4, annual additions in excess of allowable limits are "suspended;" they can't benefit your client's key employees. Therefore, your defined contribution plan should anticipate the effects of the annual limitation. Furthermore, your annual administrative policy should reflect each year's actual experience as it may impact the maximum annual addition.

Here is a checklist of suggestions along these lines:

- Don't set up a money purchase defined contribution plan calling for a maximum (e.g., 25%) contribution if you anticipate voluntary key employee contributions;

- Anticipate the skewing effect of integration for plans contributing close to the maximum. For example, suppose your integrated profit sharing plan received a full 15% contribution and that forfeitures to be reallocated represented another 10% of the total payroll (total allocable contributions equal 25%). The effect of integration would be to give higher paid participants more than 25% of pay;

- In profit sharing plans, calculate the amount of forfeitures to be reallocated as a percentage of payroll and, if it exceeds 10%, reduce the employer contribution as necessary;

- In profit sharing plans, consider making voluntary deposits on a "dump-in" basis in a year of little or no employer contributions. For example, an employee earning $40,000 could contribute as much as $10,000 to his voluntary account without running afoul of the annual limitation on additions during a year the employer makes no deposit.

¶403 HOW TO INCREASE MAXIMUM BENEFITS TO EITHER LOWER-PAID OR KEY PARTICIPANTS USING INTEGRATION

Integration of defined contribution plans with Social Security is quite flexible. Revenue Ruling 71–446 allows that the "integration level" of a defined contribution plan may be either

a. an employee's "covered compensation;" or

b. any uniformly applied dollar amount up to the taxable wage base in effect for the year of computation. For 1986, this means $42,000.

In an integrated defined contribution plan, different deposit rates or allocation methods are applied to participant compensation above and below the integration level. The maximum "additional contribution" for pay above the integration level is presently 5.7% (the amount of employer Social Security contribution attributable to retirement benefits).

FIGURE 4.2.   COMPUTATION OF EXCESS PAY
FOR SIMPLICITY CORPORATION

Employee	Age	Average Compensation	% of Total	Plan A Covered Compensation	"Excess" Pay	Plan B Taxable Wage Base	"Excess" Pay
A	50	$ 75,000	41	$15,000	$60,000	$42,000	$33,000
B	30	75,000	41	22,900	52,100	42,000	33,000
C	40	12,000	7	19,800	0	42,000	0
D	40	12,000	7	19,800	0	42,000	0
E	25	7,500	4	22,900	0	42,000	0
TOTAL		$181,500	100	N/A	N/A	N/A	N/A

Example

Consider Simplicity Corporation's effort to determine the most efficient integration level for its plan. Integrated benefits may be based either on each participant's covered compensation (Plan A is based on the 1978 Table), or the taxable wage base applied uniformly to all participants (Plan B). Integrated benefits are derived from "excess pay" determined under either method.

FIGURE 4.3.   COMPUTATION OF "EXCESS CONTRIBUTIONS"
FOR SIMPLICITY CORPORATION

Employee	Age	Average Compensation	% of Total	Plan A 5.7% Excess Deposit	% of Total	Plan B 5.7% Excess Deposit	% of Total
A	50	$ 75,000	41	$3,420	54	$1,881	50
B	30	75,000	41	2,970	46	1,881	50
C	40	12,000	7	0	0	0	0
D	40	12,000	7	0	0	0	0
E	25	7,500	4	0	0	0	0
TOTAL		$181,500	100	$6,390	100	$3,762	100

Note that there is a significant difference between the two methods. The choice would depend on whether the employer's objective was to equalize integrated benefits for all participants (in which case Plan B is preferable) or maximize deposits for the older key person (in which case Plan A is preferable).

Which integration system to use: "Covered Comp" or Wage Base? Since older employees will have lower covered compensation amounts, they would benefit most greatly from the use of covered compensation as the integration level. In most small businesses, key employees are in fact older than the average participant so that this may be a preferable integration system. However, if annual allocations must be computed by hand, then covered compensation can be unwieldy, requiring an individual determination of integration level for each employee-participant. In these cases, a uniform dollar amount integration level such as the taxable wage base is probably superior. It would also be superior in cases where key employees were actually *younger* than the average age of employee participants.

¶403.1 *How to Choose the Right Integration Level Using a Lower Dollar Amount*

The results for participants A and B under Plan B in Figure 4.3 could have been enhanced by using a lower dollar amount for the integration level. Since use of any dollar amount up to the taxable wage base is acceptable, it is worth testing several alternatives.

Example ———————————————————————————————————
Simplicity Corporation decides to try several different uniform integration levels.

Employee	Pay	$15,000 Integration Level			$9,000 Integration Level		
		Excess Pay	5.7% Deposit	% of Total	Excess Pay	5.7% Deposit	% of Total
A	$ 75,000	$ 60,000	$3,420	50%	$ 66,000	$3,762	48%
B	75,000	60,000	3,420	50	66,000	3,762	48
C	12,000	0	0	0	3,000	171	2
D	12,000	0	0	0	3,000	171	2
E	7,500	0	0	0	0	0	0
TOTAL	$181,500	$120,000	$6,840	100%	$138,000	$7,866	100%

Either the $15,000 or $9,000 integration level seems quite attractive. However, it is important to consider that any integration level lower than $12,000 will begin to draw lower-paid participants into the plan and reduce efficiency.

<u>*PLANNING TIP*</u>

Picking the right integration level is a matter of judgment. You should keep the following in mind:

- If you use too low an integration level and do not amend it in subsequent years, "wage inflation" will subvert your initial planning;

- Too high an integration level can be more costly in terms of key employee excess contributions lost than may be worthwhile; and

- Using "covered compensation" as the integration level will benefit older participants but may add a confusing element to plans whose primary attribute may be their simplicity.

¶404　*HOW TO GET BIGGER TAX-DEDUCTIBLE CONTRIBUTIONS WITH "TWO-TIERED" PLANS*

Because of the 5.7% maximum rate applied to excess compensation, even a very highly paid participant cannot derive too great a benefit from "excess only" defined contribution plans. For example, without adjusting the 5.7% deposit rate, a participant in a plan using the taxable wage base in 1986 as its integration level would theoretically need compensation of $217,439 to receive an "excess only" allocation of $10,000 ($217,439 − $42,000 = $175,439 excess pay; $175,439 × 5.7% = $10,000). Since only the first $200,000 of compensation can be considered in any plan under TRA '86, this is not even allowable, much less practical. Furthermore, plans oriented too heavily toward "excess benefits" will almost certainly run afoul of the top heavy rules (which apply to plans in which more than 60% of accrued benefits are allocated to "Key Employees," and would mandate at least a 3% of pay contribution for **all** participants).

¶404.1　*The Mechanics Are Simple*

The maximum annual addition for 1986 is the lesser of $30,000 or 25% of pay. The maximum contribution rate for pay in excess of the integration level is 5.7%. Suppose Dr. Max, who earns $150,000, establishes a base plan with a contribution rate of 15.725% and an excess plan with a deposit rate of 5.7% for pay in excess of $37,500. His maximum annual addition is $30,000. Under the plan, he gets

	Base Plan	Excess Plan	Total
Eligible Compensation	$150,000	$112,500	N/A
Times Contribution Rate	× 15.725%	× 5.7%	N/A
Equals Contribution Amount	$23,587	$ 6,413 =	$30,000

Two-tiered plans substantially improve plan efficiency.

Example

Money, Ltd., considers two defined contribution plans, one integrated (formula = 15.25% of pay, plus 5.7% of excess pay over $25,000) and the other nonintegrated (formula = 20% of pay). If Money, Ltd.'s objective is to help highly paid employees, there is not much choice:

			Two-Tiered Plan				Regular Plan	
Employee	Pay	Excess Pay	Regular Deposit	Excess Deposit	Total Deposit	% of Total	Total Deposit	% of Total
A	$150,000	$125,000	$22,875	$7,125	$30,000	67%	$30,000	63%
B	50,000	25,000	7,625	1,425	9,050	20	10,000	21
C	25,000	0	3,813	0	3,813	8	5,000	10
D	15,000	0	2,283	0	2,283	5	3,000	6
TOTAL	$240,000	$150,000	$36,596	$8,550	$45,146	100%	$48,000	100%

Not only does the regular plan cost 6% more to provide the same benefit for employee A, but it also spends the increased deposit substantially less efficiently.

¶404.2   *How to Calculate the Best Formula For Your Client*

You can save time by using the following simple formula to find the two-tiered defined contribution formula that will spend your client's deposit objective:

$$C = X \bullet T + .057 \bullet E; \text{ where}$$

C = the contribution desired for a particular employee (or the entire company);

X = the contribution rate applied to total pay (or payroll);

T = total pay (or payroll); and

E = pay (or payroll) in excess of the integration level.

Example ───

As the sole stockholder and key employee of DEF Corporation, John wants to set up a two-tiered defined contribution plan which will provide him with the maximum annual addition. His compensation is $75,000. The plan will be integrated at $15,000. John's maximum annual addition is the lesser of

- 25% of pay $18,750
- dollar limitation $30,000

Thus, the contribution rate which will most efficiently generate John's maximum annual addition is the following:

$$
\begin{aligned}
C &= X \cdot T && + .057 \cdot E \\
\$18{,}750 &= X \cdot \$75{,}000 &&+ .057 \cdot \$60{,}000 \\
\$18{,}750 &= 75{,}000X &&+ 3{,}420 \\
\$15{,}330 &= 75{,}000X \\
20.44\% &= X\text{—Best contribution rate.}
\end{aligned}
$$

By applying the rate to John's pay, we get:

Total Pay	$75,000	
Multiplied by Total Pay Contribution Rate	× .2044	
Equals Total Pay Contribution		$15,330
Excess Pay	$60,000	
Multiplied by Pay Contribution Rate	× .057	
Equals Pay Contribution		3,420
Total Contribution		$18,750

The simple formula works equally well when applied to a firm's total payroll.

Example ───

Suppose, RST Company wants to spend $25,000 for a plan integrated at $12,000. The best basic contribution rate is easy to calculate:

Employee	Total Pay	Excess Pay
A	$ 50,000	$38,000
B	30,000	18,000
C	20,000	8,000
D	10,000	0
TOTAL	$110,000	$64,000

$$C = X \cdot T + .057 \cdot E$$
$$\$25,000 = X \cdot \$110,000 + .057 \cdot \$64,000$$
$$25,000 = 110,000X + 3,648$$
$$21,352 = 110,000X$$
$$19.411\% = X$$

Checking, we see that RST Company's objective is achieved:

Employee	Total Pay	Excess Pay	19.411% Regular Deposit	+ 5.7% Excess Deposit	= Total Deposit
A	$ 50,000	$38,000	$ 9,706	$2,166	$11,872
B	30,000	18,000	5,823	1,026	6,849
C	20,000	8,000	3,882	456	4,338
D	10,000	0	1,941	0	1,941
TOTAL	$110,000	$64,000	$21,352	$3,648	$25,000

PLANNING TIP

Integrated Plans generally must use total compensation (not in excess of $2000,000) of participants to determine benefits. Nonintegrated plans often exclude bonuses, overtime, or other special compensation. Sometimes more can be achieved for key employees in a nonintegrated plan with a restrictive definition of compensation, particularly if key employees derive most of their pay from salaries, and rank and file employees earn substantial bonuses or overtime.

¶405 SUMMARIZING THE CONSIDERATIONS FOR USING DEFINED CONTRIBUTION PLANS

The implications of defined contribution plans are relatively obvious. In general, they are considered a young person's plan, since younger employees will receive the maximum number of annual allocations plus the maximum amount of time for compound interest to work.

Recall the example at 400.1 and note that our 50- and 30-year-old employees, each earning identical salaries, can anticipate vastly disproportionate retirement funds. The younger employee expects a retirement balance at 65 of $1,151,233, some five times greater than his 50-year-old counterpart.

Since most closely held company pension plans are set up for the benefit of an older key employee group, defined contribution plans often cannot fulfill one of our basic design objectives—maximum allocation of the employer's deposits for the benefit of those key individuals.

However, defined contribution plans are conceptually simple. They are often favored by accountants and attorneys. They lack the mystery of actuarial deposit determinations which are a component of the defined benefit family. For internal public relations many small businessmen prefer the contribution equalization. Thus, defined contribution plans are very popular.

The IRS, in past rulings, has tried to minimize the disparities between defined contribution and defined benefit plans. The result is a surprising amount of flexibility for the former group, at the same time sufficient to fulfill the important criteria of conceptual simplicity and allocation of the maximum percent of contributions to key personnel.

The following two Chapters describe in great detail some of the contribution/allocation methods previously approved by the IRS that help fulfill these dual objectives. Let us consider, then, profit sharing and money purchase plans.

5

Setting Up Effective Profit Sharing Plans To Compensate Employees For Inflation

Profit sharing plans are by far the most popular form of retirement programs in small- to medium-size businesses. This is not without good reason. They

- preserve flexibility in terms of contributions;

- produce an advantage from the high turnover associated with small- to medium-sized businesses and work to the benefit of those employees who remain behind; and

- are very simple and easily explained.

In the right circumstances, there is no question that a profit sharing plan ought to be the first choice of your clients.

The purpose of this chapter is to show you

1. how profit sharing plans work;

2. whom they benefit; and

3. different plan formulas you can use to accomplish different objectives.

In addition, there will be a discussion on how integration with Social Security can enhance the efficiency of profit sharing plans for key employees.

¶500   WHY PROFIT SHARING PLANS ARE SO COMMON

IRS statistics indicate that profit sharing plans are the most common of all qualified plans, particularly in small businesses. There are several good reasons for this that must be understood so you can use them to the advantage of your client.

¶500.1   *Conceptual Simplicity Allows Easy Presentation*

Profit sharing plans are conceptually the simplest of all qualified plans. Deposits are easily calculated by applying some allocation formula to your client's contribution. For example, the simplest profit sharing allocation method is salary proportion. Each participant shares in employer contributions according to the ratio his salary bears to the salary of all participants.*

Example ——————————————————————————————————

Simple, Ltd., uses a salary proportion allocation method to distribute its $10,000 contribution among participants:

Participant	Salary	Salary as a % of Total	Share of Contribution	Share as a % of Total
A	$45,000	50%	$ 5,000	50%
B	30,000	33%	3,300	33%
C	15,000	17%	1,700	17%
TOTAL	$90,000	100%	$10,000	100%

The readily understandable allocation methods used in profit sharing plans form their first significant advantage.

¶500.2   *Investment Gains Benefit Participants Directly*

Investment gains or losses in profit sharing plans are usually allocated pro rata to participants' accounts. If a participant's account balance at the end of the prior plan year represented 50% of the total, he will receive 50% of

——————————————————————

*In this simplest profit sharing plan, an individual participant's share of contributions varies as does that participant's salary to total covered payroll.

any investment gains or losses during the following plan year. Note that gains and losses are allocated according to relative account balance rather than relative compensation.

Example

Distribute, Incorporated's plan earns $3,000 during a particular plan year. Here is how participants share the gain, assuming the beginning balances shown:

Participant	Beginning Balance	Beginning Balance as a %	Share of Gain	Share of Gain as a %
A	$25,000	66%	$1,980	66%
B	10,000	26%	780	26%
C	3,000	8%	240	8%
TOTAL	$38,000	100%	$3,000	100%

Observation. Note the important distinctions, namely that investment earnings or losses are allocated in proportion to account balances rather than compensation. Participants directly reap the reward or loss of investment experience. As we discussed in Chapter 4, these earnings have added impact for your participants.

¶500.3 *The Key to Profit Sharing Plans—Forfeiture Reallocation*

Nonvested account values forfeited by terminating profit sharing participants are reallocated to the accounts of those participants who remain. The concept of forfeiture reallocation dramatically distinguishes profit sharing from most other types of qualified plans and makes them particularly attractive to younger employees. All other qualified plans (except money purchase plans) must use forfeited accrued benefits to reduce deductible employer contributions. That means your client loses a valuable tax deduction, and participants lose the opportunity to profit from their length of service.

Example

ABC, Incorporated terminates two non-vested participants, D and E. Here's what happens, assuming the beginning balances shown:

Participant	Beginning Balance	Current Deposit	Current Deposit as a %	Share of Forfeiture	
A	$10,000	$3,000	38%	$1,140	(38%)
B	15,000	3,000	38%	1,140	(38%)
C	10,000	2,000	24%	720	(24%)
D	2,000	0	0	(2,000)	(−67%)
E	1,000	0	0	(1,000)	(−33%)
TOTAL	$38,000	$8,000	100%	0	(0%)

Important. Do not underestimate the importance of reallocated forfeitures in many small- to medium-sized businesses. All other forms of retirement program (except money purchase plans) require forfeitures to be used to reduce future employer contributions. Profit sharing plans offer a highly attractive alternative that can create a powerful incentive for employees to remain. Furthermore, the reallocation of forfeitures leaves your client free to budget his profit sharing contribution to fit his cash flow position. Many other forms of retirement plan can be disrupted by unforeseen forfeitures that preclude anticipated deductions. The reallocation of forfeitures, therefore, forms a powerful reason for small businesses, *particularly* those with unusually high turnover rates, to consider profit sharing plans.

¶500.4   *Contribution Flexibility—Keeping Abreast of Your Client's Cash Flow*

The discretion to control the amount of annual contributions, if any, certainly forms the prime reason for the popularity of profit sharing plans. Your client can deposit up to 15% of covered payroll or nothing into his profit sharing plan. The volatility of profits in small businesses means that ongoing substantially fixed commitments are not palatable to accountants who have too often seen the euphoria of "good years" lead a businessman to overcommitment which can be a crushing burden when bad times arrive.

Also, your client's cash needs will change from year to year, even if there are ample profits. For instance, a small manufacturing company may, from time to time, need its surplus cash flow for plant expansion, purchase of new machinery (which may have equally attractive tax consequences), or to provide a reserve against future anticipated recessionary trends. Only a profit sharing plan provides this constant protection against unforeseen contingencies. This is very important for most small businesses.

Example ———————————————————————————————

Fallback Company and Leapahead, Incorporated, each establish retirement plans to which they expect to contribute $25,000 per year. Fallback Company uses a profit sharing approach. Leapahead uses a plan requiring a fixed annual deposit. All goes well for three years. Then a new computer package becomes available which, at a cost of $25,000, will

- substantially increase the profits of either firm in future years; or

- have virtually the same tax impact during the year of purchase as a $25,000 plan contribution.

Fallback Company skips its annual profit sharing contribution and buys the computer. Leapahead must make its regular $25,000 plan deposit and borrow the money for the computer, at an interest cost of $10,000 over the amortization period of the loan.

PLANNING TIP ———————————————————————————————

Despite all the advantages of other types of qualified plans, more favorable allocations for older key employees, bigger deductions, and greater design flexibility, the value of controlling cash flow is so important to a small business that you should strongly emphasize profit sharing plans for your client's first step into the realm of qualified plans. It is much easier to build from that base than to dismantle a more sophisticated plan when the circumstances require retrenchment.

¶501   CONSIDER THESE PROFIT SHARING LIABILITIES: EVERY SILVER LINING HAS TO HAVE A CLOUD

Profit sharing plans have several inherent liabilities. First, they generally favor younger employees. Second, profit sharing contribution plans are limited to 15% of covered payroll. Even in a profit sharing plan integrated with Social Security, this 15% limitation may generate so small a contribution as to preclude a key person from receiving a substantial enough allocation to make the time, expense, and aggravation of the plan worthwhile.

¶501.1   *You Should Consider who Are the Key Employees in the Firm*

Defined contribution plans and profit sharing in particular favor younger employees, since their relatively young age means they will receive:

- more contributions;
- more reallocated forfeitures; and
- more compound interest.

Generally, the key employees in small businesses are the older rather than the younger employees. If there is a limited budget, and the plan is primarily for the benefit of older key employees, orientation toward the wrong group may create a problem.

Example

Budget, Ltd., establishes a profit sharing plan, because the key person, employee A, needs to shelter some of his income. But he balks at the skewing of estimated retirement benefits (which assume 15% employee turnover and 7½% interest):

Employee	Age	Pay	Annual Contribution	Contribution as a %	Value @ 65
A	50	$ 50,000	$10,000	40%	$322,888
B	35	30,000	6,000	24	766,965
C	40	20,000	4,000	16	336,151
D	30	15,000	3,000	12	572,081
E	25	10,000	2,000	8	561,892
TOTAL		$125,000	$25,000	100%	N/A

Note. Forfeitures are allocated in the same manner as employer contributions, meaning that highly paid employees will derive the greatest advantage from them. That lends further force to the argument made in ¶ 500.3 regarding the importance of forfeiture reallocation to the conceptual advantages of profit sharing plans.

The prospect of a 25-year-old, who earns 20% of Budget, Ltd.'s key person's salary, receiving almost twice as large a retirement distribution as the key person may create a problem.

Observation. The philosophical differences in approach represented in profit sharing and defined benefit plans will effectively focus on your client's competing objectives—contribution flexibility versus contribution skewing. The earlier in the design process you force this confrontation, the sooner you will finalize your client's plans. The choices are often dichotomous.

¶501.2 *The 15 Percent Contribution Limitation May Thwart Substantial Planning Opportunities*

Frequently a small business owner will postpone the establishment of a qualified plan for years, preferring to reinvest surplus cash in his concern. By the time he's ready to take advantage of a plan, he's in his late 40s or 50s. At that point the 15% of payroll contribution limitation may preclude the use of a profit sharing plan for estate or income tax planning. Given the orientation of profit sharing contributions toward younger employees, it would take a large deposit to generate a meaningful annual allocation for an older key employee, and monumental annual allocations to generate substantive retirement income.

Example

LMN Company's owner and key employee, Jim Dandy, has been told by his accountant that a qualified plan is the best way to save money. He is willing to budget 15% of the company payroll but finds that that doesn't give him a large enough share of deposit to accumulate meaningful dollars before retirement; nor does it make a plan worth the effort.

Employees	Age	Pay	Share of 15% Deposit	Accumulation @ 65
Jim	50	$ 50,000	$ 7,500	$210,579
B	40	15,000	2,250	164,421
C	35	10,000	1,500	166,732
D	30	15,000	2,250	373,096
E	25	10,000	1,500	366,451
TOTAL		$100,000	$15,000	N/A

Observation. If Jim Dandy took the $15,000 contribution as a bonus and paid 28% income taxes, he'd have $10,800 in the bank. True, it couldn't be invested tax-free at the same rate, but he would also avoid the expense and ongoing responsibility associated with a plan.

¶502 *HOW PROFIT SHARING PLANS WORK*

The basic characteristics of profit sharing plans are most easily demonstrated with a simple example. Suppose your client contributes $25,000 to a profit sharing plan allocated simply according to the relationship each participant's compensation bears to the compensation of all participants. Here's what happens:

Employee	Age	Pay	% of Total	Deposit	% of Total
A	50	$ 75,000	41%	$10,330	41%
B	30	75,000	41	10,330	41
C	40	12,000	7	1,653	7
D	40	12,000	7	1,653	7
E	25	7,500	4	1,034	4
TOTAL		$181,500	100%	$25,000	100%

Observation. In this simple plan, participants' relative allocations are identical to their relative salaries. Further, the illustration highlights the most basic profit sharing plan attribute—differences in contribution rate occur primarily because of pay. The long-term implication of this observation is that young employees will ultimately derive the greatest benefit from profit sharing plans. They will receive more allocations, more interest, and will benefit from forfeitures.

¶502.1   *How Forfeitures Hold the Long-Range Key to Profit Sharing Plans*

In Chapter 4, we discussed defined contribution plans and in general pointed out that profit sharing accounting is maintained on the basis of individual accounts. To each participant's account is credited his share of employer contributions, interest, and forfeitures. In the long run, forfeitures provide the biggest boost in benefits for younger participants. The treatment of forfeitures in profit sharing plans is unique and deserves special attention.

Forfeitures result from the termination of employees with insufficient service credit to be fully vested. With the exception of profit sharing and money purchase plans, all retirement plans must use these nonvested forfeited account values to reduce subsequent employer contributions and tax deductions for the plan. Profit sharing forfeitures may be reallocated to participants who remain behind. Typically the reallocation is based on the same distribution method used for employer deposits. For a client with high turnover among his employees (a restaurateur or construction company owner, for example), these reallocated forfeitures can be a bonanza, amounting to as much as a 70% benefit increase.

Example

Quit Claim, Incorporated, and Stable Company each adopt profit sharing plans. Quit Claim is a small department store and experiences 90% turnover among its employees. Stable is a family owned and operated jewelry store with virtually no turnover. Each contributes 15% to their respective plans. After 20 years, employees A and B of Quit Claim are the only participants remaining of the initial group. All others "turned over" and were replaced. All the original participants of Stable Company stayed through the 20-year period. Compare the results:

Employee	Pay	Quit Claim, Incorporated			Stable Company		
		Status	Annual Deposit	"Pot" @ 20 Yrs	Status	Annual Deposit	"Pot" @ 20 Yrs
A	$ 50,000	Stay	$ 7,500	$581,908	Stay	$ 7,500	$349,144
B	50,000	Stay	7,500	581,908	Stay	7,500	349,144
C	25,000	Quit	3,750	N/A	Stay	3,750	174,572
D	15,000	Quit	2,250	N/A	Stay	2,250	104,743
E	10,000	Quit	1,500	N/A	Stay	1,500	69,829
F	10,000	Quit	1,500	N/A	Stay	1,500	69,829
G	6,667	Quit	1,000	N/A	Stay	1,000	46,555
TOTAL	$166,667	N/A	$25,000	N/A	N/A	$25,000	N/A

PLANNING TIP

Your clients with high turnover may want to consider more liberal eligibility requirements than normal, choosing to control participant funds through the plan's vesting schedule. Why not contribute the full 15% deposit on a broader covered payroll? If typical employees won't be there five years down the road, your client has nothing to lose, except taxes, by excluding them from his plan.

Caution. In years with substantial forfeiture reallocations, the sum of forfeitures and regular deposits may exceed the 25% limitation on annual additions. That's true particularly in integrated plans where deposits, and therefore forfeitures, are skewed toward higher-paid participants. Always test your client's proposed annual contribution to be sure that, in conjunction with forfeitures, no participant will run over the limitation.

¶502.2 *How Inflation Enhances Younger Participants' Opportunities*

If we add the reasonable assumption that employees' salaries, and therefore your client's contribution, will increase by 4% a year, the effect on 20-

year balances is further dramatized. Consider the turnover/no turnover situations illustrated in ¶502.1 with this 4% inflation factor added:

COMPARING STABLE AND HIGH TURNOVER GROUPS IN AN INFLATIONARY ENVIRONMENT

Employee	Pay*	Quit Claim, Incorporated			Stable Company		
		Status	Initial Deposit	"Pot" @ 20 Yrs	Status	Initial Deposit	"Pot" @ 20 Yrs
A	$ 50,000	Stay	$ 7,500	$741,718	Stay	$ 7,500	$445,030
B	50,000	Stay	7,500	741,718	Stay	7,500	445,030
C	25,000	Quit	3,750	N/A	Stay	3,750	222,515
D	15,000	Quit	2,250	N/A	Stay	2,250	133,508
E	10,000	Quit	1,500	N/A	Stay	1,500	89,006
F	10,000	Quit	1,500	N/A	Stay	1,500	89,006
G	6,667	Quit	1,000	N/A	Stay	1,000	59,340
TOTAL	$166,687*	N/A	$25,000	N/A	N/A	$25,000*	N/A

*Deposit and pay assumed to increase at four percent per year

Observation.   The effect of inflation on deposits and account balances will be most acutely felt by younger participants. This effect is further confirmation of a basic fact about profit sharing plans. However, this illustration uses only a 20-year accumulation period. It is not unusual among small businesses to have a 45-year-old employee. Profit sharing plans can be very attractive, therefore, to your clients with middle-aged key employees, a high turnover, or high investment return expectations.

PLANNING TIP ————————————————————
In Chapters 4 through 6 we will detail defined contribution plans and consistently conclude that this family of retirement program inherently favors those employees who are younger than age 45. That fact is clearly reinforced in the illustration above. If the objective for your client's plan is to benefit older key employees, you may want to consider the defined benefit program we discuss in Chapters 8 through 11. Defined benefit plans allow in their actuarial assumptions cost reductions based on assumed turnover rates, mortality and morbidity, and increases in the integration level, an opportunity to increase benefits allocated to the older key people. The choice of a defined contribution versus a defined benefit plan typically hinges on the dichotomous choice your client faces—contribution flexibility (obtained with profit sharing programs) versus orientation of contributions for older key employees (obtained through defined benefit plans).

¶503 *HOW TO YIELD MAXIMUM BENEFITS FOR THE KEY EMPLOYEES BY USING INTEGRATED PROFIT SHARING PLANS*

Profit sharing plans may be "integrated" with employer contributions to Social Security. A profit sharing deposit will not be considered discriminatory if different contribution rates are applied to compensation above and below a specified integration level. The integration level must be uniformly applied to all plan participants and either be:

1. the taxable wage base in effect at the end of the plan year considered; or

2. covered compensation, according to IRS tables.

The maximum allocation rate application to compensation in excess of the integration level is 5.7%.

¶503.1 *Using Covered Compensation Versus Taxable Wage Base*

As stated in ¶ 503, your client can pick his integration level. In Chapters 3 and 4 we detailed the conceptual aspects of integration. Now let's see how it works in practice.

Using a uniformly applied dollar amount integration level not in excess of the taxable wage base is the simplest alternative. Your client can deposit up to 5.7% of each employee's pay in excess of the level chosen.

How Flat Dollar Integration Works. Joe earns $30,000. His company's profit sharing plan provides for deposits of 5.7% of his pay in excess of $20,000. Joe receives an allocation of $570, 5.7% of his excess pay.

The alternative to using a uniform dollar amount integration level is the use of "covered compensation." Covered compensation is, in concept, the projected average of the taxable wage bases to which an employee will have been subject during his working life. Since the taxable wage base has historically risen, that means older employees will have been covered, on an average, by lower taxable wage bases. Thus, covered compensation tables generate lower integration levels for older employees and higher ones for younger employees. Often that fits nicely with the facts of most small businesses; key employees are usually relatively older.

How Covered Compensation Integration Works. Jim and Mark each earn $30,000. They are 50 and 30 respectively. Jim's covered compensation is $15,000, and his "excess pay" is $15,000. Mark's covered compensation is $22,900, and his excess pay is $7,100. Jim will receive $855 in a 5.7% excess plan. Mark will get $405. That's about a 50% increase for Jim, the older of the two.

¶503.2   *A Comparison of Alternative Integration Systems in a Typical Business*

The results of the alternative integration systems are best examined with an illustration comparing the two. Using a typical employee group, consider the simplest integrated profit sharing allocation. Plan I contributes 5.7% of compensation in excess of $37,500. Plan II deposits 5.7% of pay above each participant's covered compensation as determined by 1979 Table II:

Employee	Age	Pay	Plan I Integration Level	Plan I 5.7% of Pay In Excess	Plan II Integration Level	Plan II 5.7% of Pay In Excess
A	50	$ 75,000	$37,500	$2,138	$15,000	$3,420
B	30	75,000	37,500	2,138	22,900	2,970
C	40	12,000	37,500	0	19,800	0
D	40	12,000	37,500	0	19,800	0
E	25	7,500	37,500	0	22,900	0
TOTAL		$181,500	N/A	$4,276	N/A	$6,390

Either plan has the effect of drastically limiting allocation of the employer's contribution to lower-paid employees. On the other hand, if these excess-only plans were used in isolation, they would reduce key employee allocations.

Caution.   Don't forget our warning in earlier chapters about the possible impact of top heavy Rules or TRA '86 minimum participation rules on plans that attempt to exclude low paid employees! Under TRA '86 a defined contribution plan's "excess percentage," in addition to being limited to 5.7%, can't exceed 200% of the percent contribution for pay below the integration level. For example, a plan providing 3% of total pay plus 5.7% of pay in excess of the taxable wage base would not qualify because the percent for pay above the integration level (3% + 5.7% = 8.7%) is more than 200% of the rate contributed on pay up to the integration level (3%).

¶503.3   *How To Decide Which Integration Level To Use*

As we discussed in Chapters 3 and 4, covered compensation tables provide individual integration levels for plan participants depending upon their ages. The older a participant, the lower his covered compensation, since the average of the taxable wage base to which he has been subject during his working life will tend to be relatively low. Alternatively, a young employee's covered compensation level will be higher, since during the bulk of his working life he will be subject to significantly higher taxable wage bases. There are two factors to consider in choosing one integration level over another:

1. the age distribution of your client's employees; and

2. the availability of administrative support.

Given an employee group in which key participants tend to be older than the average age of employees in general, your client should naturally favor covered compensation tables at the integration levels. Using the covered compensation tables will result in a larger allocation of the employer's contribution to those older employees. However, if key participants tend to be young, the reverse would be true. Your client ought to consider using the flat dollar amount integration level designed to generate integrated benefits above that dollar level. The dollar level would be the lowest possible, to avoid bringing in a substantial additional amount of payroll.

For example, if your client's key person earns $50,000, then lowering the integration level from $15,000 to $10,000 yields an additional $285 allocation (5.7% of the additional excess compensation occasioned by the reduction to the integration level). However if, in lowering the integration level, he must provide integrated benefits to two additional employees earning $12,500, his advantage will be wiped out. That's because his own $285 additional allocation will be offset by a $285 additional allocation for the employees. In this example, the integration level might most efficiently be set at $12,500.

An additional factor to consider is the administrative support necessary in all but the smallest businesses to handle covered compensation integration levels. Hand calculations for more than five employees can be quite burdensome, and tend to produce more errors. Therefore, in the absence of administrative support, your client should consider using a flat dollar integration level for all employee-participants.

¶504   *HOW TWO-TIERED PLANS CAN BOOST DEPOSITS FOR KEY EMPLOYEES*

Most integrated profit sharing plans use a "two-tiered" format. That is, contributions are allocated in two pieces. First, each participant receives up to 5.7% of his pay in excess of the integration level. Second, whatever contribution is left over is allocated according to the ratio each participant's total compensation bears to the total compensation of all participants. A two-tiered profit sharing plan will not be considered discriminatory if the rate applied to compensation in excess of the integration level is no more than 5.7%, and the total allocation for pay *above* the integration level is not greater than 200% of the rate of allocation for pay *below* the integration level.

¶504.1   How Two-Tiered Plans Work

Two-tiered profit sharing plans utilize the most basic of integration methods. Let's consider two different contributions made to the same integrated profit sharing plan in successive years. The first year, Volatile Company has only $5,000 to spare. In the second year it has $20,000. Assume a $15,000 flat dollar integration level.

Analysis of Year One Contributions.   The first year the $5,000 deposit represents less than 5.7% of the eligible excess pay. Therefore, the 200% rule applies.

YEAR ONE CONTRIBUTIONS

Participant/Pay		Pay Below Integ. Level	Pay Above Integ. Level	Base Pay Contribution: 1.515%	Excess Pay Contribution: 3.030%	Total Contribution
A	$ 75,000	$15,000	$ 60,000	$ 227	$1,818	$2,045
B	75,000	15,000	60,000	227	1,818	2,045
C	25,000	15,000	10,000	227	304	531
D	15,000	15,000	0	227	0	227
E	10,000	10,000	0	152	0	152
TOTAL	$200,000	$70,000	$130,000	$1,060	$3,940	$5,000

The proper percentages were determined by the formula:

XY + 2XZ = Contribution, where
X = contribution for pay up to integration level
Y = total Comp. of all participants below integration level
Z = total Comp. of all participants above integration level

Thus,

$$X (\$70,000) + 2X (\$130,000) = \$5,000$$
$$X = 1.515\%$$
$$2X = 3.030\%$$

Since year two contributions are significantly higher, the 200% rule doesn't apply, and we can use the conventional rule under which excess pay gets a 5.7% contribution, while *total* pay gets a 6.295% contribution [rate of contribution for pay over the integration level (6.295% + 5.7% = 11.995%) is not more than 200% of rate of contribution for pay up to the integration level 6.295%].

YEAR ONE CONTRIBUTIONS

Participant/Pay		Pay Below Integ. Level	Pay Above Integ. Level	Base Pay Contribu- tions 6.295%	Excess Pay Contribu- tions 11.995%	Total Contribution
A	$ 75,000	$15,000	$ 60,000	$ 944	$ 7,197	$ 8,141
B	75,000	15,000	60,000	944	7,197	8,141
C	25,000	15,000	10,000	944	1,200	2,144
D	15,000	15,000	0	944	0	944
E	10,000	10,000	0	630	0	630
TOTAL	$200,000	$70,000	$130,000	$4,406	$15,594	$20,000

Analysis of Year Two Contributions. The second year's deposit of $20,000 will be allocated in two steps:

1. first on the basis of relative pay above the integration level up to 5.7%; and

2. next according to relative total pay.

¶504.2 *How to Determine the Best Contribution*

Critical to successful integration of profit sharing plans is pinpointing the most efficient contribution. Assume that your client's objective is maximization of relative deposits for key employees. In a year when cash is scarce, the following formula may help:

$$D = RB + (R + .057)E$$

D = employer deposit
R = contribution rate for base payroll
B = total employee payroll up to the integration level
E = excess employee payroll

The simple formula can be solved for any number of variables, but remember that under TRA '86, one additional restriction applies: R + .057 cannot be greater than 200% of R.

Example

Volatile Company (see ¶ 504.1) asks how much of its $25,000 deposit would be allocated to employees A and B, given an integration level of $15,000, base payroll of $70,000, and excess payroll of $130,000. First, we need the basic contribution rate:

$$\$25,000 = R \times (\$70,000) + (R + .057) \times \$130,000$$

The allocation rate for base payroll up to the integration level is 8.80% and for excess pay, 14.5%. Therefore, the allocation for employee A or B is easily determined.

Base Pay for Employee A or B	$15,000
Multiplied by Basic Allocation Rate	.088
Equals Basic Allocation	$ 1,320
Excess Pay	$60,000
Multiplied by Excess Allocation Rate	.145
Equals Excess Allocation	$ 8,700
TOTAL ALLOCATION FOR EMPLOYEE A OR B	$10,020

¶504.3 *Comparison of Integrated and Nonintegrated Profit Sharing Plans*

Let's summarize the opportunities inherent in proper integration by comparing integrated and nonintegrated alternatives, using a $12,000 integration level and $25,000 deposit.

PLAN I—INTEGRATED

Employee	Pay	% of Total	Excess Pay	9.817% Total Pay	+ 5.7% Balance	= Total Deposit	% of Total
A	$ 75,000	41%	$ 63,000	$ 7,363	$3,591	$10,954	44%
B	75,000	41	63,000	7,363	3,591	10,954	44
C	12,000	7	0	1,178	0	1,178	5
D	12,000	7	0	1,178	0	1,178	5
E	7,500	4	0	736	0	736	2
TOTAL	$181,500	100%	$126,000	$17,818	$7,182	$25,000	100%

PLAN II—NONINTEGRATED

Employee	Pay	% of Total	Total Deposit	% of Total	Change as a $ Amount	as a %
A	$ 75,000	41%	$10,330	41	−624	−6%
B	75,000	41	10,330	41	−624	−6
C	12,000	7	1,653	7	+475	+40
D	12,000	7	1,653	7	+475	+40
E	7,500	4	1,032	4	+296	+40
TOTAL	$181,500	100%	$25,000	100	N/A	N/A

Observation. Integration of the identical $25,000 deposit has dramatically shifted the deposit orientation toward the highly paid employees. Participant A, for example, receives 41% ($10,330) of the deposit under the nonintegrated approach, but 44% ($10,934) with the alternative. His deposit is 6% higher, and the $624 difference will generate an additional "pot" of more than $30,000 in 20 years.

Note. This book uses two interchangeable concepts for defined contribution plan integration. It is equivalent to consider either:

- a base rate applied to *all* pay plus 5.7% of excess pay; or

- a base rate applied to pay up to the integrating level, plus the base rate + 5.7% applied to pay over the integration level

In either case, the base rate actually applies to *total pay*, and the 5.7% applies only to excess pay.

¶504.4 *You Should Keep Deposit-Equalization in Perspective*

The greater the number of participating employees or the more restricted your client's budget, the more proper integration of a profit sharing plan becomes critical. However, even integration cannot change the fact that profit sharing plans are for young participants. Projecting the integrated deposits of 504.3 to illustrative retirement dates of each participant we find the following results:

Employee	Age	Pay	Balance @ 65
A	50	$ 75,000	$ 321,218
B	30	75,000	2,038,563
C	40	12,000	93,008
D	40	12,000	93,008
E	25	7,500	205,919
TOTAL		$181,500	N/A

Participant B will receive an estimated distribution at age 65 more than six times that of A. Even Employee E, earning 10% of Employee A's salary, could anticipate a retirement "pot" of 64% of that of his boss. The difference simply reflects compound interest. The older key employee doesn't have time to make up for his age disadvantage.

¶505 HOW TO BEST COMPENSATE LONG-SERVICE EMPLOYEES WHEN USING PROFIT SHARING PLANS

Rather than allocate participant deposits according to pure compensation ratios, you may employ a "unit" allocation system when using profit sharing plans. The plan, for example, may credit participants with a nonmonetary "unit" for each $100 of compensation and a "unit" for each year of service with the employer. An employee earning $75,000 who had been employed by your client for 10 years therefore would receive 750 "units" for compensation and 10 "units" for service, for a total of 760 "units." A participant with $7,500 of pay and 30 years of service would have 105 "units." Plan contributions (such as 15% of payroll) are allocated according to the ratio that each participant's units bear to the units of all participants. Unit allocations introduce the most rudimentary method of recognizing longstanding service.

Example

U. Knit, Incorporated, establishes a unit profit sharing plan and contributes $25,000:

Employee	Pay	% of Total	Units for yrs of Service	+	Units for Pay	=	Total Units	Share of Deposit	Share as a %
A	$ 75,000	41	30		750		780	$10,389	42
B	75,000	41	05		750		755	10,056	40
C	12,000	7	25		120		145	1,931	8
D	12,000	7	01		120		121	1,612	6
E	7,500	4	01		75		76	1,012	4
TOTAL	$181,500	100	62		1,815		1,877	$25,000	100

¶505.1 *Compare the Equal Pay/Unequal Service Participants in Unit Plans*

The example in ¶ 505 generates a dramatic departure from profit sharing allocations, whether integrated or not, based on compensation alone. By analyzing participants A and B, or C and D, you can see the dramatic shift in contributions. Each of those employee pairs is characterized by equal pay but unequal past service. The result follows:

- A's allocation is 3.31% greater than B's;
- A's retirement "pot" will increase by $1,586 over a nonintegrated plan;
- C's allocation is 19.79% greater than D's; and
- C's retirement "pot" will increase by $18,814 over a nonintegrated plan.

Observation. The higher the compensation, the lower the effect of past service units. This is because past service is simply overwhelmed by compensation at high pay levels. Note that A's past service units represent only 4% of his total units, while C's represents 17%.

PLANNING TIP

Unit plans will have their most profound effects on companies with relatively low pay levels such as banks or manufacturing companies.

¶505.2 *Compare the Unit and Integrated Profit Sharing Formats*

Unit plans are not substitutes for integrated ones. If your client's objective relates to rewarding highly paid owners, there isn't much comparison. Here's how unit and integrated plans work out, with an integration level of $15,000:

Participant	Pay	Past Service	Unit Allocation		Integrated Allocation	
			Amount	%	Amount	%
A	$ 75,000	30 Years	$10,512	42	$11,569	46
B	50,000	10 Years	6,873	27	7,428	30
C	25,000	30 Years	3,774	10	3,286	13
D	15,000	30 Years	2,426	10	1,630	7
E	10,000	5 Years	1,415	6	1,087	4
TOTAL	$175,000	105 Years	$25,000	100	$25,000	100

Observation. The real winner in the unit plan is employee D, who has relatively low pay and high past service. Employee B actually receives less than he would under a nonintegrated, salary-ratio plan.

PLANNING TIP ————————————————————————

Unit profit sharing plans may best be suited as secondary plans. If your client's primary plan maximizes integration opportunities, he may find the service emphasis of unit allocation systems philosophically attractive. Typically, a small business client will establish his first priority as rewarding higher-paid employees, with secondary emphasis on loyal, longstanding service.

¶506   WHEN AND WHERE TO USE PROFIT SHARING PLANS

Although profit sharing plans offer a unique set of advantages, they also offer potential disadvantages. Determining which type of employer should adopt a profit sharing plan is difficult to do. You should weigh for each client the advantages against the disadvantages.

1. Consider the advantages:

a. **Total contribution flexibility.** The most unique and persuasive argument in favor of profit sharing plans is that they allow you to retain complete autonomy over contribution amounts for your client. Small businesses, because of the nature of their competitive environment, simply cannot always budget a specific contribution for a pension plan more than several years in advance. From this perspective, profit sharing plans look very attractive.

b. **Conceptual simplicity.** Don't underestimate the motivational force of a plan your client's employees can readily understand. Many defined benefit programs are sophisticated and complex to explain.

Profit sharing plans, represented in simple terms of bank-account-type annual statements, are readily understood and communicated. If any type of qualified plan can motivate small- to medium-sized business employees, it is the profit sharing plan.

c. **Forfeiture reallocations.** No other form of retirement plan except money purchase plans allows those who "remain behind" to be the direct recipient of forfeitures from "those who left." The direct reallocation of forfeitures not only enhances participant account balances but also avoids irritating disruption of cash flow budgets that often result when forfeitures from other forms of plans must be used to reduce your client's tax-deductible contributions.

d. **Ease of administration.** Lacking the requirement for annual actuarial certification and Pension Benefit Guarantee Corporation supervision, a profit sharing plan enjoys the advantage of administrative simplicity over its cousins. In small- and medium-sized business retirement plans, administrative costs represent a large percentage of annual contributions. To the extent your selection of an administratively simple plan can reduce those costs, your client and his employee-participants will benefit.

2. Then consider the disadvantages: would the minuses outweigh the pluses?

a. **Contribution—orientation toward younger employees.** Profit sharing plans and all defined contribution plans favor younger employees. Frequently, smaller businesses involve key employees older than average. Even with effective use of integration, profit sharing plans can never even approach defined benefit programs in terms of their ability to skew contributions toward older key employees. That may be a fatal flaw for some of your clients.

b. **Fifteen percent deduction limitation.** Small business clients that have matured to the point of considering a qualified plan frequently wish to "make up for lost time" for key employees. That objective often requires a contribution greater than 15% of payroll. In those situations a profit sharing plan, for all its advantages, may simply not provide enough "bang" for the key employees.

c. **Corollary effect on other employer-sponsored plans—25% deduction limitation.** If a combination of retirement plans is used, then the aggregate deduction claimed for both plans cannot exceed 25% of payroll. Thus, if your client is concerned about providing big deductions or benefits for older key employees and establishes a defined benefit plan, he may not be able to use a profit sharing plan.

Given these facts about profit sharing plans, you must select with care the right clients. Here are a few situations for which profit sharing plans are recommended.

BUSINESSES WITH YOUNG KEY EMPLOYEES DERIVE THE GREATEST BENEFIT

Young, highly paid executives of small businesses, particularly high turn-over businesses, can achieve staggering results from profit sharing plans. Every advantage benefits them, because they:

- have more time for compound interest;

- will receive proportionately more forfeitures, both because of their higher pay (forfeitures are allocated with contributions), and longer future service (more service means more opportunities for recapture); and

- will have more contributions made to their account.

The most ideal candidate for a profit sharing plan would have:

- a small, centralized management of young, highly paid key employees;

- a large, low-paid labor force; and

- a high turnover rate among the labor force.

If your client fits this mold, profit sharing plans will be attractive.

BUSINESSES WITH SURPLUS CASH SHOULD CONSIDER PROFIT SHARING PLANS

All types of pension plans must use forfeited employee account values or accrued benefits to reduce employer contributions to the plan. Therefore, your clients with heavy turnover may find their hope for substantial and consistent tax deductions diminished, offsetting a substantial part of their plan's value. Profit sharing plans can reallocate forfeitures to remaining participants and, therefore, preserve continuity of the tax deduction.

BUSINESS WITH SUBSTANTIAL ACCUMULATED PROFITS CAN RECOVER SOME TAXES

Profit sharing contributions can be made even without current or accumulated profits. Therefore, if your client effectively "zeroes out" his income in a given tax year and yet still makes a contribution to his profit sharing plan from accumulated profits, he will create a net operating loss which may be carried backward or forward, to other tax years, thereby "unlocking" dollars otherwise lost. This net operating loss, when so carried backward or forward, may very well allow the business's accountant to open up prior or future years' tax returns to recover taxes. This possibility is particularly valuable to your small business clients, the bane of whose existence is taxation.

Caution. All pension plans create the opportunity for generating operating losses. However, only profit sharing plans give your client the control inherent in his ability to say when and to what extent contributions will be made.

Example ———————————————————————————

In 1986, Upandown Company, with a payroll of $200,000, has a taxable income of $40,000. Upandown makes the maximum profit sharing contribution (15% of $200,000 = $30,000) and still has taxable corporate income of $10,000, on which it pays close to $2,000 in federal and state income taxes. In 1987, with the same payroll, Upandown has a profit of only $20,000. Making a 10% of pay contribution ($20,000) would wipe out any tax liability for 1987, however. Upandown makes a $30,000 deposit and, therefore, creates a net operating loss for the year of $10,000. It carries this loss back to 1986 and, as a result, recovers the $2,000 it had paid in income taxes.

BUSINESSES THAT ARE GROWING OR HAVE SUBSTANTIALLY FLUCTUATING PROFITS CAN PROTECT THEMSELVES

Businesses without a "track record" or businesses whose track record indicates substantial profit volatility often cannot make a fixed commitment to a qualified plan, despite their attractive tax effects. Discretion over timing and amounts of profit sharing contributions eliminate the commitment that might be too heavy an ongoing cash flow burden for a struggling or volatile company.

Even in a year of substantial profit, business conditions sometimes dictate retention of working capital, notwithstanding the attendant expense of taxation. The consensus of the accounting community is probably well advised on this particular matter, and it may serve to offset all of the disadvantages otherwise inherent in the profit sharing variety of plans.

¶507   *SUMMARIZING THE RANGE OF OPPORTUNITIES*

Thus, the plan noted for its simplicity and lack of sophistication can actually become quite a manipulative tool. While inherently favoring younger employees, profit sharing plans offer broad allocation method choices to encompass a wide range of client objectives. That range, coupled with the discretion to determine contributions on an annual basis, should weigh heavily in favor of profit sharing plans as the first choice of most closely held businesses.

6

Profit Sharing Derivatives Enhance Planning Opportunities

In this Chapter we will discuss some special "cousins" of profit sharing plans, which allow creative planning opportunities in certain defined circumstances. The plans involve unique characteristics and imply a much higher level of sophistication than a straightforward profit sharing plan. The discussion should logically follow our review of profit sharing plans, but the reader is cautioned that the variants discussed herein are not used as casually as other types of plans covered in this book.

¶600 GENERAL CONSIDERATIONS FOR PROFIT SHARING DERIVATIVES

Sometimes the tax and motivational power of qualified plans can be employed to achieve very narrow business objectives. Sometimes, too, the paperwork and overhead associated with conventional qualified plans may not be warranted, particularly in the case of very small businesses. In these special circumstances, your clients may want to consider some of the alternatives enacted by Congress to deal with those special circumstances.

The special plans we will discuss—Stock Bonus, ESOP, THRIFT, and 401(k) plans—operate within the constraints of most standard profit sharing requirements. Specific exceptions will be noted. Some of the special objectives that can be achieved with these plans include:

1. Purchase and sale of securities of closely held corporations to and from shareholders, without the taint of partial redemption rules that usually haunt these transactions;

2. "Cashless" contributions to qualified plans that allow rapidly growing, cash-strapped businesses to increase working capital;

3. Additional employee saving incentives through the use of matching contributions to retirement plans;

4. Purchase of tax-deductible life insurance to indirectly support buy-sell agreements.

These techniques can be extremely powerful in the right circumstances but require considerable skill to use effectively. All of the above opportunities are derivatives of a basic profit sharing plan.

¶600.1   Thrift Plans

One of the simplest offshoots of the profit sharing plan is known as a "thrift plan." Thrift plans have been more popular in the past than they are now, due to the advent of 401(k) plans discussed below. However, there are still enough active thrift plans to warrant a brief discussion of the characteristics.

A thrift plan is nothing more than an "incentive savings plan," under which an employer commits to making a contribution to a qualified trust only if an individual employee agrees to contribute some of his after-tax pay. For example, the employer might commit to contributing $1.00 for every $2.00 the employee contributes. Under such an approach, the employer's costs are quite limited, and directed only to those employees who decide to help themselves. The employee gains the advantage of having his savings dollars accumulate within the tax-deferred shelter of the qualified trust.

The disadvantage of thrift plans, and the reason they are not currently popular is that the employee, as mentioned above, contributes to the program from his *after tax* salary. Thus, an employee in the 28% tax bracket will have to earn $1.38 in order to put $1.00 into the Thrift Plan (the first $0.38 goes to Uncle Sam). Given the availability of such vehicles as IRAs and 401(k) plans, each of which involves before tax employee contributions, it is not difficult to see why those alternatives are more popular than a thrift plan. In addition, TRA '86 imposed some tough new nondiscrimination requirements on thrift plans (and other employee-contribution plans), requirements that formerly applied only to 401(k) plans. To remain qualified, a thrift plan must meet only one of two alternative tests that compare the average contribution percentage for highly paid with those of non-highly paid employees. Under the tests, the average contribution percentage for highly paid employees cannot exceed:

1. 125% of the average percentage for non-highly paid (i.e., if non-highly paid contribute 8% on average, highly paid can contribute 10%); or

2. 200% of the average percentage for non-highly paid, with no more than a 2% spread (i.e., if non-highly paid contribute 2%, highly paid can contribute 4%).

While participants in a thrift plan enjoy modest increases in flexibility for withdrawals, these advantages are unlikely to offset the tax disadvantage, and it is unlikely that thrift plans will regain their prior appeal. For that reason, we will not discuss them further.

¶601 HOW 401(K) PLANS CAN ENHANCE EMPLOYEE RETIREMENT SAVINGS WITHOUT INCREASING EMPLOYER OVERHEAD

Dramatic changes in our society during the past quarter of a century have induced employers to redesign their retirement programs. Employees are more aware of the need to contribute toward their retirement. This has resulted from personal and corporate economic uncertainty and the problems facing the Social Security system. Profit sharing plans with 401(k) provisions allow employees to individually decide whether or not they will contribute to their own retirement fund. These plans may be tailored to meet the needs of each corporation and its employees. The response from employees of companies in which these plans have been installed has been very positive, partly because these plans are so easily explained and understood. A 401(k) plan *cannot* be a standalone program . . . it must be a supplementary provision of a conventional profit sharing plan. Thus, to retain qualification of the underlying profit sharing plan, the employer must make "substantial and recurring" contributions to the profit sharing plan itself (generally this means a significant contribution at least once every three years).

¶601.1 *The Mechanics of 401(k)*

Section 401(k) provides that an employee may make an election to reduce his taxable income by up to $7,000 by contributing the reduction to a plan that qualifies under 401(k). Such employee contributions must be nonforfeitable. The mechanism whereby this reduction is accomplished is to consider the contribution an employer deposits to the plan. As such, the contribution is eligible for many of the same tax privileges as a conventional employer deposit to a retirement plan. The incentives to contribute are strong, therefore, and include the following:

1. **Tax deduction.** The employee's money comes from *pre-tax* income and therefore avoids federal and state income taxes. Thus, a 28% bracket individual contributing to a 401(k) plan can substantially increase the amount of money he puts to work.

2. **Tax deferral.** Employee contributions accumulate on a tax-deferred basis, just like the employer's contributions. Thus, a 28% bracket taxpayer can substantially increase his yield compared to conventional personal investments.

3. **Tax-favored distributions.** Ultimate distributions from the employee's account can be eligible for special 10-year or 5-year income averaging on lump sums.

Therefore, the employee has virtually every tax incentive available to participate in the plan. The potential of these incentives is shown in the following comparison of two employees, each of whom wishes to save $5,000 per year, one contributing to 401(k), and the other trying to invest on his own, assuming a 28% tax bracket:

	PARTICIPATION STATUS	
	Not Participating	Participating
Annual Accounting		
Gross Pay	$50,000	$50,000
401(k) Deferral	N/A	(5,000)
Adjusted Income	50,000	45,000
Income Taxes	(14,000)	(12,600)
Take-Home Pay	36,000	32,400
Personal Savings Plan	(5,000)	N/A
Spendable Income	31,000	32,400
Add Back Savings	5,000	5,000
Net Worth Gain	$36,000	$37,400

| | PARTICIPATION STATUS | |
	Not Participating	Participating
Accumulation Potential		
Annual Savings	$ 5,000	$ 5,000
12% Gross Return	600	600
Less: Tax on Return	(168)	N/A
Balance, End of Yr 1	5,432	5,600
Balance After 25 Yrs	500,785	746,670
Less: Tax Due (@ 28%)	N/A	209,068
Net Funds Received	$500,785	$537,602

Observation. To those who say contributing to a retirement plan simply postpones the inevitable, consider the above opportunity.

Since 401(k) deposits are considered *employer* money, it stands to reason that the sum of employer and employee contributions cannot exceed the normal limits for profit sharing plans—15% of pay. This is, in fact, the case. Thus, if all employees contribute 10% of their pay, then the employer cannot add more than 5% in additional employer contributions. Furthermore, *individual* contribution limits are based on *reduced* compensation. For example, an employee earning $20,000 who reduced his pay by $4,000 could not receive any additional contributions, since $4,000 is 25% of his reduced ($16,000) pay. These limitations can be quite restrictive, especially in plans where the employer makes some sort of matching contribution as discussed below.

It is important to reiterate that 401(k) plans cannot stand alone, e.g., they must be a *component* of a conventional profit sharing plan. Since profit sharing plans must have "substantial and recurring" contributions, a client establishing a 401(k) plan needs to be especially careful about keeping his *total* contributions, including employee money, within the overall 15% limit.

Hardship withdrawals provide one additional pleasant feature of 401(k) plans . . . within constraints as yet not finalized, an employee may withdraw some or all of the contributions to his 401(k) (not including earnings) to deal with a major unforeseen financial emergency (such as the loss of a home). As yet, IRS has not finalized regulations on exactly what constitutes an unforeseen financial emergency, and most commentators recommend caution for the plan administrator trying to deal with requests for hardship withdrawals.

¶601.2   *Types of 401(k) Plans*

Generally 401(k) plans come in two versions: salary reduction and cash or deferred. In a salary reduction plan, employees make individual elections to reduce their income, with such reductions credited to their plan account. In cash or deferred plans, the employer usually provides an option that some or all of the annual profit sharing contribution can be designated as a 401(k) contribution. Salary reduction plans are more frequently used in small organizations, and cash or deferred plans are more common in larger businesses. An understanding of each is important.

¶601.3   *Cash or Deferred Plans*

In a typical cash or deferred 401(k) plan, the employer makes a conventional profit sharing contribution for eligible employees with the additional caveat that all (or a part) of that contribution is subject to a 401(k) election option. Under the option, each employee can elect to take his profit sharing contribution either in cash or on a deferred basis. If he elects cash, he is immediately taxed on the distribution and the elected portion obviously does not find its way into the shelter of his 401(k) account. If he elects deferral, the deferred amount is credited to his 401(k) account and is 100% vested.

The reasons that cash or deferred plans are less popular than their counterparts in smaller organizations relate primarily to their difficulty in meeting the nondiscrimination requirements discussed below. Cash or deferred elections usually relate to fairly large sums, and the fact is that lower-paid employees, when faced with the option of self-discipline or the ability to have a considerable "bird in the hand", often opt for the latter. This is especially true in those plans that deposit profit sharing contributions near the end of the year, such as at a Christmas party. The opportunity to pay Christmas bills, combined with the general attitude among the lower-paid employees that their employment is transitory, makes it difficult to elect to defer funds, no matter how attractive the tax consequences. Higher-paid employees, on the other hand, can benefit so dramatically from the deferral election that their participation will be high.

One method to help a cash or deferred plan meet the nondiscrimination requirements is to provide for some matching employer contribution on amounts the employee elects to defer. For example, the employer might provide that for every dollar the employee defers, it will contribute an additional 50 cents. The matching contribution can be variable on a year-to-year basis. At some level of matching contribution, the employer can create an environment that is too good for any employee to pass up, and thereby ensure compliance with the nondiscrimination requirements. For example, if the employer were to contribute $1 for every $1 the employee defers, there should be few employees who forego an opportunity to guarantee an immediate doubling of their funds (not counting tax advantages that may further multiply the value of a deferral). However, even with such liberal matching provisions, a cash or deferred plan, with its inherent availability of fairly large election amount possibilities, will be more difficult to qualify than a salary reduction plan, at least in a smaller business. Finally, a cash or deferred plan implies potential participation by *all* employees eligible for the profit-sharing plan. You will see that the alternative type of 401(k) plan may cover a much narrower group of employees.

¶601.4   *Salary Reduction 401(k) Plans*

The alternative to cash or deferred 401(k) plans is the salary reduction program. The basic mechanism of a salary reduction plan is an individual employee's election to reduce his salary by some percentage on a prospective basis. For example, the employee might elect to have his salary reduced, effective January 1, by 5%. Under salary reduction plans, the employee contributions are usually accomplished through payroll deduction, a far easier method of collection. In addition, the periodic payroll reduction amounts represent small enough deposits so that even the lowest-paid employees can usually justify electing into the program. This is so particularly because, due to the avoidance of income taxes, the employee's *take-home pay* will not decline by the full amount of the deferral, even for a taxpayer in the 25% bracket, deferral of 4% of income will only result in a 3% net adjustment to actual take-home pay.

One big advantage of salary reduction-type 401(k) plans in small businesses is the fact that the employer, if he makes some matching contribution to insure compliance with the nondiscrimination rules, need only be concerned with those employees who elect to participate. While the same problem of insuring adequate participation still applies, as with cash or deferred plans, there is a more pronounced bias in employer matching contributions toward those employees who "help themselves."

¶601.5   *Employee Deferral Percentage Options*

Most plans offer employees a choice as to how much of their salaries they wish to defer (or how much cash they defer under a cash or deferred arrangement). For example, the employee might be given the opportunity to defer between 4 and 8% of pay. This provision significantly increases participation of lower-paid employees. Alternatively, the plan may require a flat percentage of, say, 5% as a condition of participation. This provision may be more troublesome to lower-paid employees but has the advantage of considerably lessening the already complicated process of 401(k) plan administration. In either case, it is recommended that restrictions be placed on the number and frequency of allowed deferral percentage changes, since starting, stopping, and changing those percentages generates significant administrative costs.

¶601.6   *Employer Matching Contributions*

As discussed above, the most common method of reasonably insuring compliance with 401(k)'s nondiscrimination requirements is to provide for a minimum employer matching contribution. In many smaller organizations, your clients will find that their agreement to match employee deferrals at least 25 cents on the dollar will bring enough lower-paid employees into the plan to qualify it. Matching employer contributions may be (and probably should be) subject to a vesting schedule, which will, through employee turnover, help to reduce the ultimate costs of the plan. As discussed below, the matching contribution can be varied upward in a particular year.

Example

An employer attempts to establish a salary reduction 401(k) plan with no matching contribution and finds that he has high participation among the higher-paid employee group but insufficient coverage in the lower-paid group. He adds a provision that employee deferrals will be matched at least 50 cents on the dollar and finds that enough lower-paid employees sign up to insure compliance.

¶601.7   *401(k) Recordkeeping Requirements*

Salary reduction and cash or deferred plans can be fairly cumbersome to administer because of at least four factors:

1. Variability of employee contribution amounts;

2. Periodic accounting requirement (since most employees will contribute to the plan on a monthly basis in a salary reduction plan, they will expect to earn interest from date of deposit);

3. Number of accounts required . . . at least three accounts would be required for each employee;

   a.   Salary reduction account (100% vested);

   b.   Employer matching account; and

   c.   Profit sharing account.

Theoretically, there should be a provision for several more accounts to handle voluntary or rollover deposits.

4.   Employee investment control over his funds.

From a purely administrative perspective, these requirements dictate a fairly high operating cost for the 401(k) plan, especially the salary reduction variety. Some of the controls that can be implemented to simplify the plan and reduce its costs include the following:

1.   **Specific employee reduction percentages** can be used to streamline operations. This means dictating to the participating employees the amount of deferral they are allowed to make, rather than making it another election subject to individual variability. In this case, the employee's matching employer contribution can be fixed, allowing a general program to keep track of employee accounts. However, as discussed above, this approach has the effect of making the program somewhat less attractive to employees and therefore should be weighed against potential participation and the nondiscrimination rules.

2.   **Matching employer contributions** should be limited to an end-of-year occurrence when regular profit sharing contributions are made. This can have a very favorable impact on administrative costs and also provides the opportunity to condition the employer matching deposit on the employee's remaining employed as of the last day of the year (providing the normal coverage requirements can be met). The negative aspect of this approach is that the employer loses the benefit of immediate positive feedback associated with matching deposits made at the same time as employee contributions.

3.   **Limits on the number of employee reporting periods** can also help to reduce costs. For example, your client might provide for monthly allocation of employee contributions with *quarterly* reconciliation of interest.

4.   **Limiting employee investment discretion options** will substantially reduce administrative expenses. Most plans do not allow the employee to direct his own funds. However, ''earmarking'' has become an increasingly popular privilege, and its motivational value of involving the participant more directly with the activity of his plan is not to be

overlooked. However, by limiting investment directives to an annual event or some other combination of restrictions, at least some of the benefits of earmarking can be made available at a reasonable cost.

In general, the author's firm recommends that the administrative process involve monthly deposits with quarterly reconciliation of participating employee contributions and interest. Furthermore, earmarking is discouraged, with the possible exception of large accounts.

Caution. To avoid problems with discrimination in operation, clients should be advised not to place restrictions on earmarking potential which will have the practical effect of discriminating against lower-paid employees.

¶602 NONDISCRIMINATION REQUIREMENTS

Proper plan design is particularly critical for a 401(k) plan if the special nondiscrimination rules are to be satisfied. There must be a reasonable balance between the amount deferred by the "highly paid" employees compared to the amount deferred by the non-highly paid employees (including zeroes for employees eligible, but not participating). The participation results must satisfy one of two tests each year:

1. The average deferral percentage for the highly paid eligible employees cannot exceed 125% of the average deferral percentage for the non-highly paid; or

2. The average deferral percentage of the highly paid eligible employees cannot exceed 200% of the average deferral percentage of the non-highly paid, with the additional caveat that the difference between the two percentages may not exceed 2%.

The tests are less complex than they seem but must be constantly applied to ensure that the plan continues to be favorably qualified.

Example ──

Following are two examples of the application of the nondiscrimination rules:

EXAMPLE I: 125% TEST

Employee	Annual Payroll	Defer Amount	Defer Percent
A	$100,000	$ 5,000	5%
B	75,000	7,000	9%
C	75,000	2,250	3%
Subtotal	$250,000	$14,250	17%
Average	$ 83,333	4,750	6%
D	$ 40,000	$ 4,000	10%
E	40,000	0	0%
F	25,000	1,250	5%
G	15,000	750	5%
H	15,000	0	0%
I	10,000	400	4%
Subtotal	$145,000	$ 6,400	24%
Average	$ 24,167	$ 1,067	4%

Discussion, Example I. In the above example, the highly paid employees have an average deferral percentage of 6%; the non-highly paid, 4%. Since 6% is more than 125% of 4%, the plan would not qualify under the anti-discrimination rules. ‑ Why not the second leal

EXAMPLE II: 200% TEST

Employee	Annual Payroll	Defer Amount	Defer Percent
A	$100,000	$ 5,000	5%
B	75,000	5,000	7%
C	75,000	0	0%
Subtotal	$250,000	$10,000	12%
Average	$ 83,333	$ 3,333	4%
D	$ 40,000	$ 2,000	5%
E	40,000	0	0%
F	25,000	500	2%
G	15,000	750	5%
H	15,000	0	0%
I	10,000	0	0%
Subtotal	$145,000	$ 3,250	12%
Average	$ 24,167	$ 542	2%

Discussion, Example II. In the above illustration, the highly paid employees have an average deferral percentage of 4%, which is 200% of the ADP of the non-highly paid, and therefore would not qualify under the 125% test. However, the 200% alternative is acceptable because the spread between ADPs for highly and non-highly paid groups doesn't exceed 2%. Therefore, the plan will qualify.

PLANNING TIP ————————————————————————

A plan that fails to meet the tough antidiscrimination requirements represents an administrative nightmare; implementation of a 401(k) plan necessarily implies use of a plan administrator with the capability to constantly monitor the status of antidiscrimination.

¶602.1   *Insuring Compliance with the Nondiscrimination Rules*

Several methods have been advanced to provide "safe harbors" from the antidiscrimination rules of 401(k) plans. Most techniques have concentrated on the fact that employee contributions could be made to a qualified plan through mechanisms other than 401(k) elections, and simply recharacterizing employee contributions as something else. Another technique involves the employer making a *fully vested* contribution to eligible employees' accounts. Either approach will provide an opportunity to avoid violating antidiscrimination rules in all but the most extreme cases. TRA '86 adds the option of returning "excess" contributions within a prescribed period of time. One approach should be present in every 401(k) plan.

¶602.2   *Alternative Compliance Techniques Compared*

Recognizing that employees can generally contribute to a retirement plan through the regular (nondeductible) voluntary route, many 401(k) plans provide a simple mechanism to insure compliance with the rules. The approach recognizes that in virtually all cases where there is a problem with the rules it will be because the highly paid employees are contributing too much to the plan. One solution is to have the plan *automatically* recharacterize their contributions as regular voluntary contributions in amounts sufficient to qualify the plan. Another solution is to make *nonforfeitable* contributions to all eligible employees (whether or not participating). Let's consider some examples, first looking at a typical plan "before" being fixed:

Employee	Pay	Defer Amount	Defer %	Shift To Voluntary Contribution	Add Fully Vested 'ER Deposit	Total Deposit
A	$100,000	$ 7,000	7%	$0	$0	$ 7,000
B	75,000	6,000	8%	0	0	6,000
C	75,000	6,750	9%	0	0	6,750
Subtotal	$250,000	$19,750	24%	0	0	$19,750
Average	$ 83,333	$ 6,583	8%	0	0	$ 6,583
D	$40,000	$ 3,200	8%	$0	$0	$ 3,200
E	40,000	0	0%	0	0	0
F	25,000	1,000	4%	0	0	1,000
G	15,000	0	0%	0	0	0
H	15,000	1,200	8%	0	0	1,200
I	10,000	400	4%	0	0	400
Subtotal	$145,000	$ 5,800	24%	$0	$0	$ 5,800
Average	$ 24,167	$ 967	4%	$0	$0	$ 967

Comment. Since, in the above example, the average deferral percentage of the highly paid employees is 200% of the average deferral percentage of the non-highly paid, the plan will not qualify under 401(k). There are two commonly used solutions to this problem.

Solution I. The first solution is to recharacterize the contributions of the highly paid employees. This could be done by reducing each of their contributions designated as 401(k) deposits by 37½%. This would bring the group's average deferral percentage down to 5%, which is 125% of the 4% of the remaining employees, and would therefore allow the plan to qualify. The balance of highly paid employees' contributions would be classified as regular voluntary (nondeductible) contributions. The results of this approach appear in the table on page 106.

Observation. The qualification rules of 401(k) have now been met, at the cost of loss of executive tax deferrals totaling $7,406 and the loss of any matching contributions on that amount. The cost of this loss should be compared to the cost of solution II.

Solution II. As an alternative to recharacterization of highly paid employees' contributions, the employer might solve his 401(k) nondiscrimination problem by making a *nonforfeitable* contribution to *all* non-highly paid employees, sufficient to bring the different average deferral percent-

Employee	Pay	Defer Amount	Defer %	Shift To Voluntary Contribution	Add Fully Vested ER Deposit	Total Deposit	Revised 401(k) Deposit	Revised 401(k) %
A	$100,000	$ 7,000	7%	$2,625	$0	$ 7,000	$ 4,375	4.4%
B	75,000	6,000	8%	2,250	0	6,000	3,750	5.0%
C	75,000	6,750	9%	2,531	0	6,750	4,219	5.6%
Subtotal	$250,000	$19,750	24%	$7,406	$0	$19,750	$12,344	15.0%
Average	$ 83,333	$ 6,583	8%	$2,469	$0	$ 6,583	$ 4,115	5.0%
D	$ 40,000	$ 3,200	8%	$ 0	$0	$ 3,200	$ 3,200	8.0%
E	40,000	0	0%	0	0	0	0	0.0%
F	25,000	1,000	4%	0	0	1,000	1,000	4.0%
G	15,000	0	0%	0	0	0	0	0.0%
H	15,000	1,200	8%	0	0	1,200	1,200	8.0%
I	10,000	400	4%	0	0	400	400	4.0%
Subtotal	$145,000	$ 5,800	24%	$ 0	$0	$ 5,800	$ 5,800	24.0%
Average	$ 24,167	$ 967	4%	$ 0	$0	$ 967	$ 967	4.0%

Employee	Annual Payroll	Defer Amount	401(k) Defer Percent	Regular Nondeductible Voluntary	Total
A	$100,000	$ 6,250	6.25%	$3,750	$10,000
B	75,000	4,688	6.25%	2,812	7,500
C	75,000	1,875	2.50%	1,125	3,000
Subtotal	$250,000	$12,813	15%	$7,687	$20,500
Average	$ 83,333	4,271	5%	$2,562	$ 6,833
D	50,000	5,000	10%	0	0
E	50,000	0	0%	0	0
F	25,000	1,250	5%	0	0
G	15,000	750	5%	0	0
H	15,000	0	0%	0	0
I	10,000	400	4%	0	0
Subtotal	$165,000	$ 7,400	24%	0	0
Average	$ 27,500	$ 1,233	4%	0	0

ages into line. In the example given above, this would require a nonforfeitable contribution of 4%, determined by the formula $1.25X = Y$; where:

Y = A.D.P. for highly paid
X = Nonforfeitable contribution percentage required

Solving for X from our earlier example, we find:

$$1.25X = 8$$
$$X = 6.4.$$

Thus, if we provide an additional 2.4% *fully vested* contribution for non-highly paid employees, we should achieve protection from 401(k)'s non-discrimination requirements. How the solution would look like is shown on page 108.

Observation. Under the alternative solution, the employer has been forced to make additional plan contributions totaling $3,480. Worse yet, the contributions are nonforfeitable, so vesting schedules will not help to control final costs. Finally, it is important to note that the fully vested contribution must be made for *all* eligible, non-highly paid employees, regardless of whether they choose to participate in the 401(k) plan! In this example, as in most others you will find, the preferable solution to 401(k) discrimination problems will be the recharacterization of highly paid employees' contributions. However, you should always work through the numbers to compare results; the conclusion is not foregone.

Caution. Remember that although the *total* annual additions to an individual employee's 401(k) account, including both employee deductible and employer contributions, cannot exceed 25%, aggregate *employer* contributions to the plan cannot exceed 15% of payroll. And *employee* salary reductions are considered *employer* contributions. Under solution II above, contributions for several participants are already over 10%, therefore the matching employer contribution and regular profit sharing contributions could not exceed 5%. Also note that employer contribution limits (such as the 15%) are based on compensation as *reduced* by employee contributions to 401(k). Thus, if employees contributed 10% by salary reduction the employer would only be eligible to contribute another 3½%. Also make your clients aware that 401(k) accounts cannot be withdrawn, except for reason of death, disability, or attainment of age 59½, without a penalty tax of 10%. Hardship withdrawals, though a potential (and immediately taxable) source of relief from this distribution requirement, are, as of this writing, in too much of a state of confusion to be relied upon. Finally, TRA '86 added the additional caveat that only an employee's *contributions* (not earnings) could be drawn out in a hardship withdrawal.

Employee	Pay	Defer Amount	Defer %	Shift To Voluntary Contribution	Add Fully Vested 'ER Deposit	Total Deposit	Revised 401(k) Deposit	Revised 401(k) %
A	$100,000	$ 7,000	7%	$0	$ 0	$ 7,000	$ 7,000	7.0%
B	75,000	6,000	8%	0	0	6,000	6,000	8.0%
C	75,000	6,750	9%	0		6,750	6,750	9.0%
Subtotal	$250,000	$19,750	24%	$0	$ 0	$19,750	$19,750	24.0%
Average	$ 83,333	$ 6,583	8%	$0	$ 0	$ 6,583	$ 6,583	8.0%
D	$ 40,000	$ 3,200	8%	$0	$ 960	$ 4,160	$ 4,160	10.4%
E	40,000	0	0%	0	960	960	960	2.4%
F	25,000	1,000	4%	0	600	1,600	1,600	6.4%
G	15,000	0	0%	0	360	360	360	2.4%
H	15,000	1,200	8%	0	360	1,560	1,560	10.4%
I	10,000	400	4%	0	240	640	640	6.4%
Subtotal	$145,000	$ 5,800	24%	$0	$3,480	$ 9,280	$ 9,280	38.4%
Average	$ 24,167	$ 967	4%	$0	$ 580	$ 1,547	$ 1,547	6.4%

¶603   *STOCK BONUS, ESOP, AND PAYSOP*

Stock bonus, ESOP, and PAYSOP plans represent a special breed of retirement plan which is a direct cousin of the typical profit sharing program. In fact one of the simplest forms of stock ownership plan is a conventional profit sharing plan that has been specifically amended to own more qualifying employer securities than the normal 10% limit would allow. The basic thread running through stock bonus, ESOP, and PAYSOP is that a significant component of the plan's assets is comprised of qualifying employer securities. Thus, employees have some beneficial ownership, direct or indirect, in the company for which they work. This fact, combined with the opportunity for the employer to make ''cashless'' contributions to the plan, makes stock ownership plans both a powerful motivator and a powerful cash flow planning tool. Congressional intent in creating the stock ownership plans revolves around the perceived need for businesses to have the potential for enhanced capital formation, in conjunction with a form of ''capitalistic socialism'' that increases worker participation in the fruits of their labor. Congress and the IRS are aware, too, of the potential for abuse of the tax advantages of 'SOPs, and practitioners are cautioned that the use of 'SOPs must be strictly limited to those situations where there truly is a good fit of employer and employee needs and objectives. Given that good fit, a 'SOP can represent one of the most powerful tax, cash flow, and motivational plans currently available. The following discussion is limited to a technical review of major 'SOP opportunities; those who realize the incredible *business planning* potential of the plans are encouraged to pursue the topic, as 'SOPs are the plans of the '80s.

¶603.1   *General Characteristics Of 'SOPs*

'SOPs, as mentioned above, share a common denominator of trust fund ownership of some, or possibly all, shares of the employer. Thus, a 'SOP trust fund is similar to a conventional profit sharing plan's portfolio except that it will generally be designed *primarily* to invest in qualifying employer securities, such as common stock. For example, a typical profit sharing plan's assets include such things as common stocks and bonds, insurance contracts, CDs, or other conventional assets. A 'SOP might include these, but would also own—or plan to own—securities of the employer itself. Normal retirement plans are prohibited from allocating more than 10% of their assets to securities of the employer. Therefore, employees who are participants of a 'SOP will ultimately have part of their retirement account supported by the value of securities of the employer: since the employees can theoretically affect the performance of those securities through their own efforts, they may be more motivated in their jobs.

¶603.2   *Similarities to Profit Sharing*

In most ways, 'SOPs are like profit sharing plans. Generally, it is differences in trust fund requirements and opportunities that set them apart. Here is a list of key similarities to profit sharing plans:

'SOP AND PROFIT SHARING COMMON FEATURES

1. **Defined Contribution Plan.** 'SOPs are defined contribution plans; they involve individual bookkeeping accounts for each plan participant, representing the participant's vested and nonvested beneficial share of the underlying trust fund, whatever the composition of its assets.

2. **No Guarantee of Future Benefits.** As defined contribution plans, 'SOPs offer no guarantee as to the amount of ultimate retirement benefit. The employer simply commits to making periodic contributions to the plan and investing them, for better or worse, for the fiduciary benefit of the participants. When a participant reaches retirement age, it's a situation of "what you see is what you get" in ultimate payments . . . with good investment performance, the participant will do well, and vice versa.

3. **Flexible Contributions.** The employer is not locked into a specific annual contribution amount. Obviously, this is appealing to businessmen who cannot always predict the future cash flow and profitability of their enterprises. On the other hand, it means the participant has a less secure form of retirement benefit.

4. **Forfeiture Reallocation.** Nonvested account balances of terminated participants are usually reallocated to those participants who remain, as is the case with profit sharing plans. Thus, participants share not only in employer contributions and investment experience but also in the "turnover factor." Particularly for young employees in high turnover industries, forfeitures may represent a significant component of annual additions.

5. **Investment Experience Risk.** As with profit sharing and other defined contribution plans, participants in 'SOPs assume the investment risk element of trust fund performance. With good performance, the participant's ultimate retirement benefits may be large, and vice versa.

The above similarities to conventional profit sharing plans make 'SOPs look pretty familiar. But the differences and special characteristics of 'SOPs are equally important; we will consider those next.

¶603.3   *Special Characteristics*

'SOPs are unique in many respects, and certain types of 'SOPs have their own idiosyncrasies. The idiosyncrasies form the basis for comparing different types of 'SOPs in the following sections. Here is a list of comparative features of the different types of 'SOPs:

1. **Prudence/Diversification.** One requirement for all conventional retirement plans is that trust fund assets be invested in a prudent manner on a diversified basis. The purpose of this requirement is obviously to protect the interests of participants. Since the primary purpose of most 'SOPs is to invest primarily in a very limited list of assets (i.e., qualifying employer securities), Congress has greatly reduced or mitigated most of the diversification requirements in 'SOPs. Please note, however, that lack of diversification does not imply elimination of the fiduciary responsibility of plan sponsors and administrators. This is especially important in smaller businesses, where the risks of failure and other problems may simply make employer securities a bad (from a fiduciary point of view) investment. Remember, a 'SOP is not a panacea for a troubled business if participants' interest are threatened as a result of its implementation. Furthermore, to preclude participants having "all their eggs in one basket" and thereby being subjected to a considerable risk just short of retirement, TRA '86 added a new diversification requirement that applies to 'SOP participants who have completed at least 10 years of service and attained age 55. Under this provision, affected participants must be allowed to elect to transfer up to 25% of their year-end balances (less any previous transfers) to one of three alternative investment vehicles. This election period extends over five years, and in the fifth year the percentage available for diversification is increased to 50% (less amounts previously transferred).

2. **Key Employee Stock Redemption/Purchase.** Since 'SOPs are usually invested primarily in qualifying employer securities, the obvious question arises: Where will the stock come from? In closely held businesses, the only sources are typically existing shareholders and previously unissued treasury stock. The implication here is the potential for purchase by the 'SOP of shares directly from shareholders, which can be accomplished *without* the usual "partial redemption" problems that can plague conventional buyouts, *or* the contribution by the company of shares of stock in lieu of a cash deposit. Examples of the power of these two opportunities are presented below under our discussion of ESOPs, the most common form of 'SOP to use the privilege. In addition, TRA '86 added a special break for estates selling closely held shares to a 'SOP. Under the provision, estates are granted an *exclusion* of 50% of the proceeds of the redemption.

3. **Valuation.** In order to value a participant's account at the end of each plan year, the trust fund's fair market value must be determined. To the extent qualifying employer securities comprise a component of the fund, the employer must obtain an independent appraisal of the value of his shares. Great caution must be exercised in this area, since a casual valuation process might lead to serious problems if the IRS, on audit, found that the plan's value was over- or understated.

4. **Stock Appreciation.** One of the most unique aspects of 'SOPs is a provision that allows recipients of a plan distribution which includes employer securities to postpone taxation on the appreciation element of the value of those shares until such time as he actually disposes of the shares. See the example below under the discussion of stock bonus plans, though the opportunity is available to all types of 'SOP.

5. **Integration.** Some types of 'SOP allow integration with Social Security; others do not.

6. **Leverage.** One type of 'SOP allows the employer to *leverage* the purchase of qualifying employer securities. This opportunity opens the full potential power of a 'SOP compared to conventional plans, which cannot borrow money. Furthermore, 'SOPs are accorded two special privileges which make leveraging easier. First, if a bank or regulated investment company loans money directly to a leveraged 'SOP (or indirectly, via the employer), it may deduct from its income (for tax purposes) 50% of the interest received on the loan. This break has led such lenders to offer 'SOP loans at substantially below market rates. Second, dividends paid by a company on its shares owned by its 'SOP are *tax deductible* if either

    a. paid directly to participants; or

    b. used to repay a lender for a securities acquisition loan.

   This special privilege offers tremendous business planning potential.

7. **Distribution Requirements.** Certain types of 'SOP require that terminated participants have the right to demand that their distribution be in the form of employer securities (subject to an additional right to demand that the plan or the employer repurchase those shares within a specific time period and further subject to the employer's right of first refusal if the participant should decide to dispose of the shares.

8. **Pass Through of Voting Rights.** Certain 'SOPs require that an employee be able to vote the shares held for his benefit. Others do not.

These variables will be considered in the context of each type of 'SOP specifically discussed below. Practitioners are again advised to exercise extreme caution in the use of 'SOPs, but where there's a fit, they represent a powerful planning tool for the small- to medium-sized business.

¶604   *SPECIALLY AUTHORIZED PROFIT SHARING PLANS*

A conventional profit sharing plan can be amended to allow use of more than 10% of its assets for the purchase of qualifying employer securities. Such a plan *does not* escape any of the reduced fiduciary responsibility (i.e., diversification) aspects normally associated with 'SOPs. However, such a plan *can* be integrated in the normal sense with Social Security. It cannot use leverage to acquire employer securities, but it can use trust fund assets to effect such a purchase. ''Cashless'' contributions can also be used to enhance employer cash flow.

Example

BBB Co. is a rapidly growing business whose large profits are constantly reinvested in R & D and inventory. The company must pay significant income taxes that crimp its budget. It would like to provide some sort of employee incentive plan, such as profit sharing, but fears the additional cash flow drain. BBB asks its accountant to compare the cash flow implications of three alternatives:

1. Implementing *no* plan;

2. Implementing a conventional *profit sharing plan;* and

3. Implementing a *specially amended profit sharing plan* to which it contributes treasury stock instead of cash.

Assuming the company has $1 million in gross earnings and would like to contribute $200,000 to a plan, the results are quite interesting:

COMPANY INSTITUTES

	No Plan	Profit Sharing	''Special'' PSP
Gross Earnings	$1,000,000	$1,000,000	$1,000,000
Contribution	0	(200,000)	(200,000)
Pre-tax Earnings	1,000,000	800,000	800,000
Income Taxes @ 40%	(400,000)	(320,000)	(320,000)
Net Income	600,000	480,000	480,000
Add Back			
Noncash Contribution	0	0	200,000
Net Working Capital	$ 600,000	$ 400,000	$ 680,000

That's a pretty spectacular opportunity; not only can BBB take care of its employees, but it can also increase its working capital situation over the "no plan" situation. This opportunity for cashless contributions is available in other types of 'SOP as well.

Specially amended profit sharing plans do not need to pass voting rights through to participants under any circumstances. In addition, they do not need to provide the terminating participant with the right to demand a stock distribution, thereby allaying the frequent concern of small businessmen over having a lot of small shareholders running around. However, such plans do place a heavy fiduciary burden on the employer with respect to his decision to be less diversified than with conventional plans.

¶605   STOCK BONUS PLANS

Stock bonus plans represent the next level of sophistication in the 'SOP family. Unlike specially amended profit sharing plans, stock bonus programs are a true 'SOP in that they must specifically provide that their primary purpose is to invest in qualifying employer securities. As a true 'SOP, a stock bonus plan needs contain no provision for diversification of trust funds, thereby eliminating part of the concern about prudence that may be associated with a specially amended profit sharing plan's heavy investment in such securities. However, stock bonus plans bring into play some of the specific requirements of 'SOPs, including the following:

1. **Voting Rights** of employer shares held by the stock bonus plan must be passed through to plan participants in certain circumstances.

2. **Distributions** from stock bonus plans must include a provision for terminated participants to request their payout in the form of employer securities, subject to the employer's right of first refusal on a subsequent sale of the shares. In addition, the employer is required to repurchase the shares within a specific time period at the request of the terminated participant. This provision insures that the participant's retirement benefits under the plan have a measure of liquidity.

Stock bonus plans share many attributes with specially amended profit sharing plans, including the opportunity for use of integration with Social Security, the potential for cashless contributions, and the prohibition against "leveraging" of plan assets. One additional element added by the fact that a stock bonus plan is a true member of the 'SOP family is that a terminated participant who receives part of his distribution in employer securities can defer taxation of the appreciation element of that stock when he computes his taxes. This opportunity is only available if the employer can provide detailed cost basis information, which implies a sophisticated and costly recordkeeping system. However, the opportunity is well worth the cost.

Example

Bonus Co. invests 50% of its plan assets in employer securities. Over time, it contributes a total of $100,000 to employee G's account. When G retires, he receives a total distribution of $400,000. One half of his $300,000 investment appreciation came from shares in his employer's stock. Assuming G takes a lump sum and uses 5-year income averaging to compute his tax, here's a graphic illustration of the potential:

Gross Distribution	$400,000
Less: 'ER Security Appreciation	(150,000)
Immediately Taxable Amount	$250,000
5-Yr. Income Average Tax	(70,000)
Take-home From Tax. Portion	$180,000
Add Back Postponed Amount	150,000
Net Distribution	$330,000

Of course, when the participant ultimately disposes of the employer securities, he will pay a tax on the appreciation. In the above example, that could mean an additional $42,000. Even with that additional tax, the distribution amounts to $288,000, or 72% of the gross distribution! This opportunity is available to all members of the 'SOP family.

¶606   *LEVERAGED ESOPS*

Probably the most powerful member of the 'SOP family is the Leveraged ESOP, or LESOP. LESOPs offer all the advantages of stock bonus plans, plus more. First, we will consider how LESOPs are similar to stock bonus plans; then we will review their additional advantages. Finally, we'll look at some examples of LESOPs in action. LESOPs probably represent the most frequently used member of the 'SOP family in small- to medium-sized businesses.

¶606.1   *How LESOPs Are Similar to Stock Bonus Plans*

LESOPs are simply the next step in sophistication above stock bonus plans, which in turn are the next step in sophistication above specially amended profit sharing plans. Here is a list of the key similarities between LESOPs and stock bonus plans:

1. **Diversification** is not a requirement of a LESOP Trust. Thus, the risk of owning a disproportionate percentage of one type of asset (in this case, qualifying employer securities) that would be associated with a conventional retirement plan is mitigated. Remember, however, that this does not relieve parties in interest from the *fiduciary* responsibility associated with the decision to make an investment in employer securities, or the requirement to allow participant-directed diversification in certain circumstances as discussed earlier.

2. **Stock appreciation** components of distributions from LESOPs, like Stock Bonus Plans, represent a tax deferral opportunity. Terminated participants receiving distributions can elect taxation on their distribution, exclusive of gains from employer securities, and have that component taxed when the stock is ultimately disposed.

3. **Cashless contributions** of employer securities can benefit the employer by increasing his working capital at a cost of dilution.

All these opportunities represent a powerful tool. However, in many respects, LESOPs differ from stock bonus plans.

¶606.2   *Key Differences Between LESOPs and Stock Bonus Plans*

There are two categories of differences between LESOPs and stock bonus plans: operational considerations and planning opportunities. Let's consider the list:

1. **Integration** with Social Security is not allowed in LESOPs. The IRS has come under considerable fire for promulgating this restrictive regulation. The result, of course, is that if an employer wants a LESOP and integration, he will have to install a second plan.

2. **Distributions** from LESOPs *do not* have to be made in the form of employer securities if the employer's charter/bylaws restrict ownership of shares to active employees or qualified trusts. This is extremely important, since many smaller employers are reluctant to implement 'SOPs if they are faced with the prospect of the creation of a number of minor shareholders.

3. **Voting rights** of securities of closely held employers held by the LESOP trust *do not* have to be passed through to employees *except* in those matters which, under state law, require *more than a majority* for passage. Practitioners should consult their own state laws to determine the impact of this provision. Generally the list is short and limited to major events such as consolidation or merger. For routine corporate actions and management decisions, however, your clients will not need to be concerned about employee-participants in the LESOP looking over management's shoulder.

4. **Leverage** is allowed in LESOPs and represents the key to unlocking the power of a 'SOP in the small business environment. Leverage means that the LESOP trust can acquire blocks of employer securities through the use of borrowing—even if the collateral for such borrowing is the acquired shares.

The above differences create some interesting planning opportunities. It is beyond the scope of this book to consider all those potential uses, but the following section outlines some of the more frequently used provisions.

¶606.3 *How To Use a LESOP*

Creativity is the name of the game in using LESOPs. The potential for leverage implies that a LESOP can be used to fulfill many typical small business objectives, such as the acquisition of a retiring shareholder's interests. Here is a list of some of the most important planning uses for a LESOP:

1. **Partial or complete redemptions of key employee stock.** One of the more vexing problems facing the owners of small- to medium-sized businesses is how to dispose of their shares upon death, disability, retirement, or separation from service. When such events occur, and the shareholder wishes to sell some of his shares, he faces two problems:

    a. Without a LESOP, the transaction usually comes from after-tax income . . . for a 40% bracket taxpayer, this means it takes $1.67 of revenue for each $1 of shares purchased; and

    b. If the redemption of shares is not complete, there is a considerable risk that the advantage of long-term capital gains taxation will be lost.

A LESOP eliminates both these problems. If the shares are purchased directly by the trust, they are purchased with money that was deducted by the corporation; and even if the redemption is structured as an installment sale, the risk of loss of long-term capital gains taxation is mitigated. Furthermore, if a shareholder sells sufficient shares to his LESOP such that after the transaction the LESOP owns at least 30% of the company, and if the seller reinvests the proceeds within a prescribed period in certain non-passive investments, then his sale is *tax deferred* (until disposition of the reinvested assets). This powerful technique enables a small business owner's company to *deduct* the buyout, and the owner to receive the proceeds *without current tax.*

Warning. A LESOP cannot enter into a future buy-sell agreement with shareholders, under the theory that it is impossible to know in advance what the fair market value of shares will be in the future.

2. **Contribution limits.** In a conventional 'SOP, the maximum annual contribution is 15% of eligible payroll. However, if the funds are used for purchase of securities, an employer can contribute up to 25% of payroll to a LESOP for the principal component of purchased shares, and an unlimited amount for interest. Thus, a LESOP represents a powerful tool for the tax-deductible acquisition of employer securities. Furthermore, certain LESOPs described under Code §4975(e) are accorded an increase in the normal limit on annual additions, from $30,000 to as much as $60,000.

Your clients can truly benefit from the use of a LESOP if they are not dissuaded by the appearance of ''sharing the spoils'' with their employees.

7

How Money Purchase Plans Increase Creative Design Opportunities

Money purchase plans are the most direct examples of "defined contribution plans." In money purchase plans, the employer contribution is fixed as a percentage of eligible payroll. Thus, money purchase plans add an additional element to profit sharing plans. In addition to defining the manner in which allocations are made, the amount of contribution is also defined.

This Chapter will show you how, when, and where to use money purchase plans. In addition, it will describe the pitfalls to be avoided in planning with your clients.

Money purchase plans are the simplest type of pension plan, both operationally and conceptually. They create substantially larger tax-deductible potential than profit sharing plans and often more than a small business can afford. Like profit sharing plans, money purchase plans are powerful accumulation vehicles for young, highly paid employees. Finally, the combination of money purchase with profit sharing plans may provide the ideal mix of flexibility and tax deductibility for small- to medium-sized businesses.

¶700   KEY SIMILARITIES BETWEEN MONEY PURCHASE AND PROFIT SHARING PLANS

Money purchase plans offer substantial creative planning opportunities. To realize these opportunities you must build on the knowledge of how profit sharing plans work. Then you can capitalize on the major differences between money purchase and profit sharing plans to establish your planning strategy. Here are the essential similarities.

¶700.1   *The Accounting Is Simple*

Like profit sharing plans, money purchase plans use ***account balances*** to form the basis of each participant's benefits. Each year, a participant's account balance will be credited with employer contributions and credited (or charged) with a pro rata share of earnings (or losses). With the passage of TRA '86, forfeitures may (but need not be) used to add to participants' accounts.

Example ——————————————————————————————

A earns $70,000 while B earns $30,000. A and B establish a money purchase plan and contribute $10,000 (10% of total pay). An initial account balance is established for A in the amount of $7,000, and for B in the amount of $3,000. During the first year the plan's assets earn $1,000 interest. Since A's account balance represents 70% of the total, A receives 70% of the income ($700). B receives the balance ($300).

Every year, the account balances are updated to reflect further contributions (which are generally allocated by reference to compensation and service) and earnings (which are generally allocated according to proportionate account balances). When a participant terminates, whether for reasons of death, disability, or retirement, his benefit will be related to this account balance. There is no way to predict the exact value of a participant's share, since investment results will ultimately be such a large component of the account.

¶700.2   *Simplicity Is Its Own Reward*

As with profit sharing plans, the simple account balance system used in money purchase plans to measure participant benefits makes for easy employee communications. This enhances employee appreciation of the value of the plan. Employees will recognize a money purchase benefit as something similar to a bank book, to which the employer makes contributions, credits interest, and possibly adds forfeitures.

PLANNING TIP
If you are implementing a plan because of employee pressure, don't overlook the value of simplicity inherent in money purchase plans. Don't expect employees to appreciate something they can't understand.

¶700.3   *How Money Purchase Plans Favor Younger Employees*

Specific retirement benefits are not promised under either profit sharing or money purchase plans. Periodic contributions are simply added to employee accounts. Very often young employees, even those earning relatively small amounts, will have higher projected retirement benefits than older, higher-paid employees. It is a fact of life that defined-contribution plans favor most heavily the younger employees, for whom compound interest and a greater number of contributions will simply add up to a larger "pot" at retirement age.

Example
XYZ, Incorporated, contributes 10% of pay to its participating employees and earns 8% interest on account balances. At first glance, nothing could be more fair. But consider the results.

Participant	Age	Compensation	Annual Contribution	Account Balance at Age 65
A	55	$ 50,000	$ 5,000	$ 78,227
B	40	50,000	5,000	394,772
C	25	15,000	1,500	419,672
TOTAL		$115,000	$11,500	N/A

PLANNING TIP
Money purchase plans, like profit sharing plans, favor young employees over a period of time. Make sure your clients understand this fact. Upon considering it, many clients will opt for a program which gives older employees an opportunity to "catch-up" under a plan formula recognizing age.

¶700.4   *How Simplicity Will Conserve Your Time and Benefit Your Clients*

Pension plans of any type are inherently good, since:

1. They provide tax-deductible contributions;
2. Fund earnings are tax free; and
3. Certain distributions are accorded favorable tax treatment.

Often it is tempting, in an effort to orient the plan a little more heavily toward one or two key employees, to use more esoteric plan designs. If a money purchase or profit sharing plan comes close to fulfilling the objectives set out by your client, use them. Better to use a plan everyone understands, and for which ERISA reporting and disclosure requirements are less onerous, than to create a future "time liability" often associated with more complicated plans. The time you might have to spend explaining a more complicated plan again and again may not be justified by a marginal improvement in plan efficiency.

¶701   KEY DIFFERENCES BETWEEN MONEY PURCHASE AND PROFIT SHARING PLANS

Most similarities between money purchase and profit sharing plans are cosmetic—for instance, accounting and communication techniques. Many practitioners "piggyback" money purchase plans as secondary programs on top of existing profit sharing plans, thinking that the money purchase plan is merely an extension of the profit sharing vehicle. Do not be lulled into this feeling of complacency. The differences between money purchase and profit sharing plans are far more substantive. Use the differences to your advantage; do not be trapped by them.

¶701.1   *A Fixed Contribution May Frighten Your Clients*

Money purchase plans are subject to ERISA's minimum funding standards. Once your client adopts a money purchase plan he has a fixed, measurable, and ongoing contribution commitment, notwithstanding fluctuations in his business. This inflexibility can limit your client's options for cash flow management and be quite troublesome in times of recession or rapid growth when cash may be in short supply.

Example ———————————————————————————

Company A adopts a profit sharing plan. Company B adopts a money purchase plan. Each contributes $25,000 in the first plan year. In the second year each wishes to buy a piece of machinery which, because of depreciation, will have a comparable tax effect to a $25,000 pension or profit sharing plan contribution. Each company feels that purchase of the machinery will make it more competitive and profitable in the future. Company A skips its profit sharing contribution and uses the cash towards purchase of the machine. Company B *must* contribute again to its money purchase plan, and find other capital sources for the machine.

Guideline. Money purchase plans, because of their contribution requirements, are better for *mature* businesses whose expansion rate has slowed, or service-type businesses whose cash flow is extremely stable and for whom there is no particular need for internal cash generation. Generally, labor-intensive businesses or professional organizations will make the best prospects. Young, volatile companies usually ought to stay clear of money purchase plans.

PLANNING TIP —————————————————————————

Many defined-benefit plans discussed in later Chapters offer more contribution flexibility than money purchase plans. Their greater complexity may be offset by their ability to keep your client's options open.

What To Do. Make sure your client does not adopt a money purchase plan solely because of one or two highly profitable years. Discuss the contribution requirement and insure that for the foreseeable future adequate *surplus* cash will be available to fund the plan.

¶701.2   *How the Larger Contribution Limits of Money Purchase Plans Can Help Minimize Your Client's Taxes*

Profit sharing contributions are limited to 15% of covered payroll; money purchase plans, 25%. For the client whose salary is sufficient to meet his own personal needs and yet whose business still has surplus cash, this extra 10% deduction may make a big difference.

Example ———————————————————————————

Doctor Z's practice nets $120,000 after expenses. Assuming income not sheltered by a qualified plan will ultimately be taxed at 28%, the 15% deduction limit available under profit sharing plans ($18,000) is worth $5,040 per year in tax savings. The 25% ($30,000) money purchase deduction is worth $8,400 in tax savings. The additional $3,360 tax savings available with the money purchase plan, compounded at 8% interest for 20 years, has a future value of almost $162,273. Therefore, if the cash is available, big tax savings await.

¶701.3 *Avoiding Cash Flow Disruption Under Money Purchase Plans*

When a nonvested participant leaves a profit sharing plan, the portion of the account balance he forfeits is reallocated to remaining participants. This is not necessarily so with money purchase plans. Forfeited account balances may be used to reduce future employer contributions. This possible distinction between the use of forfeitures in profit sharing and money purchase plans can be a most substantive difference between the two types of plans, and may potentially cause a problem with the money purchase plans. If your client adopts a money purchase plan for the right reasons—stable, mature cash flow coupled with the desire for a bigger tax break—he may be displeased by the disruptive effect of forfeitures, unless he reallocates them as in a profit sharing plan.

Example

ABC Company has a profit sharing plan. DEF, Incorporated, has a money purchase plan that uses forfeitures to reduce employer contributions. Both have four participants in their plan, each of whom has a nonvested $25,000 account balance at the beginning of the plan year. Each company regularly contributes $40,000 per year to its plan. Consider the effects on the company's tax planning if one participant terminates under ABC or DEF's plans.

	Profit-Sharing ABC Company		Money-Purchase DEF, Inc.	
Beginning Account Balances (4 employees)		$100,000		$100,000
Total Contribution	40,000		40,000	
Less: Forfeitures Applied	N/A		(25,000)	
Net Tax-Deductible Contribution		40,000		15,000
Ending Account Balances		$140,000		$115,000

While the three remaining participants under each plan fare identically, the effect on ABC and DEF is dramatically different. DEF loses in two ways.

First, it must pay an additional $12,500 in taxes. Second, it now has surplus cash on hand that it had planned to put into the money purchase plan.

PLANNING TIPS

1. Unless it is unavoidable, use money purchase plans only in conjunction with profit sharing plans. The flexible contribution possibilities of profit sharing plans will cushion the otherwise disruptive cash flow aspects of money purchase plans. For instance, in a year where forfeitures would otherwise reduce your client's contribution under a money purchase plan you could boost the profit sharing plan deposit to achieve tax and cash continuity.

2. Use the most restrictive eligibility requirements possible when you implement money purchase plans. Try to eliminate your sources of turnover before they come into the plan.

3. Unless it would cause problems with the limitation on annual additions, use money purchase forfeitures as you would in profit sharing plans—reallocate them.

PLANNING TIP

Try not to use insurance or other nonliquid, or front-end loaded, products in *any* high turnover situation, but be particularly wary of money purchase plans, where relative allocations for young employees (the group most subject to turnover) will be high. If such products are attractive from other perspectives, use them only for participants who have completed some specified period of service. For instance, fund an insured death benefit with term insurance for the first five years of an employee's participation and *only then* switch to whole life.

¶702 HOW TO USE MONEY PURCHASE PLANS EFFECTIVELY

Notwithstanding their inherent limitations, money purchase plans offer practitioners substantially increased design flexibility. Maximum effectiveness will occur if you follow these steps:

1. Eliminate those clients for whom the inherent drawbacks of money purchase plans will be most acute:

    a. High turnover companies.

    b. Plans with small contributions. The combination of reporting and disclosure costs and cash flow disruption occasioned by forfeitures not reallocated will likely destroy the efficiency of the plan as a tax or cash management system.

c. Companies with older key employees. Remember, money purchase plans virtually always favor younger employees. If your goal is a big contribution for older key employees, scrap your plans for a money purchase plan.

2. **Plan**—Set your objectives in advance relative to:

a. probable budget;

b. need for flexibility; and

c. desired orientation of plan toward key individuals.

3. **Study** the following options to see whether a particular money purchase plan can achieve your goals within budget parameters.

¶703   USING EFFECTIVE COMBINATIONS OF MONEY PURCHASE AND PROFIT SHARING PLANS

Generally money purchase plans are used in conjunction with profit sharing plans by clients desiring deductions in excess of 15%. These combination plans can be effective for a variety of reasons:

- bigger deductions;
- simplicity; or
- more orientation toward key employees.

Here is how to use combination plans to provide the best of both worlds.

¶703.1   *How To Get a Big Tax Deduction With Maximum Flexibility*

The flexibility of a profit sharing plan combined with the *larger tax deduction* under money purchase plans may work well for your clients. Consider the adoption of a 10%-of-pay money purchase plan and a variable contribution profit sharing plan. The minimum required employer contribution would be 10% of payroll (less any forfeitures). The maximum tax deduction would be 25% of payroll (taking full advantage of the profit sharing plan). Consider the effect on a sample company, Flexible, Incorporated, which has wide variations in its profitability.

FIGURE 7.2.   MINIMUM AND MAXIMUM CONTRIBUTIONS UNDER TANDEM PLAN FOR FLEXIBLE, INCORPORATED

		Flexible, Inc.—**Minimum Contribution**			
Participant	Compensation	Profit-Sharing Deposit	+	Money-Purchase Deposit =	Total Minimum Deposit
A	$ 50,000	0		$ 5,000	$ 5,000
B	25,000	0		2,500	2,500
C	15,000	0		1,500	1,500
D	10,000	0		1,000	1,000
TOTAL	$100,000			$10,000	$10,000

		Flexible, Inc.—**Maximum Contribution**			
Participant	Compensation	Profit-Sharing Deposit	+	Money-Purchase Deposit =	Total Maximum Deposit
A	$ 50,000	$ 7,500		$ 5,000	$12,500
B	25,000	3,750		2,500	6,250
C	15,000	2,250		1,500	3,750
D	10,000	1,500		1,000	2,500
TOTAL	$100,000	$15,000		$10,000	$25,000

The wide choice may be very valuable to your client.

Consider also how a tandem plan can overcome the problem caused by money purchase forfeitures which are not reallocated, but rather applied to future contributions. If your client desires a constant tax deduction of 20% of payroll, he might be tempted simply to implement a 20%-of-pay money purchase plan. However, in a year of large forfeitures this tax planning may go awry. If, however, he established a 10% money purchase plan in conjunction with a variable profit sharing plan, he could simply vary the profit sharing contribution up or down to reflect forfeitures, which would otherwise limit his money purchase tax deduction.

Example

Pennywise, Incorporated, and Poundfoolish, Ltd., want to deduct 20% of covered payroll each year. Pennywise implements a 10% money purchase and variable profit sharing plan. Poundfoolish, Ltd., tries to save money by setting up a 20% money purchase plan. Each has $100,000 covered payroll and widely variable turnover. Consider the effects over a period of years:

	Poundfoolish, Ltd.	Pennywise, Inc.—Tandem Plan		
	Money-Purchase	Money-Purchase	Profit-Sharing	Total
Assumed Starting Balance	$25,000	$10,000	$15,000	$25,000
Total 1984 Allocation	20,000	10,000	11,000	21,000
Less: Forfeitures Applied (10%)	(2,500)	(1,100)	N/A	(1,000)
Net Tax-Deductible Contribution	17,500	9,000	11,000	20,000
1984 Fund Earnings (8%)	2,000	800	1,200	2,000
Ending 1984 Balance	44,500	19,800	27,200	47,000
Total 1985 Allocation	20,000	10,000	10,000	20,000
Less: Forfeitures Applied (0%)	0	0	N/A	0
Net Tax-Deductible Contribution	20,000	10,000	10,000	20,000
1985 Fund Earnings (8%)	3,560	1,584	2,176	3,760
Ending 1985 Balance	68,060	31,384	39,376	70,760
Total 1986 Allocation	20,000	10,000	13,138	23,138
Less: Forfeitures Applied (10%)	(6,806)	(3,183)	N/A	(3,138)
Net Tax-Deductible Contribution	13,194	6,862	13,138	20,000
1986 Fund Earnings (8%)	5,445	2,511	3,150	5,661
Ending 1986 Balance	$86,699	$40,757	$55,664	$96,421

(handwritten annotation near Money-Purchase column, 1984 Forfeitures: "100")

Pennywise, Incorporated, has achieved several important objectives:

- It has maintained a 20% of payroll per year tax deduction, thereby saving significant *income taxes;*

- It has managed its *cash flow* more efficiently, with a common dollar outlay each year;

- The employees in Pennywise, Incorporated, have substantially more *assets* in their accounts.

Furthermore, there may be years in which Pennywise or Poundfoolish wishes to contribute *more* than 20% of payroll. Poundfoolish will be out of luck unless it adopts a profit sharing plan at that point. Even then the profit sharing plan would not particularly enhance Poundfoolish's flexibility, being limited in a normal year to 5% of payroll. It would seem then that everybody gains, except the government, when a tandem plan is utilized.

¶703.2 *How ''Piggyback'' Plans Retain Simplicity and Hold Down Costs*

Tandem money purchase and profit sharing plans are much simpler to explain to employees than defined benefit plans. To the extent motivation of employee-participants is an objective to be achieved by the plans, simplicity is important. Even though the benefits under a defined-benefit approach might be more substantial, employees may prefer a plan they can readily understand.

Apart from improved employee public relations, in some respects tandem plans can actually *reduce* employer maintenance costs as compared to other plan alternatives. First, by generating more questions, more complicated alternatives will necessarily involve a greater amount of your clients' time, if only to respond. Further, neither profit sharing nor money purchase plans require actuarial certification: they therefore enjoy one cost advantage over defined benefit plans.

Finally, there is somewhat less pressure for stability in the value of plan assets with defined contribution plans than with defined benefit plans. Participants in defined contribution plans are guaranteed no specific benefits. Their retirement income will simply reflect an account balance to which periodic gains and losses are attributed. Defined benefit plans, on the other hand, promise specific retirement benefits. Actuaries must periodically certify that plan investment performance appears adequate to meet such future liability. To the extent periodic asset fluctuation occurs, situations may arise in which the actuary will require a larger or smaller annual deposit.

PLANNING TIP

If a defined contribution plan appears to fit the bill, start with a profit sharing plan. Use a money purchase plan primarily as an adjunct to the profit sharing program.

¶703.3   *Who Scores Big Gains With Tandem Plans?*

Before considering specific types of money purchase plan formulas it is important to restate who wins and loses when tandem plans are utilized. The employer achieves the following:

- He retains control over cash flow;

- He retains control over tax planning; and

- He maintains an administratively simple and highly motivating plan format.

Employees win too:

- Forfeitures stay where they should, in accounts of long-term employees;

- To the extent forfeitures occur, employees will actually receive allocations in excess of amounts contributed by the employer; and

- Since the size of profit sharing contributions will be somewhat dependent upon overall business profitability, the employee may recognize that his efforts enhance his position.

The only loser appears to be the IRS, for the following reasons:

- It loses revenue because of larger tax deductions;

- It loses revenue to the extent forfeitures under tandem plans are reallocated to participants as opposed to reducing the employer's tax deduction; and

- It loses revenue on income earned by the more substantial trust fund balance available with tandem plans.

¶703.4   *Don't Overlook These Drawbacks*

Along with the possibilities of tandem plans come some drawbacks. Make sure you tell your clients these in advance so as to avoid the potential for misunderstanding.

Watch Out For Costs. Two plans of *any* type double your client's costs *both* for determination letters *and* for annual reporting and disclosure. Your client could easily face an initial qualification bill of $2,000–$3,000, plus recurring administrative costs of $1,500–$2,500.

PLANNING TIP ————————————————————————————

Unless it appears certain your client will need the full 25% tax deduction, start him off with just a profit sharing plan. Consider a second plan only when the first plan has thoroughly proven its value and the need for additional tax deduction has been clearly established.

Confusion May Reign. Even though profit sharing and money purchase plans are quite similar and conceptually simple, they are different. This dissimilarity may, in some instances, breed confusion which could lower the motivational value of the plans.

PLANNING TIP ————————————————————————————

Consider using a single summary plan description to emphasize the commonality of the plans. Accent the size of employer contributions as opposed to the more complicated subject of forfeitures.

LIMITATION ON ANNUAL ADDITIONS—A TRAP FOR THE UNWARY

It is important to remember that in 1987 no more than $30,000 (or 25% of compensation) may be added to a participant's account for **all** defined contribution plans in any one limitation year. Reallocated forfeitures under profit sharing plans *are included* in the definition of annual additions. Particularly in an integrated plan, your client must be careful that none of his highly paid participants exceed this maximum annual addition.

Example ————————————————————————————

XYZ, Incorporated implements, in Year 1, a 10% money purchase with forfeitures used to reduce contributions and variable profit sharing plan and contributes the full 15% under the profit sharing plan. In Year 2, forfeitures of $3,000 in the profit sharing and $2,000 in the pension plans occur. XYZ, Incorporated, tries to offset the reduced tax deduction occasioned by the forfeiture in the money purchase plan by increasing the contribution to the profit sharing plan. If either plan is integrated, this will not work. Here is why (integration level of profit sharing is $15,000):

Employee:	Employee A	Employee B	Employee C	Total
Compensation	$50,000	$15,000	$10,000	$75,000
I. Profit-Sharing (15%)				
a. Share of Contribution	$ 8,317	$ 1,760	$ 1,173	$11,250
b. Reallocated Forfeitures	1,995	469	313	2,777
c. Total Addition	10,312	2,229	1,486	14,027
II. Money-Purchase (10%)				
a. Employer Contribution	3,667	1,100	733	5,500
b. Plus Forfeitures	1,333	400	267	2,000
c. Total Addition	5,000	1,500	1,000	7,500
III. Total Allocations				
(c + f)	$15,312	$ 3,729	$ 2,486	$21,527
IV. Allocations as a Percent of				
Pay	31%	25%	25%	N/A

Since, through the combination of forfeiture-reallocation and integration, plan efficiency has been boosted, Employee A receives a combined addition greater than the 25% limitation. The excess will have to be held in a suspense account, and may be subject to excise tax. The problem would be even worse if money purchase forfeitures were reallocated.

What To Do.   Use the simple formula appearing at 604.4 to find the best contribution to maximize benefits for your client's key employees.

¶704   HOW TO INCREASE PLAN EFFICIENCY USING INTEGRATED MONEY PURCHASE PLANS

Like profit-sharing plans, money purchase plans are integrated with Social Security by reference to the percentage the employer must contribute to the government system. Basically, the employer chooses an "integration level" and contributes different amounts to his money purchase plan for employee compensation above and below this integration level. The rate of deposit for compensation above the integration level cannot exceed the rate applied to compensation below the integration level by more than 5.7% (which will increase in future years).

Example ———————————————————

XY, Incorporated, establishes a money purchase plan to which it contributes 10% of pay below the integration level and 15.7% above. The plan qualifies since the spread for pay above and below the integration level does not exceed 5.7%, and the percentage contributed for excess pay (15.7%) is not more than 200% of the percentage below. If XY, Incorporated, had established a plan calling for contributions of 15% of pay up to the integration level and 23% for the excess, the plan would not have qualified. The spread, 8%, exceeds the allowable amount.

Proper use of integration can dramatically boost plan efficiency. Many employers, however, balk at providing a somewhat lower level of benefits (contributions) to lower-paid employees, almost all of whose pay generally is below the integration level. But *not* integrating a plan would really be unfair. Highly paid employees are only *partially* covered by Social Security. Without the catch-up opportunity afforded by integration, lower-paid employees would reap the most substantial benefits from a money purchase plan. They would receive Social Security contributions on virtually all of their salaries **and** a full allocation under the money purchase plan. Higher-paid employees would receive only partial Social Security contributions (for 1986, only on compensation up to $42,000) plus a regular money purchase contribution. Remember, the purpose of integration is to allow employers to provide *uniform,* continuous coverage for employees across the entire spectrum of compensation.

¶704.1 *Choosing the Right Integration Level*

There is quite a variety of possible integration levels. Key questions will help you choose the right one:

* Does your client wish to maximize the percentage of his contribution allocated to higher-paid employees?

* Does your client think there will continue to be substantial wage inflation?

* Does your client have a specific dollar amount of annual contribution in mind, or is he willing to "let the chips fall where they may" with a particular plan formula?

The answers to those key questions will make selecting one of the following integration approaches easier.

¶704.2 *A Flat Dollar Amount May Fit Your Client's Needs Perfectly*

The integration level in a money purchase plan may be any dollar amount up to the taxable wage base effective during that plan year. Thus, for plan years beginning in 1986, a flat dollar integration level of $42,000 could be applied uniformly to all participating employee compensation under a money purchase plan. Generally speaking, however, employers use a somewhat lower flat dollar amount, chosen to fit the character of the employer's payroll more exactly. For instance, if the employer has three employees earning $12,000 or less and one key employee earning $50,000, he would be far better off using $12,000 as his integration level than $42,000.

Example

Wasteful, Incorporated, and Frugal Company each wish to spend $10,000 on a money purchase plan. Wasteful, Incorporated, uses an integration level of $37,500; Frugal Company, $12,000. Consider carefully the annual and cumulative effect of their decisions (assuming continuity of the plan and 8% fund earnings):

$(10000 - 456) * (50/80)$
$* (12/80)$

$8000 * .057$

WASTEFUL, INC.: $10,000 WITH $42,000 INTEGRATION LEVEL

Employee	Pay	Excess Pay	5.7% Excess Allocation	+	Regular Allocation	=	Total Alloca- tion	Total Allocation as a %	Account After 20 Years
A	$50,000	$8,000	$456		$5,965		$ 6,421	64%	$317,363
B	12,000	0	0		1,432		1,432	14%	70,777
C	10,000	0	0		1,193		1,193	12%	58,955
D	8,000	0	0		954		954	10%	47,134
TOTAL	$80,000	$8,000	$456		$9,544		$10,000	100%	

$.057 * 38000$

FRUGAL COMPANY: $10,000 WITH $12,000 INTEGRATION LEVEL

A	$50,000	$38,000	$2,166		$4,896		$ 7,063	70%	$349,037
B	12,000	0	0		1,175		1,175	12%	58,077
C	10,000	0	0		979		979	10%	48,397
D	8,000	0	0		783		783	8%	38,718
TOTAL	$80,000	$38,000	$2,166		$7,833		$10,000	100%	

Properly chosen, flat dollar amount integration levels can be very effective. They are readily explainable, ostensibly fair, and easily administered.

PLANNING TIP

Flat dollar amounts would almost always be preferred in situations where higher-paid key employees are, on the average, younger than most of the other employees. This is because the other option for integrating money purchase plans discussed later—covered compensation tables—generate high integration levels for young employees and low integration levels for older employees. Always check to see where your key employees sit on the age continuum. (For covered compensation tables, see Chapter 3, ¶302.2)

Caution. If you permanently fix your integration level, inflation may do you in. If we assume merely a 4% wage inflation, look what happens to Frugal Company's cleverly designed plan after 20 years. Note that the $10,000 plan contribution has also been adjusted to reflect inflation.

FIGURE 7.4(b).   WASTEFUL, INC., AFTER 20 YEARS WAGE INFLATION (INTEGRATION AT $37,500)

Employee	20-Yr. Projected Pay	Excess Pay	5.7% Excess Allocation +	Regular Allocation =	Total Allocation	Total Allocation as a %
A	$109,556	$72,056	$4,107	$11,127	$15,234	70%
B	26,293	0	0	2,672	2,672	12%
C	21,911	0	0	2,225	2,225	10%
D	17,529	0	0	1,780	1,780	8%
TOTAL	$175,289	$72,056	$4,107	$17,804	$21,911	100%

FRUGAL COMPANY AFTER 20 YEARS' WAGE INFLATION (INTEGRATION AT $12,000)

Employee	20-Yr. Projected Pay	Excess Pay	5.7% Excess Allocation +	Regular Allocation =	Total Allocation	Total Allocation as a %
A	$109,556	$ 97,556	$5,560	$ 9,160	$14,720	67%
B	26,293	14,293	815	2,198	3,013	14%
C	21,911	9,911	565	1,832	2,397	11%
D	17,529	5,529	315	1,466	1,781	8%
TOTAL	$175,289	$127,289	$7,255	$14,656	$21,911	100%

Clearly the plan has lost a lot of its efficiency, reflected by the lower percent of deposit for employee A.

THE SOLUTION—USE A "FLOATING INTEGRATION LEVEL"

Consider tying your plan's integration level to some published wage statistic. For instance, your plan might automatically provide that the integration level would be the taxable wage base effective for a particular plan year. Or, you might use a lower flat dollar amount pegged to increase (or decrease) at the same rate as the taxable wage base. This should help stop erosion of your plan's efficiency.

¶704.3 *Capitalizing on Covered Compensation*

Usually, key employees are *older* than the average age of the participants. If this is the case with your plan, covered compensation tables may provide the right integration level for you. Oversimplified, covered compensation tables provide nothing more than the average of taxable wage bases to which an employee might have been subject during his working life. For instance, an employee who will turn 65 in 1989 would have covered compensation (Table 1, 1983) of $16,800. On the other hand, an employee who will turn 65 in the year 2010 has an estimated covered compensation of over $20,000. It is readily apparent that the greater the spread between ages of key and regular employees, the greater the opportunity for efficiency through the use of covered compensation tables. (For covered compensation tables, see Chapter 3, ¶302.2) As discussed earlier, the author tends not to use the most current covered compensation tables because they are too high relative to typical current employee compensation.

Example

XYZ, Incorporated, and ABC Company each established money purchase plans with $20,000 contributions. XYZ uses a flat $12,000 integration level; ABC, 1978 covered compensation. Refer to the table below for a comparison of the strategies. Consider the annual and cumulative effect of their decisions.

XYZ, INC.—$12,000 FLAT INTEGRATION LEVEL

Employee	Age	Pay	Integration Level	Excess Pay	5.7% Excess Allocation	Excess+ Regular Allocation	= Total Allocation	Total Allocation as a %	Account After 20 Years
A	55	$ 50,000	12,000	38,000	2,166	8,461	10,627	53%	525,217
B	45	20,000	12,000	8,000	456	3,384	3,840	19%	189,784
C	30	20,000	12,000	8,000	456	3,384	3,840	19%	189,784
D	25	10,000	12,000	0	0	1,693	1,693	9%	83,673
TOTAL		$100,000		54,000	3,078	16,922	20,000	100%	

ABC, COMPANY—COVERED COMPENSATION

A	55	$ 50,000	11,712	38,288	2,182	8,684	10,866	54%	537,029
B	45	20,000	14,412	5,588	319	3,474	3,793	19%	187,441
C	30	20,000	17,700	2,300	131	3,474	3,604	18%	178,150
D	25	10,000	17,700	0	0	1,736	1,736	9%	85,838
TOTAL		$100,000		46,176	2,632	17,368	20,000	100%	

¶704.4 *Maximizing Integration for Key Employees*

Frequently employers approach pension plans not from the perspective of a formula but rather a contribution. For instance, your client may know he wants to spend $15,000 on a money purchase plan, but may have no idea of how that dollar amount translates to a formula. A simple method of determining the most effective contribution rate to achieve your client's funding objective is provided by the following formula, solved for R:

$$C = R \times T + .057 \times E$$

Where: C = The employer's desired deposit
R = Contribution rate applied to total pay
T = Total payroll
E = Excess payroll (above integration level)

The formula works equally well for flat dollar and covered compensation integration levels. See the table below for an illustration of a business trying to decide whether to spend $20,000 on a plan with a flat dollar or covered compensation integration level. The objective is to maximize plan efficiency for employee A.

Note that the calculation confirms our earlier conclusion that covered compensation provides a more efficient integration level than a flat dollar amount.

OPTION I
$15,000 FLAT INTEGRATION LEVEL

Employee	Age	Pay	Integration Level	Excess Pay	Excess Pay × 5.7%	Total Pay × 9.7%	Total Allocation	% of Total
A	55	$ 75,000	$15,000	$60,000	$3,420	$ 7,292	$10,712	54%
B	40	35,000	15,000	20,000	1,140	3,403	4,543	23%
C	30	30,000	15,000	15,000	855	2,917	3,772	19%
D	25	10,000	15,000	0	0	973	973	4%
TOTAL		$150,000		$95,000	$5,415	$14,585	$20,000	100%

$$C = R \times T + .057 \times E$$
$$\$20,000 = R \times \$150,000 + \$.057 \times \$95,000$$
$$\$20,000 = \$150,000 + \$5,415$$
$$\$13,350 = \$150,000R$$
$$.09723 = R$$

OPTION II
1978 COVERED COMPENSATION

Integration Level	Excess Pay	Excess Pay × 5.7%	Total Pay × 9.61%	Total Allocation	% of Total
$11,712	$63,288	$3,607	$ 7,207	$10,814	54%
12,564	22,436	1,279	3,364	4,643	23%
17,700	12,300	701	2,883	3,584	18%
17,700	0	0	959	959	5%
	$98,024	$5,587	$14,413	$20,000	100%

$$C = R \times T + .07 \times E$$
$$\$20,000 = R \times \$150,000 + \$.057 \times \$98,024$$
$$\$20,000 = \$150,000 + \$5,587$$
$$\$14,413 = \$150,000R$$
$$.0961 = R$$

¶704.5 A Trap for the Unwary—Forfeitures Can Hurt Higher-Paid Participants

Remember, the *maximum* annual addition for any participant cannot exceed the lesser of 25% of pay or (1986) $30,000. The maximum annual addition is composed of employer contributions, reallocated forfeitures, and voluntary contributions. You might be tempted to set up a 25%-of-pay money purchase plan integrated with Social Security. Don't! The excess contribution for higher-paid participants resulting from integration of the plan will push these participants "over the top." To the extent 25% of pay is exceeded, the balance will have to be held in a suspense account to be allocated in a later year, and may be subject to an excise tax.

PLANNING TIP
Use the technique discussed in 704.4 to find a contribution formula. Then *apply* the formula to key participants' compensation. Make sure you have a "safe haven." Ensure that the formula chosen *maximizes* the contribution share for your key employees. Do not necessarily go for the biggest tax deduction possible.

¶705   *USING PAST SERVICE EFFECTIVELY ACHIEVES YOUR GOALS AT LOWER COST*

Profit sharing plans sometimes utilize a "unit" allocation system to partially weigh contributions in favor of employees with substantial past service. That simple concept gives way in money purchase plans to a much more elaborate and powerful planning technique—the amortization of a "past service liability." Since money purchase plans must have definitely determinable contribution formulas, it is possible to pretend that an employer always had his money purchase plan in place. Given that hypothesis, one may reasonably ask what would cumulatively have been contributed to the plan in the past. Computing the answer leads to the determination of an unfunded "pot" of money—the past service liability that can theoretically be paid off over some future period. There are two methods of measuring and amortizing this liability.

¶705.1   *Creating a Flexible Past Service Liability*

The simplest approach is to assume that a money purchase plan has always been in force. Applying the plan's contribution formula to average compensation for the number of years of an employee's past service yields a separate "pot" for each participant. Under the money purchase plan approach, this pot can be amortized over anywhere from 10 years to the number of years remaining until the employee's retirement. The annual amortization is subject to the discretion of the employer. Therein lies the flexibility with this approach. In a good year the employer can make his contribution for current compensation plus a large amount (based on the most rapid amortization—10 years) for past service. In a bad year he can pull in his horns and make his contribution for current compensation plus a minimum (based on the least rapid amortization system). Let's consider the latitude this provides.

Example ————————————————————————————————

GHIJ, Incorporated, establishes a 10%-of-pay money purchase plan, including years prior to implementation of the plan. The company wishes to know

- how much past service liability the plan creates; and

- how broad a range of deposits will be created by this method.

For purposes of our illustration, average compensation and future compensation are presumed to be the same. Here's how we determine the calculation of (a) the initial amount of past service; and (b) minimum and maximum contributions.

GHIJ, INC., CALCULATION OF PAST SERVICE LIABILITY

Employee	Age	Past Service	×	Pay	×	Contribution Rate	=	Past Service Liability
A	55	30 yrs.		$ 50,000		10%		$150,000
B	45	20 yrs.		30,000		10%		60,000
C	35	10 yrs.		20,000		10%		20,000
D	35	5 yrs.		20,000		10%		10,000
E	25	0 yrs.		10,000		10%		0
TOTAL				$130,000				$240,000

GHIJ, INC., CALCULATION OF PLAN CONTRIBUTIONS

				Past Service Amorization		Contribution Requirements	
Employee	Pay	Future Service	Regular Contribution (10% of Pay)	10-Yr. Payoff	Future Service Payoff	Minimum – Columns 4 + 6	Maximum – Columns 4 + 5
A	$ 50,000	10 yrs.	$ 5,000	$15,000	$15,000	$20,000	$20,000
B	30,000	20 yrs.	3,000	6,000	3,000	6,000	9,000
C	20,000	30 yrs.	2,000	2,000	667	2,667	4,000
D	20,000	30 yrs.	2,000	1,000	333	2,333	3,000
E	10,000	40 yrs.	1,000	0	0	1,000	1,000
TOTAL	$130,000		$13,000	$24,000	$19,000	$32,000	$37,000

Note: Any time proper planning can enhance a client's flexibility it should be an important goal.

Obviously, this use of past service mitigates one potential problem with money purchase plans—the disruption of cash and tax planning due to forfeitures.

Watch Out For This Drawback. Keeping track of past service liability as it is amortized by periodic employer contributions can be an administrative nightmare. Thus, in a larger plan, if the flexibility associated with this past service liability were particularly attractive it might be better achieved simply by adding a profit sharing plan.

¶705.2 *Past Service Integration—a Tricky Boost for Your Plan's Performance*

Since employers have contributed to Social Security in the past it stands to reason that they ought to be able to create a past service liability based on *integrated* allocations. This is okay *as long as* the spread between the contribution rates above and below the integration level does not exceed 5% for past service. The calculation of an integrated past service liability is somewhat cumbersome, but sometimes the results can be worthwhile.

Example ⎯⎯⎯⎯⎯⎯⎯⎯⎯⎯⎯⎯⎯⎯⎯⎯⎯⎯⎯⎯⎯⎯⎯⎯

The principals of WXY, Incorporated, have been employed there since they got out of college; most of their employees are of relatively recent vintage. The company sets up a past and future service money purchase plan. Benefits for past service are 1% Total × Years of Past Service plus 5% for pay above the integration level ($9,000); future service contributions are 1.4% of pay and 5.7% of excess pay. On page 142 is the calculation of the initial past service liability, and the minimum and maximum deposit allocations. Note how heavily contributions are skewed in favor of the principals.

Observation.   Can you see some problems with our results? They include the following:

1. The integration of future service contributions (1.4% of pay below the integration level and 7.1% of pay above) doesn't qualify under TRA '86 rules! Even though the "excess only" percentage is 5.7, we fail the test because our rate of contribution for pay *above* the integration level is more than 200% of the rate for pay *below* that level; and

2. It is unclear at the time this manuscript is being prepared whether plans will continue to be able to use "old" integration rules (without the 200% rule) to calculate past service benefits. Probably not.

It would be a most instructive exercise to back into contribution rates that maximize integration while keeping employee A within the 25% limit!

PLANNING TIP ⎯⎯⎯⎯⎯⎯⎯⎯⎯⎯⎯⎯⎯⎯⎯⎯⎯⎯⎯⎯⎯⎯⎯

If the facts otherwise warrant a money purchase plan, check participant dates of employment to provide an indication of the effectiveness of past service. If the average of the years of service of the key employee group is greater than the average of the years of future service for regular employees, test a past service plan.

FIGURE 7.9. WXY, INC., INTEGRATED PAST SERVICE MONEY-PURCHASE PLAN

	Age	Past Service	Future Service	Pay	Excess Pay	Past Service Liability		
						Integrated 5% Excess × Yrs.	+ Regular 1% Total × Yrs.	= Total
A	55	35	10	$ 50,000	$ 41,000	$ 71,750	$17,500	$ 89,250
B	55	30	10	40,000	31,000	46,500	12,000	58,500
C	50	25	15	40,000	31,000	38,750	10,000	48,750
D	30	5	35	40,000	31,000	7,750	2,000	9,750
E	30	5	35	30,000	21,000	5,250	1,500	6,750
TOTAL				$200,000	$155,000	$170,000	$43,000	$213,000

WXY, INC., CALCULATION OF MINIMUM AND MAXIMUM CONTRIBUTIONS

	Future Service Contributions			Past Service Contributions		Total Contributions		
	5.7% Excess	+ 1.4% Total	= Allocation	Minimum Pay to 65	Maximum Pay in 10 Yrs.	3 + 4 Minimum	3 + 5 Maximum	Maximum as a %
A	$2,337	$ 700	$ 3,037	$ 8,925	$ 8,925	$11,962	$11,962	38%
B	1,767	560	2,327	5,850	5,850	8,177	8,177	25%
C	1,767	560	2,327	3,250	4,875	5,577	7,202	22%
D	1,767	560	2,327	279	975	2,605	3,302	10%
E	1,197	420	1,617	193	675	1,810	2,292	7%
TOTAL	$8,835	$2,800	$11,635	$18,497	$21,300	$30,131	$32,935	100%

Note: If past services were not used, it would take a total contribution (with no flexibility) of $49,398 to generate the same $11,962 deposit for employee A. That's a 40%–50% increase in employer costs without any improvement for the key man.

¶705.3 *Doing it the Hard Way May Pay Off Big*

The second alternative for creating a past service liability is to build a defined benefit plan, unit benefit variety, to pay off the past service element. Complete discussion of the unit benefit approach appears in Chapter 10. However, if you must use a money purchase plan and if most of your key employees are relatively old, your persistence in studying the potential of a unit-benefit approach to past service under a money purchase plan will be rewarded.

¶705.4 *The Unit-Benefit Concept Made Simple*

The concept of a unit benefit plan is simply that during each year of service an employee accrues a specific "chunk" of retirement income. Upon retirement, the participant's benefit will be equal to the sum of these chunks earned during his working life. For example, an employer might establish a 1% per year of service unit benefit plan. Under such a plan, a 45-year-old employee earning $20,000 would earn, each year, a chunk equal to 1% of $20,000 or $200. After 20 years of service, his cumulative chunks would provide him with a retirement benefit of $4,000 per year. Determining the retirement benefit therefore is relatively easy. Computing the annual cost is more difficult.

Using the $4,000 retirement benefit as an illustration may help clarify the funding. To pay a $4,000 retirement benefit we know that we need to have approximately $40,000 on hand at age 65. Annual contributions to fund this benefit are like the reverse of a mortgage—the sum of contributions plus interest earnings should provide the necessary sum if systematically paid over the working life of the employee.

It is readily apparent that the primary variable in determining annual contributions is the number of years a participant has to go before retirement; a young employee will require very small contributions, since compound interest will do most of the work. An older employee, on the other hand, will require larger principal deposits. For example, the cost at 6% interest to provide the $4,000 per year retirement income is as follows for the indicated ages:

Age	Annual Deposit To Provide At Retirement Age
25	$244/yr.
35	477/yr.
45	$1,026/yr.
55	2,863/yr.

WHAT THIS CAN MEAN TO THE TYPICAL CLIENT

The annual accrual percentage would generally be 2% or less since the sum of accruals cannot provide a benefit greater than 100% of pay. Let's see how this works out for Sample Company, Incorporated, which establishes a money purchase plan providing a past service benefit of 1% for each year of service and a future money purchase contribution of 2.633% of pay.

FIGURE 7.10.   SAMPLE COMPANY, INCORPORATED

Employee	Age	Service	Pay	Past Service Benefit 1% × Yrs. × Pay	Contribution	Normal Contribution— 2.633% of Pay	6 + 7 Total Deposit	Total as a %*
A	55	30	$ 50,000	$15,000/yr @65	$11,183	$1,317	$12,500	71%
B	45	5	30,000	1,500/yr @65	401	790	1,191	7%
C	45	20	30,000	6,000/yr @65	1,603	790	2,393	13%
D	35	10	30,000	3,000/yr @65	373	790	1,163	7%
E	25	0	10,000	N/A	N/A	263	263	2%
TOTAL			$150,000		$13,560	$3,950	$17,510	100%

* This hybrid method of using Past Service in money-purchase plans gives a sneak preview to the power of defined-benefit plans. The ability to allocate 71% of a money-purchase contribution to a participant whose compensation represents only 33% of the total is a dramatic boost in efficiency.

PLANNING TIP ──────────────────────────────────────
While the past service approach to money purchase plans looks favorable, keep in mind that it works best for older employees. By the same token, defined benefit plans provide far more heavily skewed contributions for this group. After you have studied the defined benefit plans in later Chapters, come back and compare them to past service money purchase plans. Finally, study the material on Topheavy Plans in Chapter 13 to make sure all participants in your "high powered" plans receive appropriate "minimum contributions."

¶706   THE WHO'S, WHAT'S, WHERE'S, AND WHEN'S OF MONEY PURCHASE PLANS

Notwithstanding some of the opportunities provided by past service amortization, the use of money purchase plans should generally be restricted to the following situations:

- businesses with a stable employee pool;

- businesses where the key employees are young; and

- situations in which simplicity is of paramount importance.

If you must use money purchase plans, *be certain* to show your client the alternatives. Better that he hear about defined benefit plans from you and reject them than hear about them later from one of your competitors. Most small employers, when pressed, will choose a plan whose contributions are heavily weighted to their key employees, even though the plan may be slightly more onerous in terms of administration and cost.

¶706.1 *Because of Their Simplicity, Money Purchase Plans Do Have a Cost Advantage*

Money purchase plans do not require actuarial certification. They do not present the potential Pension Benefit Guaranty Corporation liability associated with defined benefit plans. Simple accounting lowers record-keeping costs, and greater simplicity means a minimized "time liability" for you in the future—you will not have to explain money purchase plans over and over to employees.

¶706.2 *When Should Money Purchase Plans Be Used?*

The recurrent dogma with money purchase plans is to use them when key employees are young. Even though the use of past service allows some "catch-up" for older key employees under money purchase plans, the fact remains that the combination of contribution frequency and compound interest will weigh heavily in favor of younger key employees. Unless the average age of key employees is less than 40 years old, you should, as a general rule, steer clear of money purchase plans.

¶706.3 *What To Do When Turnover Is a Major Factor*

If the tax deduction afforded by a pension plan is important to your client, and his employee group has relatively high turnover, *do not* use a money purchase plan. If you have no choice, then make sure you do the following:

- Use the most restrictive eligibility requirements possible.

- Avoid funding media with high front-end loads.

- Use forfeitures for reallocation, like profit sharing plans.

¶706.4   *Your Client's Cash Flow May Hold the Key*

Critical to the decision to implement a money purchase plan will be an analysis of your client's cash flow. If it is quite erratic, he may not like the fixed commitment of a money purchase plan. In situations where a relatively young, stable group of employees forms the participant group for a business with good, stable cash flow, money purchase plans may be an attractive and inexpensive way to get a big tax deduction.

8

How Defined Benefit
Pension Plans
Can Boost
Plan Efficiency

Defined contribution plans offer a simple and flexible series of alternatives for your clients. However, the key objective of most small businessmen is to maximize the percentage of the plan's contribution allocated to them. Assuming the vast majority of your small- to medium-sized business owners are comparatively old (over 45), then defined contribution plans may have a fatal flaw: they inevitably favor younger participants.

Defined benefit plans offer an alternative, albeit with increased complexity, which may achieve a contribution distribution more favorable to your client's key employees. Chapters 8, 9, 10, and 11 will show you how to:

- radically skew deposits toward older key employees;
- simplify the complicated jargon peculiar to defined benefit plans;
- determine when defined benefit plans can be most effective; and
- overcome the most frequent objections to defined benefit plans—the problem of a fixed contribution.

More specifically, Chapter 8 will lay the groundwork by discussing the differences between defined benefit and defined contribution plans and how to identify and take advantage of situations where defined benefit plans offer the most efficient use of your client's funds.

¶800   *IMPORTANT DIFFERENCES BETWEEN DEFINED BENEFIT AND DEFINED CONTRIBUTION PLANS*

In defined contribution plans, the *deposit* is "definitely determinable." That is, application of the plan formula or allocation method to eligible employees' compensation will, if the plan is properly designed, result in uniform, nondiscriminatory treatment of plan participants. Future *account values,* on the other hand, are indeterminable. They are clearly a function of several variables: time, interest, and contributions.

VARIABLE 1—TIME

The first and most important variable is time. Recall that an annual deposit of $100 for 10 years generates a future value of $1,397; $100 per year deposited for 25 years generates a future value of $5,816. However, the converse is also true if we set a specific age-related accumulation goal for all participants. For example, if two employees, ages 25 and 50, are promised a "pot" of $10,000 at age 65, the annual deposits required would be $61 and $405 in the cases of the younger and the older employee respectively. Due to a longer remaining working life, younger participants will benefit from time. Compound interest will do most of the work. Chapters 4 through 7 concluded that defined contribution plans inherently favor younger employees in terms of contributions. Defined benefit plans reverse that orientation.

VARIABLE 2—INTEREST

The second important variable in defined contribution plans is interest. $100 per year for 20 years at 4% generates a future value of $3,097; $100 per year for 20 years at 8% interest generates a future value of $4,942; and $100 per year for 20 years assuming an annual *loss* of 4% results in a future value of $1,339. However, defined contribution plans meet the IRS qualification requirements of providing "definitely determinable benefits," since the *benefit* of plan participation is an employee's right to receive a specific share of *contributions.* Those benefits are "definitely determinable" simply by application of the formula. Investment results do not affect a participant's status in a defined benefit plan.

VARIABLE 3—CONTRIBUTIONS

Unlike defined contribution plans, which commit an employer to a specific contribution constrained by the dollar limits we have discussed (the lesser of $30,000 or 25% of a participant's compensation), defined benefit plans have no fixed limitation on contributions; contributions are a function of the amount of benefit promised. As long as benefit limits to be discussed are not exceeded, the contribution can be whatever is reasonably required to fund those benefits. The implication of this approach is, for older employees, contributions that are far in excess of 25% of pay. It is not uncommon for a defined benefit plan to generate contributions for a particular employee which are in excess of 100% of his pay. The elimination of the "cap" on contributions represents one of the defined benefit plan's most powerful advantages, and allows older employees to "make up for lost time" with truly massive annual contributions.

¶801 *HOW DEFINED BENEFIT PLANS WORK: A TOTALLY DIFFERENT APPROACH TO "DEFINITELY DETERMINABLE BENEFITS"*

Defined benefit plans represent a wholly different group of plans, both conceptually and mechanically. As the name implies, the benefits of these plans are *defined* in advance, generally determined by application of the plan formula to compensation. However, the result of formula application is not a current *contribution* to the plan, but rather a specific stated benefit which the plan commits to pay at retirement age and which the plan must fund.

Example —————————————————————————

A simple defined benefit plan formula promises all participants a retirement benefit at age 65 equal to 50% of their pay. A participant earning $10,000 prior to retirement is entitled to a pension benefit of $10,000 × 50% or $5,000 per year for life. The contribution to fund the benefit is actuarially determined. It is the amount which, together with interest, should be sufficient to pay the promised benefit. For instance, to follow our example above, suppose that the employee to whom we have promised $5,000 per year at age 65 is currently 45 years old. Annuity tables indicate that for every $1,200 per year of benefit to be paid at age 65, you will need to have a "pot" of about $13,333 on hand. Therefore, to fund a benefit of $5,000 per year, the plan needs to accumulate $55,422 during the next 20 years.

Thus, this plan's objective would be to put a sufficient amount of money away each year which, with assumed interest, would accumulate $55,422 in the 20 years remaining until retirement. Assuming that fund deposits consistently earn 6%, the annual deposit is $1,421.

¶801.1   *Applying the Concept to a Typical Situation*

Here's how the simple defined benefit plan would work for Definitely, Incorporated. The formula calls for each participant receiving 50% of pay as a retirement benefit.

Employee	Age	Pay	50% Retirement Benefit @ 65	Annual Deposit
A	50	$ 75,000	$37,500/yr.	$15,832
B	30	75,000	37,500	3,307
C	40	12,000	6,000	1,075
D	40	12,000	6,000	1,075
E	25	2,500	3,750	238
TOTAL		$181,500	N/A	$21,527

The key to understanding defined benefit plans lies in the relationship between employees A and B. Although each earns the same income and is therefore entitled to the same benefit at retirement (50% of $75,000 = $37,500), the *time* available to accumulate sufficient funds to pay the promised benefit differs dramatically—15 and 35 years respectively. Thus, employee A's annual funding deposit for those 15 years must be five times that of B. The example graphically highlights the potential for rewarding older key employees, which makes defined benefit plans so attractive.

¶802   *WHAT IS A "FUNDING STANDARD ACCOUNT"?*

Interest assumptions in defined contribution plans were only valuable for *projecting* future accumulations; however, defined contribution plans don't *promise* any future accumulations. With defined contribution plans, your client simply makes deposits on a regular basis; a participant's benefit at retirement age is whatever he has in his plan, no more and no less.

Defined benefit plans make a specific *promise* of future benefits, and ERISA provides that your client is "on the hook"—potentially up to 30% of his net worth—to fulfill the commitments of his defined benefit plan. Therefore, the extent to which the plan assumptions deviate from actual experience will affect whether your plan will generate too much or too little money for the "pot" to pay future benefits. For example, suppose you assume your plan will earn 6% per year, and it actually earns 8%. Your plan will be overfunded because of the excess interest earned. But since the "pot" is predetermined, under- or overfunding is not acceptable. There needs to be a system to compare hypothetical with actual plan experience.

¶802.1 *How the Funding Standard Account Works*

This introduces the concept of the "funding standard account." Conceptually, a funding standard account is a plan's "perfect balance." That is, the funding standard account represents the balance that should be in the plan, assuming all plan variables exactly duplicate your projections. At least every three years, an "enrolled actuary" must review the plan's actual performance and compare it to the assumed performance predicted by the actuarial method and the funding standard account. To the extent that the plan is under- or overfunded, the plan trustees must amortize surpluses or shortages over a specific time period.

Thus the funding standard account provides a conceptual framework for comparing a plan's assets and liabilities—its income with its outgo. Since the cost of future benefits can be expressed as a present value, it is easy to consider that, for the plan to be "in balance," some simple arithmetic must work.

THE FUNDING STANDARD ACCOUNT SIMPLIFIED

A Plan's Assets	Must Equal	Its Liabilities
Present Value of Future Contributions		
+		
Accumulated Assets	=	Present Value of Future Benefits
+		+
Employer Deposits		Investment Losses
+		+
Investment Earnings		Payables to Vested Terminees

Periodically an actuary reviews the balance of the account to reflect:

- additional costs generated by new participants or changes in pay;
- savings generated by investment performance in excess of estimates; and
- distribution to retirees.

¶802.2 *Minimum Funding Standards*

Minimum funding standards apply to defined benefit, money purchase, and target benefit plans because they are considered to be pension plans; that is, they guarantee something to the participating employee. In the case of a money purchase or target plan, the guarantee is that the employer will fund the plan on a regular basis in compliance with complex rules established pursuant to ERISA. These rules are fairly straightforward for money purchase plans: the employer simply must make the annual contribution implied by the plan's formula. Target plans follow the same course, though the actual determination of the appropriate contribution is somewhat more complex. Defined benefit plan minimum funding standard rules are extremely complicated, and their application depends on the particular actuarial method employed.

The primary purpose of an actuary for a defined benefit plan is to ensure that, given the actuarial method employed, contributions are determined that fall within the acceptable range established by the minimum funding standard rules. The important detail here is not to understand the ins and outs of these rules, but rather to be aware of their existence, and the consequent commitment an employer makes when he implements a pension plan other than profit sharing.

In situations of demonstrable hardship, an employer can apply for a waiver from the minimum funding requirements for a particular year. Such a waiver requires a detailed plan for repayment, with considerable administrative complexity, so your clients should be forewarned that the adoption of a plan with minimum funding standards represents a high level of responsibility.

¶803 *HOW TIME AND INTEREST AFFECT THE DESIGN OF DEFINED BENEFIT PLANS*

It is important to consider how different variables affect defined benefit plans' funding. Keep in mind, however, that funding of defined benefit plans is based on a purely hypothetical set of assumptions. Experience will never duplicate plan assumptions. Therefore, to the extent your client develops plan parameters because they generate a more favorable allocation of deposits, he will create future problems—when your actuary compares actual plan experience to unrealistic assumptions. TRA '86 has added the potential of excise taxes for unjustified contributions based on unreasonable assumptions.

Example

Because of the powerful long-term effect of interest, it is very easy to reduce defined benefit contributions for younger employees simply by predicting a high rate of interest. You might be tempted to use an 8% assumption, since that rate is readily available in today's interest market. However, there has never been a 20- or 30-year period in our economic history in which an 8% interest rate was sustained. Therefore, using an 8% rate, we might build a future liability for younger employees. And sooner or later, your client will have to increase his deposits to make up for earnings that never materialized.

A Close Look At Interest.   The most important variable affecting defined benefit pension plans is interest. Consider the annual deposit required to generate a lump sum of $10,000, using the following time and interest variables:

| | Annual Deposit to Accumulate $10,000 If Time Period Is | | |
Interest Rate	10 Years	20 Years	30 Years
4%	$801	$323	$171
5%	757	288	143
8%	639	202	82

Observation of the 10-year column reveals that doubling the interest rate from 4% to 8% reduces the contribution required by 20%, from $801 to $639. That is not a substantial difference because the ***effect of compound interest is felt most strongly over long periods of time.***

For example, consider the 30-year column. Here, doubling the interest rate from 4% to 8% reduces the contribution required by 52% from $171 to $82! This simple exercise demonstrates a major advantage at least in *contribution* terms for defined benefit plans. Whereas the key employee of most small business organizations is older than the average age of his employees, the older an employee, the *less* interest will do the job of funding his promised retirement benefit. However, recall that ***unreasonable*** interest assumptions, as discussed earlier, may reduce or increase contributions at the expense of creating future liabilities in the form of amortizable experience gains or losses.

As a final point, however, it is clear that the higher the interest rate assumed, the more younger participants' benefits will derive from interest rather than employer deposits. Since in most small businesses the prime determinant for choice of one qualified plan over another is the relative contribution schedule for key versus regular employees, this is often an important fact.

¶804   HOW TO CHOOSE THE RIGHT ACTUARIAL METHOD FOR YOUR CLIENT

Actuarial assumptions and methods affect plan contributions quite significantly. Actuarial assumptions include many factors (mortality, turnover, interest, settlement factors, and so on). However, a prime consideration for small businesses is the actuarial method you choose. A thorough discussion of actuarial methodology is beyond the scope of this book; however, see the Appendix for an excellent review reprinted with the kind permission of Datair, Inc.

Two philosophically different approaches provide the extremes of actuarial choices for small plans. They are Attained Age Level and Entry Age Normal With Frozen Past Service Liability. Many variations lie in the middle. Your client's choice will generate dramatic variations in deposit structure. Let's consider the two divergent alternatives, not to preclude any particular actuarial methodology, but simply to avoid lengthy digression.

¶804.1   *Choose Attained Age Level Funding if Your Client Wants to Keep Things Simple*

Attained Age Level Funding is the actuarial method traditionally favored by many insurance companies and therefore a large segment of the small business pension market. This is because:

- It generates a specific "cost" for each employee and hence lends itself to individual funding products like annuities; and

- It is quite robust—it can absorb the problems caused by the historical instability of small business payrolls.

The major concept of Attained Age Level Funding is that your client deposits the *exact* amount required to fund a participant's retirement benefit over the years of service remaining in his employment *assuming* level compensation from the date of computation to date of retirement. For instance, if the employee is 55, then we fund his benefit over the 10 remaining years of employment; if he is 45, over 20 years, etc. Whenever salary increases (or decreases) *actually occur,* they are recognized and funded as incremental "blocks" of funding. Finally, investment experience gains (or losses) are amortized over 15 years.

The concept of Attained Age Level Funding can easily be demonstrated by Figure 8.1, which assumes a participant has annual salary increases.

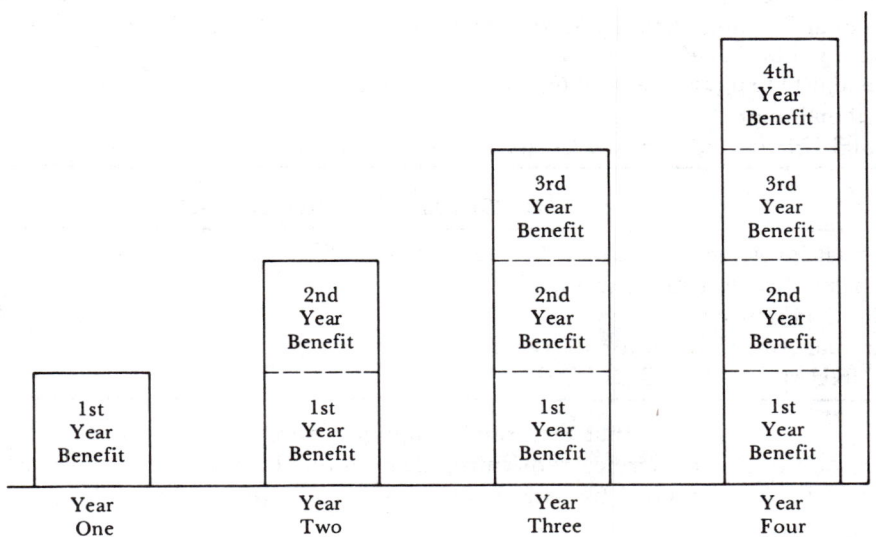

FIGURE 8.1. Cumulative Retirement Income

Example

B. Block becomes a participant in his company's pension plan at age 45, when he is earning $30,000. The plan promises a 50%-of-pay retirement benefit and assumes a 5½ percent rate of return. In his second year of participation, B. Block earns $40,000 and the plan actually earns 12% interest.

The $5,776 annual deposit will continue until either additional investment differentials or compensation changes require further adjustment.

A.   COMPUTING B. BLOCK'S BENEFITS

Compensation, Year One	$30,000	
Times Benefit Rate	× 50%	
Equals Estimated Retirement Benefit		$15,000
Compensation, Year Two	$40,000	
Minus Original Compensation	(30,000)	
Equals Incremental Compensation	$10,000	
Times Benefit Rate	× 50%	
Equals Incremental Retirement Benefit		$ 5,000
Cumulative Incremental Benefits, End of Year Two		$20,000

B.   COMPUTING B. BLOCK'S FUNDING COSTS

Initial Benefit (Age 45)	$15,000	
Annual Funding Deposit (5½% interest, 20 yrs. remaining)		$4,248/yr
Incremental Benefit, Year Two	$ 5,000	
Unadjusted Funding Deposit (5½% interest, 19 yrs. remaining)		$1,538/yr.
Total Unadjusted Funding Costs, End of Year Two		$5,786/yr.

C.   ADJUSTMENT FOR EXPERIENCE GAIN

Actual Investment Return on $4,248 Deposit (12%)	$ 510	
Assumed Investment Return (5½%)	(234)	
Net Experience Gain	276	
Annual Amortization for 15 Years		($10/yr.)
ANNUAL FUNDING DEPOSIT		$5,776/yr.

Note that each time a change is recognized, B. Block will have fewer years of service remaining. Therefore, the funding cost for an identical incremental benefit change will become progressively larger.

PLANNING TIP ──────────────────────────────

Plans using the Attained Age Level Funding Method should consider *not* recognizing benefit changes occurring within five years of retirement, since the cost of amortizing even a small benefit increase over five years could disrupt your client's budget. For example, if B. Block had his $5,000 benefit increase at age 60, your client would have to pay an **additional** $8,846 for the next five years.

¶804.2   *How Attained Age Level Funding Works in Real-Life Situations*

The Attained Age Level method of funding can be illustrated with a typical small business employee census. Assume a 25%-of-pay retirement benefit and a 10% pay increase from year one to year two.

Observation.   Employee A receives 83% of the first year deposit. In year two, despite uniform pay increases, he receives 84% of the incremental change. (The closer he gets to retirement, the higher share of his funding.) This is because there is less time to accumulate the specific sum necessary to pay the incremental retirement income.

Additional Observation.   Decreases in compensation (and therefore benefits) result in a "negative block" of retirement benefit and cost.

PLANNING TIP ———————————————————————————————————
The closer a participant is to retirement, the more sensitive his funding costs are to changes in benefits. Many plans using the Attained Age Level Funding Actuarial Method exclude from computations changes in compensation (and benefits) which occur within five years of normal retirement date.

   Note how Attained Age Level Funding (and in general all different benefit funding) orients deposits heavily in favor of an older employee.

FIRST YEAR PLAN

Employee	Age	Annual Pay	25% Benefit @ 65	Annual Deposit
A	50	$ 75,000	$18,750	$13,979
B	30	75,000	18,750	1,654
C	40	12,000	3,000	537
D	40	12,000	3,000	537
E	25	7,500	1,875	119
TOTAL		$181,150	N/A	$16,826

SECOND YEAR INCREASES

Employee	Age	Annual Pay Increase	Additional Benefit @ 65	Additional Annual Deposit
A	50	$ 7,500	$1,875	$1,603/yr.
B	30	7,500	1,875	177
C	40	1,200	300	54
D	40	1,200	300	54
E	25	750	188	13
TOTAL		$18,150	N/A	$1,901

CUMULATIVE BENEFITS AFTER 2 YEARS

Employee	Age	Annual Pay	Benefit @ 65	Annual Deposit
A	50	$ 82,500	$20,625	$15,582
B	30	82,500	20,625	1,831
C	40	13,200	3,300	591
D	40	13,200	3,300	591
E	25	8,250	2,063	132
TOTAL		$199,650	N/A	$18,727

When compared to a nonintegrated defined contribution plan, defined benefit plans are clearly superior for older employees *in terms of contributions.*

Example

Compare, Inc., is considering a defined contribution or a defined benefit plan, and has $18,727 to spend. Without introducing integration into the picture, here are the choices offered by the two alternatives:

Employee	Age	Pay	Defined-Contribution Deposit Amount	% of Total	Defined-Benefit Deposit Amount	% of Total
A	55	$ 75,000	$ 7,738	41%	$15,582	83%
B	30	75,000	7,738	41	1,831	10
C	40	12,000	1,238	7	591	3
D	40	12,000	1,238	7	591	3
E	25	7,500	775	4	132	1
TOTAL		$181,500	$18,727	100%	$18,727	100%

Observation.   Doubling employee A's allocation creates quite an opportunity, but it can create problems too. Consider employee B's reaction to the two alternative plans.

¶804.3   *Choose Entry Age Normal with FIPSL if Your Client Wants More Flexibility*

Entry Age Normal with Frozen Initial Past Service Liability (FIPSL) is a second common actuarial method that allows your client to choose from a range of contributions. Rather than a fixed deposit, there is a maximum and minimum contribution. While sooner or later your client must provide an identical "pot" to provide identical benefits, this actuarial method provides the flexibility that small businesses need so badly.

¶804.4   *How Entry Age Normal with FIPSL Works in Real-Life Situations*

In effect, Entry Age Normal assumes that your client has always had a pension plan. The actuary asks, "If the plan had always been in effect, how much money would already have been accumulated?" The answer to that question is an "unfunded past service liability." Therein lies the key to flexibility. This "unfunded past service liability" represents nothing more than a hypothetical pool of money that would be available if the pension plan had always been in effect. Your client funds future benefits currently, as with the Attained Age Level. He may *selectively amortize* the initial unfunded past service liability over a more extended period. In general, he can "pay off" the amount over anywhere from 10 to 30 years, *at his discretion.*

Thus, he could aggressively pay off the unfunded past service liability in good years and limit bad years' funding to current and minimal past service costs only. The range generated can be quite substantial. Assuming your client's actuary determines a $150,000 FIPSL, the annual amortization could be as little as $10,281 or as much as $19,227. Your client has complete discretion, *on an annual basis,* to decide whether to deposit the maximum, minimum, or somewhere in between. Such broad flexibility may give your client exactly what he wants:

1.   contributions heavily oriented toward older key employees; and

2.   a safety valve for years when the business needs to retain its cash to weather economic storms or expand.

Example

Up and Down Corporation is in the building trade and has seen successive boom and bust times. The firm's owner wants a plan that will give him a big deduction but worries about the possibility of a recession. He likes what Entry Age Normal with FIPSL can do for him.

Employee	Age	Yrs. Past Service	Pay	% of Total	Minimum Contribution	Maximum Contribution	% of Total
A	50	10	$ 75,000	41%	$14,861	$21,028	71%
B	30	10	75,000	41	3,553	5,027	17
C	40	01	12,000	7	1,398	1,479	5
D	40	20	12,000	7	1,335	2,150	7
E	25	01	7,500	4	296	313	1
TOTAL	N/A		$181,500	100%	$21,443	$29,997	100%

Observation. Entry Age Normal plans combine the best of all worlds. On the one hand, they allow the favorable skewing of contributions toward older key employees. On the other hand, they retain some flexibility for your client to fit his pension plan contribution to his cash flow.

¶804.5   *Watch Out for These Problems*

If all this seems too good to be true, you might be right. Your client must understand that more flexibility requires more self-discipline. The fact that there is a range of acceptable deposits does not reduce the amount of money ultimately necessary to pay retirement benefits. Two problems frequently trap small businesses that use Entry Age Normal with FIPSL:

1.   **Underfunding** when key participant's benefits will mature soon; or

2.   **Overfunding** when the real plan objective was a big tax deduction.

¶804.6   *How Underfunding Can Undo Your Client's Plans*

Most small businesses' key employees are closer to retirement age than regular employees. If your client promises big benefits to these key employees and then makes minimum contributions to his plan (amortizing the Past Service Liability over 30 years) he will be in trouble. If a key employee asks for a lump-sum settlement in 15 years, it may not be there.

Example ─────────────────────────────

Up and Down Corporation's president's worst fears come true: high interest rates, slow construction, and she needs cash. She makes minimum contributions to her pension plan. Just as she's about to retire, the business turns around and the future looks bright. She asks for a lump-sum distribution from the plan to obtain the favorable 5-year income averaging. Annual plan contributions of $21,443 plus interest have generated a trust fund balance of $529,053. Her lump sum will cost $458,355, leaving a balance of $70,698. Up and Down's president can take a lump sum. However, if she had been 55 rather than 50 when the plan was set up, there would have been nowhere near enough plan assets to pay her a lump sum. She would have had to forego the favorable tax treatment of 5-year averaging, and paid a lot of taxes.

Solution.   The best solution is not to need a solution. Exercise extreme caution with Entry Age Normal. However, if you have to use it in a marginal situation, consider these options:

1. **Plan to amortize the past service liability over no more than the re-maining years of service of the older key employees**. For example, if key employees are 45 years old, use no more than a 20-year amortization period. Save the slower, 30-year amortization for dire emergencies; and

2. **Restrict the availability of lump-sum distributions, or eliminate them altogether**. Your tax loss may be more than offset by enhanced flexibility.

PLANNING TIP —————————————————————————————
Make sure your actuary provides an ***Emerging Liability Report***, which will compare the projected fund assets with projected payouts on a year-by-year basis. The Emerging Liability Report will tell you when and where to expect trouble.

¶805 *HOW ACTUARIAL ASSUMPTIONS CAN ALSO AFFECT COSTS*

Your choice of actuarial method clearly has significant impact. However, certain actuarial assumptions cut across all actuarial methods in a powerful manner. These are:

1. interest;

2. turnover;

3. salary scales; and

4. benefit costs.

The influence of interest has been thoroughly detailed in ¶803. The other three deserve brief attention.

¶805.1 *How Turnover Assumptions Can Lower Your Client's Costs*

Certain types of businesses—construction companies or restaurants are good examples—historically show exceptionally high levels of turnover. Employees in those industries tend to be transient, staying at most for several years and departing. Why should your client make contributions for a group of employees who, though eligible to participate, will in all probability never become fully vested? This is the question that ''turnover tables'' can help answer.

''Turnover tables'' are nothing more than statistical compilations of the *probability* of termination of different categories of employees. Usually the primary factor reviewed by these tables is participant *age*, since that most closely correlates to termination rate. However, some tables incorporate morbidity and mortality estimates, since some participants may not receive estimated pension benefits due to sickness or death.

This application of turnover tables to your client's plan will result in a discount to his costs, the size of his discount depending on the age distribution of participants. Since, in many tables, the probability of a participant between ages 25 and 30 receiving retirement benefits is assumed to be practically zero, your clients with a young employee pool may benefit from this discount. The money saved, as with any other plan, can be used either to

1. increase benefits for selected key employees; or

2. reduce costs.

A typical table of withdrawal probabilities assigns a percentage to various age categories. Usually the younger a participant is, the higher the probability of withdrawal. Here's a sample of withdrawal rates combining termination, mortality, and morbidity factors:

Age	Withdrawal Probability	Age	Withdrawal Probability
25	.0843	45	.0335
30	.0640	50	.0289
35	.0492	55	.0288
40	.0400	60	.0364

Example

Eat Company is a large restaurant chain with average employment duration of less than five years. The key employees of Eat Company are in their mid-50s and want to receive the maximum benefit out of a $25,000 deposit. Use of an aggressive turnover table, they find, unlocks about 20% of their budget for higher key employee benefits.

Warning.   Like all assumptions, turnover will never equal the predicted amount. Sooner or later actual experience will require some modification of assumptions. Don't use too aggressive a turnover table unless:

1. there's a large enough population of employees to allow "nature to take its course," or

2. there's history to back up the reasonableness of your assumption.

¶805.2 *Salary Scales Are Important Too*

The inflation of the last decade has left many defined benefit plans underfunded. This is because when the plans were implemented, the actuary didn't feel compelled to use assumptions about wage increases. Thus, he might have felt benefit increases occurring because of salary changes would be small enough either:

1. to ignore until they actually occurred; or

2. to be covered by excess investment performance.

However, the doubling of salary levels that has occurred during the last decade has countered that assumption.

"Salary scales" are assumptions about ultimate salaries. For example, a young participant's salary might be expected to climb by an average of 5% per year during his working life. An older participant may show less dramatic change. Alternatively, an actuary might simply apply an "inflation rate" to the entire payroll. Whatever the method, it has become increasingly important to avoid the funding cost disruptions that will occur without adequate inflation planning.

Example

Look what happens to benefits and plan costs if we project a 4% salary increase.

Employee	Age	Pay	Plan I: No Salary Projection		Plan II: 4% Salary Projection	
			Retirement Benefit	Annual Contribution	Retirement Benefit	Annual Contribution
A	50	$ 75,000	$43,908	$18,260	$50,088	$16,338
B	30	75,000	43,908	3,560	90,000*	4,423
C	40	12,000	7,020	1,439	11,856	1,656
D	40	12,000	7,020	1,439	11,856	1,656
E	25	7,500	4,392	302	11,356	529
TOTAL		$181,500	N/A	$25,000	N/A	$24,602

* Maximum benefit is currently $90,000 per year.

Observation. Note how benefits and contributions shift with the introduction of the 4% assumption. The effects depend on relative age. Observe that employee A's retirement benefit increases only marginally; four percent over 15 years doesn't make a tremendous difference. However, 25-

year-old employee E, has almost *three times* the estimated retirement income. On the other hand, employee A's contribution decreases by about 10%, while employee E's almost doubles. Assuming a common $25,000 budget, the Salary-Scaled Plan must spend more of its funds to prepay inflation and boost benefits of younger participants.

In the long run, salary scale assumptions will reduce plan costs for younger employees. This is because initially boosting contributions for a young participant because of projected increases in salary allows compound interest to work for a longer period and to provide a greater ultimate percentage of the future value needed to pay the promised benefit. Salary scales theoretically avoid the problem of incrementally increasing salaries and decreasing remaining years of service inherent in the Attained Age Level Funding actuarial method.

However, if salaries don't increase at the assumed inflation or projection rate, or if a participant terminates employment early in his career, a salary-scale plan will probably have overfunded benefits and when that occurs, your client must either

1.   reduce his tax-deductible contribution, in the case of terminated employees; or

2.   amortize the experience gain, in the case of lower-than-estimated payroll increases.

However, many actuaries prefer that potential risk to the alternative of unfunded benefit increases close to retirement age.

¶805.3   *What Will These Benefits Ultimately Cost?*

Defined contribution plans make no specific promise of retirement benefits. However, the "definitely determinable benefits" requirement in defined benefit plans creates a specific, easily computed future liability for each plan participant. If an employee earning $10,000/year participates in a 50%-of-pay pension plan, he *must* receive $5,000/year when he retires. But how much money will the plan need to meet the liability? The answer can affect plan costs by as much as 25%.

Some insurance companies prefer to use their minimum guaranteed settlement option rates to compute the lump sums required to pay benefits. (A "settlement option rate" is nothing more than a commitment to distribute funds at some future date over a participant's estimated remaining lifetime.) These minimum guaranteed rates reflect the company's worst case scenario and are usually far less attractive than the company's current rates.

For example, one major insurance company currently guarantees that its future payout won't be less than $6.25 per month for each $1,000 of principal. However, for the same $1,000 received **today,** the company will pay $8.10 per month. (Based on 10-Year Certain and Continuous Option.)

Alternatively, many actuaries favor using the 1971 Group Annuity or UP-84 Table for estimating the cost of future pension liabilities. The tables predict that the plan will be able to pay out approximately $7.80 for each $1,000 of plan assets. That makes benefits far less expensive. A ''middle-of-the-road'' approach finds many actuaries utilizing a *graded* settlement cost table, which assumes employees retiring in the near future will benefit from high current settlement option rates, but that more remote retirements will cost progressively more.

Example ───

Option, Ltd., wants to know the funding costs associated with conservative and more aggressive settlement cost assumptions.

FUNDING COSTS TO PRODUCE $5,000/YEAR OF RETIREMENT INCOME

	With Conservative Assumption		With Aggressive Assumption	
Employee Age	Lump Sum	Annual Deposit	Lump Sum	Annual Deposit
25	$67,313	$ 410/yr.	$52,083	$ 317
35	67,313	803	52,083	622
45	67,313	1,726	52,083	1,336
55	67,313	4,818	42,083	3,728
TOTAL	N/A	$7,757	N/A	$6,003

That's quite a difference! The conservative plan assumes that for every dollar per month of retirement increase, the plan will need to have accumulated $161.55. The aggressive plan assumes that only $125 will be necessary to provide $1 of retirement income.

Caution.   In the long run, only actual experience will determine plan costs. Artificially conservative or aggressive settlement cost assumptions will, like unreasonable interest projections, ultimately require some adjustment.

¶806   HOW COMMON REDUCTIONS TO AND LIMITATIONS ON BENEFITS WILL IMPACT YOUR DESIGN

Defined contribution plans are limited primarily by one factor—the Maximum Annual Addition. A participant's account cannot be increased in any year by the lesser of $30,000 or 25% of pay, including

1. employer contributions;

2. forfeitures; and

3. employee contributions.

Defined benefit plans, on the other hand, are subject to several restraints primarily designed to prevent your client from establishing a qualified plan for a short period of time (for instance, within two years of normal retirement) and thereby artificially increasing contributions for one or two key participants. It is important to consider these limitations during the design process.

¶806.1   *How Maximum Retirement Benefits Are Computed*

The maximum annual pension benefit that may be provided by a defined benefit plan is the lesser of (a) $90,000 or (b) 100% of a participant's average pay over his three highest years. For example, an employee earning $150,000 at retirement date would be limited to a retirement benefit of $90,000 per year. A participant with final pay of $25,000 could have a retirement benefit of $25,000 per year. Usually these maximum benefits require further reduction.

¶806.2   *What Is the Normal Form of Retirement Benefit?*

Maximum retirement benefits assume payment in the form of life only annuities. If payment is made under any other settlement form, for instance 10-year certain and continuous, then plan benefits must be actuarially reduced. This is because the life contingencies involved with alternative settlement options make them actuarially more valuable than the basic form.

Example ————————————————————————

Here is how some of the more common settlement option forms will affect your client's benefits. Assume a $10,000 retirement income under the life only option:

Benefit Form	Reduction Required	Net Annual Benefit
Life Only Annuity	None	$10,000
10-Yr Certain and Continuous	91%	9,100
20-Yr Certain and Continuous	75%	7,500
Joint and 100% Survivor	Approx. 70%	7,000

¶806.3 *Using Earlier Normal Retirement Ages Can Further Enhance Your Client's Deduction*

Your client can use a retirement age earlier than 65 provided he makes appropriate adjustments to the $90,000 maximum benefit. Even with the deductions he may improve contribution distribution, because an earlier retirement age will

- shorten his funding period; and

- require a larger expense for an equivalent annuity.

Reductions to the $90,000 maximum benefit (but not to the 100% of pay limit) are required when the retirement age is less than 65; for earlier ages, the $90,000 must be reduced actuarially.

¶806.4 *Special Reduction for Employees With Less Than 10 Years of Participation*

IRS requirements mandate that maximum benefits must be reduced by one-tenth for each year of participation less than 10 years. Therefore, an employee who became a participant at age 59 in a plan specifying a normal retirement age of 65 will be entitled to only six-tenths of the otherwise normal retirement benefit. As a practical matter, this restriction seldom applies, since many defined benefit plans set retirement age as the later of 65 or completion of 10 years plan participation. However, the pension plan designer must then always review employer census data to pinpoint any prospective employees who would be affected by this mandatory reduction. Note that prior to TRA '86 the 10-year rule related to *service* rather than participation.

¶807 *HOW LIBERAL RETIREMENT AGES AFFECT BENEFITS IN INTEGRATED PLANS*

The integrated portion of the benefit (that portion based on compensation in excess of the integration level) must also be reduced for each year prior to age 65 that an employee retires. By far the most commonly used formula requires that an affected employee's benefits be reduced one-fifteenth for each of the first five years and one-thirtieth for each of the next five years that Normal Retirement Age precedes age 65. This reduction will be changed slightly as a result of TRA '86, which ties the reductions to those used by the Social Security System under Regulations to be issued. It is also important to note that the reduction applies *whether or not,* overall plan benefits need to be reduced (remember the $90,000 maximum annual benefit must be reduced if paid before age 65).

Example ────────────────────────────────────

Early Bird Company's retirement plan calls for a normal retirement age of 55. For illustrative purposes only, the plan provides *excess benefits only.* The plan provides income of 26% of excess pay. C. Worm computes his excess pay as $20,000 and expects a $5,200/year benefit. *Not so,* says the IRS requirement. Mr. Worm's benefits must be reduced one-fifteenth for each of the first five years and one-thirtieth for the next five years that his age 55 retirement precedes the IRS's standard. Thus, C. Worm's "excess pay" retirement income is limited to $2,600 per year, ($20,000 × 26% × (1 − 5/15 − 5/30). The reduction may be slightly different when IRS issues Regulations pursuant to TRA '86.

¶808   *DON'T BE DISCOURAGED: THE OPPORTUNITIES FAR OUTWEIGH THE COMPLICATIONS*

Clearly, defined benefit pension plans are more complex and sophisticated than defined contribution plans. They are also less flexible and more expensive to operate. That probably accounts for small business' traditional orientation toward defined contribution plans (particularly profit sharing). However, if your client has a cash flow to meet the ongoing commitment, a good actuary to keep the plan's funding on track, and a good administrator to control the complex reporting and disclosure obligations, then the flexibility inherent in defined benefit plans is worth pursuing.

Most important, defined benefit plans, by their very nature, favor older employees in terms of relative contributions. Defined contribution plans benefit younger participants. Often a small business's key employees form an older group than their average regular employee counterparts. If that's the case with your client, and if there's a limited budget to be oriented toward the key group, try a defined benefit plan. The opportunity for real design capacity will reward the practitioner who diligently pursues his defined benefit education.

¶809   *FASB 87: EMPLOYER'S ACCOUNTING FOR PENSIONS*

It is important to note that a client's tax and cash flow decisions, which can be dramatically variable as the preceding indicates, may not necessarily be consistent with the *financial statement* implications of his plan. Late in 1985, after 10 years of deliberation, the Financial Accounting Standards

Board (FASB) issued its long-awaited rules on accounting for pension plans. Interestingly, the Board's decision was rendered after a four to three vote, indicating substantial dissent among the parties in the decisionmaking process. For many small employers maintaining defined benefit pension plans, FASB 87 will present some difficult and potentially costly dilemmas.

¶809.1   *Reasons for FASB 87*

The FASB's 10-year effort simultaneously indicates their concern over treading on areas normally reserved for actuaries and the perceived need to respond to a number of problems with traditional pension accounting. Since it is the function of the FASB to insure that readers of financial statements be adequately informed of the financial status of a particular company, the following implications of conventional actuarial valuations concerned the FASB:

- Wide choice of actuarial methods: as you can see from the foregoing, a client might ordinarily choose from among many different actuarial methods. Some tend to front-load costs, others to back-load them. Accrual of benefits might be related to service or participation. Ongoing costs might be calculated as a percentage of payroll (e.g., the Entry Age Normal method) or as a function of incremental benefits accrued (e.g., the Projected Unit Cost method).

- Assumptions: we have seen that variation in any of the implicit and explicit assumptions utilized by a valuation—assumptions such as interest, mortality, life expectancy, etc.—can dramatically affect current and future pension costs. In choosing a set of assumptions, an actuary is primarily concerned that *in the aggregate,* all the implicit and explicit assumptions are reasonable. However, without knowing what all the assumptions are, a reader of financial statements might not know whether one company's stated pension cost was equivalent to another's.

- Amortization options: clients have traditionally been able to choose the rate at which they amortize things like past service liabilities, as long as that amortization is consistently applied. However, two companies with identical past service liabilities might record dramatically different pension expenses if one chose to amortize those liabilities over 10 years and the other over 30.

In addition to the above problems with prior accounting for pension plans, the Board was concerned about the difference between plan liabilities determined in the abstract by an actuarial valuation versus the liabilities calculated in a "real world" environment of fluctuating economic conditions.

This difference between liabilities measured at a "point in time" and in the context of an ongoing pension plan contributed to a rash of defined benefit plan terminations in the early 1980s, with companies terminating their defined benefit plan in order to get their hands on "surplus assets" developed by superior investment performance or a lower current liability due to high current interest rates. It is these problems FASB 87 sought to address.

¶809.2   *Objectives of FASB 87*

FASB 87 attempts to resolve these problems by providing the following:

- standardization of information for readers of Financial Statements;

- disclosure of all major assumptions;

- Financial Statement recording of current and long-range plan liabilities and assets;

- retention of independence between reported Financial Statement expense and funding/tax decisions; and

- reduction of a need to terminate plans in order to receive the economic (Financial Statement) benefit of "overfunding."

The following chart exaggerates the relationship between pre- and post-FASB 87 accounting to highlight its impact.

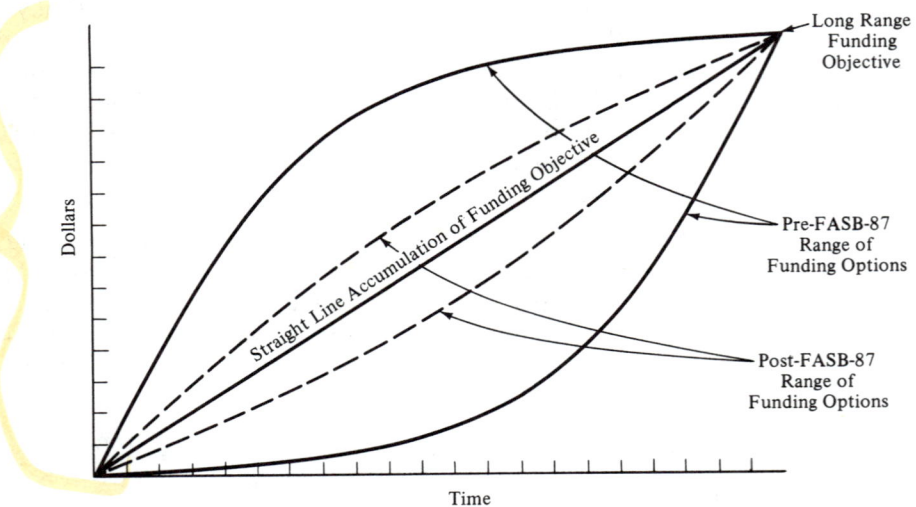

In the case of both pre- and post-FASB 87 accounting, the objective is to recognize the economic impact of a future event (retirement) over a period of time. The long-range funding goal doesn't change. However, under pre-FASB 87 accounting the wide range of actuarial methods and assumptions created broad opportunities for companies to "tailor" their reported pension expense better to their short term objectives; under FASB 87, the range of options has been significantly narrowed.

Important.   Clients will still be able to calculate pension expense according to traditional methods for purposes of *tax* and *cash flow* decisions. FASB 87 *only* relates to the amount of pension expense that will be shown on a company's financial statement.

¶809.3   *When and to Whom Does FASB 87 Apply?*

FASB 87 *must* be used by all public companies and companies with plans covering more than 100 participants for the first fiscal year beginning after 12/15/86 insofar as calculation of annual pension expense is concerned. Nonpublic companies with fewer than 100 participants in their plan must report annual pension expense as per FASB 87 during the first fiscal year beginning after 12/15/88. In either case, companies will need to reflect any FASB 87—generated liabilities on their balance sheet beginning after 12/15/88. Earlier compliance is encouraged, and many companies adopted FASB 87 as early as 1985 if its application tended to improve their balance sheets.

FASB 87 will be *de rigueur* for any company whose Financial Statements are prepared according to Generally Accepted Accounting Principals (GAAP). This includes virtually all larger companies and even smaller ones who for one reason or another (i.e., loan agreement requirements) use this form of accounting. FASB 87 will affect the client's financial statements in several key areas.

¶809.4   *Starting Point: the Transition Amount*

In drafting FASB 87, the FASB had to develop a method for measuring a company's plan's status at the time the FASB was first applied. This amount, calculated once, is amortized as a component of annual pension expense. Here's how you calculate the *Transition Amount:*

STARTING POINT: THE TRANSITION AMOUNT

	The Math	The Terms
minus	Projected Benefit Obligation (PBO)	Present value of benefits for prior service. The PBO is measured using salary scales if the formula is based on future pay.
plus	Cash Basis Assets, at Market Value	
plus	Prepaid Pension Expense	
minus	Pension Expense Liability	
Equals:	**Transition Amount**	

The resulting transition amount, whether positive or negative, is amortized on a straight line basis over the average remaining service period of active employees expected to receive benefits under the plan. If the average is less than 15 years, the employer may amortize over 15 years. The transition debit or credit becomes a component of annual pension expense as discussed below.

¶809.5   *Annual Pension Expense*

Annual pension expense, for purposes of financial statements, will be determined in a manner that may be inconsistent with contribution or tax considerations. It is the amount the employer will show as a charge or credit to earnings on his profit and loss statement. The components of *annual pension expense* are largely derived from the ***Projected Unit Cost*** actuarial method, the method that must be used. It is very important to reemphasize that a client is free to continue using conventional actuarial valuation techniques for purposes of tax and reasonable contribution determinations; FASB 87 **only** dictates the amount of charge/credit to be imposed against current reported earnings. Calculation of **annual pension expense** requires explicit statement of two interest assumptions: the **settlement rate,** which is the effective rate (such as PBGC or annuity rates used to calculate liabilities of terminating plans) at which current obligations could be settled; and the **long-term rate,** which is the expected long-term interest rate for plan assets. Here's how to calculate annual pension expense:

ANNUAL PENSION EXPENSE

The Math		The Terms
minus	Service Cost	Present value of benefits attributed to services rendered by employees during that period. A portion of the PBO unaffected by the funded status of the plan.
minus	Interest	On prior year's PBO assuming Settlement Rate.
plus	Expected Return on Assets	Prior year's assets X Long Term Interest Rate.
minus	Prior Service Credit	Amortization of increase to PBO resulting from benefit amendments with retroactive effect.
plus/minus	Gain/Loss	Difference between **expected** and **actual** rate of return **OR** changes in actuarial assumptions. Amortized over either: a. average remaining service of employees; or b. any faster rate. **IF** greater than either: a. 10% of assets; or b. 10% of PBO.
plus/minus	Transition Credit/Debit (above)	
EQUALS:	**Annual Pension Expense**	

In the case of extremely well-funded plans, or plans that have had extraordinary investment returns, annual pension expense may well be *negative,* leading to the anomalous situation in which a client may be told by his actuary to contribute at the same time his accountants tell him to report *negative expense* on his profit and loss statement.

¶809.6 *Financial Statement Disclosure*

Under FASB 87, an employer subject to GAAP Accounting will be required to report the following on his Financial Statements:

1. liability represented by plan (see discussion below);

2. general description of plan;

3. general description of funding policy; and

4. statement of settlement and long term interest rates used.

¶809.7 *Liability Calculation*

FASB 87, for the first time, requires an employer to actually reflect a liability for his pension plan under certain circumstances ***directly on his financial statements.*** This means that upon application of FASB 87, an employer whose plan is not particularly well funded may suddenly be forced to recognize a new long term liability on his balance sheet. A liability must be reported if the plan's **unfunded accumulated benefits** (the present value of accrued benefits earned to date based on past compensation) are greater than the assets of the plan available for benefit payments. However, he may simultaneously create an intangible asset **up to** any unamortized prior service or transition debit. If prior service or transition debit are insufficient, any shortfall would be charged directly against shareholder equity.

¶809.8 *Example of Disclosure Required under FASB 87*

Here's an example of the types of disclosure a company might make under FASB 87 with respect to a defined benefit plan:

The company has a Defined Benefit Pension Plan covering substantially all of its employees. The benefits are based on years of service and the employee's compensation during the last five years of employment. The company's funding policy is to contribute annually the maximum amount that can be deducted for federal income tax purposes. Contributions are intended to provide not only for benefits attributed to service to date but also for those expected to be earned in the future.

The following table sets forth the plan's funded status and amounts recognized in the company's statement of financial position at December 31, 1988 (in thousands):

Actuarial present value of benefit obligations:	
Accumulated benefit obligation, including	
Vested benefits of $XXX	$ (YYY)
Projected benefit obligation for service	
rendered to date	(ZZZ)
Plan assets at fair value, primarily listed stocks	
and U.S. bonds	AAA
Projected benefit obligation in excess of plan assets	(BB)

Unrecognized net gain from past experience different from that assumed and effects of changes in assumptions	(CC)
Prior service cost not yet recognized in net periodic pension cost	DD
Unrecognized net obligation at January 1, 1986 being recognized over 15 years	EE
Prepaid pension cost included in other assets	$ FF

Net pension cost for 1988 included the following components (in thousands):

Service cost—benefits earned during the period	$ GG
Interest cost on projected benefit obligation	HH
Actual return on plan assets	(I I)
Net amortization and deferral*	J J
Net periodic pension cost	$ KK

The weighted-average discount rate and rate of increase in future compensation levels used in determining the actuarial present value of the projected benefit obligation were 9 percent and 6 percent, respectively. The expected long-term rate of return on assets was 10 percent.

¶809.9   *Implications of FASB 87*

In its narrowing of acceptable options for measurement of plan liabilities and expenses, FASB 87 dramatically alters the traditional role of an actuary serving the defined benefit plan. Smaller clients will particularly feel the impact of FASB 87, since they will be faced with a decision of whether to have one or two actuarial valuations performed.

Many clients will opt to use FASB 87-type actuarial methods for all purposes (e.g., to satisfy contribution, tax and financial statement reporting requirements). However, it is important that they understand one

---

*The net effects of delayed recognition of certain events (for example, unanticipated investment performance) arising during the current period and amortization (recognition) of the net unrecognized effects of past similar events at a rate based on employees' average remaining service life.

significant implication of this decision: the interest rates used or suggested in FASB 87 are generally higher than those that have been traditionally employed for actuarial reports. Furthermore, FASB 87 requires those rates to be adjusted much more frequently to keep in step with the current interest environment. In periods of rapidly rising or falling interest rates, this implies potentially large volatility in pension costs.

On the other hand, a client may opt to use one FASB 87 actuarial valuation to satisfy financial statement reporting purposes or requirements and another to determine more conservative contribution levels. This approach, though it may allow for more prudent and less volatile funding, implies the expense of multiple actuarial valuations that many small employers can not afford.

¶809.10   *Conclusion*

Many commentators have expressed concern that FASB's 10-year effort to provide new accounting guidelines for pension expense goes much too far in usurping the traditional role of actuaries serving defined benefit plans. In fact, though the goal of providing better comparability among employer's reporting pension expense is laudable, it will take several years to determine its full impact. Unfortunately, its implications for smaller clients imply that fewer defined benefit plans will be installed or maintained by those employers.

9

How To Use Flat-Benefit Plans For Obtaining Minimal Complications and Maximum Flexibility

Perhaps the simplest form of defined benefit plan is the ''flat-benefit'' variety. These plans simply provide a flat benefit, expressed as a percentage of pay, to all participants when they reach retirement age. Starting with this basic concept, various levels of sophistication can be added:

- reductions for service less than a stated number of years;
- integration; and
- actuarial assumptions and parameters.

Each of these factors involves its own separate subgroup of subordinate rules and regulations, adding up to the potential for a very complicated and specifically designed retirement plan.

In this Chapter we will discuss these specific rules and regulations and how you can use them to your advantage to design a plan that fits your client's objectives. This chapter also provides a transition from the conceptual discussions of Chapter 8 to the more sophisticated defined benefit plans discussed in Chapters 10 and 11.

¶900   HOW FLAT-BENEFIT PLANS WORK

Flat-benefit plans are the simplest of the defined benefit family. They promise a specific future retirement benefit, expressed as a flat percentage of final pay. Having computed and specified the retirement benefit, your client's obligation is to make deposits which, assuming reasonable actuarial assumptions, will develop a sufficient fund at retirement age to pay the promised benefit.

Observation.   Note the discrepancy between a flat-benefit and a defined contribution (namely, money purchase) plan. A money purchase plan might promise annual *deposits* equal to 25% of pay with no guarantee of ultimate benefits, whereas a flat-benefit plan might promise a retirement *benefit* equal to 25% of pay, and whatever it costs to fund that benefit becomes a variable.

¶900.1   *How To Determine Future Benefits*

It is easy to compute retirement benefits under flat-benefit plans. Simply apply the guaranteed benefit rate to the participant's compensation (current or projected). For example, suppose your client's plan provides that at the normal retirement date a participant will receive 50% of his final three-year average compensation as a pension benefit for the rest of his life.

Example ─────────────────────────────────────

Certain Company establishes a 50%-of-pay flat-benefit pension plan. Here's what would happen:

Participant	Age	Pay	Retirement Benefit Payable @ Age 65
A	50	$ 50,000	$25,000/yr.
B	30	50,000	25,000
C	40	20,000	10,000
D	45	20,000	10,000
E	25	10,000	5,000
TOTAL	N/A	$150,000	N/A

Observation.   Participants earning the same compensation are promised the same retirement income, *regardless* of their respective ages. That highlights the major difference between defined contribution and defined benefit plans. The "definitely determinable" benefits requirement for qualified plans is met by the benefit payable at normal retirement date. Recall that defined contribution plans use their contribution rate to meet this "definitely determinable" test.

¶900.2   *How to Determine Annual Contributions*

Having computed benefits, the next step is to calculate annual contributions. Those depend on a variety of factors, primarily assumed interest and participation age. The younger the participant, the longer the funding period. The longer the funding period, the smaller the contributions because:

1. with a fixed future funding objective, more years of participation do not mean an increased benefit; and

2. compound interest will provide the bulk of the benefits.

The actual computation is complicated unless you have a present value-future value calculator. To perform the calculation, you will need to assemble the following data:

1. assumed interest rate of plan;

2. years of future participation;

3. sex of participant; and

4. settlement option factor.

Assume the plan has a 45-year-old male participant whose benefit at 65 (20 years' future participation) is predicted to be $500 per month, based on receipt of a life only annuity which requires $120 of principal for every one dollar of monthly retirement income.

Monthly Benefit	$500
Multiplied by Settlement Option	× 120
Equals Future Value Necessary @ 65	$60,000

Given this funding objective, we can consult a compound interest table to find that the annual payment necessary to accumulate one dollar after 20 years at 6% interest is .025649. Therefore, the annual deposit for our sample participant is

Accumulation Required in 20 Years	$ 60,000
Multiplied by Annual Payment Per $1	×.025649
Equals Annual Deposit To Fund Benefit	$ 1,539

The calculation process can be troublesome for plans with many participants. Also, the simple demonstration above does not apply to more complex actuarial methods. The concept, however, is the same.

PLANNING TIP ————————————————————————————————

The complexity of deposit calculations has, more than any other single factor, probably discouraged practitioners from using defined benefit plans. However, many firms such as insurance companies, pension consultants, and banks have the capacity to generate defined benefit proposals quickly and accurately. Consider using them before you reject these plans as overly sophisticated.

Example ————————————————————————————————

Certain Company asks you the cost of the 50%-of-pay flat-benefit plan it proposes. Your answer:

Participant	Age	Pay	Retirement Benefit @ 65	Annual Deposit	% of Total
A	50	$ 50,000	$25,000/yr.	$10,555	50%
B	30	50,000	25,000	2,205	13
C	40	20,000	10,000	1,791	10
D	45	20,000	10,000	2,671	15
E	25	10,000	5,000	317	2
TOTAL	N/A	$150,000	N/A	$17,359	100%

Observation.   Participants A and B earn identical salaries but have vastly disporportionate contributions, due to their different ages. Even participants C and D have widely divergent deposits and their ages differ by only five years. This illustration emphasizes the inherent nature of flat-benefit plans and defined benefit plans in general—they will always skew contributions toward older participants.

That frequently meets typical small business needs. It also demonstrates the fact that a company with a limited budget should carefully consider whether the flat-benefit type of plan offers a sufficiently weighted contribution allocation to offset its ongoing fixed commitment. Even the most aggressive defined contribution plan cannot come close to this skewing of employer funds toward older key individuals. And don't forget—defined contribution plans are limited to a $30,000/25% of pay deposit . . . defined benefit plans aren't! Many small businesses are run by one or two key individuals who started the company years ago and have now reached their late 40s or early 50s, and so flat-benefit plans become a viable alternative.

¶900.3 *How To Develop a Formula on Your Client's Budget*

In the real world, small businessmen are more concerned with their budget than with plan formulas. Therefore, our discussion in 900.1 and 900.2 puts the cart ahead of the horse. Most of your clients will want to compare alternative pension plans such as profit sharing, money purchase, or defined benefit plans, not on the basis of future benefits, but rather according to the distribution of current plan deposits.

For example, you are likely to be asked how a $25,000 deposit would be distributed in a defined benefit as opposed to a profit sharing plan. That's very easy for a defined contribution plan but not for a defined benefit program. For the practitioner without sophisticated equipment, such a calculation is almost impossibly time consuming except in the smallest cases.

PLANNING TIP ─────────────────────────────

Use the facility of insurance companies, pension consulting firms, or banks to obtain the budget-determined plan illustrations you need. That will conserve your time and, if you review the proposals with regard to planning tips discussed in this and subsequent Chapters, serve the best interests of your client.

¶900.4 *How To Maximize Contributions for Older Key Employees*

Even without capitalizing on sophisticated forms of flat-benefit plans, you can orient the program toward older key participants. The two most obvious methods for achieving that result are:

1. choice of interest assumption, and
2. service reductions.

HOW INTEREST ASSUMPTIONS CAN HELP

Defined benefit plans operate within the constraints of a hypothetical actuarial model. An integral part of that model is the assumed interest rate for the plan assets. While ultimately actual experience will replace the actuarial model, choice of assumed interest rates can have a dramatic effect on plan funding. Low interest assumptions will raise initial contributions for all plan participants but particularly younger ones; older participants are too close to retirement for compound interest to have a significant role. High interest assumptions will lower overall contributions especially for younger participants. High interest tends to create a much bigger funding gap between younger and older employees.

Example ─────────────────────────────────────

Up and Down Company wants, within reason, to skew their $25,000 budget toward the company's president, who started the company at age 25. You illustrate the effect of using a 5% or 6½% interest assumption:

ANNUAL CONTRIBUTIONS REQUIRED

Participant	Age	Service @ 65	Pay	5% Interest as a $	5% Interest as a %	6½% Interest as a $	6½% Interest as a %	% Change From 5 to 6½
A	55	40 yrs.	$ 50,000	$19,230	77%	$19,786	80%	+3%
B	45	20	15,000	2,194	9	2,063	8	−6
C	40	30	15,000	1,520	6	1,360	5	−10
D	40	25	15,000	1,520	6	1,360	5	−10
E	30	35	10,000	536	2	431	2	−20
TOTAL			$105,000	$25,000	100%	$25,000	100%	N/A

The illustration clearly shows how time and interest combine to cut costs for younger participants. Fifty-five-year-old employee A, with only 10 years until retirement, simply doesn't have much time for interest to go to work. Hence his contribution remains practically constant. At the other end of the spectrum, 30-year-old employee E gives interest 35 years to show its effect, and the result is dramatic—a 20% reduction in annual deposits. The moral of the story is that higher interest rate assumptions will allow your clients to focus their budgets to a greater extent on older participants.

Observation. This illustration held the $25,000 *budget* constant, and allowed plan *benefits* to "float." An alternative approach might hold *benefits* constant with resultant changes to the budget. Costs for younger participants will be substantially reduced.

HOW SERVICE REDUCTIONS CAN PROVIDE
FURTHER EFFICIENCY

You can achieve an even more powerful effect than interest will by including **benefit reductions** in your flat-benefit plan. The logic is simple. If the key man will have "x" years of service at retirement, why not reduce benefits for all participants with less than "x" years of service? The results can be spectacular for an organization with key employees who started young.

Example ─────────────────────────────────

Up and Down Company's president will have 40 years of service when he reaches 65. No other current employee will have that much service. Therefore, Up and Down's attorney reduces plan benefits by one-fortieth for each year of service less than 40.

Participant	Unadjusted Contribution $	Unadjusted Contribution %	×	Service @ 65 40		=	Adjusted Contribution $	Adjusted Contribution %
A	$19,786	(80%)		40/40	(1.00)		$19,786	85%
B	2,063	(8)		20/40	(.50)		1,532	6
C	1,360	(5)		30/40	(.75)		1,020	4
D	1,360	(5)		25/40	(.63)		760	3
E	431	(2)		35/40	(.88)		377	2
TOTAL	$25,000	(100%)		N/A	N/A		$23,455	100%

With the service reduction, plan costs are reduced by 7% without reducing either benefits or contributions for key employee A. Alternatively, your client could spend the saving generated by the service reduction for higher benefits, approximately 85% of which will accrue to his benefit.

Observation. Many real-life situations do not start out with contributions so heavily skewed in favor of a key employee as in the above illustration. In more typical cases, benefit reductions for service can make the difference between successful plan design and a waste of time.

¶901 *HOW TO INTEGRATE FLAT-BENEFIT PLANS FOR MAXIMUM RETURN*

Defined contribution plans have relatively simple integration rules that allocate an extra percentage (usually 5.7%) to compensation above a specified integration level. Thus, a defined contribution plan could provide a contribution equal to 10% of the first $25,000 and 15.7% of the balance of any participant's compensation. A "floating 5.7% rule" was the key to correct integration under the plan. Further, defined contribution plans can use any flat dollar amount integration level up to and including the taxable wage base in force at the time your client's plan year begins.

Flat-benefit defined benefit plans promise specific future *benefits*, rather than a *rate* of current contribution. It seems reasonable, therefore, that the integration of such plans should also be tied to ultimate benefit levels. In fact, that is how integration of flat-benefit plans is achieved.

The basic theory is that since Social Security provided benefits for "covered compensation" of each employee (roughly the equivalent of the average of all taxable wage bases in effect during his years of employment) at his normal retirement date, your client should be able to provide "catch-up" benefits for pay in excess of covered compensation.

Example

If the estimated Social Security benefit for one of your client's participants amounts to $500 per month, which benefit your client funded through payroll taxes, shouldn't it be reflected somehow in the formula for plan retirement income established by your client? Flat-benefit plans recognize Social Security benefits by allowing an extra benefit for participant compensation not covered by the Social Security system. The theory is that under a properly integrated plan, the sum of benefits provided by Social Security and your client's plan ought to provide uniform retirement benefits for all participants, regardless of their compensation.

¶901.1   *How to Determine the Integration Level*

The integration level of a defined benefit plan must be derived from one of the following three alternatives, each of which is directly related to covered compensation. Covered compensation, you will recall, is approximately the average of taxable wage bases to which an employee has or will have been subject during his working life.

Table I simply reflects an average maximum covered compensation for any employee retiring (e.g., turning age 65) in a certain calendar year. Since the taxable wage base has progressively been rising through the history of the Social Security system, employees reaching age 65 some years from now have relatively high covered compensation levels. A flat-benefit plan may specify an integration level which is each participant's covered-compensation according to Table I.

ALTERNATIVE ONE

The first choice for integration level is the IRS's "Table 1." Reproduced below is the 1979 table. Any year's table can be used up to the current year's.

TABLE I

Year Age 65	Amount	Year Age 65	Amount
1979	$ 9,000	1998	$16,800
1980	9,600	1999	17,400
1981	10,200	2000	18,000
1982–1983	10,800	2001–2002	18,600
1984	11,400	2003	19,200
1985	12,000	2004	19,800
1986–1987	12,600	2005–2006	20,400
1988–1989	13,200	2007	21,000
1990–1991	13,800	2008–2009	21,600
1992–1993	14,400	2010–2011	22,200
1994	15,000	2012–2013	22,800
1995–1996	15,600	2014 or later	22,900
1997	16,200		

Example

Integral Company's flat-benefit defined benefit plan is integrated according to 1979 covered compensation. Your job is to determine each participant's excess pay:

TABLE II INTEGRATION

Participant	Age	Pay	Calendar Yr. of 65th Birthday	Covered Compensa-tion	Excess Pay
A	55	$ 50,000	1989	$13,200	$36,800
B	48	40,000	1996	15,600	24,400
C	43	15,000	2001	18,600	0
D	38	15,000	2006	20,400	0
E	32	15,000	2012	22,800	0
TOTAL	N/A	$135,000	N/A	N/A	$61,200

The older the participant, the lower his covered compensation, and the higher his excess pay. Since integrated plan benefits are a derivative of excess pay and will accrue primarily to the benefit of higher-paid key employees, use of this integration level will obviously fit well into the situation of a typical defined benefit plan candidate.

ALTERNATIVE TWO

The second alternative for flat-benefit plan integration level is the IRS's Table II, which is nothing more than *individualized* covered compensation. Table II provides a more exact method for determining excess compensation and can be worth the effort if your client's facts are right. Table II, from 1979, is produced below:

1979 TABLE II

Year Age 65	Amount	Year Age 65	Amount	Year Age 65	Amount
1979	$ 8,724	1991	$14,040	2003	$19,344
1980	9,396	1992	14,304	2004	19,776
1981	10,008	1993	14,556	2005	20,208
1982	10,572	1994	14,796	2006	20,640
1983	11,088	1995	15,312	2007	21,072
1984	11,556	1996	15,828	2008	21,468
1985	12,000	1997	16,344	2009	21,816
1986	12,396	1998	16,860	2010	22,092
1987	12,768	1999	17,388	2011	22,344
1988	13,116	2000	17,904	2012	22,560
1989	13,452	2001	18,420	2013	22,740
1990	13,752	2002	18,888	2014 or later	22,900

Example

Integral Company decides that an individual determination of covered compensation is not too complicated and asks how Table II would work. It is worth comparing the results obtained with several years' tables. The difference in excess compensation resulting from the use of Table II as opposed to Table I is small. However, to maximize benefits for older key employees—for whom funding even relatively small additional benefits is quite expensive—use of Covered Compensation Table II frequently provides the most efficient system.

TABLE II Integral Co.—Integration

Participant	Age	Pay	Calendar Yr. of 65th Birthday	Covered Compensation	Excess Pay
A	55	$ 50,000	1989	$13,452	$36,548
B	48	40,000	1996	15,828	24,172
C	43	15,000	2001	18,420	0
D	38	15,000	2006	20,640	0
E	32	15,000	2012	22,560	0
TOTAL	N/A	$135,000	N/A	N/A	$60,720

ALTERNATIVE THREE

The third alternative for integrating flat-benefit plans is a uniformly applied flat dollar amount. This flat dollar amount cannot exceed the lowest covered compensation of any person who is or might become a participant in the plan. For example, employees turning 65 in 1989 have covered compensation of $16,800. Therefore, defined benefit plans implemented in 1989 could use a flat dollar integration level for all participants of $16,800. Using a flat dollar amount integration level simplifies the task of determining benefits under the plan by streamlining the process.

When Can a Higher Integration Level Be Used? Your client can select a uniformly applied flat dollar amount integration level higher than that described for alternative three (above) if he applies a reduction to excess benefits otherwise available. The formula for defined benefit plan reductions is the following:

$$\frac{\text{maximum flat dollar integration level (Alternative Three)}}{\text{integration level chosen by your employer}} \times \begin{array}{l}\text{integrated} \\ \text{benefits} \\ \text{otherwise} \\ \text{available}\end{array}$$

Example

Suppose your client wants to use a flat $20,000 integration level. He can, as long as he reduces excess benefits otherwise available by the percentage resulting from the formula:

$$\frac{\$16,800 \text{ (maximum from Alternative Three)}}{\$20,000 \text{ (desired integration level)}} \times 26\% \text{ (maximum ''excess'' benefit)}$$

Therefore your client's flat-benefit plan can provide excess benefits equal to 22%.

¶901.2   *How To Select An Integration Level For Your Client*

The above discussion and illustrations yield several conclusions. Here are some situations where one or another integration level ought to be considered:

- Key employees are relatively old—use covered compensation from either Table I or Table II. Covered compensation tables will establish lower integration levels (and therefore higher integrated benefits) for older participants;

- Key employees are relatively young—use a flat dollar amount selected to be just above the median compensation level for all plan participants;

- The budget is limited—consider a flat dollar amount higher than $16,800 so as to isolate key employees; and

- Calculations must be hand done—for preliminary purposes, use a flat dollar integration level. Though slightly less efficient, it will greatly simplify the calculation procedure and conserve your time.

¶902   *HOW TO DETERMINE MAXIMUM INTEGRATED BENEFITS*

What ''catch-up'' benefits are available for compensation in excess of the integration level? TRA '86 allows that an employer may provide benefits for excess participant compensation not to exceed the ''maximum excess allowance,'' which is ¾ of 1% for each year of service with the employer and considered by the plan not to exceed 35. In other words, the excess percent cannot exceed 35 × .75, or 26.25%. For purposes of simplicity, we will use 26% as the maximum. Under pre-TRA '86 rules, the maximum was 37½% **but** that amount had to be reduced actuarially for ''ancillary'' benefits (such as death or disability benefits). Now the excess percentage does not have to be reduced, except for early retirement (pre-65). In addition, the excess percent (applicable to pay *above* the integration level) cannot be greater than the base percent (applicable to compensation *below* the integration level). For practical purposes, the minimum plan formula is therefore 26% of pay up to the integration level, and 52% of pay above the integration level. An alternative way to express this is 26% of *total* pay plus 26% of pay over the integration level.

Example ─────────────────────────────────────

Assume John earns $15,000 per year in a plan with a $9,000 flat integration level. His maximum integrated benefit is the following:

Total Pay		$15,000
Less: Integration Level	(9,000)	
Equals: Excess Pay		$ 6,000
Times: Maximum Benefit Rate	× .26	
Equals: Maximum ''Integrated'' Benefit		$ 1,560/yr.

¶902.1   *Consider That There May Be a Reduction for Retirement Prior to Age 65*

Nonintegrated defined benefit plans can specify a normal retirement date earlier than 65, but the normal $90,000 maximum benefit must be actuarially reduced. Since Social Security benefits are not available (at full rates) until age 65, integrated benefits require adjustment for early retirement provisions. The most commonly used reduction is $1/15$ for each of the first five years, and $1/30$ for each of the next five years by which normal retirement date preceded age 65. However, this reduction may be altered slightly as a result of TRA '86.

Observation.   Note that non-integrated benefits only need to be reduced if the $90,000 benefit limit (or its actuarial equivalent) is a factor; *integrated* benefits (the 26%) must *always* be reduced for retirement ages prior to 65.

Example ─────────────────────────────────────

John's plan is amended to specify a normal retirement age of 55. His excess benefit must be reduced as follows:

Excess Compensation	$50,000
Maximum Excess Rate	× 26%
Maximum Excess Benefit	$13,000
Reduction For Early Payment (5/15 + 5/30)	(6,500)
Net Maximum Integrated Benefit @ 55	$ 6,500

Example ———————————————————————

Even with these significant reductions certain key employees, particularly those in the 40- to 45-year age range, will profit from an early normal retirement age. Consider two plans, both integrated at $9,000, one providing retirement at 65, the other 55.

Participant	Age	Pay	Excess Pay	Plan I: Retire at 65		Plan II: Retire at 55	
				26% of Excess Benefit	Annual Contribution	13% of Excess Benefit	Annual Contribution
A	45	$ 50,000	$41,000	$10,660	$2,390	$5,330	$3,439
B	40	15,000	6,000	1,560	231	780	281
C	35	50,000	41,000	10,660	1,074	5,330	1,195
D	30	15,000	6,000	1,560	110	780	115
E	25	10,000	1,000	260	13	130	13
TOTAL		$140,000	$95,000	N/A	$3,818	N/A	$5,043

Observation.   Older participants profit from a shortening of their potential funding period. The 45-year-old key employee contribution increases by over 40%; the 35-year-old's by only 10%. This reinforces our earlier observation that the effects of interest are most strongly felt by participants with the longest to go until retirement. In this example, we have, even with a 50% reduction in benefits, increased plan costs by about 30%, but 85% of that increase goes to one participant.

¶903   *HOW TO USE TWO-TIERED FLAT-BENEFIT PLANS*

The integration spread discussed at 902 can be used in two-tiered flat-benefit plans. Two-tiered plans can dramatically increase budget and benefit options for your client, while retaining all-important contribution-efficiency for older key employees.

Your client will want to use a two-tiered flat-benefit plan if:

1. he needs a bigger deduction;

2. he wants to provide more than miniscule benefits for lower-paid employees;

3. he wants to provide more benefits for himself than can be generated by an excess only program; or

4. he is required to, under TEFRA's top heavy rules discussed later.

¶903.1 *How Two-Tiered Flat-Benefit Plans Work*

Your plan can provide one level of benefits for compensation up to the integration level and another, higher level of benefits for excess pay. In other words, the plan might provide one level of benefit for total pay with an additional benefit for excess pay. As discussed above, the spread between benefit levels cannot exceed 26%. Thus, your plan could provide a benefit equal to, for example, 50% of *total* pay plus 26% of pay above $9,000 (assuming an age 65 retirement).

Example ———————————————————————————————

Dr. Kelly is persuaded to:

1. lower his salary so he can put more away; and

2. provide more substantial benefits for his employees.

He decides to implement a formula of 40% of *total* pay plus 26% of pay in excess of $9,000. Let's see the results:

Employee	Age	Pay	Excess Pay	26% Excess Benefit	40% of Pay Benefit	Total Benefit	Annual Contribution
A	55	$ 75,000	$66,000	$17,160	$30,000	$47,160	$30,418
B	40	14,000	5,000	1,300	5,600	6,900	1,020
C	35	14,000	5,000	1,300	5,600	6,900	695
D	35	12,000	3,000	780	4,800	5,580	562
E	25	9,000	0	0	3,600	3,600	178
TOTAL		$124,000	$79,000	N/A	N/A	N/A	$32,873

The two-tiered formula increases the plan's contribution substantially, without significantly compromising its efficiency. Dr. Kelly receives over 90% of the contribution. Furthermore, he's providing meaningful retirement benefits for his employees.

Example ─────────────────────────────────

Dr. Kelly asks about the maximum plan deposits possible under a two-tiered flat-benefit plan. The formula works out to be 77.12% of total pay, plus 26% of excess pay.

Employee	Age	Pay	Excess Pay	26% Excess Benefit	77.12% Total Benefit	Total Benefit	Annual Contribution
A	55	$ 75,000	$66,000	$17,160	$57,840	$75,000	$48,374
B	40	14,000	5,000	1,300	10,797	12,097	1,788
C	35	14,000	5,000	1,300	10,797	12,097	1,219
D	35	12,000	3,000	780	9,254	10,034	1,011
E	25	9,000	0	0	6,941	6,941	344
TOTAL		$124,000	$79,000	N/A	N/A	N/A	$52,736

This illustration highlights the opportunity for dramatic plan deductions available to higher-paid, older key employees who participate in integrated flat-benefit plans. Dr. Kelly's contribution represents 72% of his salary—not many clients would be able to afford the luxury of putting that much away. Yet his share of the total deposit is still 92%, so he cannot use the cost of covering employees as an excuse for not establishing a plan.

¶904   WHEN AND WHERE TO USE FLAT-BENEFIT PLANS

Flat-benefit plans work well whenever

1. key employees are relatively old;

2. key employees are middle-aged, but the plan's budget is somewhat limited (use an earlier normal retirement date);

3. your client believes that retirement income should be equated; or

4. your client can live with a fixed annual commitment (tempered, perhaps, by using the Entry Age Normal with FIPSL actuarial method).

However, notwithstanding their potential for large, highly skewed contributions, there are more potential situations in which flat-benefit plans do not make sense;

1. your client feels length of service should be the prime benefit determinant;

2. your client's profits and cash flow fluctuate dramatically from year to year;

3. key employees are young relative to other employees;

4. the plan might have to be terminated within 10 years of its inception;

5. employee ill-will might be a controlling factor.

Flat-benefit plans provide the simplest defined benefit formula and are frequently utilized. They are easily explained. They work particularly well for small businesses where principals tend to be older. Make sure your clients are aware of their potential.

10

When and How Unit-Benefit Plans Can Be Effective

Unit-benefit plans present an opportunity to reward longstanding service in the most direct and visible way. Retirement income in unit-benefit plans is a multiple of compensation and years of service or participation. Participants accrue a small "portion" of their retirement income annually, adding another "portion" each year until they retire, at which time the portions earned cumulatively are totaled. Thus, the longer the period of a participant's service, the higher his retirement benefits.

Frequently, the owner or key employee of a small- to medium-sized business will have worked for the organization since he was quite young, and therefore will have substantial service accumulated as he approaches retirement. He may value most highly those employees who, like himself, have contributed the better part of their lives to the business. Here, unit-benefit plans can be the answer.

This chapter will show you how unit-benefit plans work, how they compare to their flat-benefit counterparts, and how to use them effectively. It will explain the peculiar integration rules that apply and highlight the situations most amenable to unit-benefit plans. The information will add measurably to your "bag of tricks" and enhance your ability to match your client's objectives with the right plan.

¶1000   HOW A UNIT-BENEFIT PLAN WORKS

Conceptually, unit-benefit plans are as simple as flat-benefit plans. Flat-benefit plans promise future benefits equal to a percentage of compensation (such as 50% of pay). Unit-benefit plans simply translate these calculations to an annual event. Each year a plan participant accrues another "unit," and at retirement, his pension will be the sum of all units earned during his working life. In other words, a participant earns a new benefit each time he completes a year of service.

You can visualize a unit-benefit plan in the same manner we had you view the Attained Age Level Actuarial Funding Method. You will recall that in that method, each year's change in compensation was reflected in an incremental and cumulative change in funding. In unit-benefit plans each year's service adds a new incremental benefit to the total. Therefore, employees with substantial amounts of service at retirement age will have accumulated the greatest number of incremental blocks. For example, if a plan provided a benefit for each year of service equal to 1% of pay, then a participant retiring after 40 years of service would receive 40% of his pay; a participant retiring after 10 years of service would receive 10% of his pay.

Example ───────────────────────────────

U. Knit Company establishes a simple unit-benefit plan. The plan promises each participant a retirement benefit equal to 2% of his pay for each year of service. The result is a plan offering vastly disproportionate benefits to participants with different service at retirement date.

Participant	Age	Pay	Service @ 65	2% Annual Benefit Increment	Benefit @ 65	Annual Contribution
A	50	$ 50,000	40 yrs.	$1,000/yr.	$40,000	$14,397
B	45	30,000	20 yrs.	600	12,000.	2,690
C	45	30,000	40 yrs.	600	24,000	3,547
D	35	15,000	30 yrs.	300	9,000	907
E	30	10,000	35 yrs.	200	7,000	491
TOTAL		$135,000	N/A	N/A	N/A	$22,032

Observation.   The illustration clearly shows how unit-benefit plans work. Participant A receives an annual increment of 2% of his $50,000 pay. That works out to $1,000. Assuming 40 years of service at that compensation rate, his retirement benefit will simply be the sum of 40 annual increments or $40,000. The real key to unit-benefit plans is shown by the relationship between participants B and C. Each earns $30,000 and each is 45 years old. Their annual increments are $600. But participant B will only have 20 years of service at age 65; participant C will have 40 years. Therefore, participant C will retire with twice as much income as his counterpart. Unit-benefit plans, more than any other discussed in this book, specifically reward longstanding service. That can be a plus or a minus depending upon your client's situation.

¶1000.1 *Why Incremental Benefits Can Add Up Big for Longstanding Participants*

The illustration in ¶1000 for U. Knit Company generated a whopping benefit for participant C because of that employee's having 40 years of service at retirement. The beneficiaries of the unit approach are typically young employees, who are assumed, for purposes of the plan, to be employed for the duration of their working lives. Therefore, a 25-year-old participant will generally receive the maximum possible benefit under the unit approach.

¶1000.2 *How Unit-Benefit Plans Can Work Against Older Key Employees*

Frequently, your client's older key employees will have either

- joined the company during middle age; or
- purchased the business (and therefore commenced employment) during middle age.

Either of those two situations can disrupt the efficacy of a unit-benefit plan. This is because an employee hired at, for example, age 45 would—except for adjustments discussed below—find, at best, he receives a smaller benefit than average employees of the firm who are probably much younger (and therefore have more future service).

Example

Joe had worked as general manager for a paint store for 20 years before he managed to save enough money to start his own business. When he finally started his own store, he hired one of his competitor's key employees, a 50-year-old buyer. Business boomed and the company soon employed 10 sales, clerical, and stock personnel with an average age of 30. Joe considered setting up a unit-benefit plan—but only for a moment. He and his key employee were 45 and 50 respectively and therefore couldn't receive more than 15 or 20 incremental units. The younger employees could receive up to 40 units thus yielding twice the retirement income. A flat-benefit plan would be a better bet.

¶1001   *HOW TO MAKE THE PLAN WORK BEST FOR KEY EMPLOYEES*

Your client can improve the performance of his unit-benefit plan in several ways. One is to make the threshold decision of whether or not a unit-benefit plan is likely to work given the client's basic census information. Another is to restrict eligible service.

¶1001.1   *What Are the Critical Factors for Evaluating Census Information?*

A cursory review of your client's basic census data may reveal hidden opportunities or pitfalls critical to the selection of a unit-benefit plan. You will generally reject unit-benefit plans if any of the following factors are present:

1. The key man has less than 20 years service at normal retirement date;

2. The average service potential of regular employees is significantly (e.g., more than five years) greater than that of the key man or men; and

3. The key man plans to retire early, thereby further shortening his relative service span.

On the other hand, certain census or subjective factors may favor adopting a unit-benefit plan:

1. Is the business your client's lifelong work? Frequently, small businesses will have been started and operated by one individual for many years. In those cases, the key employee may have as many as 40 or 45 years of service when he reaches retirement age.

2. Does your client want to reward service above all else? If your client's motivation is to reward longstanding service, no plan can do it better than a unit-benefit program.

3. Does your client's business tend to hire older employees? Certain industries have traditionally hired older, more mature employees. If this is the case with your client, and if he started the business when he was fairly young, his employee pool is likely to have a shorter average working life than his own. That would be a good situation for a unit-benefit plan.

¶1001.2 *How To Use the Key Employee Past Service for Optimal Efficiency*

To insure that none of your client's employees will receive benefits greater than those of the key employee, consider a limitation on credited years of service under the plan's formula. For example, if the key employee will have 30 years of service at age 65, the plan's annual increment should be limited to 30. That way, employees who will have more service upon retirement than the key employee will not receive larger pension benefits.

Example

Limit, Ltd.'s key employee will have been employed for 25 years when he reaches age 65. He purchased the business at age 40. While he is oriented toward rewarding service, he doesn't want to provide benefits for any employee that are greater than his own. He considers two alternative unit-benefit plans. The first provides 2½% of pay for each year of service. The second provides 2½% for each year of service not to exceed 25. Since Limit, Ltd., when purchased by the key man, retained some of its existing employees who had substantial service, the results are dramatic.

Participant	Age	Pay	Service @ 65	Plan I 2½%/yr. Benefit	Annual Deposit	Plan II 2½% to 25 yrs. Benefit	Annual Deposit
A	40	$ 50,000	25 yrs	$31,250	$ 4,619	$31,250	$ 4,619
B	50	30,000	40 yrs	30,000	10,798	18,750	6,749
C	50	20,000	15 yrs	7,500	2,699	7,500	2,699
D	45	20,000	20 yrs	10,000	2,242	10,000	2,242
E	30	15,000	40 yrs	15,000	1,053	13,124	921
TOTAL		$135,000	N/A	N/A	$21,411	N/A	$17,230

Observation. Limit Ltd.'s president has saved $4,181 without reducing his own benefits! By limiting eligible service to 25 years, he has excluded from benefit computations 15 years of service for employees B and E, who—except for limitation—would have received retirement income equal to 100% of their pay (2½% × 40 years = 100%).

PLANNING TIP

Always review your client's census information to see how many years of service the key employee will have when he reaches age 65. If it is more than 30, then a unit-benefit plan is worth considering. And if a unit-benefit plan is worth considering, make sure you include a limitation on credited service that corresponds to the amount of service your key employee will have when he retires.

¶1002   HOW TO OBTAIN MAXIMUM BENEFITS USING UNIT-BENEFIT PLANS

Maximum benefits under unit-benefit plans are the same as those for flat-benefit plans (e.g., the ultimate retirement benefit cannot exceed the lesser of 100% of an employee's average compensation or $90,000, with the exception of the $10,000 minimum retirement benefit option). Also, benefits paid in a form other than a life annuity must be reduced to actuarial equivalencies.

PLANNING TIP

The best way to attain maximum benefits for your key employee is to divide his pay (not in excess of $90,000) by the years of service. This will be the exact annual increment necessary to achieve the highest benefit level.

Example

Jim earns $150,000 and will have 30 years of service at normal retirement age. If Jim wants maximum benefits, the plan's formula should be 2% for each year of service not in excess of 30 ($90,000 ÷ 30 = $3,000/yr., which = 2% of $150,000).

¶1003   HOW TO INCREASE MAXIMUM BENEFITS USING INTEGRATED UNIT-BENEFIT PLANS

If the facts of your client's situation warrant consideration of a unit-benefit plan, then proper integration can only make things better. Integration of unit-benefit plans is quite similar to that of flat-benefit plans except that the integration system is applied to the annual incremental benefit rather than aggregate retirement income. In addition, unit-benefit plans offer added flexibility for choosing an integration level.

All these options make unit-benefit plans a potentially sophisticated tool for solving your client's problems.

¶1003.1 *How Integration Works in Unit-Benefit Plans*

Like integrated flat-benefit plans, integrated unit-benefit programs establish separate benefit levels for compensation above and below integration levels. Ultimate retirement benefits are therefore a combination of years of service times compensation up to the integration level and years of service times compensation in excess of the integration level.

Note. The total of excess "increments" cannot exceed 26.25%. Therefore, determine the best *annual* accrual for excess pay by dividing 26.25% by your key person's years of service at retirement. Also, the full 26.25% is only available for employees with 35 years of service with the employer.

Example ───────────────────────────

Integral Corporation's president participates in a unit-benefit plan which recognizes all his 35 years of service with a benefit formula providing 1% of total pay for each year of service and .75% of pay in excess of the plan's $10,000 integration level for each year of service. Based on his $50,000 salary, benefits are easy to compute:

Excess Pay over $10,000	$40,000	
Excess Pay Benefit Rate	× .75%	
Annual Increment, Excess Pay		$ 300
Total Pay	50,000	
Benefit Rate	× 1%	
Annual Increment, Basic Pay		$ 500
Total Annual Increment		$ 800
Times Years of Service		× 35
Total Retirement Benefit		$28,000

Clearly the integration of unit-benefit plans is not complex. However, there are more alternatives and variations with unit-benefit plans than with flat-benefit plans. Let's consider some of those now.

¶1003.2 *How To Choose the Right Integration Level*

Unit-benefit plans offer the same choices as their flat-benefit counterparts. (See Covered Compensation Table I, Covered Compensation Table II, and flat dollar amounts. Higher flat dollar amounts can be used here assuming you make certain benefit reductions.) The application of integration levels to employee compensation in unit-benefit plans is virtually identical to flat-benefit programs. Note that any Covered Compensation Table up to the current year's may be used. The 1979 Table is used in most of the examples that follow.

ALTERNATIVE ONE

Table I. Covered Compensation Table I (reproduced in ¶901.1, Alternative One) is your first alternative for calculating participant's "excess pay." Table I applies an averaged covered compensation amount to each participating employee. Here's how it would apply to a typical situation:

TABLE I: COVERED COMPENSATION

Participant	Age	Calendar Year of 65th Birthday	Pay	Covered Compensation	Excess Pay
A	55	1989	$50,000	$13,200	$36,800
B	48	1996	45,000	15,600	29,400
C	43	2001	20,000	18,600	1,400
D	38	2006	20,000	20,400	0
E	32	2012	20,000	22,800	0

ALTERNATIVE TWO

Table II. Covered Compensation Table II presents a comparable alternative based on individual participant ages. While Table II offers more specificity, it also complicates calculation of a participant's covered compensation. Table II is reproduced at ¶901.1 (Alternative Two) and can apply as follows:

TABLE II: COVERED COMPENSATION

Participant	Age	Calendar Year of 65th Birthday	Pay	Covered Compensation	Excess Pay
A	55	1989	$50,000	$13,452	$36,548
B	48	1996	45,000	15,828	29,172
C	43	2001	20,000	18,420	1,580
D	38	2006	20,000	20,640	0
E	32	2012	20,000	22,560	0

ALTERNATIVE THREE

Taxable Wage Base. Flat-benefit plans can use a uniform flat dollar integration level not to exceed the *covered compensation* of the oldest employee who is or might be a participant of the plan. As discussed in ¶901.1, (Alternative Three), that effectively limits flat dollar integration levels to $16,800. Unit-benefit plans can utilize flat dollar integration levels up to and including the *taxable wage base* in effect at the beginning of a particular plan year. Since the taxable wage base for 1986 is $42,000, that's a substantial increase that allows for the exclusion of substantially more lower-paid employees. Continuing with the examples given above, let's consider how a $20,000 uniform dollar amount integration level can maximize excess pay for key plan participants.

FLAT DOLLAR AMOUNT INTEGRATION LEVELS

Participant	Age	Calendar Year of 65th Birthday	Pay	Integration Level	Excess Pay
A	55	N/A	$50,000	$20,000	$30,000
B	48	N/A	45,000	20,000	25,000
C	43	N/A	20,000	20,000	0
D	38	N/A	20,000	20,000	0
E	32	N/A	20,000	20,000	0

¶1003.3   *Which Integration Level to Use*

As we discussed with respect to integration level choices for flat-benefit plans, the choice of which integration level to use should not be taken lightly. Certain situations lend themselves to the use of one integration system over another. Here are some tips:

1. Use Table I Covered Compensation when your key employees are relatively old and in situations where there will be so many participants that the individual calculations of Table II might become burdensome.

2. Table II will be most productive in situations where key men are relatively old and the plan's budget is limited enough to warrant getting every dollar's worth of excess benefit. Particularly in plans with relatively few participants, the extra effort for an individual calculation is not so burdensome that it needs to be avoided.

¶1003.4   *How Final Average Pay Plans Can Ease Your Administrative Burdens*

Unit-benefit plans can provide retirement income based on a three-year average. In these cases, benefits are a multiple of the plan's accrual rate, years of service, and final average compensation. The big difference is in the compensation averaged. Typically, an employee's three final years' compensation will be substantially higher than pay averaged over the employee's entire working life. Therefore, this approach will generate higher retirement income.

Even so, the incremental benefit that can be earned for pay in excess of the integration level is still .75% per year of service to a maximum of 35.

Example

Fred, who will have 15 years of service at retirement, wants to know what his excess benefits would be under a final average pay plan. For that we need only consider his compensation averaged over the last three years.

Average Pay, Last 3 Years	$50,000
Less: Assumed Integration Level	(10,000)
Equals: Excess Pay	40,000
Times: Max. Excess Accrual Rate	× .75%
Equals: Annual Excess Increment	300
Times: Years of Service	× 15
Equals: Excess Portion of Benefits	$ 4,500

Caution.   Unit-benefit plans, like flat-benefit plans, are also subject to a limitation that benefits paid on excess pay cannot be any greater than for those paid on pay up to the integration level. For an employee with 35 years of service at retirement, that means the *minimum* formula for a fully integrated plan is:

$$(.75\% \times 35 \times \text{Total Pay}) + (.75\% \times 35 \times \text{Excess Pay}).$$

¶1003.5   *How a Two-Tiered Final Average Pay Plan Works*

The spread discussed in Paragraph 1003.3 applies to two-tiered unit-benefit plans as well. Therefore, subject to the constraints of the $90,000/100% rule, in 1986 your client could establish a unit-benefit plan, providing, for example, 1% for each year of service up to $42,000 and 1.75% for each year of service for compensation for each year in excess of $42,000.

Example ───

U. Fural Company considers a final average pay plan providing just such a formula, but using an integration level of $30,000. Because final average pay will tend to be higher than career average, compensation is assumed to be 25% higher than under the alternative approach discussed in ¶1003.5.

Participant	Age	Pay	Service @ 65	1%/yr. Total Pay Benefit	+	.75%/yr. Excess Benefit	=	Total Benefit	Annual Deposit
A	50	$ 62,500	30 yrs.	$18,750		$7,313		$26,063	$10,357
B	40	37,500	40	11,250		2,250		13,500	2,276
C	40	37,500	20	7,500		1,125		8,625	1,454
D	35	18,750	30	5,625		0		5,625	567
E	30	15,000	35	4,500		0		4,500	316
TOTAL		$171,250		N/A		N/A		N/A	$14,970

Observation. The above illustration assumed a 25% increase in participant payroll over the comparable example in ¶1003.5. As a practical matter, any assumption about inflation as it relates to payroll will mean that younger participants will derive the greatest additional advantage from final average pay unit-benefit plans. This is because the effect of compound interest on the younger participants' salaries will be much stronger than it will be for the older participants' salaries.

¶1004 A CHECKLIST OF KEY QUESTIONS WHEN USING UNIT-BENEFIT PLANS

Most of what can be done with a unit-benefit plan can also be done with a flat-benefit program and vice versa. Therefore, the choice will often boil down to which approach you and your client feel most comfortable with. The key, under either approach, is to maximize your client's key employee share of benefits and contributions. In situations where the use of a unit-benefit plan is dictated, use the following checklist to cover your bases:

- Have you limited maximum credited service to years your key employee will have accumulated at normal retirement date?

- Does the sum of excess pay increments for the key employee equal 26.25%?

- Does the sum of excess and regular pay increments fall within the 100%/$90,000 limitations?

- Does the sum of excess pay increments exceed the sum of increments for pay below the integration level by more than .75% per year of service?

- Does an average or final pay plan make more sense?

- If a career average plan is selected, who will be responsible for the potentially troublesome recordkeeping responsibilities?

- Will your client's level of sophistication make a unit-benefit approach more or less attractive?

¶1005   PRINCIPAL ADVANTAGES AND DISADVANTAGES OF UNIT-BENEFIT PLANS

Because of their orientation toward relative service, unit-benefit plans can present challenging limitations or opportunities. While completing the checklist in ¶1004 you should be constantly aware of these obstacles and challenges. Most can be overcome or avoided by diligent review of your client's census information.

¶1005.1   *Situations Where Unit-Benefit Plans Can Work*

Unit-benefit plans can be a powerful tool where one or more of the following factors are present:

1. The key employee will have substantially more service than the average employee.

2. Your client is philosophically attuned to a plan where he recognizes service above all else.

3. Your client finds the annual benefit increment approach to ultimate pensions conceptually simpler than the flat-benefit approach.

¶1005.2 *Situations Where Unit-Benefit Plans Can Work Against You*

The converse of the positive statements in ¶1005.1 can be equally true. The presence of some or all of the following factors might mitigate against using the unit-benefit approach:

1. Potential service of regular employees exceeds that of key employees.

2. The business was acquired relatively recently by the key employee, thereby limiting his potential for eligible service under the plan.

3. Your client finds the flat-benefit approach conceptually simpler.

4. Your client does not feel that relative service should be a controlling factor for determining plan benefits.

The brevity of this Chapter underscores the similarity of unit- and flat-benefit plans. Flat-benefit plans that provide a pro rata reduction for service less than the number of years that key employees will have to achieve virtually the identical result as unit-benefit plans. More often than not, the ultimate decision about which approach to use will be based on a particular practitioner or client's comfort with an aggregate versus annual approach to pension benefits. The only defined benefit plan to offer significant, substantive differences from unit- and flat-benefit plans is discussed in the following Chapter dealing with offset plans.

11

Offset Plans Provide a Simple Integration Alternative

Unit-benefit and flat-benefit pension plans recognize Social Security benefits indirectly by providing separate benefits for compensation above and below the integration level. Very often it is difficult to explain to plan participants how these two-tiered computations affect them. Offset plans provide a simple two-step alternative. First, offset plans provide all participants with a pension benefit that ignores Social Security. However, then the benefit is reduced by (offset by) a portion of Social Security benefits. Theoretically, an offset plan provides uniform retirement income, considering the sum of Social Security and employer-provided benefits, for all participants. The offset amount cannot exceed the lesser of:

1. the "maximum offset allowance" (¾ of 1% of a participant's final average compensation for each year of service with the employer); or

2. 50% of the benefit that would have been provided without regard to the offset.

This Chapter will explain in detail what offset plans are, various alternative formats you can choose, and how or when to use them. In addition, it will discuss "tricks" to improve the efficiency of your offset plan.

¶1100   *WHAT IS AN OFFSET PLAN?*

Offset plans provide a unique and easily explained alternative to the more sophisticated unit- and flat-benefit plans. While unit- and flat-benefit plan integration is governed by complex rules about the relationship of plan benefits above and below the integration level, offset plans use a much more basic approach.

Offset plans theoretically provide benefits for **all** plan participants, under a traditional nonintegrated unit- or flat-benefit formula. There is no annual computation of "spread" or "excess-benefit" rates. Whenever a participant reaches retirement age, however, his benefits are simply *reduced* by a portion of his Social Security payments. The maximum reduction, or "offset," is 26.25% of final average pay (or 50% of the benefit computed without regard to the offset). Because of the rapid escalation of Social Security benefits—bound to continue with the advent of cost-of-living and coupling adjustments—this offset can provide a more effectively integrated plan than traditional flat- or unit-benefit plans. This is because Social Security benefits replace a high percentage of lower-paid employees' salaries and that percentage is often higher than the retirement benefits provided by the employer's underlying plan.

¶1100.1   *How Offset Plans Qualify*

Virtually any defined benefit plan can use an offset format. Either a flat- or unit-benefit plan can establish a benefit level from which a Social Security offset may be deducted.

Example ──────────────────────────────

Offshore, Ltd., establishes a 50%-of-pay flat-benefit plan with an offset equal to 60% of primary Social Security. John has worked for Offshore for 35 years, always earning more than the taxable wage base. His final pay is $28,000. Here's his plan benefit computation:

Compensation		$28,000
Times Benefit Rate		× 50%
Plan Benefit		$14,000
Social Security Benefit	$7,935	
Times Percentage of Offset	60%	
Net Offset	($4,761)	
John's Benefit From Offshore, Ltd.		$ 9,239

Note that the maximum offset in this example would have been $7,000, because the offset amount cannot exceed the lesser of

a. the "maximum offset allowance" (.75% × 35 × $28,000 = $7,350); or

b. 50% of the benefit determined without regard to the offset (50% of (50% of $28,000), or $7,000).

This additional requirement was added by TRA '86, and adds considerable complexity to offset plans.

Example ———————————————————————————————————

John's brother Jim has worked for Exit Company for 30 years and earned $30,000. Exit Company gives exiting employees a retirement benefit of 3% of pay for years of service offset by 70% of primary Social Security. Jim can look forward to:

Compensation		$30,000
Times Annual Benefit Accrual Rate		× 3%
Annual Benefit Increment		$ 900
Times Years of Service		× 30
Gross Retirement Benefit		$27,000
Social Security Benefit	7,935	
Times Offset Percentage	70%	
Net Offset	($5,553)	
Jim's Benefit		$21,447

Observation. Many lower-paid employees have such a high percentage of their income replaced by Social Security that a high level of offset may exceed the additional tests added by TRA '86. The implication is that a fairly high base benefit may be required.

Example ———————————————————————————————————

Savit, Incorporated, provides employees with 40% of their pay, less 70% of Social Security. Mark's average pay is $15,000/yr. Therefore, his employer-sponsored benefit is

Compensation	$15,000
Benefit Rate	× 40%
Plan Benefit	$ 6,000
Social Security Benefit	$8,000
Offset Percentage	× 70%
Offset Amount	$5,600
Net Employer Benefit	$ 400

This plan won't qualify because it fails *both* of the additional tests of TRA '86, even assuming Mark worked 35 years:

> **Test One.** Maximum Offset: 35 yrs. × .75% × $15,000 = $3,938

> **Test Two.** Maximum Reduction: 50% of (40% of $15,000) = $3,000

Better go back to the drawing board on this one!

¶1100.2   *Choosing the Best Combination for Your Client—Critical Choices*

The best combination of benefits and offset depends on your client's objectives. Assuming his objectives center around maximization of contributions for older key employees, he will naturally choose a high Social Security offset.

Example ————————————————————————

In the interests of good public relations, Fair Play Company decides to compare a 100% offset plan with a 50% offset program. Basic plan benefits are held constant at 75% of pay. The results illustrate the dramatic shift of benefits in favor of the lower-paid participants as shown in the following table.

The illustrations clearly show how significant effective integration can be, particularly for lower-paid employees. Make sure that your client understands that any reduction in the maximum integration rate or offset rate will skew benefits toward the lower-paid people. That may be a high price to pay for a simpler, or more equitable plan. Remember that, assuming integration rules that have been worked out over the last several decades accurately reflect the proper relationship between private plan benefits and Social Security, the only discriminatory plan is one that *does not* maximize integration. On the other hand, be prepared to meet TRA '86's additional tests—you can't take away all lower-paid employee's benefits!

COMPARISON OF NET FAIR PLAY COMPANY BENEFITS

Participant			100% Offset Plan			50% Offset Plan		
#	Comp.	S.S. Benefit	75% Basic Benefit	Less: 100% Offset	= Net Fair Play Benefit	75% Basic Benefit	Less: 50% Offset	= Net Fair Play Benefit
A	50,000	6,000	37,500	6,000	31,500	37,500	3,000	34,500
B	30,000	6,000	22,500	6,000	16,500	22,500	3,000	19,500
C	30,000	6,000	22,500	6,000	16,500	22,500	3,000	19,500
D	20,000	6,000	15,000	6,000	9,000	15,000	3,000	12,000
E	10,000	6,000	7,500	6,000	1,500	7,500	3,000	4,500

COMPARISON OF TOTAL RETIREMENT INCOME

Participant	100% Offset Plan			50% Offset Plan			
	Net Fair Play Benefit	+ Social Security	= Total Benefit	Net Fair Play Benefit	+ Social Security	= Total Benefit	% Increase
A	31,500	6,000	37,500	34,500	6,000	40,500	+ 8%
B	16,500	6,000	22,500	19,500	6,000	25,500	+13%
C	16,500	6,000	22,500	19,500	6,000	25,500	+13%
D	9,000	6,000	15,000	12,000	6,000	18,000	+20%
E	1,500	6,000	7,500	4,500	6,000	10,500	+40%

Observation. The 100% offset plan won't qualify because of Participants D and E; the 50% offset plan won't because of Participant E. See if you can tell why.

¶1101 *HOW TO USE FLAT-BENEFIT OFFSET PLANS EFFICIENTLY*

Flat-benefit plans are most amenable to an offset format. This is because basic benefits under the plan are computed in a parallel fashion to the offset amount. Flat-benefit offset plans will work best in the same situations where traditional flat-benefit or flat-benefit excess plans will be effective. The differences will be in slight contribution discrepancies.

¶1101.1 *When Flat-Benefit Offset Plans Will Work Best for Your Clients*

Chapter 9 described in considerable detail situations warranting consideration of flat-benefit plans. Those situations include:

1. key employees older than average employees;

2. key employees higher paid than average employees; or

3. client wants all retiring employees to receive a comparable retirement income.

Virtually any time a flat-benefit excess plan makes sense, so does an offset program.

Example
Reduction Company considers establishing an 80%-of-pay flat-benefit plan offset by 50% of a participant's assumed Social Security, but asks how that plan would compare with a traditional flat-benefit (excess) plan spending approximately the same amount. Here's your answer:

80% PAY LESS 50% SOCIAL SECURITY

Participant	Age	Pay	Benefits Gross	Benefits Offset	Benefits Net	Deposit	36% Total + 22% Excess Flat Benefit Plan* Benefit	36% Total + 22% Excess Flat Benefit Plan* Deposit
A	50	$ 50,000	$40,000	$4,000	$36,000	$12,957	$36,800	$13,245
B	45	15,000	12,000	4,000	8,000	1,794	6,500	1,458
C	40	25,000	20,000	4,000	16,000	2,364	12,300	1,817
D	35	50,000	40,000	4,000	36,000	3,627	36,800	3,708
E	25	10,000	8,000	4,000	4,000	198	3,600	178
TOTAL		$150,000	N/A	N/A	N/A	$20,940	N/A	$20,406

*Table 1, 1978

Observation. It is interesting to note how similar the results are under either approach. The similarity adds power to the arguments that choosing between the alternatives is more a matter of style than substance. The offset and flat-benefit excess plans provide benefits and contributions that are almost identical. Note that participant A's benefit increases by only 1%.

¶1101.2   *How Service Reductions Can Improve Your Results*

Adding another element to your benefit formula—a pro rata reduction in benefits for service less than a specified number of years—will enhance the performance of your offset plan.

Example

Reduction Company (1101.1) implements the offset plan, but adds a requirement of 40 years service for full benefits. That has a significant impact on plan benefits and costs, since employee A started working for the firm at age 25:

Participant	Age	Pay	Assumed Service	Gross Benefit	Service Reduction	Net Benefit	Deposit
A	50	$50,000	40 yrs	$36,000	N/A	$36,000	$12,957
B	45	15,000	20	8,000	20/40	4,000	897
C	40	25,000	30	16,000	30/40	12,000	1,773
D	35	50,000	30	36,000	30/40	27,000	1,372
E	25	10,000	40	4,000	N/A	4,000	198
TOTAL		$150,000	N/A	N/A	N/A	N/A	$17,197

Observation. The participants with less than 40 years of service at retirement receive a substantial reduction in their benefits and therefore, contributions. *Don't forget:* employees with less than 35 years of service with the employer may not be eligible for fully integrated benefits!

Participant B, except for the service reduction, receives a retirement benefit of $8,000. But since participant B is assumed to have only 20 years of service at retirement, his plan benefits can be reduced by twenty-fortieths and his contribution cut in half. The effect of these service reductions can be quite dramatic, particularly with relatively old employees who, under a flat-benefit alternative, require a much larger deposit. This illustration reinforces the fact that flat-benefit plans, used in conjunction with the right modifications and reductions, can be a powerful planning tool for your client.

¶1102   HOW UNIT-BENEFIT OFFSET PLANS PROVIDE FURTHER DESIGN OPPORTUNITY

If your client's key employees will have substantially more service at retirement than most employees, or if your client believes retirement benefits should be directly tied to years of service, then a unit-benefit offset plan can be effective. The arguments in favor of unit-benefit offset plans are obviously the same as those for regular unit-benefit programs.

¶1102.1   *How Unit-Benefit Offset Plans Work*

Unit-benefit offset plans are simple to operate. There are two basic approaches:

1. Compute the gross retirement benefit and subtract a *flat* percentage of Social Security; or

2. Compute the gross retirement benefit and subtract an *incremental* percentage of Social Security.

Under the first approach, your client would compute total retirement benefits in the conventional unit-benefit manner, such as the following:

- Years of service times the benefit rate equals retirement income; subtract a portion of the total Social Security benefits available at age 65; or

- Retirement income minus X% of Social Security equals net plan benefits.

This first approach, therefore, uses a flat offset to a unit-benefit format.

The second approach uses a unit-benefit offset, as well as a unit-benefit retirement income calculation. The total plan benefit is calculated in an identical manner. But the offset is determined on an incremental approach.

$$\text{Years of Service} \times \text{Offset Rate} = \text{Total Offset}$$

With this latter approach, participants with the most service will have the largest offset. In many small- to medium-sized businesses, this is contrary to typical objectives.

PLANNING TIP ————————————————————————————————

The incremental approach to offset amounts is most effectively used in the unusual circumstance where your client has key employees who do not have more service than typical employees, but still insists on a unit-benefit approach.

Example ——————————————————————————————————————

Reduction Company changes its corporate mind and sets up a 2%-of-pay-per-year-of-service unit-benefit plan offset by 74.07% of Social Security. Here's the result:

Participant	Age	Pay	Service	Basic Benefit 2% × Yrs. × Pay	Offset Amount	Net Benefit	Annual Deposit
A	50	$ 50,000	40	$40,000	$5,803	$34,197	$12,308
B	45	15,000	20	6,000	5,387	613	137
C	40	25,000	30	15,000	5,803	9,197	1,359
D	35	50,000	30	30,000	5,803	24,197	2,438
E	25	10,000	40	8,000	4,462	3,538	175
TOTAL		$150,000	N/A	N/A	N/A	N/A	$16,417

The above example illustrates a unit-benefit plan with a flat-offset. Basic plan benefits were a multiple of years of service and the incremental benefit rate. For example, employee C receives a benefit of 60% (30 years of service × 2% per year) of pay. Offset amounts are a flat 74% of estimated Social Security benefits, without regard to years of service at retirement. That results in a larger offset for participants with less service. But the plan won't qualify. Why? (Hint: Remember, the offset amount can't be greater than 50% of the benefit determined without regard to the offset!)

Example ——————————————————————————————————————

Unite, Incorporated, has identical census facts as Reduction Company, but elects a 2%-of-pay-per-year-service unit-benefit plan offset by 1.85% of Social Security for each year of service. This is a more complicated approach, but adds consistency to the plan:

Participant	Age	Pay	Service	Basic Benefit 2% × Yrs. × Pay	Offset– 1.85% × Service × S. Sec.	Net Benefit	Annual Deposit
A	50	$ 50,000	40 yrs.	$40,000	$5,803	$34,197	$12,308
B	45	15,000	20 yrs.	6,000	2,690	3,309	742
C	40	25,000	30 yrs.	15,000	4,348	10,652	1,574
D	35	50,000	30 yrs.	30,000	4,348	25,652	2,584
E	25	10,000	40 yrs.	8,000	4,462	3,538	175
TOTAL		$150,000	N/A	N/A	N/A	N/A	$17,383

Unite, Incorporated's plan generates identical basic retirement benefits. For example, employee C still receives 60% (30 years of service × 2% per year) of pay. However, the *offset amount* is calculated on an incremental approach. Employee C's offset, rather than being a flat 74% of Social Security, is now 30 years times 1.85% times Social Security. Thus, his offset is $4,348 (55.5% of Social Security). Note that net plan benefits to be provided by Unite, Incorporated, for employee C are now $10,652 and the annual deposit is $1,574. Under the flat offset approach, net plan benefits were $9,197 and the deposit was $1,359. This 12% increase in benefits and costs may be in opposition to your client's objectives. **But** the plan will not quite follow the rules under TRA '86. Why? (Hint: Does employee E's offset amount exceed 50% of his benefit without regard to the offset?)

Observation.   The latter approach, using an incremental offset technique, dramatically boosts benefits and contributions for participants with **less** service and **lower** pay. That's an unusual goal for most businessmen and may well limit the utility of this type of unit-benefit offset plan.

¶1102.2   *When Your Clients Should Use These Plans*

Unit-benefit offset plans work best in the same situations where traditional unit-benefit plans are effective. That means you should consider them in the following situations:

1.   When your client is philosophically oriented towards long service as a prime determinant of pension benefit;

2.   When key employees have substantially more service than the average participant;

3.   When key employees are relatively young; and

4. When your client finds the incremental approach to benefits conceptually simpler than the flat-benefit alternative.

The opportunity to use either a flat offset amount (i.e., 70% of Social Security) or an incremental offset (i.e., 2% of Social Security for each year of service up to 35) allows you virtually endless choices in designing hybrid plans. Thus, the potential sophistication of unit-benefit offset plans is limited only by your creativity.

¶1103 OTHER IMPORTANT PRACTITIONER CONSIDERATIONS WHEN USING OFFSET PLANS

There are some additional factors which might warrant or preclude more detailed analysis of offset plan alternatives. Most of them represent positive opportunities, and include special options to enhance benefits for key participants who were employed late. Simplicity and cost control can be improved dramatically by using these factors. Each has important ramifications and may influence your attitude toward offset plans.

¶1103.1 *How Offset Plans Can Help Key Employees Who Started Late*

Unit-benefit and flat-benefit plans integrated in the traditional manner must contain a provision that reduces excess benefits for each year of service less than 35. For a client whose key employees were employed by their corporations late in their careers, offset plans may be uniquely attractive. This is because a different reduction is applicable to offset plans. Basically, the **offset** is reduced (remember, it can't exceed .75% × years of service up to 35) so a key employee who started late would have a **smaller** offset, and **larger** employer-provided benefits.

¶1103.2 *The Inherent Value of Simplicity*

Many employers feel that offset plans are the simplest defined benefit plan to explain. If you agree, do not underestimate the importance of that fact. Defined contribution plans, like money purchase and profit sharing plans, are often chosen by default. Many clients prefer something they can understand and explain as opposed to an alternative that is cumbersome or overly complicated, no matter how attractive it appears. Saying to a key employee or other participant, "Your benefit is X% of pay minus Y% of your Social Security Benefit" is much easier than explaining the complicated relationship between integration level and excess benefits under the other defined-benefit approaches. If your client has decided on a defined benefit plan, he might as well (given approximately comparable contributions) use one that everyone understands. On the other hand, the *operation* can be **very** complex and therefore expensive because of the difficulty of calculating appropriate Social Security Benefits. Caveat emptor.

¶1103.3 *Effective Control of Future Costs*

Because Social Security benefits are inflation-indexed and coupled, they have been rising dramatically over the last several years. So have Social Security taxes, to which any of your clients will testify. The higher Social Security benefits climb, the higher the offset they will provide to an offset defined benefit plan. Therefore, your client may, if he sets up that sort of plan, have a built-in cost-control mechanism for his pension plan—one that will probably keep pace with, or even exceed, his payroll costs. Furthermore, a Social Security offset plan is self-adjusting, that is, it does not require annual amendment of the plan's integration level to keep benefits in perspective. That helps simplify the administration of the plan and adds the simplicity that makes offset plans an attractive option for your clients.

Alternative integrated plans—flat-benefit or unit-benefit—typically require periodic amendments to the integration level (with the exception of unit-benefit plans that use the taxable wage base as their integration level). The amendments can be irritating from several points of view:

1. Someone needs to keep track of the required amendments.

2. Someone needs to prepare the amendments.

3. After three amendments, pension plans typically need to be resubmitted to the Internal Revenue Service for approval.

Therefore, any type of plan that can decrease the need for future administration and qualification functions can be a long-range advantage to your client. On the other hand, benefit calculations in offset plans, as mentioned above, are quite cumbersome—especially in plans using salary scales—because of the need to accurately calculate projected Social Security benefits. This can make offset plans a "high overhead" form of program, not to be taken lightly in a small business.

12

Target Benefit Plans: The Best Choice for Many Small Business Employers

Target benefit plans are a cross between defined contribution and defined benefit plans. If the facts of your client's situation are right, this plan can provide the best of both worlds.

Target plans are infrequently used, primarily because they are little known or understood. This chapter will explain the intricacies of target benefit plans so that you can use these effective tools. Target benefit plans come in all forms—flat-benefit, unit-benefit and offset. In general, they work similarly to defined benefit programs. Chapter 12 will explain the differences and help you use them to your advantage.

¶1200 HOW TO EXPLAIN TARGET BENEFIT PLANS TO YOUR CLIENTS

Target benefit pension plans share attributes of both defined benefit and defined contribution plans. They are hybrid creatures operating within a unique sphere in the pension industry. Unfortunately, this uniqueness implies some additional complexity. In fact, target benefit plans are more sophisticated than some of the other plans but the opportunity they present for additional flexibility should not be overlooked.

The best way to understand target benefit plans is to compare them to defined contribution and defined benefit plans. By understanding which aspects of target plans fit in the defined contribution realm and which in the defined benefit, you will enhance your effectiveness at explaining target plans to your clients.

¶1200.1   *A Checklist of Similarities to Defined Contribution Plans*

In many respects target plans closely resemble defined contribution plans, particularly the money purchase variety. Both in terms of the "maximum annual addition" and the "account balance" system of measuring benefits, they fit the mold quite well.

In one other important respect, too, target benefit plans share a relationship with the defined contribution plans: they do not require annual actuarial certification. That will obviously help your small clients to keep costs to a minimum.

Maximum Annual Addition.   No participant in a target benefit plan can have his account increased during a limitation year by more than the lesser of

- $30,000; or

- 25% of compensation.

You will recall from Chapters 4 through 6 that the maximum annual addition includes the following components:

- employer contributions;

- forfeitures; and

- employee voluntary contributions.

Example —————————————————————————————

Mr. Bullit participates in his employer's target benefit plan. He earns $20,000 per year. His employer's contribution is $4,000. In addition, he receives $1,000 in forfeitures. Finally Mr. Bullit makes a $2,000 contribution to his voluntary account. He has exceeded maximum annual addition as is evident here:

Employer Additions To Account	$4,000	
Forfeitures	1,000	
Total Employer Addition		$5,000
Voluntary Contribution		2,000
TOTAL ANNUAL ADDITION		$7,000
MAXIMUM ANNUAL ADDITION, LESSER OF—		
a. 25% of pay	5,000	
b. Dollar limitation	$30,000	
MAXIMUM ANNUAL ADDITION		$5,000
EXCESS ANNUAL ADDITION		$2,000

Account Balances.   The most striking similarity between target plans and other defined contribution plans is that they utilize account balances to record participant benefits. As with regular defined contribution plans, a target benefit account balance is composed of the following:

* employer contribution;

* forfeitures; and

* earnings (or losses).

When a participant retires, his benefit is simply the account balance that has been accumulated. If investment results have been good, benefits might be quite substantial. If investment experience has been disappointing, then his benefits may be less than attractive.

No Actuarial Certification.   Since benefits are not ***guaranteed,*** there is no reason for a plan's funding to be certified by an actuary. Therefore, like defined contribution plans, target benefit plans have a less expensive administrative process. Since actuarial certification can represent a significant expense component of small plans, programs that avoid it will be well received by your clients.

¶1200.2   *A Checklist of Similarities to Defined Benefit Plans*

Target benefit plans are also quite similar to defined benefit programs. Contributions are computed in virtually the same fashion—through actuarial determinations.

Maximum Benefit Limitations Applicable to Target Benefit Plans. Your client's target benefit plan cannot call for estimated retirement benefits that require a contribution greater than the lesser of:

- $30,000 (for 1986); or

- 25% of pay.

What is ultimately paid out of the plan is irrelevant as long as the assumptions used for generating deposits were reasonable.

Example _____

XYZ Company establishes a target benefit plan providing estimated retirement income of 200% of pay for plan participants. Contributions are determined with an implicit assumption that fund earnings will average 2%. Fund earnings actually average 8%. The plan will not qualify because the targeted benefits were computed by reference to unreasonable assumptions.

Observation. Target benefit plans will generally be considered reasonable if they utilize an assumed interest rate of 5½% to 6½%.

Actuarial Computations. Target plans set up estimated retirement benefits for plan participants and then fund toward those estimated benefits. Actual investment experience (which would affect the funding standard account of a traditional defined benefit plan) is ignored during the accumulation period. However, contributions *are* based on the estimated retirement income. Therefore actuarial computations are necessary to determine annual contributions.

Example _____

Mr. Ring is 45 years old and earns $50,000 per year. He participates in a target benefit plan which provides an estimated retirement income of 70% of pay. Assuming 6½% interest, his annual plan contribution is computed as follows:

Compensation	$50,000	
Benefit Percentage	× 70%	
Estimated Target Benefit		$35,000/yr.
Funding Period	20 years	
Assumed Interest	6½%	
Annual Contribution		$ 7,846

If Mr. Ring's contributions actually earn 9% interest, the excess earnings will simply be *added* to his account. The contribution won't change. Therefore, when he reaches age 65, he will have a retirement income of $47,200. On the other hand, if the $7,846 contribution only earned 1% interest, his retirement income would be $18,824 per year. *Participants* bear the risk of investment loss. Contributions, once actuarially determined, remain level except for incremental benefit changes.

¶1200.3 *The Biggest Advantage—the Allocation of Excess Interest*

The allocation of excess interest to participant accounts can benefit everyone.

- It can benefit the employee because actual retirement benefits can exceed targeted estimates.

- It can benefit the employer because his annual cash flow requirement for the plan is not disturbed by a Funding Standard Account amortization of excess or interest.

If conservative assumptions are used and actual investment performance exceeds expectations, the results can be pretty spectacular.

Example

Consider five employees of varying age who participate in a target benefit plan whose benefit formula calls for 50% of pay. Each of the participants earns the same income. Depending upon investment performance, results can vary widely.

Partici-pant	Age	Pay	Target Benefit	Deposit @ 65	Pot @ 65 Assuming 6% Return	Pot @ 65 Assuming 2% Return	Pot @ 65 Assuming 10% Return
A	50	$20,000	$10,000	$3,757	$92,695	$66,271	$131,306
B	45	20,000	10,000	2,377	92,686	58,910	149,757
C	40	20,000	10,000	1,594	92,701	52,077	172,422
D	35	20,000	10,000	1,106	92,701	45,766	200,123
E	25	20,000	10,000	565	92,687	34,810	275,071

Observation. Since deposits, once computed, remain fixed, target benefit participants are directly affected by interest higher or lower than the assumed rate. For example, participant E, who is youngest and therefore has the greatest to gain or lose from interest, could receive as much as $275,071 or as little as $34,810, depending on whether the average rate of return is 2% or 10%. Unlike a defined benefit plan, which would require amortization or "spreading" gains or losses above or below the assumed plan interest rate, target benefit plans, like defined contribution plans in general, simply add surplus gains or losses to participant accounts.

Note that the contribution initially fixed for each participant assumes level compensation for that participant from the time of entry to the plan to retirement. Each time a participant's pay changes, a new deposit increment is added to the previous total and funded on a level basis to retirement. You'll recall that this sort of computation is comparable to the attained age level funding method used by many defined benefit plans. The only difference is the absence of a provision to handle interest differentials between the hypothetical plan model and actual experience.

¶1201 HOW FLAT-BENEFIT TARGET PLANS CAN FULFILL MOST SMALL BUSINESS EMPLOYERS' NEEDS

Flat-benefit target plans are substantially similar to their flat-benefit cousins. Benefits are simply a percentage of compensation. The only difference is that excess (or shortfall) earnings do not increase or decrease plan contributions. They are simply added to accounts.

Example

Center Company implements a 40%-of-pay flat-benefit plan using a 6½% interest assumption. Here are the results:

Participant	Age	Pay	40% Target Benefit	Lump Sum Necessary	Annual Contribution	Contribution as a %
A	54	$ 50,000	$20,000	$185,391	$11,325	80%
B	40	15,000	6,000	55,617	887	6
C	30	50,000	20,000	185,391	1,403	10
D	30	12,000	4,800	44,494	337	3
E	25	10,000	4,000	37,078	198	1
TOTAL		$137,000	N/A	N/A	$14,150	100%

Since target benefit plan contributions are calculated similarly to defined benefit ones, you might have anticipated that contributions would be skewed heavily toward older participants. This in fact occurs, as illustrated above. Participants A and C each earn comparable salaries and are entitled to the same estimated retirement benefit. Yet participant A's contribution is eight times that of his counterpart. Target benefit plans can, therefore, often provide the orientation toward older key employees. Your clients will want the convenience and simplicity of account balances as opposed to the more cumbersome actuarial model and funding standard account with which defined benefit plans must constantly be reckoned.

Observation.   The allocation of the $14,150 deposit is so favorably inclined toward key employee A that your client may ask why he should bother with a traditional defined benefit plan when he can accomplish the same funding objectives through the target benefit alternative. For many small clients that is a good question but keep two facts in mind:

1. No participant's contributions can exceed 25% of pay—and employee A is quite close to that ceiling.

2. Target benefit plans cannot use the Entry Age Normal actuarial method, which means the contribution is an annual fixed amount with no flexibility for troublesome economic times.

¶1201.1   *What Are the Special Problems With Integration and How To Avoid Them*

Integration of target benefit plans is traditionally troublesome because IRS requires excess benefits to be limited to "properly" integrated levels. Since target benefit plans do not provide a *guarantee* of either integrated or basic plan benefits, it is impossible to predict in advance whether benefits ultimately paid at retirement will be properly integrated. In addition, Revenue Ruling 83-110 conformed target benefit plan integration with defined contribution plans. The upshot of this is that normal defined benefit integration "spreads" must be reduced to seven-ninths of conventional limits. Remember, the maximum integration spread is 26.25% (assuming 35 years of service); therefore, the maximum spread for a target benefit plan is $\frac{7}{9}$ × 26.25%.

Caution.   Since TRA '86 cut back integration possibilities it is reasonable to expect Revenue Ruling 83-110 to be reconsidered. Practitioners are well-advised to keep abreast of changes in this area.

Example

Guess Company establishes a flat-benefit excess target plan with an assumed interest rate of 6%. Based on the assumed interest rate, benefits in excess of the integration level will not exceed the 20.42% (26.25% × $\frac{7}{9}$)

limitation associated with this plan form. However, the plan earns an average rate of return of 12%. That means ultimate benefits will be far in excess of those assumed and will exceed what IRS deems properly integrated.

There are two possible solutions to these issues:

1. Distribute excess earnings attributable to benefits above the integration level *evenly* to all employee-participants (i.e., according to relative total payroll); or

2. Use the ''safe harbor'' provision that allows unit-benefit target plans using an assumed interest rate not less than 5½% to let the actual investment return of each participant's account ''stay where it is'' without artificial reallocation.

Because of the cumbersome nature of flat-benefit excess plan integration, most of your clients will opt for the second solution discussed in ¶1202.2.

¶1201.2   *When Flat-Benefit Plans Will Be Most Effective*

Flat-benefit target plans are effective any time defined benefit plans would be, with some additions:

1. When key employees are older and higher-paid than the average employees;

2. When the plan's budget is limited enough so that the 25% maximum annual addition requirements are not troublesome;

3. When the business includes few enough employee-participants to preclude using the Entry Age Normal method that might, in some circumstances, make defined benefit plans more attractive; or

4. When your client wishes to stabilize his budget and avoid the funding disruptions that would occur in defined benefit plans as a result of earnings above or below the assumed rate.

¶1201.3   *Do Not Forget Service Reductions in Your Flat-Benefit Target Plans*

Like traditional defined benefit plans, target programs can include benefit reductions based on service less than a certain number of years. If the key employees in your client's organization will have more service at retirement than an average participant, you'll want to include a provision requiring a certain number of years' participation for full benefits.

Example ───

Center Company (1201) adds a provision to its plan requiring that participants have 40 years service at retirement for full benefits. Here's the impact on plan funding:

Partici-pant	Age	Pay	Assumed Yrs. Service	40% Target Benefit	×	Target Benefit Yrs. 40	Annual Contri-bution	Contri-bution as a %
A	50	50,000	40 yrs.	20,000		$20,000	$11,325	83%
B	45	15,000	25 yrs.	6,000		3,750	554	4
C	40	5,000	35 yrs.	20,000		17,500	1,228	9
D	35	12,000	35 yrs.	4,800		4,200	295	2
E	25	10,000	40 yrs.	4,000		4,000	198	2
							$13,600	100%

The illustration for Center Company reinforces the utility of one of the simplest and most overlooked design tools. Recalling the illustration in ¶1201 and comparing it to the above, note that without reducing the contribution or benefit for participant A we have increased his share of the total contribution dramatically. Alternatively, we have cut down substantially on costs for other employees, which reduction we used to increase the benefit level of participants—and participant A would receive substantially all increased funding to pay for those additional benefits.

The illustration at 1201 uses the same compensation level for all plan participants to drive home a point about the interrelated age, interest, and service. In the real world of your clients' situations, key employees will not only tend to be older, but also higher paid than the typical employee. Any such differential in compensation will further enhance efficiency of a target plan, particularly when the plan will be integrated.

¶1202 HOW UNIT-BENEFIT TARGET PLANS PROVIDE MORE FLEXIBILITY

Unit-benefit target plans are considerably more useful than their defined benefit counterparts because they provide the one specific "safe harbor" for integration (see ¶1202.2). These plans will give you and your client traditional planning flexibility and lessen the risk for problems if you choose an integrated format. Your goal in designing a unit-benefit target plan will be the same as for any other plan—to maximize benefits (and therefore, contributions) for key employees.

¶1202.1   *How To Use Unit-Benefit Target Plans*

Generally you will want the sum of annual benefit increments for your client's key employee to provide the highest percentage of pay above any plan participant. Typically that will mean your annual benefit increment will be equal to retirement income desired divided by years of service of the key man at normal retirement date.

Example ——————————————————————————————————

Mr. Bullseye will have 40 years of service when he retires. He wants to replace 40% of his preretirement income. Therefore, his target plan should call for annual benefit increments of 1% of pay. Furthermore, the plan should limit credited service to 40 years. That way, no participant can receive a higher benefit than Mr. Bullseye. Here's how the plan would work out.

Partici-pant	Age	Pay	Assumed Service @ 65	Annual Increment	Target Benefit	Annual Contri-bution	Contri-bution as a %
A	50	$ 60,000	40 yrs.	1%	$24,000	$ 8,638	74%
B	45	40,000	20	1	8,000	1,793	15
C	40	15,000	25	1	3,750	554	5
D	35	15,000	30	1	4,500	453	4
E	30	10,000	35	1	3,500	246	2
TOTAL	N/A	$140,000	N/A	N/A	N/A	$11,684	100%

Observation.   A nonintegrated unit-benefit plan provides no particular advantage over a flat-benefit alternative, unless your client finds it easier to understand. In the example above, participant A receives 40% of pay at retirement. All other participants receive less, based on their relative service. A flat-benefit plan could have achieved *exactly* the same result by using a formula calling for 40% of pay at retirement reduced pro rata for each year of service less than 40. Therefore, whether you use a flat- or unit-benefit target plan in *nonintegrated* situations is primarily a matter of personal preference or of the philosophical approach of your client. However, if you wish to integrate a target benefit plan, the story is different. Here, unit-benefit plans offer a substantial advantage.

¶1202.2   *"Safe Harbor" From Integration Problems*

Revenue Ruling 71-446, Section 18.01, provides that unit-benefit excess plans can allocate earnings in excess of the assumed rate and can be allocated according to relative benefits, **as long as** the assumed interest rate under the plan is at least 5½%. Therefore, your client could set up a unit-benefit target plan which provides annual benefits for pay in excess of the integration level equal to .584% per year of service not in excess of 35.

Furthermore, keep in mind that the integration level of a unit-benefit plan can be:

- covered compensation; or

- a uniform dollar amount up to and including the taxable wage base in effect for a particular plan year.

Example ———————————————————————————————

Aim, Incorporated, establishes a target benefit plan integrated with Social Security. The plan uses average compensation and provides a retirement benefit equal to 1% of total pay plus .583% of pay in excess of $15,000 to plan participants.

Participant	Age	Pay	Service @ NRD	1%/Yr. Basic Benefit	.583%/Yr. Excess Benefit	Total Benefit	Annual Deposit
A	50	$ 50,000	35 yrs.	$17,500	$7,142	$24,642	$ 8,869
B	45	20,000	20 yrs.	4,000	583	4,583	1,027
C	40	15,000	30 yrs.	4,500	0	4,500	665
D	35	40,000	35 yrs.	14,000	5,101	19,101	1,925
E	30	15,000	35 yrs.	5,250	0	5,250	368
Total		$140,000	N/A	N/A	N/A	N/A	$12,854

The efficiency of Aim, Incorporated's plan is equal to that of a conventional defined benefit program. Yet, this exceptional efficiency is achieved:

- without cumbersome and expensive actuarial certification; and

- while maintaining the conceptually simple account balance method of recordkeeping.

The disadvantages are the same as for any target plan:

- Participants can't be *certain* of the benefits they will ultimately receive;

- Maximum contributions are 25% of pay, which may be a limiting factor; and

- The flexibility of Entry Age Normal with its attendant range of contributions is not available.

Observation.   Aim, Incorporated's plan is very efficient for employee A. He receives 36% of total payroll but 73% of the plan contribution. If you're going to use a target plan as your primary retirement accumulation vehicle, the unit-benefit variety can be used safely and effectively.

¶1202.3   *How to Maximize Plan Efficiency for Key Employees*

Most of the methods for increasing the efficiency of defined benefit unit programs are applicable to target hybrids as well. Make sure your plan does the following:

1. Places a "cap" on the number of years key employees will have when they reach retirement age;

2. Uses a relatively high interest assumption in order to keep contributions lower for younger participants; and

3. Provides annual benefit increments that generate exactly the right benefit or contribution for the key employee. Once the plan is designed for him, you may let the other "chips fall where they may."

¶1203   *HOW OFFSET TARGET BENEFIT PLANS WORK*

Offset target benefit plans offer substantially similar opportunities to those of more traditional defined benefit programs. In order to determine a net benefit received under such a plan, first compute a participant's **gross** retirement benefit under the plan. Then, subtract the amount of offset to determine the net plan benefit for which the employer must fund. The resultant benefit is an estimate only. Each year, changes in compensation are reflected in incremental benefit/contribution increases or decreases.

Example ————————————————————————

Mr. Bumble participates in a target benefit offset plan promising 50% of pay less 50% of Social Security benefits as an assumed benefit at normal retirement age. Mr. Bumble is 45 years old earning $100,000 per year and will receive estimated Social Security benefits of $8,000 per year at 65. His target benefit under the plan would be calculated as follows:

Gross benefit (50% of pay)		$50,000
Less: Estimated Social Security at 65	$8,000	
Times Offset percentage	× 50%	
Net Social Security Offset		($4,000)
Net Plan benefit		$46,000

The annual deposit for Mr. Bumble based on this preliminary calculation will be $12,450. If, in his second year of participation, Mr. Bumble receives a $5,000 pay increase but his estimated Social Security benefits do not change, then the plan administrator must begin funding for an additional retirement benefit of $5,000, the cost of which is $1,507. Thus, after two years, Mr. Bumble's contribution is pegged at $13,957. Regardless of whether investment performance yields a larger or smaller benefit, these funding amounts will be continued and future amounts added or subtracted depending on changes in pay. Do not forget the additional requirements of TRA '86 with respect to offset plan integration:

1. The offset amount can't exceed ⅞ of 26.25% of a participant's estimated 3-year high average salary; and

2. The offset amount can't exceed 50% of the estimated benefit determined without regard to the offset amount.

¶1203.1   *What Types of Offset Target Benefit Plans Will Qualify?*

All the traditional defined benefit formula approaches are available in the target offset domain. The major alternatives in defined benefit plans—flat- and unit-benefit—are the major alternatives here as well. Flat-benefit alternatives are illustrated above with the example of Mr. Bumble. Unit-benefit plans offer a second important alternative. Under a unit plan, benefits are calculated on an incremental annual basis.

Example

Suppose Mr. Bumble will have 30 years of service when he retires, and that he participates in a **unit-benefit** offset plan rather than the flat-benefit program indicated above. The plan's formula calls for 1.666% for each year of service less 1.666% of estimated Social Security benefits for each year of service. Mr. Bumble's retirement benefit would be calculated as follows:

Gross benefit (1.666% × $50,000 × 30) ..		$25,000
Offset amount (1.666% × $8,000 × 30) ..	($4,000)	
Net retirement benefit		$21,000

Also keep in mind that unit-benefit programs have traditionally been a safe harbor as long as they use an assumed interest rate of not less than 5½%.

¶1203.2   When Will Target Benefit Offset Plans Work Best?

Many employers find the "offset approach" to integration the simplest of their alternatives. Offset plans are fairly easy to describe to employees. Therefore in cases where a defined benefit or target benefit approach is wanted because of key employee parameters, the offset approach may have some advantage because of its relative simplicity.

¶1204   WHY TARGET PLANS SHOULD BE USED MORE OFTEN BY SMALL BUSINESS EMPLOYERS

Target plans are quite sophisticated and difficult to explain because they contain attributes of both the defined contribution and defined benefit families of retirement plans. However, in many situations the effort will be well rewarded. Target plans provide some unique opportunities that many clients can utilize with great efficiency.

¶1204.1   Stability of Cash Flow Preserves Tax Budgeting

Traditional defined benefit plan contributions are affected by a variety of factors. Two significant factors are forfeitures, which reduce contributions directly, and investment gains and losses, which reduce contributions indirectly through the amortization or "spreading" process. Since each of these factors is largely uncontrollable, they reduce your client's ability to budget the cash flow and tax aspects of this plan. Target benefit plans enhance this management ability by eliminating one source of volatility—investment experience. The fact that in target plans excess earnings (or losses) are simply added to account balances means that annual plan funding will be subject to less fluctuation.

¶1204.2 *Simplicity Means Reduced Costs for Your Clients*

The absence of actuarial certification requirements means that the client who adopts a target plan can eliminate a substantial annual expense. This is a significant factor for many small employers. Furthermore, the requirement for actuarial certification attendant with traditional defined benefit plans creates an aura of complexity and inflexibility that frightens many potential clients. Finally, a simpler plan will obviously, in the long run, minimize the amount of *your* time spent explaining and re-explaining how a particular retirement program works. For the same reason, employees should be more highly motivated by a plan they understand.

¶1204.3 *Interest Earnings Have a Major Effect*

Today's inflationary environment has created a unique opportunity to "lock in" high rates of return. High rates of return in a defined benefit plan are often counterproductive because they will eventually reduce plan costs. Most small businessmen implement defined benefit plans in order to *create* tax deductions of a certain magnitude and will be irritated by a constant decrease occasioned by superior investment performance.

Target plans, on the other hand, can utilize excess earnings very effectively. They are simply added to participant accounts. The effect of these high rates of return over a long period of time can be staggering. ¶1200.3 illustrated this dramatic opportunity. Therefore, assuming your client can afford to "live with" a *fixed* annual commitment that goes along with a target benefit plan, today's investment environment may provide additional incentive for target plans.

¶1204.4 *Few Employers Can Spare 25% of Payroll*

As a practical matter, the 25% of payroll limitation on annual additions affects only a very few potential clients. Twenty-five percent of payroll is a very large amount of money for most individuals to save. For all but the highest paid professionals, it will probably create a sufficient tax deduction and retirement benefit.

¶1204.5 *Summing Up Target Plans*

Target plans provide some unique opportunities. Their only drawbacks appear to be the following:

1. They lack contribution flexibility that may be obtained through use of the Entry Age Normal actuarial method with a defined benefit plan; and

2. They limit an employee's contribution to 25% of pay which, for some older participants, may not build up a retirement benefit quickly enough.

However, these drawbacks, plus the complexity of the target plans, should not serve to diminish their utility. Particularly in the current inflationary environment, the target benefit plans provide, for many small businessmen, the best of all possible worlds.

13

Special Considerations in Plan Design

The rules discussed in prior Chapters generally apply to single plans with a reasonable level of common law employee participation. However, the practitioner will commonly run into situations where the standard rules are "overridden." This is primarily due to the passage of the Tax Equity and Fiscal Responsibility Act (TEFRA), which placed severe constraints on plans that "push the limits" of deductions and benefits, or which are designed to minimize the level of participation of employees in general. The purpose of this Chapter is to discuss the special cases where there are exceptions to the standard rules. Although a complete digression into every exception and its impact is beyond the scope of this book, the discussion should make practitioners aware of the areas of primary concern.

The special circumstances to be explored herein include the following:

1. Unrelated business income;

2. Multiple plan limits;

3. Controlled group and affiliated service organization rules;

4. Top heavy plan requirements;

5. Super top heavy requirements; and

6. Special distribution notification rules.

Each of these areas has its own set of rules and regulations, some of which are not entirely resolved as of this writing. Practitioners are cautioned to consult the latest promulgations if client situations touch upon one or more of the special areas.

¶1300   UNRELATED BUSINESS INCOME

The purpose of a pension plan is to enhance the future security of employees; pension trusts are offered exceptional tax advantages to provide an incentive to employers to support this socially valuable objective. The tax shelter of a qualified plan's trust is not to be used as a shelter for extraneous activities. This is the theory and background to the fairly simple rules on unrelated business income.

Basically, these rules proscribe trust activities which are considered ancillary or extraneous to the creation of secure retirement benefits for employees. For example, trusts (except LESOPs) cannot borrow money or otherwise "leverage" their assets because that activity is not deemed a prudent method to develop retirement benefits.

Example
Lever Co.'s pension trust includes life insurance policies on the lives of participants. The policies contain the privilege of letting contract holders borrow accumulated cash values at 6% interest. Lever Co. borrows all cash values ($100,000) at 6% and invests the proceeds in corporate bonds yielding 14%, thinking that the net gain (8% interest) represents an efficient way to enhance the plan's return. Unfortunately for the company, the 8% interest will be considered unrelated business income since it was generated through a technique which is prohibited.

Example
Profitminders, Inc., with three or four profitable subsidiaries, has an even more clever idea: why not have the pension trust purchase one of the subsidiaries? The trustees of the plan could operate the company, and all its profits would be sheltered in the plan from corporate income taxes. Why, the parent corporation and other subsidiaries could actually diminish their own profits and somehow push them into the trust-owned subsidiary. This is a good idea, but one that won't fly. Pension trusts are not supposed to be in the business of running businesses. They are supposed to be in the business of investing funds for the benefit of retirement.

The consequence of plan income being characterized as unrelated business income is simply that the trust must file an income tax return and pay taxes on that income. Thus, to the extent that tax would occur at a lower rate than if the income had not been shifted, the plan may actually benefit from having unrelated business income. However, the two most common applications of these rules are given in the above examples, and the best advice is usually the following:

1. Do not put life insurance in a qualified plan if you intend to borrow;

2. Profitable businesses are better off making larger contributions to their plan than to shift profits to the plan.

Although unrelated business income is a problem seldom encountered in the retirement plan field, it is worth avoiding.

¶1301   *MULTIPLE PLAN LIMITS*

Notwithstanding the design flexibility and tax power of qualified plans, situations sometimes arise in which a single retirement program will not fulfill the objectives of a business. In those situations, a good solution may be to install a second plan.

Example ─────────────────────────────────

Dr. Wait has always earned a large income. However, between his expensive lifestyle, education costs for four children, and some tax shelter investments that did not pan out, he finds himself at age 50 with very little net worth and no way to provide for maintaining his lifestyle if he slowed down his practice. He asks his attorney if he can put more money into a retirement plan than the contribution associated with an aggressive defined benefit plan. The answer is ''yes,'' with an important caveat: with the passage of TRA '86 the maximum contribution by a company for **multiple** plans is 25% of eligible payroll. Often a defined benefit plan spends more than this by itself, thereby precluding installation of a second plan.

Example ─────────────────────────────────

GGG Co. wants to provide a strong incentive for its employees as well as a special benefit for key managers. An ESOP fits the bill for employee motivation and cash flow planning, but it does not do anything special for key employees since it cannot be integrated with Social Security. The solution: a combination of LESOP and an integrated target benefit plan.

To limit the large deductions and unreasonable accumulations that would occur with no constraints on plans, rules have developed over time and have been considerably tightened under TEFRA. The rules place limits on total plan benefits by imposing the requirement that the percentage utilization of maximum benefits under combined plans can't exceed 1.0, under a complicated formula discussed below. Opportunities are further restricted if the employer has a so-called Top heavy plan, discussed later in this Chapter.

Caution. The multiple plan limit rules considered herein do not take into account one of the most complicated parts of TEFRA: special considerations, in the form of transitional rules, for pre-TEFRA programs. Practitioners are cautioned to consult those transitional rules when they encounter situations involving pre-TEFRA programs.

¶1301.1   *The 1.0 Rule Explained*

Multiple plan limits are defined by a complicated "1.0 Rule" that compares the utilization percentage of the multiple plans. Utilization percentage means the percentage of the maximum available benefit under a particular form of plan. For example, if an employer established a defined benefit plan with a 50%-of-pay formula, he obviously has used 50% of the available limit of defined-benefit programs, 100% of pay. Different computations are required if a particular plan is calculated with reference to the *dollar limits* (i.e., maximum benefit of $90,000, or maximum contribution of $30,000), or the *percentage limits* (i.e., 100% of pay for a defined benefit plan, and 25% of pay for a defined contribution plan). Let's consider the application of each to both defined contribution and defined benefit programs.

¶1301.2   *How the 1.0 Rule Applies to Defined Benefit Plans*

The portion of the overall 1.0 limit comprised by the defined benefit plan is calculated by the fraction:

ACTUAL DEFINED BENEFIT UNDER THE PLAN

Either:

1.25 × Maximum Defined Benefit ($90,000) If $ Limits Apply, or
1.40 × Plan Compensation, If % Limitations Apply

The effect of this "either/or" formula is that lower-paid individuals get more flexibility in their use of multiple plans, while those pushing the limits of available benefits are somewhat more restricted. This is in line with Congressional intent that the use of the retirement plan tax shelters be limited for very highly paid individuals. Let's consider the application of the rules to two situations: one in which the $ limits apply, and one in which the % limits dominate.

Example With Dollar Limits ————————————————

Dr. Em's defined benefit plan promises him a benefit, based on his compensation, of $90,000. Since the $ limits apply, Dr. Em is restricted by the 1.25 denominator:

1. Actual Benefit $90,000

2. 1.25 × $90,000 .... $112,500

3. Defined Benefit Use (1 ÷ 2) 0.8

Thus, Dr. Em could establish a defined contribution plan whose percentage use under the defined contribution plan formula discussed below was 0.2 or less . . . if the combined contribution for the two plans did not exceed 25% of eligible compensation.

Example with Percentage Limits ————————————————

Dr. Bedside's manner is somewhat less extreme. He earns a salary of $50,000, and his defined benefit plan promises a benefit of just that, or 100% of pay ($50,000). Since he isn't pushing the limits of maximum benefits, he can have a somewhat more liberal determination of his defined benefit utilization:

1. Actual Benefit $50,000

2. 1.4 × Plan Comp $70,000

3. Defined Benefit Use (1 ÷ 2) 0.7

Thus, Dr. Bedside could establish a defined contribution plan that used no more than 0.3 of the available defined contribution limit. The slightly more liberal opportunity available for Dr. Bedside reflects the fact that he is not in a position to overuse the retirement plan tax shelter.

¶1301.3 *How the 1.0 Rule Applies to Defined Contribution Plans*

The application of the 1.0 Rule to defined contribution plans is somewhat more difficult, since it involves a ''look-back'' provision that allows participants to consider not only the current year but also what they **could have done** in prior years. As with the defined benefit determination, defined contribution plan calculations allow a more liberal interpretation for those who have not used the full dollar limits available to those plans. The rule can be stated as follows:

TOTAL ANNUAL ADDITIONS CUMULATIVELY MADE

Total Annual Additions Which Could Have Been Made ×
1.25, If the $ Limits Applied in a Particular Year; or
1.40, If the % Limits Applied in that Year

This rule is obviously more complicated to apply, for two reasons:

1. It involves **historical data;** and

2. That historical data must be reviewed from an annual perspective to see whether the dollar or percentage limits apply.

The best way to understand the rules is to review an example.

Example

Dr. Med maintains a defined contribution plan and wishes to know what his defined contribution fraction amounts to so he can establish a second plan. He has maintained the defined contribution plan for three years, one of which involved a contribution less than the maximum:

Year	Salary	Actual Plan Contribution	Available Contribution	Applicable Factor	Denominator
1982	$150,000	$30,000	$30,000	1.25	$ 37,500
1983	$ 90,000	$22,500	$22,500	1.40	$ 31,500
1984	$120,000	$25,000	$30,000	1.25	$ 37,500
TOTALS	N/A	$77,500	$82,500	N/A	$106,500

Note in the above table how either the 1.4 or the 1.25 factor may apply in a given year, depending on whether the dollar or the percentage limits apply to that particular year. You can easily see that the calculation of defined contribution limits can be extremely difficult when a business has been in existence for some time . . . especially when you consider the fact that present rules allow practitioners to "look back" to **all prior years.** Given the above data, the calculation of Dr. Med's defined contribution fraction is fairly simple:

1. Actual Contributions Made .... $ 77,500
2. Contributions that Could Have Been Made × Factor $106,500
3. Defined-Contributions Factor (1 ÷ 2)................................. 0.7

Therefore, Dr. Med could theoretically implement a defined benefit plan with a formula which, when applied under the defined benefit multiple plan rules, did not exceed 0.3. Since the dollar limits would obviously apply to such a second plan, that means its formula could be as follows:

$$\frac{X\% \text{ of Pay}}{\$90,000 \times 1.25} = 0.3$$

Solving for X, we find that the formula, given a $120,000 salary, could be 30% of compensation.

Caution.   Remember that the defined contribution fraction is a **variable,** so you will have to check *every* year that your cumulative defined contribution fraction, together with the defined benefit fraction, do not exceed 1.0. Further, remember that TRA '86 imposes the additional requirement that multiple plans can't have aggregate contributions greater than 25% of eligible payroll.

¶1301.4 *Summing Up the Multiple Plan Limits*

As discussed above, the multiple plan limit rules, characterized by the 1.0 formula limitation, represent a significant "override" to the normal opportunities available under individual qualified plans. Application of the rules is certain to cause both practitioner and client frustration: practitioners because of the voluminous paperwork required to track the annually variable defined contribution fraction, and clients because of the expense and uncertainty involved. Particularly if the plans involve pre-TEFRA history, your clients will need to pay special attention to take maximum advantage of the multiple plan limits.

Caution. Please review the section on super top heavy plans appearing later in this Chapter. It places an even greater constraint on the availability of multiple plan benefits and deductions for those plans where 90% or more of the benefits accrue to key employees.

¶1302 *CONTROLLED GROUPS AND AFFILIATED SERVICE ORGANIZATIONS*

Frequently, smaller businesses wish to exclude as many common law employees as possible from coverage under their qualified plans. The usual reason for such efforts is that most employees do not appreciate, and therefore do not warrant the expense of, a retirement benefit. Most employers feel that their employees would welcome a bigger paycheck (e.g., **direct compensation**) much more than a deferred benefit with vesting and other risks. The available rules for excluding employees from coverage are really quite liberal. They can be excluded because:

1. they haven't attained age 21;

2. they haven't completed a year of service (or 1,000 hours);

3. they aren't employed on the last day of the plan year (defined contribution plans); or

4. they are part of an excluded *class* of employee not exceeding 30% of those otherwise eligible.

Notwithstanding this list of exclusion mechanisms, some employers have gone further, perhaps by setting up a second organization that hires the employees in question and does not establish a plan.

Another common situation finds a businessman setting up several organizations for completely valid business reasons and wishing to implement different plans in the respective organizations. Or a company with a qualified plan might acquire another organization that does not have a retirement plan.

In order to insure that a fair cross-section of retirement plan coverage exists throughout the related organizations, a complicated set of controlled group and affiliated service organization rules have been developed over time and substantially tightened by TEFRA and TRA '86. The purpose of this section is to explore those rules in detail, with the warning that the rules are intricate and need review every time a specific situation is presented.

¶1302.1   *The Controlled Group Rules Explained*

There are two situations where the controlled group regulations are brought into play: with a parent-subsidiary relationship and with a brother-sister relationship. The implication of either classification is the same: all members of the controlled group must be considered for purposes of meeting eligibility and nondiscrimination requirements. Here are the rules which relate to the two classes of controlled group:

   Parent-subsidiary relationships exist for controlled group purposes when there is a group of organizations with a common parent, and each of these under control of one or more of the other, **and** the common parent has direct control over at least one member of the group. This rule is fairly clear compared to that which applies to brother-sister organizations.

   Brother-sister relationships exist if two conditions are met:

1.   Five or fewer shareholders own more than 80% of the **voting power** or 80% of all **value** (excluding classes of stock which are nonvoting and limited with preference for dividends); and

2.   The same five or fewer shareholders own more than 50% of the voting stock, taking into account ownership only to the extent of identical ownership for each corporation.

These rules are a little more difficult to interpret, so a couple of examples are in order:

EXAMPLE I

Shareholders	Corporations			Identical Ownership
	D	O	C	
A	40%	20%	40%	20%
B	15%	40%	30%	15%
C	10%	10%	20%	10%
D	20%	15%	5%	5%
E	15%	15%	5%	5%
TOTALS	100%	100%	100%	55%

Example I Comments.   D, O, and C are members of a controlled group because five or fewer shareholders own 100% of the shares of the relevant corporations, and, with respect to *identical ownership*, own more than 50% of the voting stock. The "identical ownership" issue is sometimes difficult to grasp: note that it is the *smallest* ownership interest that applies.

EXAMPLE II

Shareholders	Corporations D	R	Identical Ownership
F	15%		
G	15%		
H	15%		
I	55%	55%	55%
J		20%	
K		20%	
L		5%	
TOTALS	100%	100%	55%

Example II Comment. D and R are not members of a controlled group because five or fewer individuals do not own 100% of the stock of both corporations.

Example III depicts a slightly more difficult situation, which has taken some time to resolve.

EXAMPLE III

Shareholders	Corporations D	R	Identical Ownership
A	75%	100%	75%
B	25%		
TOTALS	100%		75%

Example III Comments. It would appear that this represents a controlled group, since five or fewer individuals own 100% of both companies and, to the extent of identical ownership, own more than 50% of the voting stock. This issue has been litigated for years, because considering the above a controlled group seems somehow unfair to shareholder B, who owns *none* of Corporation R. The issue was litigated in several key cases, including Fairfax, Baloian, and Hunt, with inconclusive results. Finally, in Vogel Fertilizer, the Supreme Court settled the matter: D and R are *not* a controlled group. This was good news for practitioners, and knowledge of the exception may prove helpful in planning situations.

The controlled group regulations and requirements comprise a difficult planning obstacle for many small- to medium-sized businesses. They are further complicated by the fact that *attribution* applies to ownership determinations among various family, trust, and business entities. In the case of a parent-subsidiary relationship, only stock that the corporation has an option to acquire is included; in the case of brother-sister situations, the list is more far-reaching and includes certain partnerships, trusts, corporations, spouses, children, grandchildren, parents, and grandparents. Specific potential attribution situations should be reviewed from the perspective of the regulations.

¶1302.2 *Affiliated Service Organizations*

One of the more creative techniques employed to circumvent the controlled group regulations had been applied in the area of professional corporations. The technique involved, in its most basic form, a professional who incorporated himself (i.e., practiced as a PC and was the only employee) and established a second organization to employ clerical or support staff. The second organization provided services to the first and was in form an independent entity. As such, the argument went, it should be free to establish its own set of fringe benefits. The professional should be able to implement a rich retirement plan in his PC without being required to do anything for the service organization. One other common variant of this approach was to contract the support services out to a truly independent organization specializing in office management. This variant was typically called "employee leasing."

I say "the argument **went**" because TEFRA has considerably narrowed the allowable schemes to accomplish the objectives implied by affiliated service organizations and employee leasing. Let's consider the rules that govern each type of transaction.

¶1302.3 *Affiliated Service Organizations Explained*

The rules for affiliated service organizations are contained in IRC 414(m). The consequence of being characterized as an affiliated service group is that the *entire* group and all its employees must be included in retirement plan eligibility, coverage, and vesting tests. The implication is that the professional who separately incorporates cannot escape providing the same retirement plan terms, conditions, and coverage for related employees that he provides for himself. Service organizations, by the way, are broadly defined as those whose principal business is the performance or delivery of services.

An affiliated service group consists of two components: a "first service organization" (let's call it the "FSO"), and second, one or more of the following:

1. An "A" organization, which is another service organization that

   a. is a shareholder or partner in the FSO; and

    b.   regularly performs services for the FSO **or** is regularly associated with the FSO in performing services for third persons; and/or

2. A ''B'' organization, which is any other organization if

    a.   a significant portion of the business of such B organization is the performance of services for the FSO, and ''A'' organization, or both, which services are of a type historically performed in such service by employees; and

    b.   10% or more of the interest in such organization is held by persons who are officers, highly compensated employees, or owners of the FSO or the ''A'' organization.

Comment.   Note that the ''control'' tests (10%) are far more narrow than those applicable to the conventional controlled group regulations discussed above.

Example ——————————————————————————

Drs. Bed and Side each practice as professional corporations. They are service organizations. Support Staff, Inc., is a separate organization, 15% each owned by Drs. Bed and Side, consisting of nurses and clerical help and is regularly associated with Drs. Bed and Side in the delivery of services to patients. Drs. Bed and Side, together with Support Staff, Inc., are members of an affiliated service group, and all employees of Support Staff, Inc., must be included in determinations of eligibility, vesting, and benefits of any retirement plan established for the group. It does not matter what the respective ownership interests of Drs. Bed and Side are, as each one owns at least 10%.

Example ——————————————————————————

Assume the same facts as in the first example, except that Drs. Bed and Side cease performing services directly to the public, instead delivering them only through Support Staff, Inc. Result: They are still included in an affiliated service group.

    Thus, it is clear that shell games involving delivery of services divided among multiple organizations will generally not allow professionals to escape the tentacles of IRC 414(m); most attempts will result in failure, with the consequence of retirement plan coverage for employees. But what of the situation where support services are provided by a truly independent organization which specializes in ''practice management'' through the technique of employee leasing?

¶1302.4 *Employee Leasing*

Let's consider the example of Lease-Your-Staff, Inc., which is an **independent** organization whose sole business is the management of the office environment of a professional practice. Lease-Your-Staff, Inc., assumes all responsibility for hiring and firing, testing, management, placement, and payroll taxes of employees, which services it leases to professional practices on a contractual basis. Since the professionals truly have no control or ownership in Lease-Your-Staff, Inc., there is no affiliated service group problem. However, to preclude professionals' swarming en masse to this apparent safe harbor, TEFRA also includes provisions governing retirement plan coverage for leased employees.

A ''leased employee'' is one employed by the leasing company (Lease-Your-Staff, Inc., in our example) and made available to the professional under an agreement or contract. Furthermore, the leased employee must have performed such services full time for more than one year, and the services must be of a type historically performed by employees of the profession in question.

If an employee qualifies as leased, then he is treated as **an employee of the recipient** (e.g., the professional) for purposes of retirement plan coverage and eligibility, although contributions are to be made by the leasing organization (Lease-Your-Staff, Inc.). A ''safe harbor'' benefit was provided in TEFRA and TRA '86—a 10% of pay, fully vested, money purchase contribution with immediate eligibility for leased employees who earned at least $1,000 in the current or any of the prior three plan years. This is the smallest benefit Lease-Your-Staff, Inc., can provide for the leased employees; these contributions will be deemed to have been made by the recipient.

Leasing organizations enjoyed increased popularity in the wake of TEFRA. After all, it is no small task to run an office, and professionals' time is probably better spent practicing than managing employees. Furthermore, the 10% contribution level required under the leased employees rules is considerably less than most professionals historically contribute to their **own** retirement programs, thus representing a reduction in both costs and headaches. However, TRA '86 added one additional bombshell: if more than 20% of the recipient organization's employees are leased, then the safe harbor (10% contribution) is not available, and the leased employees must be covered under the recipient organization's plans.

¶1303 *TOPHEAVY PLANS*

Without question the most controversial aspect of TEFRA was its punitive provisions for so-called ''topheavy plans.'' The intent of the Topheavy

Rules, like much of TEFRA, was to thwart the use of retirement plans as a tax shelter for highly paid employees. The impact of the Topheavy Rules will be felt by *all* retirement plans, big and small, because these rules must be incorporated into every qualified plan, whether or not they could ever apply to that plan. From a benefit/cost point of view, most larger retirement plans will not be affected by the Topheavy Rules; virtually **all** small- to medium-sized businesses will, however, be pinched. The uproar over the impact of the Topheavy Rules in the small business environment has been strong enough to lead to several legislative proposals to ameliorate or postpone their impact. But TRA '86 affirmed and even strengthened the rules, so it is clear they are here to stay.

¶1303.1   *Topheavy Plan Defined*

A topheavy plan is one in which more than 60% or more of specifically enumerated benefits (account balance, in the case of a defined contribution plan; present value of accrued benefits, in the case of a defined benefit plan) accrue to the benefit of key employees. A key employee is defined as any of the following:

1. an employee with one of the 10 largest ownership interests;

2. any more than 5% or more owner;

3. any more than 1% owner with annual compensation of $150,000 or more; or

4. corporate officers earning at least 150% of the currently applicable limit on annual additions (which is $30,000 in 1986, therefore officers earning more than $45,000 are key.)

Clearly, this is a far-reaching list and encompasses most small business situations where one or two key men have the bulk of the accrued benefits in their retirement plan. The list is even more encompassing when one considers the nature of the accrued benefits to be counted and the "lookback" nature of this review, which includes benefit values of separated employees for the last five years.

¶1303.2   *Contributions, Benefits, and Distributions To Be Recognized*

The accrued benefits to be reviewed for the 60% test include more than simply routine employer contributions. Included in the accrued benefit determination are the following:

1. all benefits earned from employer contributions;

2. all benefits earned through nondeductible employee contributions (whether mandatory or voluntary);

3. most rollover contributions, unless made from an *unrelated* plan *after* 12/31/83; and

4. all distributions made from the Plan Year or the *preceding four plan years.*

The implications of this broadly defined group of contributions, benefits, and distributions is obvious: a plan which is topheavy may well have to wait four or five years to change its status, and even then it will be tough.

¶1303.3   *What Are the Consequences of Being Topheavy?*

The implications of being topheavy range from minimal to dire, depending on the unique circumstances of a particular business and retirement plan. Generally, the consequences include

1. accelerated vesting;

2. minimum contribution requirements; and

3. special multiple plan limitations.

Some of these consequences, such as accelerated vesting, have a hidden cost effect, since the impact of employee turnover on retirement plan costs takes some time to be felt; others, such as minimum benefits, may be highly visible and immediate. We will consider each consequence separately in the paragraphs that follow.

¶1303.4   *Special Vesting Requirements for Topheavy Plans*

If a plan is topheavy, then the standard TRA '86 vesting options are not available. Instead, the plan must provide for vesting under one or the other of the following options:

1. Three-year ''cliff'' vesting, e.g., all accrued benefits would be nonforfeitable after three years of service; or

2. A graded schedule with vesting not less rapid than 20% after two years of service, with 20% additional vesting for each subsequent year (full vesting after six years).

For purposes of years of service determinations, topheavy plans must essentially recognize all service with the employer from age 22 or the plan effective date, including years of service prior to the topheavy period. In other words, an employee hired at age 22 but precluded from participation by a plan's 2-year eligibility provisions until age 24 would be 20% vested at the end of his or her first year of participation. Also, the vesting schedule must be applied to *all* accruals, not just those accumulated during the topheavy period. Thus, it may have considerable retroactive impact.

The employer costs of this accelerated vesting requirement are significant, but "invisible." Over time, there will be fewer forfeitures in profit sharing or money purchase plans and smaller "credits" to employer contributions under target benefit or defined benefit plans. These hidden costs will be quite significant in the case of high turnover industries such as restaurants, construction, etc.

¶1303.5   *Minimum Contributions and Benefits*

In order to discourage the use of so-called "excess only" plans (those providing benefits only for compensation of an integration level most employees will never reach), TEFRA's Topheavy Rule calls for the implementation of *minimum benefits* for all employees eligible for a topheavy plan. The rules are different for defined contribution and defined benefit plans, *but either type of plan can be used to satisfy the minimum benefit requirements.* Keep in mind that TRA '86 added new integration requirements that effectively preclude "excess only" plans *by themselves*—regardless of whether or not a plan is topheavy.

In the case of defined contribution plans that are topheavy, the program must provide a contribution allocation equal to at least 3% of compensation or, if less, the percentage contributed for key employees. In addition, the minimum contributions must be made for all eligible non-key employees, *even those unwilling to comply with a plan's mandatory contribution requirements.* What's more, under proposed regulations, contributions would be due employees *regardless of the number of hours of service worked,* as long as the individual is employed as of the first day of the plan year. In other words, part-time employees traditionally excluded from retirement plan coverage will have to be provided a 3% contribution if the plan is topheavy.

In the case of a defined benefit plan, a Topheavy program must provide a minimum benefit, payable at normal retirement date, equal to 2% of an employee's highest five-year average compensation for each Year of Service earned by the employee *while the plan is topheavy,* to a maximum of 20% of such average annual compensation. Note that the 2% benefit is *fully accrued* in the year earned. This is different from most conventional defined-benefit accruals, which are earned on a ***linear basis*** between date of employment (or participation) and retirement age. The impact here is the potential for underfunding under most actuarial methods, which assume a smooth "accruing of benefits" over a much longer period.

Example

Let's compare the actuarial value of a $250/month accrued benefit under the minimum benefit requirements of TEFRA and a conventional actuarial method:

Employee	Payout Age	Actuarial Value of TEFRA Benefit	Funding Accumulation	Potential Underfunding
A	35	$ 5,508	$2,368	$3,140
B	55	$17,666	$9,963	$7,703

Implication. FASB 87 Reporting Requirements in re: present value of a plan's accumulated benefits and unfunded liabilities . . . clients' balance sheets may be negatively impacted.

Comparing the cost of providing minimum benefits under a defined benefit or defined contribution plan is important to practitioners, because small companies will often have a choice as to which plan to use to comply with the requirements. As you might expect, age plays a key role in determining the most viable option. Here's a comparison of the annual contribution required to ***fully fund*** minimum benefits for an employee earning $15,000 at various ages:

Age	Defined-Contribution Minimum Benefit Funding	Defined-Benefit Minimum Benefit Funding
25	$450	$ 394
35	$450	$ 706
45	$450	$1264
55	$450	$1990

Comment. Employers with a relatively ***young*** group of participants will wish to use a defined benefit plan to provide minimum benefits; those with ***older*** non-key employees will benefit from the use of a defined contribution plan.

Caution. If a defined contribution plan is *implemented* for purposes of meeting the Minimum Benefit requirements, it will probably be required to provide a contribution of *at least* 5%, rather than 3%, to insure actuarial equivalency between the different forms of plan. Also, the minimum benefits may need to be higher in the case of plans which take advantage of the multiple plan limits (e.g., a combination of plans using the 1.0 rule described earlier in this Chapter).

¶1303.6   *Multiple Plan Limits Changed*

If a plan is topheavy, the employer desiring to utilize the multiple plan limits available under the 1.0 rule must reduce the denominator of the relevant plan's calculation of its percentage utilization from 1.25 to 1.0 if the program provides benefits or contributions limited by the dollar ceilings ($90,000 for a defined benefit plan; $30,000 for a defined contribution plan). The effect of this change to the normal 1.0 rule is that an employer maintaining either a "maximum" defined-benefit or defined contribution plan is precluded from implementing a second plan.

Exception.   An important exception to the above is available to the employer who is willing to increase the otherwise applicable minimum benefits to 4% of pay per year in the case of a defined contribution plan and 3% of pay for a defined benefit plan. In other words, if the employer is willing to increase appropriately minimum benefits, he may continue to utilize the conventional 1.25 rule with its implications for multiple plan deductions. The approximate funding costs of these higher minimum benefits may be compared to those we discussed earlier for the $15,000-a-year employees of different ages:

Age	Defined-Contribution Minimum Benefit Funding	Defined-Benefit Minimum Benefit Funding
25	$600	$ 591
35	$600	$1059
45	$600	$1897
55	$600	$2985

The implications of our earlier analysis of minimum benefits still remain the same: employers with young employees will prefer the defined benefit plan for minimum benefits; employers with older employees, the defined contribution alternative.

¶1304 SUPER-TOPHEAVY PLANS

A Plan is "super-topheavy" if 90% of the benefits accrue to key employees. Super-topheavy plans are not uncommon in small professional corporations. If a plan is super-topheavy, then the denominator used in multiple plan limitation tests (normally 1.25 with respect to dollar limits and 1.40 with respect to percentage limits) is reduced to 1.0 for plans utilizing the dollar limits and stays at 1.4 for those with percentage limits. This effectively precludes the implementation of a second plan in a small organization that uses its first plan to the maximum extent possible. There is *no exception* for higher minimum benefits, probably because TEFRA's drafters realized that many super-topheavy plans involve just one employee, such as an incorporated professional: so the impact of additional minimum benefits would be nil.

¶1305 JOINT AND SURVIVOR ANNUITIES

A Qualified Joint and Survivor Annuity (QJSA) is an annuity for the life of the participant with a survivor annuity for life for his or her spouse. In certain situations, it must be offered to plan participants. In addition, certain complex notification requirements apply. When applicable, payments to the surviving spouse must be at least 50% but no greater than 100%, of the amount that was provided to the participant and his or her spouse while they both were alive. The QJSA must be actuarially equivalent to a single annuity for the life of the participant according to IRC Section 417(b)(2). A single annuity is one that provides benefits until the person receiving the annuity dies, with no further benefits provided after the annuitant dies. Regulations, however, do not dictate the form such an annuity must take within these parameters.

Plans must offer qualifying annuities not only for married participants but unmarried participants as well, although distributions in the form of a single sum and/or installments for unmarried participants are an acceptable alternative. The code provision indicates that a QJSA need not be provided for participants who have been married less than one year on the annuity starting date. Regulations seem to mandate the provision for unmarried participants and for participants who have been married at least one year, but not for newlyweds.

There are two survivor annuity requirements:

1. A trust will not be qualified unless the plan provides for payment of accrued benefits in the form of a QJSA to a vested participant who retires; and

2. In addition, if participant dies before his annuity starting date, the plan must provide a qualified preretirement survivor annuity to the participant's surviving spouse.

A Qualified Preretirement Survivor Annuity (QPSA) is a survivor annuity for the life of a participant's spouse which provides payments that are not less than the amounts that would have been paid to a surviving spouse under a QJSA (or actuarially equivalent payments) if:

1. The participant dies after attaining the earliest date on which, under the plan, he could elect to receive retirement benefits (earliest retirement age) it is assumed that he retired the day before his death with an immediate QJSA; or

2. The participant dies prior to attaining the earliest retirement age, it is assumed that he:

   a. Separated from service on the day he died;

   b. Survived to the earliest retirement age;

   c. Retired with an immediate QJSA; and

   d. Died the day after attaining the earliest retirement age.

Although Code Section 417 requires certain plans to provide a deceased vested participant's spouse with a Preretirement Survivor Annuity, the participant during his/her lifetime can waive the requirement, provided his/her spouse consents in writing.

Plan administrators are strongly urged to follow through with beneficiary designation forms to all participants and to monitor the return of the newly signed forms as well as the previously filed ones to avoid lawsuits by nonspouse beneficiaries.

¶1305.1 *Which Plans Must Comply*

According to Section 401(a)(11)(B) requirements of both QJSAs and QPSAs apply to any defined benefit plan and to any defined contribution plan subject to the minimum funding standards of Code Section 412 (for example money purchase plans and target benefit plans). The requirements are applicable to benefits paid pursuant to annuity contracts purchased by the plan and distributed to a participant or his or her spouse.

Generally employee stock ownership plans are subject to QJSA and QPSA requirements; however, the statute excepts that portion of ESOP benefits relating to employer securities.

Certain conditions can be met to escape the application of the QJSA and QPSA rules for certain defined contribution plans. Below are the three conditions:

1. Upon the death of a participant, the entire nonforfeitable accrued benefit is payable to his or her spouse unless there is no surviving spouse or unless the spouse consents to the designation of an alternative beneficiary;

2. The participant does not elect payment of benefits in the form of a life annuity. Many defined contribution plans do not offer an annuity as a form of benefit; and

3. The plan is not a direct or indirect transferee of a plan which is required to provide QJSAs and QPSAs.

¶1305.2 *Application of QJSA and QPSA Coverage Requirements to Annuity Contracts*

The regulations indicate that the requirement of Sections 401(a) and 417 apply to any annuity contract that is purchased and distributed to a participant by a plan to which such requirements apply. This means a participant who obtains a contract could not agree with the issuer of the contract to vary the form of benefit or change the death beneficiary without consent of his or her spouse.

Regulations also indicate the annuity requirements apply to benefits derived from employee contributions as well as employer contributions. Therefore, participants that wish to withdraw voluntary contributions from a plan would not be able to obtain the refund of such contributions (unless in the form of a QJSA) without consent of their spouses.

A participant has the opportunity to elect **not** to receive his benefits in a joint and survivor annuity. The election period can be made in a 90-day period ending on the date his annuity payments are to begin. While the code specifies a definite time period in which the election must be made, it merely requires that the information needed to make this election be provided to the participant within a ''reasonable time'' before the starting date.

The election period for waiving the preretirement survivor annuity begins on the first day of the plan year in which the vested participant reaches age 35 and ends on the date of his death. Also, within the period beginning with the first day the participant reaches age 32 and ending with the plan year preceding the plan year in which the participant reaches 35, the participant must be provided with a written explanation of the preretirement survivor annuity. The spouse's consent must meet the same criteria as the election not to receive a joint and survivor annuity.

¶1305.3 *Summary*

The annuity requirements are very complex. Practitioners should exercise extreme care to insure that proper notifications are provided. Otherwise, a nonspouse intended to be the beneficiary may be unintentionally disenfranchised, opening the door for litigation.

¶1306 *SPECIAL LIMITATIONS SUMMARY*

The special limitations and multiple plan opportunities discussed in this Chapter will frequently be applicable to the small business environment, so they are not to be taken lightly. Practitioners are advised to develop their own checklist or "screen" to pass their plan designs through before carving them into granite. While the use of multiple plans represents a tremendous opportunity for large deductions, controlled group, topheavy, and other restrictions discussed represent difficult obstacles to overcome.

14

A Practitioner's Guide to Overseeing Qualification, Administration, and Investment Aspects of the Plan

¶1400 HOW TO CHOOSE THE RIGHT PLAN FOR YOUR CLIENT

The success of your client's pension or profit sharing plan will not be determinable for several years. By then it will be difficult or impossible to recover the time, expense, and aggravation that went into the qualification and ongoing administration of the plan if it proves to have been a bad choice. Success will be dependent upon both controllable and uncontrollable events, such as the following:

1. How accurate are your client's forecasts about wage inflation, profitability, and stability?

2. Will the plan end up benefiting the group it was designed for?

3. Will timely and complete qualification and administration preclude necessary and disconcerting problems with participants or the government?

Many of these issues, profitability for example, cannot always be determined in advance, but most fall at least partially within your domain of control.

Frequently a client will become so enamored of the tax advantages of *any* qualified plan that he may tend to minimize the balance of the design process. It is easy to opt for a simple profit sharing plan and, therefore, avoid the more sophisticated and complex discussion that would have to surround implementation of a defined benefit program. However, it is essential that you *force* your client to thoroughly focus on his objectives and the entire range of alternatives which could, theoretically, fulfill them. That may, at times, seem an exercise in futility, but it is not. The extra time you spend during the design process, following through with and illustrating the results of your client's hypothetical questions, will be well worth the effort.

¶1400.1   *Checklist of Key Questions: How To Get the Right Information*

Your client will not understand the semantic implications of pension jargon. Therefore, it is important to clearly define your terms. Frequently, when you are at the design stage of pension planning, your client may think that *estimates* of dates of birth, dates of employment, and other pertinent employee age or service discrepancy for an employee close to normal retirement age would be very significant.

One of the least addressed topics during design discussions is the definition of "pay." Yet the plan's ultimate definition of compensation can affect benefits and contributions more directly than virtually any other parameter. Integrated plans must use *total* compensation when determining benefits. And actually, that's generally more favorable for your client's key employees.

Following are some questions whose accurate answers early in the design process will save a significant amount of time:

- Who is the president of the firm?

- Who is the secretary/clerk of the firm?

- What is the tax identification number?

- When does the fiscal year end?

- Is the business a Subchapter S Corporation?

- What, if applicable, is the original date of incorporation?

- What is the name, date of birth, date of employment, Social Security number, and projected **total** compensation for the fiscal year for all employees who will complete 1,000 hours of service during the fiscal year?

- Of the total compensation, how much is base pay and how much bonus or overtime?

- Who is the business's attorney?

- Who is the business's accountant?

- What is the exact legal name, address, and telephone number of the business?

The frequency with which the items above are necessary warrants your concerted effort to obtain them as accurately and early as possible. Forcing your client through the exercise of obtaining this data will have an additional advantage: it will emphasize to him the technically demanding, detailed-oriented world he is entering. His early recognition of this will save time further down the road.

¶1400.2 *Identifying Your Client's Objectives*

Having gathered accurate information about your client's employees and business you must force him to commit himself to increasingly narrow goals. Since most small businesses have a limited budget, they can only achieve so much with their plans. Therefore, it is extremely important for your client to focus specifically on *who* should benefit most under his plan and *why.*

Frequently small businessmen may, in the preliminary stages of designing a plan, emphasize altruistic motivation. For instance, they may discuss an ethical obligation to help employees save money. As a practical matter, most common-law employees would be more highly motivated by a cash bonus than a deferred pension benefit. Furthermore, the tax advantages of qualified plans are not as meaningful to low-paid plan participants. Generally, as the design process unfolds, your client will become more oriented toward a plan that favors him.

To conserve your time, energy, and expense you must focus your client on key questions. To the extent he provides sincere and realistic answers, plan design time and expense can be minimized. Here are some of the philosophical questions your client should answer:

- What is a reasonable, sustainable budget?

- How widely does cash flow vary from year to year?

- In the worst of the last three fiscal years, how much cash would have been available to fund a retirement program?

- If it were technically possible, would your client spend the *entire* plan budget on the two or three highest paid employees?

- Who are the most important non-owner employees?

- Who should reap the greater benefit from the plan: employees with past service or employees with high pay?

- Which is more important to participating key employees: income tax deferral or asset accumulation?

- Is the company likely to have continuity after the departure of the key employee?

- Will there be any extraordinary demands on cash flow for personnel expansion during the next several years?

Discussions in previous chapters should have given you an impression of why these questions are important. You'll want to add more and tailor the list to your particular client, but you'll find that the above will sharpen your client's focus appreciably.

¶1400.3   *Plan Design: How to Match Objectives, Client Data, and Plan Alternatives*

¶s 1400.1 and 1400.2 discuss the information you need to evaluate alternatives. Now, what do you do when you get it? That's the substance of plan design. Figure 14.1 compares various census statistics with client objectives. See how many times a particular type of plan results when you apply your client facts. If one type of plan consistently results when you compare census statistics to your client's objectives, chances are that that is a good place for you to start your analysis.

HOW TO USE THE CHART

To use the chart shown in Figure 14.1, simply compare your client's answers to the simple "yes or no" questions you ask during the plan design interview. If he answers "yes" to a particular question, then cross out the "no" line. If he answers "no," then cross out the "yes" line. If a particular question is not applicable, cross out both lines. When you are done, simply add up the column totals for each type of plan. Whichever plan results in the highest total is likely to be the first plan you should consider for your client.

¶1400.4   *What Are the Penalties or Problems of Underfunding?*

Many of the pension plans that are most attractive for older key employees are of the defined benefit or target benefit variety. Money purchase plans,

FIGURE 14.1 Census Statistics vs. Client Objectives

Questions		Profit-Sharing, Nonintegrated	Profit-Sharing, Integrated	Money-Purchase, Nonintegrated	Money-Purchase, Integrated	Flat-Benefit, with Past Service	Flat-Benefit, Nonintegrated, Integrated	Flat-Benefit, Integrated	Unit-Benefit, Integrated	Unit-Benefit, Nonintegrated, Integrated	Unit-Benefit, Nonintegrated EAN/FIPSL*	Offset, Flat-Benefit Format, Integrated EAN/FIPSL*	Offset, Flat-Benefit Format EAN/FIPSL*	Offset, Unit-Benefit, Format EAN/FIPSL	Offset, Unit-Benefit, Format	Target plan, Nonintegrated	Target plan, Integrated	Unit-Benefit, Integrated
Is Cash Flow Stable?	N	5	5	-1	-1	0	-4	0	-4	-4	-4	0	-4	-4	-4	0	-4	-4
	Y	-2	0	3	4	2	3	2	4	3	4	2	4	4	3	2	4	4
Are Key Men Older?	N	4	5	2	5	-2	-3	-3	-1	-2	-3	-3	-4	-3	-4	-3	0	-3
	Y	-4	-3	4	-4	4	2	4	3	2	4	5	4	5	5	5	4	4
Is A Second Plan Likely?	N	3	4	1	1	0	2	1	2	3	5	3	3	2	3	4	1	2
	Y	2	2	0	3	3	0	0	2	2	5	5	4	0	4	0	2	2
Will Key Men Have Substantial Service at N.R.D.?	N	2	3	2	2	-4	2	0	4	0	3	3	5	-3	0	4	0	-5
	Y	2	3	4	0	0	0	-2	2	-1	0	2	0	2	-4	2	-2	0
Is There High Turnover?	N	2	3	-3	1	3	-2	2	0	-2	2	2	3	3	2	3	2	2
	Y	4	5	4	-2	2	0	2	1	-2	1	3	3	1	-2	-2	0	-2
Is Flexibility Necessary?	N	0	0	2	2	3	0	3	3	0	3	0	3	3	0	3	3	3
	Y	4	5	4	3	-2	3	-4	0	-3	-4	1	0	-4	0	-4	-3	-3
Will Key Men Have Less Than 15 Yrs Service at N.R.D.?	N	2	4	3	3	2	-3	2	1	2	1	1	1	0	1	0	0	0
	Y	-1	0	-1	-1	0	-1	0	-3	-5	-3	0	3	3	4	-3	0	-5
Will Key Men Have Less Than 10 Yrs Service at N.R.D.?	N	2	3	2	2	1	-2	3	3	1	2	2	3	2	2	2	1	2
	Y	-3	-3	-3	-3	-3	-4	-3	-5	-3	-4	-5	-5	-3	-3	-5	-2	-5
Is Plan Likely To Be Terminated Within 10 Yrs?	N	4	4	0	0	0	-3	0	0	0	0	0	0	0	0	0	0	0
	Y	0	5	0	-2	2	-4	-3	0	-2	-4	-3	-5	-3	0	-1	-2	-5
Early Normal Retirement Age?	N	0	0	0	0	0	0	-3	0	0	0	0	0	-2	0	0	0	0
	Y	1	1	-2	-1	-3	0	0	2	3	4	0	0	-2	0	1	0	0
Is Simplicity Important?	N	2	2	1	1	1	-2	2	3	2	2	3	3	2	2	3	2	2
	Y	2	3	2	1	1	2	3	2	0	3	-1	0	0	-2	3	1	0
Used As A Second Plan?	N	0	0	0	0	0	0	0	0	0	0	0	0	0	0	0	0	0
	Y	3	-3	4	-3	4	-2	0	0	-2	-2	-2	-2	0	-2	5	0	-2
Plan Invests Aggressively?	N	0	0	0	0	0	0	0	-1	-3	-3	-1	-3	-1	-3	-1	0	0
	Y	5	5	4	4	4	-1	-3	-1	-3	-3	-1	-3	-1	-3	-1	4	-3

*EAN/FIPSL — Entry age normal with frozen initial past service liability.

263

too, are often in the background as secondary programs. Your client may have problems with any of these plans if he decides he has "bitten off more than he can chew." Defined benefit, target benefit, and money purchase plans all require a "funding standard account" that helps measure the exact amount of money that *must* be contributed to the plan each year. Failing to meet the requirements of the funding standard account may result in automatic termination of the plan, which could cause:

1. retroactive disqualification of the plan and loss of previous tax deductions; or

2. 100% immediate vesting for all plan participants.

The consequences of disqualification and 100% vesting should be explained carefully to your client. There are two possible remedies:

1. Built-in flexibility: always try to design a plan or combination of plans that offers the greatest amount of flexibility. In the case of a defined benefit plan, try to use the Entry Age Normal with FIPSL actuarial method to provide a range of contributions. Suggest to your client that he cut back his budget by 20% to allow for unforeseen contingencies. Remember, a plan can almost always be amended to *increase* benefits, but a decrease is difficult to accomplish without some punitive consequences.

2. Obtain a temporary waiver of the funding standard account from IRS. Businesses showing need can usually obtain such a temporary waiver by filing various forms (in advance) with the government. Any portion of the funding standard account requirement waived must be repaid under rigid supervision. This remedy should only be considered in the case of dire, unforeseen emergencies.

The message of underfunding is loud and clear: do not do it. Proper plan design, including an allowance for future downturns in business, will probably prevent the issue of underfunding from arising.

¶1400.5 *What Your Client Can and Cannot Do When Dealing With a Pension Fund—Prohibited Transactions*

Because of the potential conflict of interest involved in transactions between the pension plan, its sponsor, the trustee, stockholders, and plan administrators, ERISA sought to create a class of actions which are automatically disallowed. This class is known as "prohibited transactions." ERISA added muscle to its intentions by specifying certain nondeductible excise taxes applicable in even more punitive steps to prohibited transactions which go uncorrected.

In general, prohibited transactions are those that involve a relationship between "interested parties" where there is a potential for gain—whether economic or otherwise. Interested parties include

- plan administrator;

- plan participant;

- trustee;

- employer;

- plan sponsor;

- "the prohibited group" (highly paid shareholders and other employees);

- salesmen purveying assets to the plan; and

- close relatives of any of the above.

This subject of prohibited transactions is complex and fraught with exceptions. As a general concept, however, you and your client should be aware that small businesspeople often wear several hats when they set up a pension plan—agent of the plan administrator, trustee, plan sponsor, and plan participant—and that any transaction your client is involved in where he simultaneously wears two hats is likely to be problematic. For example, the sale or lease of goods and services by the employer to a plan is typically disallowed. The loaning of money by a plan to the employer or a key employee is generally forbidden. The use of more than 10% of a plan's assets for the purchase of employer securities is forbidden (except in an ESOP or specially amended profit sharing plan).

All these transactions have obvious potential for conflict of interest and it is easy to see how the concept of prohibited transactions could apply. However, many more subtle activities are prohibited, and your client would be well advised to review the latest regulations before attempting any transaction that involves an interested party. Since it is a cumbersome process to obtain an exemption from the prohibited transaction penalties, there is no reason for your client to be caught in this trap.

¶1401 SPECIAL CONSIDERATIONS WHEN CHANGING PLANS MIDSTREAM

What happens if your client adopts the wrong type of qualified plan or "outgrows" one that initially matched his objectives? It is possible to change plans, but depending on the circumstances, that can be quite a cumbersome job. In general, it is fairly easy to switch from profit sharing to money purchase or from money purchase to defined benefit plans, since participants theoretically have more determinable and secure benefits under the latter. However, going from defined benefit to money purchase or profit sharing certainly constitutes a formal plan termination which triggers some potentially troublesome liabilities and responsibilities.

Good advance planning and design work usually precludes the need for a change in approach. For example, your client's financial situation may change on a year to year basis as well as in more permanent terms. The use of defined benefit pension plans with Entry Age Normal/FIPSL, as well as profit sharing plans, builds in a substantial amount of flexibility for your client in terms of contributions. But in a rapidly growing and changing business, even this might not be enough. But if the facts dictate a restructuring, here are some of the issues you and your client should address.

¶1401.1   *Is the Change a Termination?*

Virtually, any significant change in the format of a qualified plan will constitute a termination. Depending upon the severity of the termination (is it a complete termination or does it reduce benefits for participants, and are all benefits preserved under the new plan?) and the nature of the successor plan, a termination will result in one or more of the following events:

1. Participants will have to be guaranteed that their accrued benefits (in the case of a defined contribution plan, that means account balance) will never be less than their accrued benefits at the time the plan was changed.

2. Participants' accrued benefits will not only have to be guaranteed but also 100% vested at the time of transition.

3. Participants' accrued benefits will not only have to be 100% vested but also "frozen."

Terminating a defined benefit plan has extremely complicated and far-reaching effects, including potential employer liability. A complete discussion of defined benefit termination is far beyond the scope of this book, but you should be aware of its substantive impact. The degree to which vesting and benefit freezing are required depends on how similar the successor is to the predecessor plan. Also, TRA '86 added a new wrinkle to terminations in which "surplus assets" revert directly or indirectly to the employer—a 10% excise tax! Be careful.

Example _____

Change-of-Heart Company establishes a profit sharing plan integrated with Social Security. Five years later, increased profit stability leads Change-of-Heart's owner to the conclusion that his employees would be more highly motivated by the security offered by a money purchase plan. Therefore, Change-of-Heart amends and restates his profit sharing plan to an integrated money purchase plan. In all likelihood, 100% immediate vesting would not be required in this case.

Example _____

Turnaround, Incorporated, implements a defined benefit plan primarily for the benefit of its 55-year-old owner. One week after the owner retires at age 65, the company's successor managers amend and restate the defined benefit to a profit sharing plan. That would constitute the most dangerous form of termination, with 100% vesting of accrued benefits and employer liability up to 30% of net worth for unfunded accrued benefits.

Observation. Despite volumes of case histories, rulings, and regulations, the severity of the ramifications of plan termination is largely a subjective issue. Be prepared to discuss the issue with the IRS when you submit an amended and restated plan. Emphasize how the new plan improves participants' benefits, and discuss the issues with the IRS **prior** to submitting the new plan. An adverse response may have impact on your decision to move forward with your restatement. And remember: the cost and aggravation of terminating a defined benefit plan often makes clients extremely unhappy.

¶1401.2 *How To Avoid Hidden Problems With Defined Benefit Terminations*

Defined benefit plan terminations create special problems. The principal upon which these problems are built is that defined benefit plans in small businesses are generally constructed for the benefit of some older key employees. The IRS is justifiably concerned that once the benefits for these older key employees are funded, the company will abandon the plan. That means younger participants, whose benefits are actuarially funded over a longer working life, will suffer. To prevent that result, the IRS and the Pension Benefit Guaranty Corporation (PBGC), **particularly** in the first 10 plan years, have considerable power. The two most onerous solutions are:

1. imposition of the 10-year early termination rule; and

2. reallocation of assets.

Under the 10-year early termination rule, the IRS may require that members of the "prohibited" (higher-paid) group may not receive any distributions from the plan unless they post security far in excess of that distribution until such time as all obligations for regular employees are met.

Example ————————————————————————————————

King-Pin, Incorporated, adopted a defined benefit plan eight years ago for the benefit of its owner-president, Mary Blake. Mary Blake retires with fully funded benefits and asks for her $500,000 lump sum. Fine, says the IRS, as long as she provides collateral in the amount of $600,000.

Reallocation of assets may be far worse. In situations where the IRS feels that the plan was not "for the exclusive benefit of employees" but rather discriminated highly in favor of one or more key employees, the agency may act to protect the benefits of rank-and-file employees by reallocation of assets.

Example ————————————————————————————————

Dr. Platt sets up an integrated defined benefit pension plan that nets her 96% of the total contribution. The 58-year-old doctor has six rank-and-file employees in their mid-20s and early 30s. Several years later she decides to close up her practice and take her pension benefits with her. However, the IRS does some surgery and cuts out what it feels is a malignant part of her contribution. Assets are reallocated to rank-and-file employees.

What To Do.   If there is a significant chance for a plan termination within the first 10 years, consider using an *insured* plan. If a plan qualifies as being "fully insured" (all benefits guaranteed by level premium contracts issued by an insurance company) then it is not subject to ERISA's minimum funding standard *or* to PBGC supervision. Furthermore, accrued benefits under fully insured plans are defined as the reserve of the contracts providing the insured benefits. Many annuity contracts, with various expense factors, qualify under the fully insured definition, and the expenses associated with the contracts may well be justified if:

1. the plan needs to be terminated; and

2. the servicing agent can provide ancillary services such as plan administration as a part of his coverage.

¶1401.3   *Step-By-Step Termination Procedures*

If you have to deal with a *formal* termination procedure, such as the suspension of a defined benefit plan, here are the steps to follow:

1. *Discuss* the circumstances of termination in advance with the IRS and the PBGC;

2. Fully *report* the termination to the PBGC and request a *letter of sufficiency*;

3. Request a letter of determination from the IRS stating that the termination will not have adverse tax consequences. Your letter must include the PBGC letter of sufficiency; and

4. *Communicate* to participants their options under the terminated plan, i.e.:

   a. rollover to IRAs;

   b. cash distributions;

   c. nontransferable annuity contract; or

   d. "frozen" account left at interest.

¶1402 AN EASY GUIDE TO THE QUALIFICATION OF PLANS

Qualification of pension or profit sharing plans is a routine process which, with proper supervision, can be effectively delegated to upper-level clerical employees. The process needs control from two perspectives:

• chronological; and

• qualitative.

Effective plan qualification involves step-by-step chronological activities. Generally, one activity or sequence of events must be completed before another is begun. Therefore, your profit potential is largely dependent upon your planning.

Example ——————————————————————————

Attorney Reed spends eight weeks preparing the plan and trust documents for XYZ's pension plan. Then he realizes he has forgotten to post the "Notice of Submission" for XYZ's employees. He'll have to wait several weeks to submit the plan to the IRS, a wait he could have avoided if he had done first things first.

Qualification also involves a mechanical or qualitative checklist of specific **items** that must be submitted or prepared at some point during the lengthy process. Since most of the items will be required again and again, it is a good idea to develop a list.

Example ———————————————————————————

Attorney Scatter submits an integrated defined benefit plan to his regional IRS office. Several months later, he is informed that the designated reviewer has put his plan in a suspense file awaiting receipt of data showing how integrated benefits were calculated.

¶1402.1   *Step-By-Step Chronological Checklist for Controlling the Qualification Process*

The Exhibit A form shown on page 271 includes all the items in chronological order, plus columns to designate whether a particular item is applicable to the plan being qualified, whether it has been completed, when followup was accomplished, and when the answer or information necessary arrived from the respondent. The chart is followed with a line-by-line explanation of how it is used in the author's office. It will be easy for you to adapt the form to your own office's procedures and responsibilities.

Below is a line-by-line discussion of the first segment of the chart. In the breakdown of the chart that follows, let's assume you are responsible for qualifying a corporate integrated profit sharing plan for a company whose fiscal year (and plan year) ended December 31, 1979.

Signature Materials.   First, those items which require client, trustee, or the plan administrator's signature appear in sequence:

Function	Req.	Completed	Followup	Rec'd	Comments
Signature Materials:					
Administration Control Card	Yes	12/15/79			
Contract	Yes	12/15/79	12/26	1/9/80	
Bill −1/2 fee	Yes	12/15/79	12/26	1/9/80	check "In the mail"
*Plan & Trust	Yes	12/15/79	12/26	1/9/80	
*5300/5301/5307	Yes	12/15/79	12/26	1/9/80	
*Clerk's Certificate	Yes	12/15/79	12/26	1/9/80	

Administration Control Card.   The author's office establishes a "fail-safe" control card for each case, which is coded with key recurring administrative dates. For any of the work that is done on a particular client, we establish this 3 × 5 card and insert it in the proper sequence in a chronological filing system. Since the card does not leave our office, the columns "Followup" and "Rec'd" are not applicable and therefore they are filled in. Let's assume the 3 × 5 card is prepared on December 15, 1979.

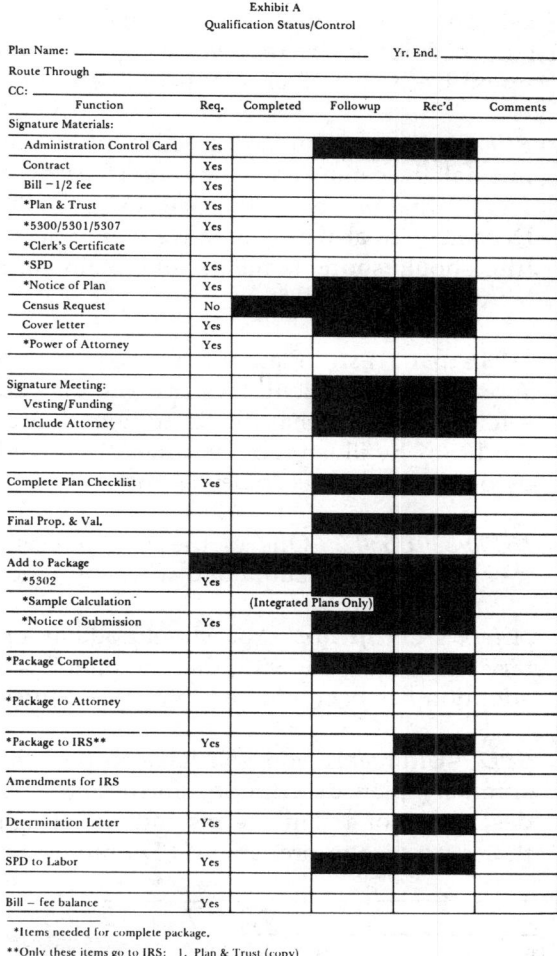

Exhibit A
Qualification Status/Control

Plan Name: _____   Yr. End. _____

Route Through _____

CC: _____

Function	Req.	Completed	Followup	Rec'd	Comments
Signature Materials:					
Administration Control Card	Yes				
Contract	Yes				
Bill −1/2 fee	Yes				
*Plan & Trust	Yes				
*5300/5301/5307	Yes				
*Clerk's Certificate					
*SPD	Yes				
*Notice of Plan	Yes				
Census Request	No				
Cover letter	Yes				
*Power of Attorney	Yes				
Signature Meeting:					
Vesting/Funding					
Include Attorney					
Complete Plan Checklist	Yes				
Final Prop. & Val.					
Add to Package					
*5302	Yes				
*Sample Calculation		(Integrated Plans Only)			
*Notice of Submission	Yes				
*Package Completed					
*Package to Attorney					
*Package to IRS**	Yes				
Amendments for IRS					
Determination Letter	Yes				
SPD to Labor	Yes				
Bill − fee balance	Yes				

*Items needed for complete package.

**Only these items go to IRS: 1. Plan & Trust (copy)
2. 5300/5301/5307 (orig. & copy)
3. 5302 (2)
4. 2848 (orig.)
5. Sample Calculation (when required)

Contract. Most pension consulting firms use a service contract or engagement letter to specify the services and limitations applicable to the qualification process. Since the job originates in the service provider's office, the column "Completed" is left blank. When the responsible person in the office has prepared the service contract, it is forwarded with the other materials to the client. The "Followup" column provides space for noting dates when our office pursued the matter. When the item is finally received, the "Rec'd" (received) column is dated. Now since the entire line is filled in, the person responsible for following through with the process can move on to the next chronological item. In this case, we have assumed that the contract was completed and sent December 15, followed up on December 23 and January 3, and finally received January 8, 1980.

Bill – 1/2 fee. Standard practice at the author's firm involves obtaining one-half the estimated qualification fee prior to commencement of the work. The illustration shows that we sent our bill December 15, followed up on December 26 at which time we were told that a check was "in the mail" (this should sound familiar), and finally received payment for one-half our fee on January 2, 1980.

*Plan and Trust. Plan and Trust documents must also be prepared and submitted to the client, trustees, and plan administrator for signature. The asterisk indicates that this is an item that ultimately will be submitted to the IRS. The illustration assumes that all plan materials were completed by our office on December 17 and mailed.

*5300/5301/5307. One of these "Application for Determination" forms must generally be submitted with any type of qualified plan.

*Clerk's Certificate. You should obtain a sealed copy of the clerk/secretary's certificate showing that the plan has been adopted, and that formal adoption has been entered into the minutes of the corporation.

SPD. Ultimately you will have to provide each plan participant with a summary plan description. Furthermore, IRS usually requires a general description of a plan's terms and operating procedures. Thus, it is the author's practice to prepare a SPD draft as a part of the initial package.

*SPD	Yes	12/17	12/25	1/9/80	
*Notice of Plan	Yes	12/17			
Census Request	No				
Cover Letter	Yes	12/17			
*Power of Attorney	Yes	12/17	12/25	1/9/80	

*Notice of Plan. Participants should be notified by letter or by clear posting that a plan has been adopted and that they will be given more details soon. Since no response from participants is required at this point, the followup and received columns are inapplicable.

Census Request. Preliminary proposals are based on estimated census information. Since IRS uses the data you supply, it is important to make sure census data is updated and accurate prior to submission. This example assumes, however, that our office already had accurate, up-to-date census information on hand. Therefore, the preparer of the form wrote ''no'' in the ''Req.'' column and crossed out the balance of the columns as not applicable.

Cover letter.   You will want to prepare a standard cover letter for submitting the qualification letter to the IRS.

Power of Attorney.   To prevent the IRS from calling your client and asking questions about the plan (questions your client will not be able to answer) you should include a Power of Attorney to ''field'' IRS inquiries.

Signature Meeting:

Vesting/Funding	465	12/21		discuss 4-40 and 5-15
Include Attorney	465	12/21	°	

Signature Meeting.   Once the above materials are complete you should plan a meeting with your client, including all parties to the plan. The meeting will serve to

1. iron out any last minute difficulties;

2. reiterate relative responsibilities; and

3. obtain signatures.

Vesting/Funding.   One subject for this meeting might be a last-minute analysis of the plan's vesting or funding provisions. Often decisions about where to invest plan assets is held off till the last possible moment. The illustration assumes our office wishes to discuss two alternative vesting schedules—IRS 4–40 and the 5 to 15 schedule.

Include Attorney.   Generally, your client's attorney should be present at this signature meeting. The balance of illustrative form will be left blank so you can think through the chronological process by yourself.

Complete Plan Checklist	Yes		
Final Prop. & Val.			
Add to Package			
*5302	Yes		
*Sample Calculation		(Integrated Plans Only)	
*Notice of Submission	Yes		

Pending Correct.   Before submitting the plan to the IRS make any last minute changes occasioned by:

1. the census information you get back from your client; or

2. points raised at the signature meeting.

Complete Plan Checklist.   At this point, with all data in hand, you are in the best position to transfer plan data to the administrative system which will use them for ongoing reporting and disclosure. It is important at this point to coordinate plan provisions with administrative functions.

Final Prop. and Val.   If you are using computer-generated reports to illustrate plan parameters and benefits, now is the best time to prepare a finalized version for use in the first plan year reporting and disclosure process.

Add to Package.   Now you should have the information necessary to prepare the remaining items for your IRS submission package.

*Form 5302.   Form 5302 applies the plan's provisions to current census information to show the IRS reviewer benefits and/or contributions under the plan.

*Sample Calculation.   If the plan is integrated you must include a sample calculation to show how the plan's integrated provisions work.

*Notice of Submission.   Prior to IRS submission, you must notify plan participants of the submission and give interested parties an opportunity to be heard.

*Package Completed					

*Package to Attorney						

*Package to IRS**	Yes				

Package Completed.   A supervising party should review all of the above before forwarding to the IRS.

Package to Attorney.   Your client's attorney should have one last chance to review the completed package.

Package to IRS.   With approval of counsel, you are ready to forward plan, trust, and associated materials to the IRS.

Amendments for IRS				■	
Determination Letter	Yes			■	
SPD to Labor	Yes		■		
Bill — Fee Balance	Yes				

Amendments for IRS.   Presumably, the IRS will require some amendments to plan language. This line provides for that contingency.

Determination Letter.   Ultimately, the IRS (it is to be hoped) will issue a favorable determination letter regarding the qualification of the plan.

SPD to Labor.   The initial draft of the SPD should be amended to reflect the changes resulting from IRS amendments, and that should be forwarded to the Department of Labor.

Bill—Fee Balance.   It is the practice of the author's firm to bill for the balance of the qualification fee when all tasks are completed.
   You will have to experiment with your own chronological checklist. With adequate planning, qualification is a simple, routine function. Your problems will be commensurate with your ability to organize, delegate, and supervise this process.

¶1402.2   *When and Where to Use Prototype Plans*

Supervised by qualified counsel, prototypes provide an efficient, cost-effective alternative to individually designed plans. However, counsel should view the prototype primarily as a starting point only and evaluate its provisions as if they were rough drafts. Here are some questions to ask about any prototype:

1.   What limitations does the instrument place on plan investment?

2.   What limitations does the instrument place on distribution alternatives?

3.   Does the prototype allow the death beneficiary an opportunity to elect 5-year income averaging?

4. Do the plan's eligibility requirements maximize the legal waiting period without creating undue administrative burdens?

5. Who is responsible for ensuring that the prototype will remain consistent with changing IRS rules and regulations?

6. Does the instrument restrict actuarial methodology?

Although this list is by no means complete, it should serve as a reminder that use of a prototype requires professional supervision.

PLANNING TIP _____

Always keep in mind that prototypes, with amendments, may be submitted as individually designed plans. If you want to make certain changes to a prototype instrument, the qualification instrument will still be dramatically simplified and expedited because the reviewer will feel comfortble with virtually all the plan provisions not affected by your amendments. Too often, prototypes are "sold" as inexpensive, "take-it-or-leave-it," no-changes-necessary substitutes for good legal advice. Your constant vigilance against that attitude will make prototypes an effective tool without sacrificing your client's best interests.

¶1403 *HOW TO CONTROL PLAN ADMINISTRATION AND AVOID PROBLEMS*

The ongoing liability and responsibility for timely and complete reporting and complete disclosure to the government, interested parties, active plan participants, and the employer certainly contributed to the massive number of plan terminations after ERISA. Now that the dust has settled, the functions included in plan administration are more clearly defined. Administration requires constant oversight by a qualified individual or organization to insure that

1. administrative practices reflect the latest IRS and Department of Labor requirements;

2. chronological deadlines are met; and

3. distributions of information and benefits to plan participants are accurate.

Since the components of plan administration extend beyond the ability of one individual or organization to provide everything, the real role of the plan administrator is to lead the team of plan advisors who monitor the plan's performance.

¶1403.1 *The Functions and Liabilities of the Plan Administrator*

The administrator is the individual or organization charged with primary responsibility for carrying out the operational requirements of the plan documents. In addition, ERISA specifies certain specific functions that fall within the plan administrator's province. In short, the plan administrator is charged with the day-to-day responsibility for "running" the plan. That includes many diverse elements, such as

1. obtaining information from various plan service providers (i.e., asset information from the trustee);

2. computing accrued and vested accrued benefits for active and retired participants;

3. authorizing payouts to terminated or retired plan participants;

4. filing various reporting and disclosure forms with the IRS, the Department of Labor, and the PBGC;

5. distributing summary plan descriptions and summary annual reports to plan participants; and

6. arbitrating claims that may arise because of ambiguity or disagreement over the terms of the plan.

The nature and extent of the above enumerated responsibilities obviously cast the plan administrator in a fiduciary capacity. In fact, ERISA specifies that the plan administrator *is* a fiduciary. As such, he is liable for discharging his responsibilities in a prudent manner and can be sued for a breach of his fiduciary capacity.

Because it is impossible for most small firms to assign an employee the task of monitoring ERISA's rules and regulations to insure ongoing plan administrative compliance, many of these small firms rely on a "ministerial assistant" who provides most of the back-up reports necessary to complete the job. For example, a life insurance agent may sell a plan to your client on the assumption that his home office will provide most of the ancillary plan administrative services required. However, the agent would undoubtedly *not* agree to act as the named plan administrator and in fact is probably precluded from doing so by ERISA's ban on performing multiple services for a qualified plan.

¶1403.2 *Choosing the Right Administrator*

Probably over 75% of the small business clients are named in their plan documents as the plan administrator. This is fine, *as long as* your client understands the ongoing responsibilities associated with maintaining a plan and the potential liability for problems.

Many firms that provide prototype, master, or specimen pension plan materials have excellent back-up capability for plan administration. The key is for your client to ensure that, in fact, these services are available from the individual or organization who provided the plan, that they can be expected to have substantial continuity, and that, in the absence of those circumstances, your client has a specific service provider available to perform the necessary services.

Presuming the plan has been initiated and largely set up by a sponsoring organization (such as an insurance or mutual fund company that is providing these services in order to sell some assets to the plan), you should obtain a letter from the representative's home office detailing the ancillary services regularly provided, their costs, and the commitment the company has made to long-term involvement in the pension industry.

You should also discuss the effect of your client's decision to buy other assets in the future. In other words, if the basis for setting up the plan was the sale of a particular type of plan asset, what will happen to administrative services if there is a change in your client's investment philosophy that precludes his dealing with the original asset providers?

The ministerial assistant should be able to provide substantial details about his own involvement, historically and educationally, in the pension field. You should query the client as to the number of qualified plans he currently maintains and obtain three references. Discuss with these references the ongoing plan administrative services you foresee and find out whether the individual has received adequate service relative to those items. You should also be concerned about the nature of the organization providing the ancillary services. You should ask the following questions about the organization:

1. What computer capacity does it have?

2. Does it have administrative personnel beyond the salesman or key employee that is "selling" the services?

3. How long has it been in the pension business?

Do not let your client underestimate the time and financial expense that can be incurred if diligent plan administrative services are not provided on a timely, expeditious basis.

Many small- to medium-size pension consulting and actuarial firms have sprung up since ERISA. Your client's best bet may be the use of such a firm. As a disinterested third party specializing in qualified plan administration, such a consulting firm may be well worth the price.

¶1403.3   *A Chronological Checklist for Controlling Administrative Functions*

The plan administrator has two major concerns:

1. that he does everything; and
2. that he does everything on time.

Those concerns lend themselves well to the use of the chronological checklist described in ¶1402.1. The use of a chronological checklist also has the advantage of allowing delegation of most of the administrative process to a lower level and less expensive person. The form used in the author's office is shown in Exhibit B. This form allows for the initial review of the plan to determine **what** functions must be performed. Further, these functions are listed in the order they must proceed and are "fail-safed" at various points at chronological deadlines that must be met. Following the complete checklist you will find a breakdown with explanations showing step-by-step instructions on how each item is prepared.

- *Job Description* refers to an item that may or may not be applicable to a particular plan administrative cycle.

- *Yes/No* queries whether or not a particular item is applicable.

- *?* indicates whose responsibility a particular function is.

- *Completed* asks for the date an applicable job was completed.

- *Followup* refers, if applicable, to any followup made on a particular date to obtain information or materials requested.

- *Received* provides an opportunity for the responsible party to note the date that requested material was received.

- *Tag to info. cycle* indicates that the first job in the administrative cycle is to put the name of the plan on a card which we maintain as a visual display in our office.

- *Deadline—FYE–60* indicates that our procedure dictates that the plan be reviewed jointly by the administrative staff and the partner assigned to the plan 60 days prior to the end of the plan year.

Exhibit B
Chronological Plan Administrative Checklist

Job Description		Y/N	?	Completed	Followup	Received	Comments
Tag to Info. Cycle		Yes	C				Deadline — FYE — 60 / /
Special Letterhead			O				
Annv. Notice Cover Letter		Yes	M				
Notice of Val/or Census Sheet		Yes	M				
Contract			U				
Change Schedule			N				
Deposit Schedule			I				
Insurance Fund Values/w/Auth			C				
Side-Fund Values w/Auth			A				Go on to Prop I/A
			T				
Package to Employer			I	Tag "Deposit" Deadline — FYE — 10 / /			
			O				
			N				
Prepare Prop I/A		Yes	I				
Run Prop I/A		Yes	N				
Prepare Actuarial Request			T				
Cont. Let. cc: Advisors		Yes	E				
Prep and Run Pending Corrects			R				
New Contrib. Let. cc: Advisors			N		Tag "Finalize" Deadline — FYE + 60 / /		
			A				
			L				
Prepare Cash Flow Summary		Yes					
Prepare: Prop. Final		Yes	I				
Eliab			N				
Val		Yes	T				
Run: Prop. Final		Yes	E				
Eliab			R				
Val		Yes	N				
Prepare Vested Payment Sched			A				
			L				
Report Cover Letter Advisor	A	Yes	C				
5500 C/K	D	Yes	O				
Schedule A	V		M				
Schedule B	I		M				
PBGC-1/Instruct/Bill	S		U				
Cash Flow Summary	O	Yes	N				
Termination Summary	R		I				
Cover Letter-Employer		Yes	C				
Bill		Yes	A				
Amendments			T				
Participants			I				
Cover Letter		Yes	O				
Termination Ltr/1099			N				
Accounting		Yes	S				
Summ. Ann. Report		Yes	T				
Benf. Design New Parts		Yes	A				
Ins. Policies			F				
SPD's New Parts		Yes	F		Tag "Gov't" Deadline — FYE + 120 / /		
Report Delivery		Yes					
Forms to Government		Yes					
Prepare Amendments cc: Advisor							
Amendments to IRS							
PBGC-1 to Labor					Tag "Garbage" Deadline — FYE + 180 / /		

Job Description	Y/N	?	Completed	Followup	Received	Comments
Tag to Info. Cycle	Yes	C		■■■■■■		Deadline – FYE – 60 / /
Special Letterhead		O				
Annv. Notice Cover Letter	Yes	M		■■■■■■		
Notice of Val/or Census Sheet	Yes	M				
Contract		U				
Change Schedule		N				
Deposit Schedule		I				
Insurance Fund Values/w/Auth		C				
Side-Fund Values w/Auth		A				Go on to Prop I/A
		T				
Package to Employer		I	Tag Deposit Deadline – FYE – 10 / /			

- *Special letterhead* refers to our obtaining from the client a supply of his letterhead so that employee letters and communications can be prepared on a more personalized basis.

- *Annv. notice cover letter* reminds staff members that a package of materials goes to each client prior to the end of plan year with a cover letter detailing each component of the package.

- *Notice of val* is the first item in the package and includes census information about prior plan participants. When our office has completed that, the **completed** column is filled in and we await receipt of the requested employee information.

- *Contract* means our annual service contract which is renewed each year and includes the fees that will be applicable to the administration for that particular plan.

- *Change schedule* means that if, in the review cycle, the responsible partner determines a particular change in the plan document (i.e., increased integration level), it is essential that the client be notified of the change and what it will cost prior to our implementing the administrative process.

- We also ask clients to complete a *deposit schedule* reconciling the dates, amounts, and recipients of checks they have drawn during the plan year on the account of the plan. This deposit schedule is checked against a similar one that is requested from the trustees or funding institution to make sure that all deposits are properly accounted for.

- *Insurance fund values/w/auth* and *side-fund values w/auth:* If there are any "other" materials that should be included in the employer information request package they would be itemized on these lines. While the information requests are sent to clients, funding letters with "authorization" go to those institutions or agents who, as of the end of the last plan year, held or administered assets subject to the plan.

- *Go on to Prop I/A* indicates to the administrator responsible for completion of the form that the administrative process need not be held up on account of lack of asset information at this point.

When all the above materials are prepared, you should send the package to the client. At that point, the ball will be in his court, and, other than followups, there is nothing more to be done for that particular plan.
When the information comes back, we

Prepare Prop I/A	Yes	I			
Run Prop I/A	Yes	N			
Prepare Actuarial Request		T			
Cont. Let. cc: Advisors	Yes	E			
Prep and Run Pending Corrects		R			
New Contrib. Let. cc: Advisors		N		Tag "Finalize" Deadline — FYE + 60 / /	

- *Prepare Prop I/A,* which means the input necessary for the computer to generate contributions for the plan year being administered.

- That complete, we *Run Prop I/A* to generate a computer report of increases and additions for the plan year.

- Immediately, we send a *contribution letter, cc. the client's tax advisor,* to insure that all parties are aware of the deposit that has been or will be made for the plan year.

- *Prepare & run pending corrects* and *New contribution letter, cc: advisors:* Frequently, when the client reviews this contribution letter, he finds that some of the information he provided was in error; we must then prepare and run "pending corrects"—generate a new computer report, and then send out a new contribution letter "cc. advisors" to finalize everyone's understanding of the amount of and deadline for plan contributions.

- At that point, said information should be available and you can develop a *cash flow summary* showing beginning of year assets, contributions, earnings, and ending assets. That cash flow statement allows preparation of computer input for various final reports that will be part of the administrative package.

Prepare Cash Flow Summary	Yes			
Prepare: Prop. Final	Yes	I		
Eliab		N		
Val	Yes	T		
Run: Prop Final	Yes	E		
Eliab		R		
Val	Yes	N		
Prepare Vested Payment Sched		A		

- The notations *Prop final, ELIAB* and *Val* represent our names for the computer reports prepared at this point.

- Based on the census information finally returned from your client, you should be able to prepare a *vested payment schedule* indicating distribution amounts for terminated vested or retired participants.

- Finally, with cash flow, computer reports and vested payment schedule in hand, the responsible partner will have fresh in his mind any specific matters that should be addressed and he can dictate a *cover letter.*

- With all of the above done, your administrator can prepare the mundane forms that should fulfill the government's requirements for reporting and disclosure. You may find it convenient to break the standard items down to employer and employee components. Since it is very important for various advisors of the plan to be constantly informed of administrative activity, a special report *cover letter for the advisor* ought to be prepared at this point.

Report Cover Letter Advisor	A	Yes	C		
5500 C/K	D	Yes	O		
Schedule A	V		M		
Schedule B	I		M		
PBGC-1/Instruct/Bill	S		U		
Cash Flow Summary	O	Yes	N		
Termination Summary	R		I		
Cover Letter-Employer		Yes	C		
Bill		Yes	A		
Amendments			T		

- Certain components of the client's annual report should be sent to the advisor as well as the client. The *5500-C, Schedule A, Schedule B, PBGC 1* with instructions about payment amounts, fund cash flow summary, and participant termination letter (with 1099s) would clearly be of interest to your client's accountant.

- Other materials that are employer-related but not necessarily of interest to advisors include a special *cover letter to the employer,* your *bill* for services rendered, and copies of *amendments* drafted pursuant to the change schedule discussed above.

Participants: Cover Letter	Yes	O				
Termination Ltr/1099		N				
Accounting	Yes	S				
Summ. Ann. Report	Yes	T				
Benf. Design New Parts	Yes	A				
Ins. Policies		F				
SPD's New Parts	Yes	F	Tag "Gov't" Deadline — FYE + 120 / /			
Report Delivery	Yes					
Forms to Government	Yes					
Prepare Amendments cc: Advisor						
Amendments to IRS						
PBGC-1 to Labor			Tag "Garbage" Deadline — FYE + 180 / /			

- Participants may or may not need certain materials as well. Most of your clients will wish to provide them with a *cover letter* which provides an *accounting* of their accrued and estimated retirement benefits to date, the *summary annual report* required by government regulations, *beneficiary designations* if the plan has an insured benefit of some type, and *summary plan descriptions* for new plan participants.

- The deadline for completion of all those materials included in the employer's annual report ought to be four months (120 days) after finalized amendments can be prepared for submission to counsel and the IRS.

That should complete the administrative process for virtually any type of qualified plan within the restraints of chronology and completeness mandated by regulation and common sense.

¶1403.4   *Getting from Here to There*

Frequently clients will come to you with *existing* retirement plans they would like you to take over for one reason or another. Usually the reason is either that

1. the plan is so completely messed up that years of annual administrative cycles will have to be recreated; or

2. the client thinks he is paying too much and that you will save him money.

These are bad reasons to take over a plan, since they imply that the client did not take the importance of ongoing design and administration seriously. But from time to time there are good reasons—such as a referral from a satisfied client—to take over an existing plan.

The takeover process involves collection of voluminous data and affords an excellent opportunity to rethink the plan's basic design in conjunction with the client's most current objectives. Figure 14.2 is a form

Function	Where We Are	Options To Consider
Plan Design		
Eligibility		
Vesting		
Type of Plan		
Contribution Flexibility		
Benefit Formula		
Actuarial Assumptions		
Integration		
Distribution Options		
Distribution Timing		
Documentation		
Plan Document		
Trust Document		
Language Clarity		
Summary Plan Description		
Regulatory Compliance		
IRS Submission/Approval		
Employee Notification		
Statutory Compliance		
Summary Annual Report		
IRS Forms (5500's)		
(PBGC) and DOL		
Trust Accounting		
Census Update		
Accrued Benefits		
Notice of Changes		
Regulatory Updates		
Actuarial Assumptions		
Actuarial Valuation		
Part. Recordkeeping		
Benefit Calculations		
Contribution Calculation		
Contribution Allocation		
Investment Allocation		
Forfeiture Allocation		
Vesting Determination		
Statement of Account		
Termination Calculations		
Termination Payouts/1099's		
Beneficiary Designations		
Routine Questions		
Investment Management		
Decision About Risk		
Evaluation of Options		
Competitive Appraisal		
Performance Measurement		
Annuity Purchases		
Liquidity/Timing		
Employee Earmarking		

FIGURE 14.2 Getting from Here to There

designed for these purposes by the author's firm. No discussion of individual line items is provided, since the form is self-explanatory.

¶1404   CHOOSING THE RIGHT INVESTMENTS AND MONITORING THEIR PERFORMANCE

One advantage, if not the prime one, of qualified retirement programs is the tax-free accumulation of funds they offer. Furthermore, investment performance will have a dramatic effect upon plan costs and funding stability. It is important that you help your client choose the right investments to fulfill his objectives. The key is evaluating and setting these objectives. Your client must understand the consequences of his investment philosophy and, once he has established it, set up a procedure to monitor how closely the philosophy fulfills his expectations.

As for choosing the right investments, "right" is a subjective term. The same "right" will not apply to each client or to each type of qualified plan. However, there can be more or less "right" decisions depending upon the characteristics of your client and your client's plan.

¶1404.1   *Actuarial Method Only a Model*

Keep in mind that interest assumptions in defined benefit plans are just that—assumptions. Sooner or later, actual investment performance must be recognized and will eventually control plan costs. Furthermore, the interest assumptions in defined benefit plans assume earnings stability that never occurs. Since your client can, by his investment decisions, control to a considerable extent yield stability, some investment options may be more "right" than others with defined benefit plans.

Example ───────────────────────────────

Go-Get-Them, Incorporated, and Take-It-Easy Company establish defined benefit plans with 6 1/2 percent interest assumptions. Go-Get-Them, Incorporated, invests all its money in bonds rated B or lower at a time when long-term interest rates are averaging 6 to 7%. Take-It-Easy Company invests half its money in certificates of deposit and half in long-term guaranteed investment contracts with major insurance companies. Two years later, long-term interest rates have risen to the 9 to 10% level. Go-Get-Them, Incorporated—according to fair market value—has sustained a paper loss of 40% on its bonds and must increase its annual plan contribution by almost 25%. The change in interest rates hardly affects Take-It-Easy Company and its funding remains constant.

> ***Observation.*** It is generally agreed that defined benefit funding ought to be more conservative than defined contribution funding.

¶1404.2 *The Prudent Man Rule Is Always in the Background*

ERISA requires fiduciaries to act in the highest and best interest of plan participants (note the emphasis on participants as opposed to employer). That dictates caution for the investment manager. Since the named fiduciary can be sued for a breach of this Prudent Man Rule, it is incumbent upon your client not to be too aggressive or conservative in his investment approach but rather follow a middle-of-the-road course, with aggressive investments tempered by more conservative ones to provide a balanced portfolio.

¶1404.3 *The Advantages of Conservatism*

No matter what type of plan your client adopts, a conservative investment posture will be rewarded. The effect of overshooting investment objectives could create either

- lower contributions for your client in a defined benefit plan; or

- a bigger ''pot'' for participants in a defined contribution plan.

However, the consequences of **undershooting** investment goals would be the converse and each would have a negative impact, such as

- higher employer costs in a defined benefit plan; or

- lower participant accumulations in a defined contribution plan.

Example

Mason Company sets up a profit sharing and defined benefit plan with which it hopes to achieve spectacular investment results by investing exclusively in the solar energy industry. Three years later, scientists discover a simple way to convert coal to a readily usable liquid form. All of Mason Company's stocks plummet. Participants find that their profit sharing account balances have been slashed and several consider suing the company for failure to meet the prudence requirement. Two older participants are so close to retirement that Mason's defined benefit funding costs must increase by 40% to meet the upcoming actuarial liabilities.

¶1405 ALTERNATIVE INVESTMENTS FOR THE SMALL PLAN

It has traditionally been difficult for small pension plans to obtain high quality investments or investment advice. In recent years, however, the competition for small plan business has led to the development of some really attractive alternatives, so that your client should have an excellent opportunity to "shop" among a number of excellent "products." The following is a brief description of four alternatives that you or your client might consider.

¶1405.1 *Pooled Investment Funds—A Poor Man's Diversified Portfolio*

Many bank and trust departments currently offer pooled or common funds in which your client can participate. The size of the pooled fund is sufficient to warrant aggressive full-time investment management and thus your client has the advantage of professional money management. Most pooled investment funds have a small custodial or trustee's fee that generally covers some of the ancillary services provided by the funding institution. Usually the pooled funds are quite liquid and most major funding institutions offer the opportunity for switching among several different pooled funds that have significantly different investment goals.

For example, many trust companies have a pooled fund composed primarily of common stocks with an orientation toward long-term growth, one designed to produce high current yields (a bond fund), or one emphasizing liquidity (for example, a money market instrument fund). The investment expense associated with these funds is so low that they generally are not the basis for decision making.

Observation. Mutual funds offer a comparable opportunity with similar "portfolio-hopping" potential. Make sure you compare pooled funds on the basis of reasonable long-term investment performance rather than the short-term investment achievements that are often so highly touted.

¶1405.2 *Guaranteed Investment Contracts: The Perils, Pitfalls, and How They Work*

Major insurance companies have been creatively responsive to investment fears engendered by the stock market's and other traditional investment media's cyclical performance. The response has been guaranteed investment funds alternatively known as group deposit administration contracts, group annuities, or "bullets." These insurance contracts can, at their best, provide virtually an ideal small plan funding vehicle; at their worst, they can be an expensive trap that locks your client into a long-term commitment.

HOW GUARANTEED INVESTMENT CONTRACTS (GICs) WORK

Most GICs share a common format. Your client commits either an initial lump sum or a series of payments to an insurance company which, in turn, invests those funds, either as part of its general assets or in a segregated fund. Generally, the underlying investments are mortgages, private placements, or other long-term debt instruments. In exchange for the use of your client's funds, the insurance company shares "the portfolio investment returns," usually providing a relatively long-term guarantee on interest and principal.

Example ————————————————————————

One major company offers a five-year guarantee of interest and principal. It will set up a guaranteed rate of interest on all deposits received during the five-year period, with the interest rate renegotiated at the end of that time frame.

Example ————————————————————————

Another company uses a declining balance format. Under this approach, the company guarantees a specific rate of interest for each year's "new" money. The interest guarantee lasts 15 years and is payable on a declining balance. Each year, the company returns to your client one-fifteenth of his principal with "no strings attached." The guaranteed rate of interest is payable on the remaining balance. Assuming a series of deposits over a period of years, the combination of changing "new money" rate, plus rollovers effectively gives your client a "rolling interest rate" that simultaneously protects him from being "locked in" and offers substantial principal and interest stability.

Example ————————————————————————

Recently "bullet" contracts have been popular. In these, the insurance company typically accepts a single lump-sum deposit, on which it guarantees a minimum or fixed rate of return for a specified duration such as 3 or 5 years. Usually, principal and interest are returned in a lump sum at the end of that time period, leaving the client free to reinvest his funds according to the investment environment then existing.

GETTING OUT CAN BE COSTLY

DAs boast relatively nominal expense factors. They are generally applicable either to:

- deposits; or

- accumulated assets.

Typical charges include the following:

1. **Sales Charge:** Some DAs have a specific sales charge, usually expressed as a percentage of each deposit (i.e., 2% of contributions). Frequently, the sales expense is graded downward for a larger deposit. For example, it might be 2% of the first $25,000 of an annual contribution and 1% of the balance.

2. **Investment Charge:** A number of DAs apply an investment or "management" charge against the accumulated assets in the contract. This charge, usually ranging from .5 to 1% covers some of these issuing companies' expenses for maintaining the contract. It, too, is frequently graded downward for larger asset accumulations.

3. **Contract Charges:** A number of GICs have an annual "contract charge." Generally the charge is between $100 and $500.

Given the high long-term interest guarantees associated with DAs, the above expenses usually are not troublesome. The real problems and expenses usually relate to contract termination provisions. Since the issuing insurance company uses long-term investments to fulfill the commitments it makes to your client, it is only fair that contract holders should be discouraged from jumping in and out of DAs. The resultant portfolio instability would adversely affect all contract holders. However, it is *extremely* important for your client to request specific illustrations of the application of the contract's termination provisions to hypothetical scenarios in which interest rates are assumed to rise or fall after the contract is purchased. Typically, a DA offers two escape valves—market value withdrawal and book value withdrawal.

HOW MARKET WITHDRAWAL WORKS

GIC market value withdrawal formulas usually "pretend" that the contract is an intermediate maturity bond. The purpose of the market value withdrawal formula is to determine what the principal value of a bond issued with the same "coupon rate" (e.g., long-term interest guarantee) would be at the time your client elects to terminate his DA.

If long-term interest rates have risen since issue, then the principal value of a bond, and therefore the GIC, will have declined. If interest rates have fallen, then the converse is true. "Pure" market value withdrawal formulas do nothing more than complete this exercise, and a check goes to your client. However, some or all of the following penalties and charges may apply to the contract you are considering:

- **Termination Charge:** Some issuers take a flat percentage of the contract's accumulated value (sometimes as high as 5% before applying the market value withdrawal formula. That can be worse than an initial sales charge since it is applied to total accumulated value (principal *plus* interest) as opposed to deposits (principal only).

- **Ceiling On Profit:** A "pure" market value withdrawal formula gives your client an opportunity to make a substantial profit if long-term interest rates decline after he purchases the DA. Many insurance companies issue DAs which, although they happily allow your client to share in a *loss*, will not allow him to receive more than accumulated principal plus guaranteed interest. In effect, under one or those contracts, your client has no downside limit on his potential loss but has a cap on his potential profit.

- **Interest Differentials:** A few GICs, when comparing the hypothetical "coupon rates" of bond equivalents, *subtract* one or two percentage points. The upshot of that is that your client can't make a profit unless long-term interest rates have moved downward at least as many percentage points. While that is not really a penalty, it does tend to preclude investment decisions based on short-term changes and interest rates. In all fairness, that may be a legitimate and sensible approach for an issuer of GICs to take.

BOOK VALUE WITHDRAWALS

Usually, GIC contract issuers will allow contract holders to take an "installment payout." By spreading the payout over several years' time, the company avoids portfolio disruption and can better anticipate its cash flow requirements. Typically, the payout period will be four to seven years. Installments are paid without applying the market value formula. The two questions to ask about a GIC's book value termination provision are

1. **What is the interest rate on the unpaid balance?** Some issuers pay their normal guaranteed interest rate on any unpaid balance. Others apply a substantially reduced rate. The reduction, if severe, is a form of penalty.

2. **What contractual expenses continue during the payout period?** Frequently, annual contract charges and investment management fees (described above) continue during the installment period. Since your client may have comparable charges in his successor funding medium, he may be paying double expenses during the payout period.

¶1405.3 *Annuity Contracts: Are the Guarantees Worth the Costs?*

Much of the marketing of small pension plans is accomplished through insurance agents. Frequently, individual annuity contracts are recommended as a funding vehicle. Individual annuity contracts have theoretical advantages:

1. **They automatically provide participant recordkeeping.** Since participant assets are segregated in individual contracts, financial reporting and disclosure is simplified.

2. **Compensation.** Commissions from contracts provide a source of compensation for the agent and the insurance company for which they may be able to provide ancillary plan services such as prototypes, administration, and reporting and disclosure.

3. **Annuity Guarantees:** The issuing insurance company usually *guarantees* the minimum payout rate applicable to distributions many years down the road. Therefore, the insurance company assumes the risk that future changes in mortality and morbidity will increase longevity so significantly that participants will outlive their annuities.

4. **Principal and Interest:** Annuity contracts generally specify guarantees of principal and periodic interest rates. Quite often the interest guarantee will take the form of a minimum with excess earnings credited at the option of the company. Historically, credited interest rates have been higher than guaranteed ones.

In a very small plan, these advantages can be quite persuasive. However, consider them in conjunction with the following potential disadvantages.

- **Are the commissions for sales or service?** Without a commitment from an insurance agent and his company, the commission may turn out to be nothing more than a reward for the agent's *sales* effort. Because of the necessity of ongoing reporting and disclosure inherent in qualified plans, that is not enough. Someone needs to perform the ancillary functions associated with the plan. Make sure there is an understanding that the commissions will support this service aspect.

- **How meaningful are the annuity guarantees?** The annuity rates guaranteed in most annuity contracts are so conservative as not to be relevant. In other words, the insurance company really is not assuming a substantial risk. If this is the case on the contracts you are looking at, there may be no justification for using the annuity structure as opposed to, for example, long-term certificates of deposit comparable in safety of principal and interest.

- **How is your client's investment freedom affected?** Using a particular insurance company's ancillary services—prototypes, for example—may carry with it an obligation to continue using that company's products forever. It is often difficult to predict what the investment environment will be like 10 or 15 years from now or that today's "products" will fulfill future corporate objectives. Make sure you consider the potential costs of amendment and transition that will occur with a change in investment orientation and philosophy.

¶1405.4   *Life Insurance—The Great Debate*

More time and energy have been expended arguing the merits of including an insured death benefit in small pension plans than virtually any other subject. Arguments on each side are powerful and sophisticated. Probably more important than these arguments are the quality and continuity of the life insurance salesman.

The value of ancillary pension services available through a qualified and conscientious insurance underwriter is immeasurable; conversely, the problems and expense that can result from the improper use of life insurance by a short-sighted or inexperienced life insurance salesman can be overwhelming. In any event, here are some of the major arguments in favor of using life insurance in qualified plans:

1. **Services available:** As discussed above, the potential value of ancillary services available from a major insurance company is a substantial savings in cost.

2. **Premiums are deductible:** If the funds used to pay premiums are part of a qualified trust or deducted by the corporation, they are, effectively, tax deductible.

3. **Policy tax matters:** Since reserves held by qualified insurance pursuant to qualified plans receive more favored tax treatment than do reserves held for other business, many companies pass these savings on to pol-

icyholders in the form of increased dividends, cash values, or settlement option rates.

4. **Conservatism:** Life insurance provides one of the safest and most conservative of all investments, and using it as a component in the plan's portfolio justifies more aggressive investments for the balance of plan funds.

The above arguments are persuasive. However, consider the arguments marshalled *against* including life insurance in the plan.

1. **PS-58 Costs:** Life insurance protection is construed to be a current economic benefit. Participants must report as taxable income the value of this economic benefit at the time it is received (e.g., the year of premium payment). Since a major incentive of small businessmen for establishing qualified plans is to defer income taxation, PS-58 costs may seem counterproductive. However, note that a taxable income charge for PS-58 costs is credited against the taxable income occasioned by later plan distributions (e.g., at retirement).

2. **Rate of Return:** Many opponents argue that the major advantage of qualified plans is the tax-free accumulation of investment income. They contend that putting life insurance (which has a very low return when viewed as an investment) in a plan in effect "robs" the plan of substantial compound interest potential.

3. **Public Relations:** Normally it is the key employees of the organization who, because of large estates and estate taxes, are motivated to include a large death benefit in the plan. Regular participants, if asked, tend to say "no, thank you" if given a choice about an insured death benefit. Is it advisable to saddle all employees with an insured death benefit to fulfill the estate planning objectives of one or two key principals?

4. **Alternatives:** Opponents point out that, for example, group term life insurance can provide the same death benefit with *no* tax liability on the first $50,000 of coverage and only a reduced tax liability on the balance. Further, they point out that group term life is one of the least expensive forms of death protection available.

5. **Transience of Most Insurance Agents:** The insurance industry has historically high levels of turnover among its agents. Since qualified plans need to be attended with continuity, it is possible to argue that some insured plans will be "sold," high front-end commissions paid, and then plans—no longer profitable—abandoned. However, most insurance companies are diligently working to create quality control at the field agent level to preclude this scenario.

Ultimately, an insurance sales organization with a good history of continuity and proven experience in the qualified plan field can pay its way for a small plan. Further, to avoid many of the potential negatives, your client might consider issuing only term insurance to plan participants during the first three years, only switching to permanent forms of insurance after that period of uncertainty about their employment longevity is past. The cost of cancelled term insurance policies is substantially less than for permanent plans.

In the final analysis, your client's decision about an insured death will be more a qualitative than a quantitative evaluation. Just make sure you inform him of the quantitative pluses and minuses discussed above.

¶1406   *CHOOSING A FIDUCIARY—COST VERSUS INVESTMENT EXPERIENCE*

The plan you implement will need a trustee. The trustee's duties are primarily investment and protection of plan assets for the benefit of participants. Responsibilities must be carried out under the guidance of various federal and local requirements for prudence and diversification. In addition, the trustee of most larger plans will be under considerable pressure to increase investment performance, since any yield in excess of assumptions will reduce employer costs.

Trustees can be sued personally for a breach of their fiduciary capacities, and therefore their job should not be taken lightly. As a practical matter, many small plans opt for an "in-house" trustee (e.g., the company president) and invest plan assets so conservatively as to fall within the safe harbor provisions of the law. Consider the advantages and disadvantages of this practice.

¶1406.1   *Advantages and Disadvantages of Self- and Corporate-Trusteed Plans*

Here are the widely acknowledged advantages of self-trusteed plans:

1. Using a corporate officer or other employee close to the employer's changing situation allows the employee to be more responsive to the individual needs of the small plan;

2. The company president, by acting as his own trustee, can avoid the expenses of a full-fledged corporate trustee (e.g., a bank);

3. By investing on the most conservative levels, the company president can fulfill the obligations imposed by the prudent man and diversification rules.

However, use of an individual trustee, such as the company president, has several potential drawbacks:

1. He may die or be disabled, thereby leaving the plan in a turmoil;

2. He probably lacks the investment experience of a corporate trustee;

3. He probably cannot diversify his assets like a corporate trustee can, who pools the assets of a number of clients; or

4. He may not have a good enough accounting or recordkeeping system to keep proper track of investment performance and account allocations.

Those are persuasive arguments both for and against an individual trustee. To further complicate the issue, consider the advantages of a corporate trustee:

1. A bank (assuming that is the most typical form of corporate trustee) spends most or all of its time depositing and monitoring investments; it, therefore, has more experience;

2. A bank has continuity that extends beyond the life of individuals;

3. Naming a corporate trustee transfers a substantial part of the fiduciary liability associated with investment and pension funds;

4. A corporate trustee's charges are generally not substantial;

5. The bank will typically have extensive computer capacity that can be used both for recordkeeping and participant allocation;

6. Because of its larger size and the pooling of its customers' funds, the bank can typically purchase investments for lower costs, and in addition, buy larger "blocks" of investment—with higher rates of return—than generally available to the small (e.g., individual trustee) investor.

Offsetting these advantages are the following potential problems:

1. Banks can't guarantee principal and interest;

2. Trustee's fees, even nominal ones, can represent a substantial amount to small plans. This is particularly so, assuming the corporate trustee has a *minimum* account charge;

3. Investment performance over the last several years has been subject to substantial fluctuation; and

4. Many owners of small businesses prefer either:

   a. investments so conservative (e.g., Treasury obligations or Certificates of Deposit) as to preclude a persuasive argument in favor of a corporate trustee; or

   b. to invest their own plan funds, reasoning (probably incorrectly) that their success in running their business presupposes general investment skill.

In general, the arguments in favor of a corporate trustee seem more powerful than those against, except for the smallest or most conservatively invested plans.

¶1407 *MONITORING INVESTMENT COST AND PERFORMANCE*

The first step for your client to take is to set his own investment objectives, including the risks he is willing to take. Some of those variables will be affected by the type of plan he has chosen; others are purely subjective. These are the components of a successful investment program.

¶1407.1 *Self-Prompting Questionnaire for Critical Investment Choices*

Partly to focus your client's attention on the critical issues he must address, and partly to eliminate various alternative investment choices, your client ought to address the following questions:

1. **How important are the pension assets to the long-term financial health of your client?** With some wealthy small businessmen, funds accumulated in a qualified plan, no matter how well invested, aren't essential. In some cases, a qualified plan is almost a "toy" that allows tax-free investment. Other resources may be so substantial that they could fulfill your client's financial objectives in and of themselves.

2. **Does your client's company have substantial profits above and beyond those deposited in the plan?** Depending on the availability of surplus cash in the business, your client may be tempted to take a more or less aggressive posture relative to investments. Less conservative assets with their attendant risks of fluctuation could lead to instability in pension funding. Some clients can tolerate that; others can't.

3. **What type of plan has your client elected?** Choice of a defined benefit plan carries with it an implication of greater conservatism, both to avoid funding fluctuation and the potential financial liability that could result

from a substantial drop in portfolio value. Alternatively, plans that promise nothing more than account balances (e.g., profit sharing, money purchase, and target benefit plans) might warrant a more aggressive investment.

¶1407.2 *Measuring Costs of Alternative Choices*

Having narrowed the field of acceptable investment choices, your client should further cull the group by comparing external and internal costs and contract features. Here are some obvious items to compare:

- What is the current rate of return?

- Is it guaranteed?

- If so, for how long?

- Is there a long-term floor on investment returns?

- What minimum settlement option rates (annuity rates) does the contract **guarantee**?

- What annuity rates does the company **currently** pay?

- What are the sales charges for years one through ten assuming a constant investment?

- What are the investment or management charges for years one through ten assuming a level deposit and a constant rate of return?

- Is there an annual contract charge?

- Are market value withdrawals available?

- If so, are they "pure," e.g., is there an adjustment to interest rates, or a holdback?

- Is there a ceiling on the profit your client can make on a market value transfer?

- What is the interest rate payable on the unpaid balance if a book value installment withdrawal is chosen?

- Which contract or investment charges continue during a book value withdrawal?

- If participants who reach retirement take annuity contracts as their distribution form, are there any contract charges?

- Do the assets used to purchase annuity contracts for participants come out at book or market value?

- What are the trustee or custodial fees, if applicable?

- Are there any other termination charges?

- What happens if your client chooses to deposit next year's allocation elsewhere?

- What ancillary services (e.g., qualification or administration) are available given the purchase of a particular asset?

- How many pension accounts does the asset-supplier actually manage— obtain three names and call them.

- How long has the supplier been in the pension business?

- Who will be the trustee if the particular investment is chosen?

Some or all of these questions may be applicable. They are all potentially important since alternative funding media vary so widely in their provisions. Even if your client is "sold" on a particular type of investment, make him aware of the alternatives.

¶1407.3 *Evaluating Performance—Setting Goals*

Ultimately, a particular investment will be chosen because its attributes most closely fulfill your client's objectives. However, objectives and investment products change. It is important to commit to writing the reasons a particular choice was made. Then, after a reasonable time, it is easy to compare actual performance with original objectives. And, periodically, you will want to go through the investment alternative exercise to make sure that your client's:

- objectives haven't changed; or

- investment products still represent the most efficient method of attaining the objectives set out.

Above all, be sure your client's plan allows for flexibility to accommodate changing times.

¶1408 *REVIEWING THE EXTRAORDINARY OPPORTUNITIES FOR THE SMALL BUSINESS EMPLOYER*

Few areas of financial planning and consulting offer the same level of rewards for both practitioner and client as the qualified retirement plan area. Because of changing regulations and the otherwise sophisticated nature of qualified plans, involvement in the retirement plan area can be intellectually stimulating and fulfilling. Likewise, a small business that finds itself in a position to implement a plan has probably been successful enough in its own right to form an interesting story.

Finally, small businessmen who implement qualified plans *enjoy* working on their programs. This is because, as opposed to estate planning, with its concommitant discussion of death and mortality, retirement plans offer **current** economic benefits in the form of tax relief. Small businessmen are likely to be frustrated. They are caught by their own productivity—further profits are so eroded by oppressive taxation that they seem pointless. Pension plans help relieve this frustration.

In spite of all the intricacies, expenses, reporting and disclosure liabilities, and complex regulations, do not let your client lose sight of these advantages:

1. Contributions are deductible—they therefore conserve for your client—money that would otherwise have been paid in taxes;

2. Tax-free accumulation—without application of immediate taxation to their yield, pension plan assets can compound at least twice the rate of more traditional alternatives. Over a 20-year period, the effect of 9% gross as opposed to 6% net interest can achieve remarkable results;

3. Distribution taxation—your client's key employees will be able to choose from a group of attractively taxed distribution options.

Your client will not find a package like that anywhere else within the investment domain.

APPENDIXES

APPENDICES

HOW TO USE THIS SECTION

So far, this book has described all the factors to be considered prior to designing a pension plan. It also examined the planning opportunities available in alternative formats for designing the plan most advantageous to the owner and key men. Finally, it set forth the administrative and investment aspects of plan design and ongoing maintenance. This section of the book outlines the following:

APPENDIX A: THE ACTUARIAL METHODS COMMONLY USED IN SMALL PLANS

The complexity and sophistication of actuarial methodology associated with defined-benefit plans has been the largest single "fly in the ointment" preventing practitioners from using the plan more frequently. Appendix A is an article describing in layman's terms the mechanical aspects of several popular actuarial methods. While it will not make you an actuary, it will give you sufficient insight into the language and concepts of these popular actuarial methods to allow you to participate in a meaningful way in planning sessions that involve actuarial choices.

APPENDIX B: ACTUAL PLAN DOCUMENT

An actual pension plan is reprinted in its entirety in Appendix B. The document offers a broad spectrum of choices both for formulas and investment media. The adoption of any qualified plan, even one approved by IRS, is a serious matter with significant legal and business consequences. It should only be contemplated in close association with your client's counsel, whose broader knowledge of the client's personal and business affairs puts him in the best position to weigh repeating and alternative suggestions.

Appendix A
Actuarial Cost Methods and the Small Plans

INTRODUCTION

In this paper, we will explain in detail six actuarial cost methods which are most popular with small plans, particularly the small split-funded plans. Three of the six we will cover are among the "acceptable six" enumerated in ERISA. The other three are variations of the "acceptable" cost methods, and these evolved because of some shortcomings inherent in the traditional cost methods especially when applied to small plans.

The following discussion will be geared to the cost methods when applied to split-funded plans. However, by simply ignoring references to the policy cash values, you can apply the principles to uninsured plans as well. By the way, a split-funded plan is one which is funded by cash value life insurance or annuity contract, which is allocable to each participant, and an auxiliary fund. The cash value at retirement supplemented by the auxiliary fund should provide the monthly pension (See chapter 2, paragraph 204.8).

This article has been reprinted with the kind permission of Datair, a Chicago, Illinois purveyor of pension consulting software programs and ancillary services.

OVERVIEW

Here are six more popular actuarial cost methods:

PTAX or Direct Code	Actuarial Cost Method
A	Individual Level Premium Cost Method
B	Entry Age Normal with Frozen Initial Liability Cost Method
C	Aggregate Cost Method
E	Modified Aggregate Cost Method
K	Modified Entry Age Normal with Frozen Initial Liability Cost Method
P	Modified Individual Level Premium Cost Method

Note that the first three cost methods are among the "acceptable" actuarial cost methods enumerated in ERISA. All the above cost methods, except the traditional individual level premium cost method, automatically spread gains and/or losses.

WHAT IS AN ACTUARIAL COST METHOD?

Section 3(31) of ERISA defines actuarial cost method as "a recognized actuarial technique utilized for establishing the amount and incidence of the annual actuarial cost of pension plan benefits and expenses." The same section also gives examples of acceptable actuarial cost methods:

> Acceptable actuarial cost methods shall include the accrued benefit cost method (unit credit method), the entry age normal cost method, the individual level premium cost method, the aggregate cost method, the attained age normal cost method, and the frozen initial liability cost method. The terminal funding cost method and the current funding (pay-as-you-go) cost method are not acceptable actuarial cost methods. The Secretary of the Treasury shall issue regulations to further define acceptable actuarial cost methods.

A cost method, for purposes of the minimum funding rules, must be systematic and consistent in its allocation of expected cost. The objective is to allocate the expected cost of the plan to the years of service that give rise to the benefit and, hence, cost.

ESTIMATING THE MONTHLY PENSION AT RETIREMENT

In most small plans, the monthly pension is estimated with the assumption that the current salary remains the same until retirement age. Therefore, it is a simple matter to apply the benefit formula to the current salary. Where the final pension is based on some averaged salary, some averaging procedure may be used. For example, where the plan provides for 50% of average salary based on the highest 5 consecutive salaries on or before age 59, and the participant is 57 years old, the current salary may be assumed to remain the same to age 59. The monthly pension may be based on the average monthly salary using actual salaries at ages 55 to 57, and projected salaries at ages 58 and 59, e.g.:

$$
\begin{array}{lll}
55 & 850 & \text{actual} \\
56 & 935 & \text{actual} \\
57 & 1000 & \text{actual} \\
58 & 1000 & \text{projected} \\
59 & \underline{1000} & \text{projected} \\
\end{array}
$$

$$4785 \div 5 = 957 \text{ averaged salary}$$
$$\underline{\times\ .50}$$
$$478.50 \text{ estimated monthly pension}$$

On the other hand, you may wish to take into consideration a salary scale. Consider the case of A. Smith who is 47 years old and is currently earning \$55,000 per year. The final pension is based on averaged salary as described above. The salary scale is based on 3% per year, and from a table of Sx we can find the projected salary.

Projected
Averaged

$$\text{Salary} = 55,000 \times \frac{(S55 = S56 + S57 + S58 + S59) \div 5}{S47}$$

$$= 55,000 \times \frac{(.7440939 + .7664167 + .7894092 + .8130915 + .8374843) \div 5}{.5873946}$$

$$= 55,000 \times 1.3450909$$

$$= 73,980 \text{ projected averaged salary}$$

Now, look for the factor MZR/Sx for age 47. Note that this is the same averaged salary projection factor we just calculated.

SOME NOTATIONS AND FORMULAE

A. Ages

1. **a** = Attained age as of valuation date (assuming this date to be as of the beginning of a plan year).

2. **e** = Entry age: for plan members who were such as of the plan effective date, the age they would have become eligible had there always been a plan; for other plan members, their age as of actual participation in the plan. For simplicity, most practitioners (including Datair) assume that e = employment age.

3. **r** = Retirement age.

4. **p** = Participation age: age at which plan member actually became eligible.

5. **i** = Issue age when dealing with split-funded plans which use an incremental approach in cost calculations. This is the age at which a particular benefit increase was recognized, the normal cost attributable to the "new" benefit being calculated from "issue" age to retirement age.

6. **f** = Age as of the beginning of the first plan year.

B. Benefits

1. **B** = Total projected benefit. When salary scale is used, the benefit formula is applied to the salary projected according to the salary scale assumed.

2. $\triangle$**B** = Incremental benefits for plans described in A5 above.

C. Salaries

1. **CS** = Current salary: the plan member's annual salary used in the current year's valuation.

D. Cost of Benefits at Retirement

1. **MV** = Maturity value: the total lump sum required at retirement to provide the projected benefit.

2. **CV@NRD** = The total cash value at normal retirement date of all policies held to partially fund the projected benefit.

3. **COC** = Cost of conversion: the amount required to convert the policies at normal retirement date to an annuity which will provide the projected benefit.

$$COC = MV - CV@NRD$$

E. Present Values

1. **$(PVB)_x$** = Present value of the projected benefit as of age x, *net* of the cash value at normal retirement.

$$(PVB)_X = (MV - CV@NRD)\,\frac{Dr}{Dx} = COC \bullet \frac{Dr}{Dx}$$

2. **$(PV\triangle B)_x$** = Present value of the *increase* in benefit as of age x, net of cash values at normal retirement of any policy attributable to the increase.

$$(PV\triangle B)_X = (MV \text{ for } \triangle B - CV@NRD \text{ attributable to } \triangle B) \bullet \frac{Dr}{Dx}$$

3. **$(PVFS)_x$** = Present value of future salaries. This is a lump-sum equivalent at age x of all salaries payable from age x until retirement. Or it may be regarded simply as the product of the current salary and a temporary annuity factor. As we shall see later, this latter concept is important in understanding the aggregate cost method.

$$(PVFS)_x = CS \bullet ax : r - x$$

$\ddot{a}_x : \overline{r-x}$ is the value at age x of a temporary annuity of \$1 payable from age x and every year thereafter until retirement age when the payment stops. It is therefore payable immediately at age x for a total of $r - x$ years. And if a salary scale is involved, an increasing annuity factor is used which is denoted by $^s\ddot{a}_x : \overline{r-x}$

F. Normal Costs and Their Present Values

1. **$(PVFNC_e)_x$** = Present value of normal cost based on total projected benefits as of age x where the normal costs themselves are calculated as of entry age.

$$(PVFNC_e)_x = \frac{(PVB)_e}{{}^s\bar{a}_{e:\overline{r-e}|}} \bullet {}^s\bar{a}_x :_{\overline{r-x}|}, \text{ where x is greater than e.}$$

(Note that the "s" in the temporary annuity is optional, i.e., a salary scale may be used.)

2. **$(PVFNC_i)_x$** = Present value of normal costs based on the incremental benefit as of age x where the normal costs themselves are calculated as of the *issue* age.

$$(PVFNC_i)_x = \frac{(PV\triangle B)_i}{\bar{a}_{i:\overline{r-i}|}} \bullet \bar{a}_x :_{\overline{r-x}|}, \text{ where x is greater than i.}$$

(Note that salary scale is not permissible here.)

3. **$(PVFNC_p)_x$** = Present value of normal costs based on the total projected benefit as of age x where the normal costs themselves are calculated as of the *participation* age.

$$(PVFNC_p)_x = \frac{(PVB)_p}{{}^s\bar{a}_{p:\overline{r-p}|}} \bullet {}^s\bar{a}_x :_{\overline{r-x}|}, \text{ where x is greater than p.}$$

(Note that salary scale is permitted here.)

G. Fund Offset

As we shall soon see, the modified individual level premium cost method requires an artificial allocation of assets among the plan members. The fund offset is the term we use to refer to this asset allocated to each employee. The way this is calculated is given by the following formula:

$$\text{Fund Offset} = \frac{(PVB)_a \bullet \dfrac{a-p}{r-p}}{\sum \left[(PVB)_a \bullet \dfrac{a-p}{r-p} \right]} \bullet \text{Total Assets}$$

H. Remaining Initial Accrued Liability

$$(RIAL)_x = [(RIAL)_{x-1} + (NC)_{x-1}] \bullet (1+i) - C_{x-1} - I_c$$

where $(RIAL)_{x-1}$ = Last year's remaining initial accrued liability
NC_{x-1} = Last year's normal cost for the plan as a whole
C_{x-1} = Actual contribution towards last year's cost
I_c = Interest attributable to the contribution
i = Interest rate

I. Gains (Losses) for the Year

$$\text{Gain (Loss)} = EUF - AUF$$

where EUF = Expected unfunded liability
AUF = Actual unfunded liability
$(EUF)_x = [(AUF)_{x-1} + (NC)_{x-1}] \bullet (1+i) - C_{x-1} - I_c$
$(AUF)_x = (\text{Accrued liability})_x - \text{Assets}$

INDIVIDUAL LEVEL PREMIUM COST METHOD (A METHOD)

This cost method originated at the time when plans were entirely funded by retirement income or annuity contracts. As increases in pensions due to increases in salaries are recognized, they are funded by new contracts. Hence, with split-funded plans, auxiliary fund deposits are calculated for each increment of benefit from the time the increase in benefit is recognized until retirement date. The total of all the auxiliary fund deposits and the life insurance premiums is the normal cost. Under this method, gains and losses are determined each year and separately amortized and added (or subtracted) as adjustments to the level deposits (normal costs) are made.

Note that the method does not lend itself to the use of a salary scale, since by its very nature salary increases are taken into account at the time of occurrence.

The advantage of this method, however, is that it is very easy to explain to the client, his accountants, or his attorney. The client knows exactly to what each dollar of cost is attributable. It is especially important in situations where a breakdown of cost per participant is required by the accountant.

MODIFIED INDIVIDUAL LEVEL PREMIUM COST METHOD (P METHOD)

The disadvantages associated with the traditional individual level premium cost method led to this modification. Let's review these disadvantages:

First, the recordkeeping associated with the incremental approach is a definite shortcoming of the method. An old plan with a multitude of policies yet with very few participants may involve a lot of records, since information is kept on each increase in benefit. It makes it almost impossible to take over an existing plan using this method because of the need to have a history of all previous increases and corresponding fund deposits.

Second, since the method by its very nature takes into account salary increases as they occur, changes in actuarial assumptions involving salary scales cannot be accommodated under the individual level premium cost method.

Third, gains and/or losses are not automatically spread out. Therefore, each year's gain (or loss) must be calculated and noted. Every year all previous years' components of gains (or losses) must be taken into consideration for the minimum funding standards.

The modification to this cost method eliminated the need to keep track of each increment of benefit, while maintaining the capability to automatically provide a breakdown of cost per participant.

The procedure of the modified method involves an allocation of the assets as of each valuation date. It is most important, however, that the participants are not led to believe that the asset allocation is in any way a measure of what they are vested in. Hence, the term "fund offset" is used to refer to this figure. Here is the step-by-step procedure:

1. Calculate the present value of benefits for each participant by determining the discounted value of the amount required from the fund to provide the expected retirement benefits. (For split-funded plans the amount required is the cost of conversion.) Note that this is the present value of each participant's *total* benefits as of the valuation date. The benefits may be calculated with or without salary scale. $(PVB)_a$

2. Multiply each participant's present value of benefits by a fraction, the numerator of which is the number of years he has participated in the plan as of the valuation date, and the denominator the total projected number of years of participation to normal retirement date. Let's call this the "fund liability."

$$\frac{a - p}{r - p} \bullet (PVB)_a$$

3. Allocate the total assets to each participant in proportion to his fund liability. Call this the "fund offset."

4. Subtract the fund offset from the present value of benefits to arrive at the present value of future normal cost.

5. Finally, the normal cost for each participant is determined by dividing the present value of future normal cost by the value of a temporary annuity with payments commencing at the participant's attained age and ending at his normal retirement age. Of course, if a salary scale is utilized, the present value of an increasing annuity should be used.

Note how gains and losses are automatically spread over the anticipated working lifetime of each participant.

Let us summarize the advantages of this modified ILPC method:

1. It greatly simplifies the entire valuation process, because it does not require the calculations associated with each incremental benefit.

2. Since gains and/or losses are automatically spread over the anticipated working lifetime of each employee, the funding standard account is simplified. There is no need to keep track of each year's actuarial gain (or loss) for separate amortization. Furthermore, the annual contribution may be based on market value valuation of assets without resulting in violent fluctuations in contributions.

3. The method is a natural for take-over cases.

4. If the case becomes such that the actuary finds a need to use a salary scale, unlike the traditional ILPC method, he does not have to change actuarial cost methods. As you know, changes in actuarial cost methods require prior IRS approval.

AGGREGATE COST METHOD (C METHOD)

The actuarial cost methods we just discussed involve the calculation of cost on an individual-by-individual basis. Under the traditional individual level premium cost method, for example, we calculate the cost attributable to an increment of benefit by spreading it over a period of time from the date the increase was realized to retirement date. The actual mathematical procedure is to divide the present value of benefit (PVB_x) by the temporary annuity of $1.00 payable from the "issue" age to a year prior to retirement age.

For large plans, this becomes very cumbersome. So, why not determine the *average* number of years applicable to the group over which cost must be spread, i.e., find the average temporary annuity factor for this group. And to find this average, we can simply add each member's temporary annuity factor and divide by the number of plan members:

($\bar{a}_a : \overline{r-a}|$ is the symbol for the present value of $1.00 per year beginning at age a and payable for $\overline{r-a}|$ years. This is the temporary annuity factor.)

$$\text{Averaged Temporary Annuity Factor (ATAF)} = \frac{\sum \bar{a}_a : \overline{r-a}|}{\text{No. of Participants}}$$

Therefore, if we divided the present value of benefits for all participants by this average factor, we should come very close to approximating the cost for this plan.

$$\text{Normal Cost} = \frac{\sum(PVB)a}{ATAF}$$

Well, in some cases, yes. If all plan members' benefits are the same, this method is appropriate and easy to use. However, most benefits are tied to the plan members' salary, e.g., benefit is 50% of salary. In this case, wouldn't it be better to give more weight to the temporary annuity factors of the plan members with higher salaries and less for those with lower salaries in the averaging process? Of course! We accomplish this by multiplying each plan member's temporary annuity factor by his current salary (PVFSa). We calculate the present vaue of future salary for the whole group and divide it by the total current salary.

$$\text{Weighted Ave. Temporary Annuity Factor (WATAF)} = \frac{\sum(PVFS)a}{\sum CS}$$

We can then determine the normal cost by dividing the present value of benefits for all participants by the weighted factor. Now, this is what the traditional aggregate cost method (C Method) is about:

$$\text{Normal Cost} = \frac{\sum(PVB)a}{WATAF}$$

This formula is good for the first plan year but must be adjusted for existing assets in subsequent years. Therefore, in subsequent years,

$$\text{Normal Cost} = \frac{\sum(\text{PVB})a - \text{Assets}}{\text{WATAF}}$$

Therefore, under this method, we are amortizing the benefits still to be funded (after reduction for amounts already in the fund) over the averaged future working lifetime of the group, with such average weighted by salary. Some people might be more familiar with the following formula:

$$\text{Normal Cost} = \frac{\sum(\text{PVB})a - \text{Assets}}{\sum(\text{PVFS})a} \bullet \text{CS}$$

Through algebra, the above can easily be shown as another way of writing

$$\text{Normal Cost} = \frac{\dfrac{\sum(\text{PVB})a - \text{Assets}}{\sum(\text{PVFS})a}}{\sum\text{CS}}$$

The aggregate cost method, therefore, is a neat and easy way of calculating plan cost. Its advantages are the following:

1. It is one of the six "acceptable" actuarial cost methods.

2. It is quite easy to calculate, and very little recordkeeping is involved when compared to the individual level premium cost method.

3. It can be used with salary scales. This is done by calculating benefits based on projected salaries. The present value of benefits are in turn calculated with salary scales taken into account. An increasing temporary annuity is then used in the denominator so that a cost based on a *level* percentage of payroll is expected instead of a level dollar amount.

4. The spread gain feature of the method makes the funding standard account easier to maintain.

MODIFIED AGGREGATE COST METHOD (E METHOD)

When ERISA's provisions on minimum funding standards became effective, the pension actuaries were faced with the problem of choosing the "acceptable" actuarial cost method. A great many of them were most concerned with using a cost method that automatically spread gains and losses. Others liked the aggregate concept, which kept the funds unallocated and helped to keep the concept of vested accrued benefits from the "my account balance" concept.

The problem with the aggregate cost method, however, lay in the fact that many plans were integrated, and the use of salaries as weights distorted the cost. A few young employees with minimum benefits could increase the average temporary annuity factor and decrease the cost, particularly when the highly paid principal was quite old. Therefore, modified aggregate cost methods became popular. Quite a few variations emerged, but they all had one thing in common—the use of a weight based on "tabular normal costs." Some actuaries used the incremental normal costs as calculated in the individual level premium cost methods as weights. Therefore, such normal costs were referred to as tabular normal costs to distinguish them from the normal costs. In cost method E, we have adopted the simpler version of calculating a tabular normal cost for each plan member as of his original participation age. This tabular normal cost is recalculated every year based on the then total projected benefit.

And this tabular normal cost is what we use as the weight in arriving at the average temporary annuity factor. Following is a step-by-step procedure of this method.

1. Calculate the tabular normal cost for each active plan participant. This is the level annual payment, calculated from each participant's date of participation in the plan, which will accumulate to the amount required in the auxiliary fund at retirement to provide the projected benefits (NCp).

2. Determine the present values of future tabular normal costs by multiplying each participant's tabular normal cost by the temporary annuity due factor from attained age to normal retirement age.

$$(\text{PVFNCp})a = (\text{NC}_p) \bullet \ddot{a}a : \overline{r - a}|$$

3. Determine the weighted average temporary annuity by dividing the total present value of future tabular normal cost for the group by the total tabular normal costs. Note that the weights used for this average annuity are the individual level amounts required from entry age for each participant's total projected benefit on the valuation date.

$$\Sigma(\text{PVFNCp})a \div \Sigma(\text{NCp})$$

4. The normal cost is determined in the aggregate for the group by dividing the present value of benefits less assets by the weighted temporary annuity for the group.

$$\text{NC} = \cfrac{\Sigma\text{PVBa} - \text{Assets}}{\cfrac{\Sigma(\text{PVFNCp})a}{\Sigma\text{NCp}}}$$

Note that at the time of plan inception, the first plan year normal cost is equal to the sum of the individual tabular normal costs required to fund for the initial benefit.

ENTRY AGE NORMAL WITH FROZEN INITIAL LIABILITY COST METHOD (B METHOD)

This actuarial cost method allows for funding flexibility. The result is to offer a range of contribution for the year. The flexibility is accomplished by establishing a past service liability which may be amortized over 10 to 30 years (40 for multi-employer plans).

This liability attributable to prior years, called the frozen initial past service liability, is calculated at the plan's inception. The excess of contributions for each plan year over the Normal Cost for that year is allocated toward funding this frozen liability. Once the initial past service liability is established, the procedure involved is very similar to the aggregate cost method. In fact, after this past service liability is completely amortized, it reverts to the aggregate cost method.

Following is a step-by-step procedure of how the initial past service liability is calculated:

1. Calculate the tabular normal cost from entry age for each plan member. This is the annual payment, calculated from each participant's date of employment (his entry age), which will accumulate to the amount required in the auxiliary fund at retirement to provide the projected benefits (NCe).

2. Determine the present value of future tabular normal costs by multiplying each participant's tabular normal cost by his temporary annuity factor from attained age to normal retirement age.

$$(PVFNCp)a = NCe \bullet \ddot{a}a : \overline{r - a}]$$

3. Calculate the present value of benefits for each participant by determining the discounted value of the amount required from the fund to provide the projected benefits at retirement (PVBa).

4. The initial past service liability is equal to the difference between the present value of all benefits and the present value of future normal costs:

$$IPSL = \Sigma(PVB)a - \Sigma(PVFNCe)a$$

The normal cost is calculated by using an average temporary annuity factor weighted by salaries:

$$NC = \cfrac{\dfrac{\sum(PVB)a - Assets - RIAL}{\sum(PVFS)a}}{\sum CS}$$

RIAL is the remaining initial accrued liability. It originated from the initial past service liability:

$$(RIAL)n = (RIAL)n - 1 + (NC)n - 1 + I - (C)n - 1$$

where n = this year
n−1 = last year
I = interest attributable to each component
C = last year's contribution

Therefore, this cost method has not only all of the advantages of the aggregate cost method, which includes "spread" gain technique and ease of calculation and recordkeeping, but in addition it provides for flexibility in contribution.

MODIFIED ENTRY AGE NORMAL COST METHOD WITH FROZEN INITIAL LIABILITY COST METHOD (K METHOD)

The modification to this cost method is in the use of "tabular" normal costs, calculated from entry age, as weights in determining the averaged temporary annuity factor for the group. It is, therefore, nothing more than a fine-tuning of the traditional entry age normal with FIPSL.
    The initial past service liability is determined as in the traditional version.
    The normal cost is determined in the aggregate for the group using the following procedure:

1. Calculate the tabular normal cost for each active plan participant. This is the level annual payment, calculated from each participant's date of employment (entry age), which will accumulate to the amount required in the auxiliary fund at retirement to provide the projected benefits (NCe).

2. Determine the present value of future tabular normal costs by multiplying each participant's tabular normal cost by the temporary annuity due from attained age to normal retirement age.

$$(PVFNCe)a = NCe \bullet \ddot{a}a : \overline{r - a|}$$

3. Determine the weighted average temporary annuity by dividing the total present value of future tabular normal cost for the group by the total tabular normal costs. Note that the weights used for this average annuity are the individual level amounts required from entry age for each participant's total projected benefit on the valuation date.

$$\frac{\sum(PVFNCe)a}{\sum NCe}$$

4. The normal cost is determined in the aggregate for the group by dividing the present value of benefits less remaining frozen initial liability less assets by the weighted average temporary annuity for the group.

$$\frac{\sum(PVB)a - Assets - RIAL}{\dfrac{\sum(PVFNCe)a}{\sum NCe}}$$

Note that at the time of plan inception, the first plan year normal cost is equal to the sum of the individual tabular normal costs required to fund for the initial benefit.

Further, note that under this method the accrued liability can easily be determined should it be needed:

$$AL = \sum(PVB)a - \sum(PVFNCe)a$$

SUMMARY

There you have it. The six more popular actuarial cost methods. The following two pages show all the formulae discussed. Have fun!

ACTUARIAL COST METHODS FOR SPLIT-FUNDED PLANS
MODIFIED METHOD

Actuarial Cost Method	Initial Accrued Liability	Normal Cost	Accrued Liability
1. Modified Individual Level Premium (P Method)	none	$\sum\left(\dfrac{(PVB)a - Fund\ Offset}{{}^{s}\ddot{a}\ddot{a}:\overline{r-a}}\right)$	$\sum\left((PVB)a \cdot \left(\dfrac{a-p}{r-p}\right)\right)$
2. Modified Entry Age Normal w/Frozen Initial Liability (K Method)	$\sum(PVB)_f - \sum(PVFNC_e)_f$	$\dfrac{\sum(PBV)a - Assets - Rial}{\dfrac{\sum(PVFNCe)a}{\sum(NC)e}}$	$\sum(PBV)a - \sum(PVFNCe)a$
3. Modified Aggregate (E Method)	none	$\dfrac{\sum(PVB)a - Assets}{\dfrac{\sum(PVFNCp)a}{\sum NCp}}$	$\sum(PVB)a - \sum(PVFNCp)a$

ACTUARIAL COST METHODS FOR SPLIT-FUNDED PLANS
TRADITIONAL METHOD

Actuarial Cost Method	Initial Accrued Liability	Normal Cost	Accrued Liability
1. Individual Level Premium (A Method)	none	$\sum\left(\dfrac{(PV\Delta B)I}{\ddot{a}\ddot{a}:\overline{r-i}\,\vert}\right)$	$\sum(PVB)a - (PVFNCi)a$
2. Entry Age Normal w/Frozen Initial Liability (B Method)	$(PVB)_f - (PVFNCe)_f$	$\dfrac{\sum(PVB)a - \text{Assets} - \text{RIAL}}{\dfrac{\sum(PVFS)a}{\sum CS}}$	none
3. Aggregate (C Method)	none	$\dfrac{\sum(PVF)a - \text{Assets}}{\dfrac{\sum(PVFS)a}{\sum CS}}$	none

Appendix B
Actual Plan Document

CORBEL & CO.

The individually designed pension plan and trust was prepared by Corbel & Co., 6620 Southpoint Dr., South, Jacksonville, Florida 32216. Corbel is a firm servicing the legal profession in the preparation of individualized qualified pension plan documents developed from a comprehensive plan design checklist. Corbel also publishes a pension plan and a VEBA forms manual that contain variable clauses and phrases used for drafting plan documents.

To utilize Corbel's services for the design of a plan, have an all-embracing plan design checklist completed by an attorney. The specific features you desire for your plan should be indicated on the checklist and the checklist returned to Corbel for processing. An individual document with supporting forms, based upon answers to the checklist questions and ready for execution, is then prepared by Corbel. If you are in need of expert help in designing and drafting a pension plan or preparing a plan for qualification, you may obtain specialized assistance by contacting Corbel & Co. This and other Corbel services are also available in online mode.

Corbel & Co.®
6620 Southpoint Drive, South
Jacksonville, Florida 32216-6193
(904) 731-4455

Mailing Address:
P.O. Box 17548
Jacksonville, Florida 32245-7548

PLEASE NOTE: There is an initial pension document preparation set-up fee of $25 (one-time charge). See page 2 for CREDIT POLICY. Modification of language is charged at a rate of $25 per hour.

CHECKLIST COMPLETED BY: CLIENT NO. _____

Name _____

Firm Name _____ Telephone (_____) _____

Address _____

City _____ State _____ Zip _____

PLEASE be thorough in completing this form to help us efficiently generate your documents.

Plan Name: _____

☐ This is an Amendment & Restatement of a complete plan and supporting forms package previously prepared by Corbel – a special 20% discount *(if plan type remains the same)*. Inquiries should be directed to our Client Service Department.

USE THIS CHECKLIST TO GENERATE:

☐ Defined Benefit $165.00
(Corporate or Noncorporate)

☐ Thrift (special request)

☐ Floor Plan $165.00

☐ Supporting Forms Package $95.00
Includes the following:
Summary Plan Description ($55)
Notice to Employees ($10)
Plan Index (Abstract) ($15)

☐ 5300 OR ☐ 5307 ($45) (additional Application for Determination form $15)

☐ Certificate of Corporate Resolution with Funding Policy & Method $15.00

☐ Administrative Forms Package $15.00

PAPER SIZE (FINAL):

☐ Letter (8½ x 11)

☐ Legal (8½ x 14)

SPACING (FINAL):

☐ Single

☐ Double ($7 additional)

MARGIN (FINAL):

☐ Ragged

☐ Right Justified ($5 additional)

DOCUMENT IS TO BE PREPARED IN

☐ Final Form (25 lb. rag bond–office quality)

☐ Draft Form ($30 additional) (Plan & Trust only)
(Letter, double-spaced, Xerox copy)
☐ Paragraph numbers & codes in margin
☐ No paragraph numbers & codes

☐ Draft copies _____ ($11.90)
NUMBER

ADDITIONAL COPIES OF PLAN & SUMMARY

☐ Letter size plan _____ $5.95 (double-spaced $11.90)
NUMBER

☐ Legal size plan _____ $5.35 (double-spaced $10.70)
NUMBER

☐ Copies to be Bound _____ $3.00
NUMBER

☐ Bind Original $3.00

☐ Summ. Plan Desc. _____ $2.50 (double-spaced $5.00)
NUMBER

TURN-AROUND

☐ Normal (10 business days) (plus postage)

☐ Rush (1-2 business days)
($40 additional plus postage)

☐ Telephone Rush (phone-in checklist)
($70 additional plus postage)

DELIVERY BY: This plan is needed in my office by (date)_____

☐ UPS Overnight

☐ UPS Blue Label (2nd day air)

☐ UPS Regular (5-6 business days)

☐ Federal Express (overnight)

☐ Federal Express Standard Air (2 business days)

☐ 1st Class (non-traceable)   ☐ Other _____

SPECIAL INSTRUCTIONS: _____

_____

_____

Prices subject to change without notice

CORBEL & CO.®

CREDIT POLICY

Corbel understands how important it is that your plans are processed in a timely fashion, and we want to help you avoid any unnecessary delays. Therefore, it is important that you read the following carefully.

(a)   Payment of all invoices are due within ten (10) days of receipt.

(b)   Charges not paid within thirty (30) days will result in a finance charge of 1½% on the outstanding balance.

(c)   *Equally important,* please be aware that once your account is sixty (60) days in arrears, no plans will be processed until your account becomes current.

If you feel that your situation is exceptional, contact David Verre, Accounting Manager, to provide him with additional credit information.

DEFINED BENEFIT
W20L
FIXED BENEFIT--UNIT BENEFIT
W2

EMPLOYER INFORMATION

A1 Name   a. _____

           b. _____

A2 Address   a. _____   Telephone e. (   ) _____
                           (street)

           b. _____   c. _____   d. _____
                  (city)   (state)   (zip)

A4 Employer Identification Number a. _____   b. ☐ Applied For

A5 Business Code Number (same as shown on 1120) _____

A6 Date of Incorporation _____
                     (month)   (day)   (year)

A7 Type of Entity   a. ☐   Sub-S Corporation   f. ☐ Partnership
                 b. ☐   Professional Service Corporation   g. ☐ Trade
                 c. ☐   Corporation   h. ☐ Unincorporated Business
                 e. ☐   Sole Proprietorship   d. ☐ Member of Controlled Group (if yes, check applicable box above)
                                                 i. ☐ Member of Affiliated Service Group (if yes, check applicable box above)

A8 **TRUSTEE NAME(S)**

     a. _____   c. _____
            (if bank, enter here)   (if individual, enter here)

     b. _____   d. _____
            (2nd line for bank)   (2nd line for individual)

                                        e. _____
                                                   (3rd line for individual)

A9 Trustees' Address   a. ☐ Use Employer Address   f. _____
                                                      (4th line for individual)

     c. _____
                        (street)

     d. _____   e. _____   f. _____
                (city)   (state)   (zip)

A10 Name of any insurance Co. or mutual fund that maintains a fund of the Plan   a. _____
                                                           (applicable for fully insured or guaranteed annuity contract plans)

PLAN INFORMATION

This Plan is to include **"top heavy"** provisions.   top. ☐ Yes   ntop. ☐ No

B1 This is   a. ☐ a New Trust   b. ☐ An Amendment & Restatement of
                                       ☐ Same Plan   pr1. ☐ Prototype Plan   pr2. ☐ Master Plan

                              (Name of Master or Prototype Plan (XYZ Bank Master Plan #1)

                           ☐ conversion of cv1. ☐ Profit Sharing Plan   cv2. ☐ Money Purchase Pension Plan into   this Plan,
                           AND Participants' account balances shall be used to
                           cva. ☐ provide additional retirement benefits.   cvb. ☐ offset such Participants' Accrued Benefits.
                           ☐ Other (merger, consolidation, etc.)

B3 Title of Document...indicate **exactly** how the title on the first page is to appear, e.g., ABC COMPANY
                                                         DEFINED BENEFIT PLAN AND TRUST

     a. _____

     b. _____

     c. _____

     d. _____

     e. _____

B4 Plan Name **(original)**   a. _____
[c.] [d.]

                        b. _____

B6 Effective Date of Plan (Generally 1st day of Plan Year) _____
                                           (month)   (day)   (year)

B7 Effective Date of Amendment _____
                                  (month)   (day)   (year)

B8 Plan Year Beginning (e.g., May 1st)   a. _____   Plan Year End   b. _____
                                      (month)   (day)   (month)   (day)

B9 Anniversary Date of Plan   a. _____   b. _____
                               (month)   (day)   (year--must include year for which Plan is effective)

B10 Plan Number assigned by the Employer (circle one)   001   002   003   004   005

B11 Name of Plan Administrator:

    a. ☐ Employer

    b. ☐ Name _____ i. ☐ use Employer address

    c.   Address _____ Telephone g. (   ) _____

    d. _____ e. _____ f. _____ h. _____
             (city)   (state)   (zip)   (I.D. number)

K1 Plan's agent for service of legal process   a. _____ d. ☐ use Employer address

    b.   Address _____

    c. _____ , _____ _____
             (city)   (state)   (zip)

K2 Years of Service shall be based upon   a. ☐ 1000 hours   b. ☐ elapsed time method (see commentary)

C10 **ACCRUED BENEFIT** means a participant earns a portion of his normal retirement benefit equal to:

    New Plan   Amended Plan   **Fractional Method--A fraction based upon the number of**

    a. ☐   d. ☐   Plan Years of service to Normal Retirement Date.

    g. ☐   g. ☐   Total Years of service to Normal Retirement Date.

    b. ☐   e. ☐   **3% Method** - For each year of Participation - **(May not be used in an integrated plan.)**

    c. ☐   f. ☐   **133% Method--(Must be used with career average Plans.)** (type and attach definition)

    For an Amended Plan, Accrued Benefit shall be determined prior to

    x. ☐   date Plan became subject to Code Section 411(b) (may be applicable to pre-ERISA plan)

    y. ☐ _____(for post-ERISA plan) **PLUS** future accruals based on d. or e. above.
            month-day-year

    ☐ N/A (g. was checked)

C10 Benefit accruals will **not** be effective until Participant completes 2 continuous Years of Service   h. ☐ Yes   i. ☐ No

C11 **ACTUARIAL EQUIVALENT** (as provided by Employer's Actuary) means amounts of equal value when computed using

    a. ☐ _____
                           (i.e. pre or post retirement interest, mortality, turnover)

    AND, in calculating the Present Value of Accrued Benefit in the determination of **"top heavy"** status the following actuarial assumptions shall be used.

    b. ☐ _____

    c. ☐ Same as a. above.

C12 **AGE** shall mean age at   a. ☐ nearest birthday   b. ☐ last birthday.

C0 **AVERAGE MONTHLY COMPENSATION** shall be based on   w. ☐ Plan   **or**   x. ☐ total Years of Service   & shall be averaged over

    a. ☐   highest _____ consecutive years within the last 10 years to date of termination of employment.*

    b. ☐   highest _____ consecutive years to date of termination of employment.*

    c. ☐   years to date of termination of employment. (career average)

    d. ☐   highest _____ years within the last 10 years excluding the 5 years preceding Normal Retirement Date.*

    e. ☐   final _____ years to date of termination of employment.*

    ☐   N/A Flat benefit formula used.
    *A minimum of 5 years is required for integrated plan unless adjustments are made.

CO Shall Compensation be recognized subsequent to Normal Retirement Date?   y. ☐ Yes   z. ☐ No

C1 **COMPENSATION** [☐ **paid only**] [c1. ☐ **paid or accrued**] with respect to any Participant means:

    a. ☐   total Compensation excluding overtime, commissions and discretionary bonuses.

    b. ☐   total Compensation excluding overtime, commissions and bonuses.

    c. ☐   total Compensation excluding commissions.

    d. ☐   total Compensation excluding bonuses.

    e. ☐   total Compensation.

    v. ☐   Other (draft, title as C1v & attach)
    NOTE: If total compensation is not used, plan may, in operation, discriminate in favor of employees who are stockholders, officers, or highly compensated. If so, your plan will not remain qualified.

C1 **AND, shall be based on a**   x. ☐ Plan   y. ☐ Calendar   z. ☐ Fiscal Year (defines Plan's "limitation year").

C2 **EARLY RETIREMENT DATE means,** prior to **Normal Retirement Date:**   d. ☐ any Anniversary Date   e. ☐ the 1st day of the month

    ☐   coinciding with or next following the date on which a Participant attained his a. _____ birthday and has

    completed at least b. _____ Years of Service

    c. ☐   No Early Retirement provision provided.

    v. ☐   Other (draft, title as C2v & attach)

C3   **ELIGIBLE EMPLOYEES shall mean:**
    a. ☐ all Employees who have satisfied the eligibility requirements.
    b. ☐ only Employees who are compensated on a salaried basis (Salaried only Plan)
    c. ☐ all Employees EXCEPT Employees receiving compensation in the form of commissions or sales incentives.
    v. ☐ Other (draft, title as C3v & attach)

    AND
        x. ☐ Employees whose employment is governed by a collective bargaining agreement under which retirement benefits were the subject of good faith bargaining **WILL NOT** be eligible. ☐ N/A
        y. ☐ Only Employees whose Compensation exceeds the Plan's integration level **SHALL** be eligible. ☐ N/A
        z. ☐ Employees who participate in another plan maintained by the Employer **WILL NOT** be eligible to participate in this Plan. Name of plan: _____ ☐ N/A
        w. ☐ Owner-Employees or Self-Employed Individuals **WILL NOT** be eligible to participate in this Plan. ☐ N/A
        q. ☐ Key Employees **WILL NOT** be eligible to participate in this Plan. ☐ N/A
        r. ☐ Non-Key Employees **WILL NOT** be eligible to participate in this Plan. ☐ N/A

C4   **LOCATION OF EMPLOYER'S PRINCIPAL OFFICE:**   a. ☐ (state)   b. ☐ (commonwealth) of c. _____ and this trust shall be governed under the same.

C4   **Include provisions for plan adoption by affiliated or other corporations**   e. ☐ No   d. ☐ Yes
    If Yes, each Participating Employer's contributions are for the exclusive benefit of that Participating Employer's Employees.
    f. ☐ Yes
    g. ☐ No
    ☐ N/A (May be checked only if C4e above was checked.)

C5   **FISCAL YEAR means:**
    ☐ 12 months commencing on   a. _____ and ending on b. _____
                                (month)   (day)   (month)   (day)
    ☐ **for plan year only** .. 12 months commencing on   c. _____ and ending on d. _____
                                          (month)   (day)   (month)   (day)
        except for the first Fiscal Year which commenced on   e. _____
                                                (month)   (day)
    ☐ accounting year based on 52 to 53 week year ending on the   f. _____ nearest g. _____ of each year and commencing on the next day thereafter.
                                          (day of week)   (month)   (day)

C6   **NORMAL RETIREMENT AGE ("NRA") means date Participant attains his** a. ☐ 65th birthday (maximum) b. ☐ _____ birthday
                                                                                            (max. 65)

C7   **NORMAL RETIREMENT DATE shall commence as of the:**   p. ☐ first day of the month   q. ☐ Anniversary Date
    a. ☐ coinciding with or next following the Participant's "NRA".
    b. ☐ nearest the Participant's "NRA".
    c. ☐ coinciding with or next following the Participant's "NRA", or the _____ anniversary of joining the Plan, if later.
    d. ☐ nearest the Participant's "NRA", or the _____ anniversary of joining the Plan, if later.
    ☐ coinciding with or next following the Participant's "NRA", or the e. _____ anniversary of joining the Plan, if later, but in no event later than his f. _____ birthday.
    ☐ nearest the Participant's "NRA", or the g. _____ anniversary of joining the Plan, if later, but in no event later than his h. _____ birthday.

C8   **TOTAL AND PERMANENT DISABILITY...Disability Benefits will be payable when a**
    a. ☐ Participant has become totally and permanently disabled as determined by a licensed physician chosen by the Administrator.
    b. ☐ Participant has become totally and permanently disabled and is receiving disability benefits under the Social Security Act.
    c. ☐ N/A This Plan does not provide disability benefits.

C9   **WILL PLAN RECOGNIZE SERVICE WITH PREDECESSOR EMPLOYER?** NOTE: If plan was maintained by a predecessor Employer, b or c must be checked.
    a. ☐ No
    b. ☐ Yes: Years of Service with _____ shall be recognized for the purposes of this Plan.
    c. ☐ Yes: Years of Service with _____ during such years that a qualified plan was maintained by such Employer.

E1   **CONDITIONS OF ELIGIBILITY (Check only one of the choices below.) Any employee who**

    a. ☐ is employed on an Anniversary Date. (No waiting period) (no minimum age)

    b. ☐ has completed _____ Year(s) of Service (No minimum age) (Use fractions for less than 1 yr.)

    c. ☐ has reached _____ birthday. (No service requirement)

    d. ☐ has completed _____ Year(s) of Service (Use fractions for less than 1 yr.) and has reached his e. _____ birthday.

    [OR] Any Employee who was employed on the first Anniversary Date. Thereafter, any employee who has...

    f. ☐ completed _____ Year(s) of Service (No minimum age) (Use fractions for less than 1 yr.)

    g. ☐ reached his _____ birthday. (No service requirement)

    h. ☐ completed _____ Year(s) of Service (Use fractions for less than 1 yr.) and has reached his i. _____ birthday.

    [OR] For Amended Plans

    Any Employee who was a Participant in the Plan prior to the Effective Date of this Amendment. Thereafter, any Employee who has...

    j. ☐ completed _____ Year(s) of Service (No minimum age) (Use fractions for less than 1 yr.)

    k. ☐ reached his _____ birthday. (No service requirement)

    l. ☐ completed _____ Year(s) of Service (Use fractions for less than 1 yr.) and has reached his m. _____ birthday.

       ☐ Other

    NOTE: Years of Service cannot exceed three. If Years of Service is greater than one, 100% vesting is required.

E1   Is the above eligibility requirement less than 1 year?   x. ☐ Yes   ☐ No

E1   **SHALL THOSE EMPLOYEES employed within 5 years of their normal retirement age be excluded from the plan?**
    (Must be No if C7 c or d are checked.)   p. ☐ Yes   ☐ No

E2   **EFFECTIVE DATE OF PARTICIPATION...An Eligible Employee shall become a Participant as of**

    a. ☐ the first day of the Plan Year in which he met the requirements.

    d. ☐ the first day of the Plan Year **next following** the date on which he met the requirements. (Eligibility must be 6 mo./24-1/2 or less.)

    b. ☐ the first day of the Plan Year in which he met the requirements, if he met the requirements in the first 6 months of the Plan Year, or as of the first day of the next succeeding Plan Year if he met the requirements in the last 6 months of the Plan Year.

    c. ☐ the earlier of the _____ or 1st day of Plan year next following the date in which he met the requirements.
                      (1st day of the seventh month)

E3   **BENEFIT FORMULAS...Participant's Monthly Retirement Benefit shall be equal to**
      Fixed Benefit

a. ☐ _____% of such participants's monthly compensation. (No Table)

b. ☐ _____% of such participant's monthly compensation in excess of c. $_____ (No Table)

d. ☐ _____% of such participant's monthly compensation in excess of the amount shown in the table for the calendar year in which Normal Retirement Date/65th birthday occurs. (Check Applicable E16 Table)

e. ☐ _____% of monthly compensation, plus f. _____% of monthly compensation in excess of g. $_____ (No Table)

h. ☐ _____% of monthly compensation, plus i. _____% of monthly compensation in excess of the amount shown in the table for the calendar year in which Normal Retirement Date/65th birthday occurs. (Check Applicable E16 Table)

Unit Benefit

j. ☐ _____% of monthly compensation, multiplied by the participant's total number of years employment. (No Table)

k. ☐ _____% of monthly compensation in excess of l. $_____, multiplied by the participant's total number of years of employment. (No Table)

m. ☐ _____% of monthly compensation in excess of the amount shown in the table for the calendar year in which Normal Retirement Date/65th birthday occurs, multiplied by the participant's total number of years of employment. (Check Applicable E16 Table)

n. ☐ _____% of monthly compensation, multiplied by the participant's total number of years of employment, plus o. _____% of monthly compensation in excess of p. $_____, multiplied by the total number of year of employment. (No Table)

q. ☐ _____% of monthly compensation multiplied by the participant's total number of years of employment, plus
      r. _____% of such monthly compensation in excess of the amount shown in the table for the calendar year in which Normal Retirement Date/65th birthday occurs, multiplied by the participant's total number of years of employment. (Check Applicable E16 Table)

Flat Benefit

s. ☐ $_____ per month for each Year of Service with the employer. (No Table)

Offset Formulas

t. ☐ _____% of monthly compensation offset by u. _____% of the primary Social Security benefit he would be entitled to immediately following retirement. (No Table)

w. ☐ _____% of monthly compensation multiplied by the participant's total number of Years of Service, offset by
      x. _____% of the primary Social Security benefit he would be entitled to immediately following retirement. (No Table)

E18   **Floating Benefit Formulas**

a. ☐ _____% of such participant's monthly compensation in excess of the Social security Table I in effect for the calendar year in which normal retirement date occurs. (No Table)

b. ☐ _____% of monthly compensation, plus c. _____% of monthly compensation in excess of the Social Security Table I in effect for the calendar year in which normal retirement date occurs. (No Table)

d. ☐ _____% of monthly compensation in excess of the Social Security Table I in effect for the calendar year in which normal retirement date occurs, multiplied by the participant's total number of years of employment. (No Table)

e. ☐ _____% of monthly compensation multiplied by the participant's total number of years of employment, plus f. _____% of such monthly compensation in excess of the Social Security Table I in effect for the calendar year in which normal retirement date occurs, multiplied by the participant's total number of years of employment. (No Table)

E3   v. ☐ Other (draft, title as E3v & attach)

EE   **INCREASING ANNUITY...the monthly Retirement Benefit shall be increased by**

a. ☐ _____% annually following such participant's normal retirement date.

b. ☐ N/A

Page 5

331

E16   **TABLES FOR INTEGRATED FORMULAS** (E3d, h, m, q)...Monthly Covered Compensation shall be based on Calendar Year of
    w. ☐   Retirement   x. ☐   65th Birthday **AND** Integration shall be based on
    y. ☐   Table I   z. ☐   Table II.

a. ☐ **1971 Table I**	b. ☐ **1975 Table I**	c. ☐ **1976 Table I**	d. ☐ **1977 Table I**
1971 $ 450	1975 $ 550	1976 $ 600	1977 $ 650
(See Section 5.1 of Master Text)	(See Section 5.1 of Master Text)	(See Section 5.1 of Master Text)	(See Section 5.1 of Master Text)
2004 or later 750	2006 or later 1150	2011 or later 1275	2012 or later 1375

a. ☐ **1971 Table II**	b. ☐ **1975 Table II**	c. ☐ **1976 Table II**	d. ☐ **1977 Table II**
1971 $ 460	1975 $ 578	1976 $ 613	1977 $ 650
(See Section 5.1 of Master Text)	(See Section 5.1 of Master Text)	(See Section 5.1 of Master Text)	(See Section 5.1 of Master Text)
2010 or later 750	2010 or later 1175	2011 or later 1275	2012 or later 1375

e. ☐ **1978 Table I**	f. ☐ **1979 Table I**	g. ☐ **1980 Table I**	h. ☐ **1981 Table I**
1978 $ 700	1978 $ 700	1978 $ 700	1978 $ 700
(See Section 5.1 of Master Text)	(See Section 5.1 of Master Text)	(See Section 5.1 of Master Text)	(See Section 5.1 of Master Text)
2013 or later 1475	2014 or later 1908.33	2015 or later 2158.33	2016 or later 2475

e. ☐ **1978 Table II**	f. ☐ **1979 Table II**	g. ☐ **1980 Table II**	h. ☐ **1981 Table II**
1978 $ 688	1978 $ 688	1978 $ 688	1978 $ 688
(See Section 5.1 of Master Text)	(See Section 5.1 of Master Text)	(See Section 5.1 of Master Text)	(See Section 5.1 of Master Text)
2000 or later 1232	2014 or later 1908	2015 or later 2158	2016 or later 2475

i. ☐ **1982 Table I**	j. ☐ **1983 Table I**
1982 $ 900	1983 $1000
(See Section 5.1 of Master Text)	(See Section 5.1 of Master Text)
2015 or later 2700	2018 or later 2975

i. ☐ **1982 Table II**	j. ☐ **1983 Table II**
1982 $ 917	1983 $ 991
(See Section 5.1 of Master Text)	(See Section 5.1 of Master Text)
2017 or later 2700	2018 or later 2975

E4   REDUCTIONS AND LIMITATIONS The above monthly retirement benefits may be modified as follows:

    ☐ Benefit shall be reduced by a. _____* (e.g. 1/20th) for each year of service less than b. _____* (e.g. 20)

    ☐ The excess portion of the benefit shall be reduced by c. _____ (e.g. 1/20) for each year of service less than d. _____* (e.g. 20)

    ☐ Before applying Social Security offset, the basic benefit shall be reduced by e. _____* (e.g. 1/20th) for each year of service less than f. _____* (e.g. 20)

    ☐ Other

    ☐ N/A

    *NOTE: Integrated plans must provide for excess percentage reduction of at least 1/15 for each year of service less than 15, if the maximum integration percentage is used.

E5   ☐ Years of service with the employer shall be limited to a. _____ years.

    ☐ N/A

E6   ☐ Years of service prior to a. _____ shall not be recognized.
                      (month-day-year)

    ☐ N/A

E7   ☐ Notwithstanding the above, each participant shall be provided with a monthly benefit of not less than a. $_____ (standard **"top heavy"** provision provides minimum accrual).

    ☐ N/A

E8   ☐ Notwithstanding the above, a participant's monthly retirement benefit shall not exceed a. $_____ .

    ☐ N/A

E14   a. ☐ The minimum increase or decrease to be taken into consideration in monthly retirement benefits shall be $_____ . (May be applicable if insured death benefits will be provided.)

      ☐ N/A

E15   a. ☐ Increases in benefits due to compensation changes shall be recognized as of each Anniversary Date, but decreases shall not be recognized until 2 years after such decrease has been in effect. (May be applicable if insured death benefits will be provided.)

      ☐ N/A

E19   a. ☐ Retirement benefits shall be reduced by the Actuarial Equivalent of compensation received by a Workmen's Compensation award.

      ☐ N/A

E20   a. ☐ Benefits reduced by monthly pension of any other defined benefit plan to which Employer contributes on behalf of a Participant.

      ☐ N/A

E9   EARLY RETIREMENT BENEFITS (must coordinate with C2) payable at Early Retirement shall be equal to the

    a. ☐ accrued retirement benefit reduced by 1/15th for each of first 5 years, and 1/30th for each of next 5 years, & actuarially thereafter.

    b. ☐ present value of accrued benefit.

    c. ☐ accrued benefit reduced by 1/2 of 1% for each month early retirement precedes normal retirement date. (May not be used if plan is integrated.)

    d. ☐ No early retirement benefits. Participants retiring prior to normal retirement shall be considered to be terminated.

      ☐ Other

E10   THE NORMAL RETIREMENT BENEFIT payable to a participant shall be

    a. ☐ a life annuity or the actuarial equivalent.

    b. ☐ an annuity for life and _____ months certain, or the actuarial equivalent.

    ☐ a 100% joint and survivor annuity, or if any other form of payment is elected, the actuarial equivalent of a straight life annuity using*

      c. _____
                      (i.e. the Actuarial Equivalent pursuant to Section 1.3)

      AND for unmarried Participants, the normal form shall be d. _____
                                        (i.e. 10 yrs. certain, life only)

    *NOTE: Cannot exceed actuarial equivalent of a straight life annuity using maximum annual benefit under IRC Section 415.

E11   LATE RETIREMENT BENEFIT shall be

    a. ☐ the actuarial equivalent of the benefit he would have received at his Normal Retirement Date.

    b. ☐ paid as though he had actually retired. (No deferred benefits)

    c. ☐ the same monthly benefit that he would have received at his Normal Retirement Date.

    d. ☐ the actuarial equivalent of the Normal Retirement Benefit plus the net income or losses incurred to actual retirement date. However it shall not be less than the benefit due at his Normal Retirement Date.

      ☐ Other

E12   DISABILITY RETIREMENT BENEFITS

    a. ☐ Shall be the value of total prior contributions determined under the typical individual level premium cost method.

    b. ☐ Early retirement benefit without regard to age and service requirements.

    c. ☐ 100% of present value of accrued benefit.

    d. ☐ No disability benefits, disabled Participants shall be treated in the same manner as Terminated Participants.

    v. ☐ Other (draft, title as E12v & attach)

333

E13   **DEATH BENEFITS** ... Will death benefits be provided?   a. ☐ Yes   b. ☐ No   If yes, death benefit will be equal to:

For Non-insured Death Benefits

   c. ☐   the Present Value of Accrued Benefit.

   d. ☐   The Value of Total Prior Contributions.

   e. ☐   a Participant's total compensation for _____ calendar years prior to date of death.

   f. ☐   _____ times monthly benefit.

For Insured Death Benefits (Insurance purchases are **OPTIONAL**, but if purchased, must be purchased uniformly.)

   g. ☐   proceeds of policies **ONLY** (Administrator will establish amount of coverage),

   h. ☐   proceeds of policies **PLUS** m. or n. below.

   i. ☐   the greater of proceeds of policies **OR** m. or n. below.

For Insured Death Benefits (Policies **MUST** be purchased)

   j. ☐   _____ times monthly benefit.

   k. ☐   _____ times monthly benefit **PLUS** m. or n. below.

   l. ☐   the greater of _____ times monthly benefit **OR** m. or n. below.

      m. ☐ Present Value of Accrued Benefit

      n. ☐ The Value of Total Prior Contributions

   o. ☐   Other (Type & attach)

With respect to g-l above (more than one may be checked)

   p. ☐   Policies shall be purchased only for Participants who have completed _____ Plan Years of Service.

   q. ☐   Policies shall be purchased only for Participants who have **NOT** attained Age _____

   r. ☐   No additional policies shall be purchased for Participants who are over Age _____

   s. ☐   Policies shall be purchased only in multiples of $_____

     ☐   N/A

The above benefits (c-l) shall be (check one only)

   t. ☐   limited to the greater of 100 times the monthly benefit or the reserve under the Typical Level Premium Cost Method.

   u. ☐   limited to 100 times the monthly benefit.

   v. ☐   limited to the reserve under the Typical Level Premium Cost Method.

   w. ☐   equal to the insurance in force plus the reserve calculated under the Typical Level Premium Cost Method (less than 2/3 of the cost to be used to purchase insurance - Rev. Rul. 74-307).

     ☐   Other

     ☐   N/A (May be checked **ONLY** if c. or d. above were checked.)

F5   **PARTICIPANT ROLLOVER ACCOUNTS:** (may be accepted at discretion of Administrator)

   e. ☐   Yes

   c. ☐   N/A   Rollover Accounts are not permitted in this plan.

F6   **AFTER TAX EMPLOYEE VOLUNTARY CONTRIBUTIONS are to be allowed. (not to exceed 10% of pay)**

   e. ☐   Yes, not to exceed _____ % of Compensation.

   c. ☐   No, Voluntary Contributions will not be allowed.

F7   **AGGREGATE PRIOR CONTRIBUTIONS For Amended Plans ONLY!** Were Voluntary Contributions allowed prior to 1/1/76?

   a. ☐ Yes   b. ☐ No

F8   **DIRECTED INVESTMENT ACCOUNTS** are permitted for the Vested interest in any one or more accounts (Accrued Benefit excluded).

   a. ☐   Yes, at the Administrator's discretion (creates onerous administrative problems.)

   b. ☐   No

F15   **TAX DEDUCTIBLE QUALIFIED VOLUNTARY EMPLOYEE CONTRIBUTIONS (QVEC)**

At the Administrator's discretion, up to $2,000 (not to exceed 100% of Compensation) may be allowed.

   b. ☐   Yes, and accounts will be invested as part of the general Trust Fund.

   f. ☐   No, **QVEC** will not be allowed.

H2 **PAYMENT OF VESTED BENEFITS** will normally be paid at normal (early) retirement date, death or disability. Shall the administrator have the power to direct earlier payment?

    d. ☐ Yes   e. ☐ No

If the vested amount is less than $1,750, payment shall be made on the anniversary date following termination.

    f. ☐ Yes   g. ☐ No

H4 **VESTING...In determining Years of Service for vesting purposes:**

Service prior to the Effective Date of the Plan shall be **excluded**	a. ☐ Yes	b. ☐ No
Service prior to the time an Employee attained age 22 shall be **excluded**	c. ☐ Yes	d. ☐ No

NOTE: If 4.40 Vesting Schedule is used, b. & d. must be marked. If Rule of 45 Vesting Schedule is used, d. must be marked. Unless 5-15 or 10 year Vesting Standard is satisfied, d. must be marked.

H6 **VESTING OF PARTICIPANT'S INTEREST...The vesting schedule, based on number of Years of Service shall be as follows:**

a. ☐

4 Years	40%
5 Years	45%
6 Years	50%
7 Years	60%
8 Years	70%
9 Years	80%
10 Years	90%
11 Years	100%

Note: If this Vesting Schedule (a.) is elected, the answers to H4 MUST BE NO.

b. ☐

2 Years	10%
3 Years	20%
4 Years	40%
5 Years	45%
6 Years	50%
7 Years	60%
8 Years	70%
9 Years	80%
10 Years	90%
11 Years	100%

c. ☐

1 through 9 Years	0%
10 Years	100%

d. ☐

1 Year	10%
2 Years	20%
3 Years	30%
4 Years	40%
5 Years	50%
6 Years	60%
7 Years	70%
8 Years	80%
9 Years	90%
10 Years	100%

e. ☐

5 Years	25%
6 Years	30%
7 Years	35%
8 Years	40%
9 Years	45%
10 Years	50%
11 Years	60%
12 Years	70%
13 Years	80%
14 Years	90%
15 Years	100%

h. ☐

4 Years	40%
5 Years	50%
6 Years	60%
7 Years	70%
8 Years	80%
9 Years	90%
10 Years	100%

i. ☐

1 Year	20%
2 Years	40%
3 Years	60%
4 Years	80%
5 Years	100%

j. ☐

1 Year	25%
2 Years	50%
3 Years	75%
4 Years	100%

l. ☐

2 Years	20%
3 Years	40%
4 Years	60%
5 Years	80%
6 Years	100%

k. ☐

1 through 2 Years	0%
3 Years	100%

    f. ☐ Rule of 45

    g. ☐ 100% upon entering Plan. (Required if eligibility requirement is greater than 1 year.)

    v. ☐ Other

Years of Service	Percentage	Years of Service	Percentage
_____	_____	_____	_____
_____	_____	_____	_____
_____	_____	_____	_____
_____	_____	_____	_____
_____	_____	_____	_____
_____	_____	_____	_____

However, if this Plan becomes **"top heavy"**, the following vesting schedule shall become effective.

    ☐ N/A, H6g., i., j., k., or l. above was checked.

    p. ☐ 100% upon entering Plan. (Required if eligibility requirement is greater than 1 year.)

q. ☐

1 through 2 Years	0%
3 Years	100%

r. ☐

2 Years	20%
3 Years	40%
4 Years	60%
5 Years	80%
6 Years	100%

u. ☐

1 Year	20%
2 Years	40%
3 Years	60%
4 Years	80%
5 Years	100%

w. ☐

1 Year	25%
2 Years	50%
3 Years	75%
4 Years	100%

335

IF THIS IS A RESTATED PLAN and the vesting schedule has been amended, enter pre-amended schedule below:

H6   s. ☐   Years of Service   Percentage   Years of Service   Percentage

_____   _____   _____   _____
_____   _____   _____   _____
_____   _____   _____   _____
_____   _____   _____   _____
_____   _____   _____   _____

    t. ☐   Vesting schedule has not been amended.

H9   **FORFEITURE OF BENEFITS FOR CERTAIN CAUSES**
    a. ☐   Yes   Participant shall forfeit accrued benefit if terminated for cause in accordance with a modified 4.40 vesting schedule.
    b. ☐   No

H12   **LIMITATION OF BENEFITS (Code Section 415) the dollar limitation applicable for the calendar year in which the Plan Year ends is**
    a. ☐ $_____ ($90,000 for all TEFRA Plans. Language automatically reduces maximum benefit for retirement ages under 62.)

    AND

    b. ☐   shall automatically be adjusted annually for cost of living increases, when permitted by law.
    c. ☐   shall **not** be adjusted annually for cost of living increases. (The dollar limit in a. above shall remain unchanged.)

H13   **If the sum of the defined benefit fraction and the defined contribution fraction exceeds 1.0, the numerator of the:**
    a. ☐   defined contribution plan fraction shall be adjusted.
    b. ☐   defined benefit plan fraction shall be adjusted.

F2   **IS THE PLAN INTEGRATED WITH SOCIAL SECURITY?**   k. ☐ Yes   l. ☐ No

J1   **INVESTMENT POWERS AND DUTIES OF TRUSTEE...If bank trusteed, is the insertion of the bank's name and/or the common trust fund or funds to be used for investment required?**
    a. ☐   Yes, Type & Attach exact language   b. ☐ No

J4   **OTHER POWERS OF TRUSTEES...is this trust governed by Georgia Law?**   a. ☐ Yes   b. ☐ No

J5   **PENSION BENEFIT GUARANTEE CORPORATION COVERAGE** (only P.A.'s and P.C.'s with **less** than 26 participants are exempt from P.B.G.C. coverage.)
    Will the plan be covered by the P.B.G.C.?   c. ☐ Yes   d. ☐ No

    LOANS TO PARTICIPANTS
J7   Trustee directed loans may be made as an investment of the Trust Fund (maximum flexibility).   a. ☐ Yes   b. ☐ No

J6   Loans **for financial necessity or hardship only** may be granted. (Generally applicable only to rank & file Employees.)
    a. ☐   Yes   b. ☐ No

Should the execution page provide for...
@M1   a. ☐ Yes   b. ☐ No   Witnesses as to the employer's signature?
@M2   a. ☐ Yes   b. ☐ No   Attest line for Employer?
@M3   a. ☐ Yes   b. ☐ No   Attest line for Corporate (Bank) Trustee?

Plan is to be submitted to _____ **IRS office for approval.**
                                        (City)

L1   a. **Name of Attorney** _____   Telephone g. (_____) _____
    b. Name of Firm _____
    c. Address _____
    d. _____   e. _____   f. _____
            (City)   (State)   (Zip)

All items must be complete and should be verified. If a question is N/A enter either "None" or N/A. Otherwise all questions should be answered; any unanswered questions may result in errors in the Plan produced by using the information from this worksheet.

I understand that in preparing the document requested, Corbel & Co. is utilizing information shown on this checklist to produce legal documents using a Format which has been designed by Corbel & Co. with advice and assistance of its attorneys and programmed by Corbel & Co. on their Generation of Legal Documents (GOLD)^TM system. Corbel & Co. has made NO REPRESENTATION OR WARRANTY OF ANY KIND, expressed or implied, including no warranties of MERCHANTABILITY OR FITNESS FOR A PARTICULAR PURPOSE, nor is any opinion, expressed or implied, rendered by their attorneys as to the legal effect, sufficiency or tax qualification of any document utilizing Corbel & Co.'s Format. If a check is not enclosed, the undersigned agrees to pay Corbel & Co. within ten days after receipt of such documents at the prices in effect when this order is received by Corbel & Co. I hereby RELEASE Corbel & Co. and its attorneys from any and all liability attributable to any legal or other defect in the requested document.

                         Signed _____

SAMPLE COMPANY, INC.
DEFINED-BENEFIT PLAN AND TRUST
SUMMARY PLAN DESCRIPTION

TABLE OF CONTENTS

IV
BENEFITS

V
ONE-YEAR BREAK IN SERVICE

VI
NONTRANSFERABLE INTEREST

VII
CLAIMS BY PARTICIPANTS OR BENEFICIARIES

VIII
STATEMENT OF ERISA RIGHTS

SAMPLE COMPANY, INC.
DEFINED-BENEFIT PLAN AND TRUST

SUMMARY PLAN DESCRIPTION

I

TYPE OF PLAN

(1) EFFECTIVE DATE OF PLAN

Sample Company, Inc. (hereinafter referred to as the "Company"), has adopted, effective January 1, 1984, a Pension Plan for the exclusive benefit of the Eligible Employees and their Beneficiaries. The purpose of the Plan is to reward Eligible Employees for long and loyal service by providing them with Retirement Benefits. It may also provide some additional benefits in the event of death, disability, or other termination of employment. The Plan is subject to the provisions of the Employee Retirement Income Security Act of 1974 (ERISA).

Upon retirement, an Eligible Employee will be entitled to receive a monthly pension. Each year between now and his retirement, the Company will contribute to a trust fund an amount necessary to fund his benefit and the benefits of all other Eligible Employees. Since there are no employee contributions required, the Plan will cost employees nothing; the entire cost of the Plan is paid by the Company.

This announcement is a brief description of the Plan and Trust Agreement (the "Plan"). It is not meant to interpret, extend, or change the Plan in any way. The provisions of the Plan can only be determined accurately by consulting the Plan itself. A copy of the Plan is on file at the Company office and may be read by any employee at any reasonable time. In the event of any discrepancy between this announcement and the actual provisions of the Plan, the Plan shall govern.

II
TYPE OF ADMINISTRATION

(1) USE OF TRUST

The Plan is administered under a written Plan and Trust Agreement entered into between the Trustee(s) and the Company.

(2) THE TRUSTEES

The Trustee(s) are responsible for the investment of the Plan assets. They may appoint such persons or companies as they deem necessary to carry out their responsibilities. The name(s) and address of the Plan's Trustee(s) are the following:

James Sample
1234 West Forsythe
Chicago, Illinois 60601

The Plan number assigned by the Sponsor is 001.

(3) PLAN YEAR

January 1 is the first day of the twelve (12) month Plan Year, December 31 is the last day, and December 31 is the Anniversary Date. Plan records are maintained on this basis.
The first Anniversary Date of the Plan is December 31, 1984.

(4)   PLAN ADMINISTRATOR

The Plan Administrator is responsible for the administration of the Plan.

The name, address and business telephone number of the Plan Administrator is

> Sample Company, Inc.
> 1234 West Forsythe
> Chicago, Illinois 60601
> (312) 555-9876

The Employer Identification Number is 59-1234567.

(5)   SERVICE OF PROCESS

The Plan's Agent for Service of Legal Process is

> Trustee
> 1234 West Forsythe
> Chicago, Illinois 60601

Legal process can also be made upon the Plan Trustee or Plan Administrator.

III
PARTICIPATION

(1)   SPECIFIC REQUIREMENTS FOR PARTICIPATION

If you are an employee of the Company, you will be eligible to participate in the Plan under the following conditions:

An employee becomes eligible to participate when he has completed one (1) Year(s) of Service and has reached his 25th birthday.

Employees employed within 5 years of their Normal Retirement Date will be excluded from the Plan.

An Owner-Employee and a Self-Employed Individual shall be eligible to participate as employees in the Plan. "Owner-Employee" means a sole proprietor or partner who owns more than 10% of either the capital interest or the profits interest in the Company and who receives income for personal services from the Company. "Self-Employed Individual" means, with respect to an unincorporated business, those individuals who have earned income as defined in the Plan.

(2) EFFECTIVE DATE OF PARTICIPATION

If you meet the above eligibility requirements, you will become a Participant in the Plan as of the first day of the Plan Year in which you met the requirements.

IV
BENEFITS

(1) RETIREMENT BENEFIT

At Normal Retirement, as an Eligible Employee you will receive (subject to the limitations imposed by the Internal Revenue Code) a monthly benefit called a Normal Retirement Benefit equal to 24% of your Average Monthly Compensation, as defined below, in excess of the amount shown below for the calendar year in which your 65th birthday occurs, computed to the nearest dollar.

Calendar Year of 65th Birthday	Monthly Covered Compensation
1983	$1,000
1984	1,050
1985	1,150
1986	1,200
1987	1,250
1988	1,350
1989	1,400
1990	1,450
1991	1,500
1992	1,550
1993	1,550
1994	1,600
1995	1,700
1996	1,750

Calendar Year of 65th Birthday	Monthly Covered Compensation
1997	1,850
1998	1,900
1999	2,000
2000	2,050
2001	2,150
2002	2,200
2003	2,250
2004	2,350
2005	2,400
2006	2,450
2007	2,550
2008	2,600
2009	2,650
2010	2,700
2011	2,750
2012	2,800
2013	2,850
2014	2,900
2015	2,950
2016	2,950
2017	2,950
2018 or later	2,975

Such monthly retirement benefit shall be reduced by one-nineteenth for each Year of Service that your Years of Service are less than 19.

"Average Monthly Compensation" means your monthly Covered Compensation averaged over the five consecutive total Years of Service which produce the highest monthly average from your date of employment to your date of termination. If you have less than 60 Months of Service from your date of employment to your date of termination, your Average Monthly Compensation will be based on your monthly Covered Compensation during your Months of Service from your date of employment to your date of termination.

Covered Compensation shall not be recognized subsequent to your Normal Retirement Date.

"Month of Service" means any calendar month during which you completed an Hour of Service.

"Covered Compensation" means total wages paid or accrued during a Plan Year excluding bonuses. For Self-Employed Individuals, Covered Compensation means that individual's earned income as defined in the Plan.

Your benefit is normally payable in the form of a 120 months certain and life annuity, that is, you will receive a monthly payment for as long as you live. Should you die before you have received your monthly benefit for 120 months, benefit payments will be made to your beneficiary for the re-mainder of that certain period.

However, upon the attainment of an age that is 10 years prior to your Normal Retirement Age, and if you are married on the date your annuity commences, you will automatically receive a 50% joint and survivor annuity in lieu of the above, which is the actuarial equivalent of your monthly retire-ment benefit. This means that should you die and be survived by a spouse, your spouse will receive a monthly annuity for the remainder of his or her life equal to 50% of the monthly pension you were receiving at the time of your death. You may elect a 75% or 100% joint and survivor annuity, which is the actuarial equivalent of your monthly retirement benefit, in lieu of the standard 50% joint and survivor annuity. It should be noted that a joint and survivor annuity may provide a lower monthly benefit than other forms of payment. You should find out the differences before making such election.

However, if you are married on the date your annuity commences, you will automatically receive a 50% joint and survivor annuity in lieu of the above, which is the actuarial equivalent of your monthly retirement benefit. This means that should you die and be survived by a spouse, your spouse will receive a monthly annuity for the remainder of his or her life equal to 50% of the monthly pension you were receiving at the time of your death. You may elect a 75% or 100% joint and survivor annuity, which is the actuar-ial equivalent of your monthly retirement benefit, in lieu of the standard 50% joint and survivor annuity. It should be noted that a joint and survivor annu-ity may provide a lower monthly benefit than other forms of payment. You should find out the differences before making such election.

You may also elect not to take a joint and survivor annuity at all, in which case you will automatically receive the life annuity described above. If you desire some other form of payment such as a single lump sum or other form of annuity, the Administrator will, in his sole discretion, determine the alternative form of payment. Whichever form of payment you elect to re-ceive and/or are given at the direction of the Administrator, its "value" to you will be the same value of each other form of payment.

All benefits payable to you under the Plan are in addition to any bene-fits to which you may be entitled under Social Security.

(2) *BENEFITS INSURED BY PBGC*

Benefits under this plan are insured by the Pension Benefit Guaranty Cor-poration (PBGC) if the Plan terminates. Generally, the PBGC guarantees most vested normal age retirement benefits, early retirement benefits, and certain disability and survivor's pensions. However, PBGC does not guarantee all types of benefits under covered plans, and the amount of benefit protection is subject to certain limitations.

The PBGC guarantees vested benefits at the level in effect on the date of plan termination. However, if a plan has been in effect less than five years before it terminates, or if benefits have been increased within the five years before plan termination, the whole amount of the plan's vested benefits or the benefit increase may not be guaranteed. In addition, there is a ceiling on the amount of monthly benefit that PBGC guarantees, which is adjusted periodically.

For more information on the PBGC insurance protection and its limitations, ask your Plan Administrator or the PBGC. Inquiries to the PBGC should be addressed to the Office of Communications, PBGC, 2020 K Street, N.W., Washington, D.C., 20006. The PBGC Office of Communications may also be contacted by calling (202) 254-4817.

(3) RETIREMENT DATE

Your Normal Retirement Date is the first day of the month nearest your 65th birthday.

However, you shall become 100% Vested in your account upon attaining your 65th birthday.

(4) ACCRUED BENEFIT

You may also receive benefits for reasons other than Normal Retirement. When you have completed two Years of Service, you accrue or earn for each year you are in the Plan a portion of the benefit you are projected to receive at Normal Retirement. This portion is called your Accrued Benefit.

(5) DEATH BENEFIT

The Plan provides preretirement death benefits. Also, the Administrator may instruct the Trustee to purchase life insurance policies on your life with a face amount to be determined by the Administrator using a uniform, nondiscriminatory policy consistently applied (assuming you are insurable at standard rates—there are special procedures in other cases).

Insurance policies shall be purchased only for parties who have participated in the Plan for three (3) years.

Additional insurance policies will not be purchased after you attain the age of 57.

Insurance policies will not be purchased or surrendered until the change in coverage is at least $10,000.

If you die before retirement, your beneficiary will receive a benefit equal to the Value of the Total Prior Contributions applicable for you as of the Anniversary Date following your death plus any insurance proceeds in effect at the time of your death.

If less than ⅔ of the Plan's normal cost under the Typical Level Premium Cost Method (defined below) has been used to purchase whole life insurance (or less than ⅓ if term insurance is purchased), then the total death benefit payable to your beneficiary shall be equal to the insurance in effect at the time of your death minus the cash value of such policies, plus the reserve calculated under the Typical Level Premium Cost Method.

However, if more than ⅔ of the normal cost is used to purchase whole life insurance (or more than ⅓ if term insurance is purchased), then the total death benefit payable to your beneficiary shall be equal to the insurance that would have been in effect at the time of your death if the premium payments satisfied the above requirement, minus the cash value, plus the reserve calculated under the Typical Level Premium Cost Method.

The Typical Level Premium Cost Method is, in layman's terms, the calculation made by the Plan's independent actuary to determine the amount needed each year to provide your Normal Retirement Benefit, beginning with your age at date of hire to your Normal Retirement Date.

If you die before any insurance policy to which you were entitled becomes effective, the insurance proceeds your beneficiary will receive from such coverage will be limited to the standard rated premium that was or should have been used to purchase the policy.

(6) DISABILITY BENEFIT

If you become totally and permanently disabled in accordance with the terms of the Plan while you are a Participant in the Plan and your condition continues for a period of six (6) months, you will receive a Disability Benefit equal to the value of your Accrued Benefit.

(7) ANNUAL STATEMENT

Each year you will be given a statement showing your benefits under the plan.

(8) *LOSS OF BENEFITS AND VESTING*

Your Vested Interest will be determined in accordance with the following schedule:

VESTING SCHEDULE

Years of Service	Percentage
4	40%
5	45%
6	50%
7	60%
8	70%
9	80%
10	90%
11	100%

This Plan is designed to encourage you to stay with the Company until retirement. Payment of the vested interest in your Accrued Benefit to which you have become entitled will normally be made at the time you would have received a benefit had you remained in the employ of the Company (e.g., in the event of retirement, death, or disability).

The Administrator in his sole discretion (based on uniform principles consistently applied) may direct the Trustees, on or after the Anniversary Date following a One-Year Break in Service, to distribute your Vested Interest to you prior to the date it would normally be distributed; provided, however, that your written consent is given for amounts in excess of $1,750.

Vested Benefits of less than $1,750 will be automatically distributed on or after the Anniversary Date following a One-Year Break in Service.

If the value of your vested interest in your Accrued Benefit equals or exceeds the cash surrender value of any life insurance contracts issued on your life under the Plan, you may, at your request, be assigned those contracts as part of your distribution. If the value of your vested interest in your Accrued Benefit is less than the cash surrender values, you may request the Administrator to permit you to make other efforts to secure distribution of the contracts.

"Year of Service": You will be credited with a Year of Service for each Plan Year during which you work at least 1000 hours for the Company.

"Hour of Service": You will be credited with an Hour of Service for each hour that you are directly or indirectly compensated by the Company for performing duties during a Plan Year.

(9) *TOPHEAVY RULES*

Under a complicated set of rules and mathematical calculations set out in the Plan, as required by the Internal Revenue Code, the Plan may be a Topheavy Plan. Simply stated, a Topheavy Plan is one where more than 60% of the contributions or benefits have been allocated to "Key Employees." "Key Employees" are generally owners, officers, shareholders, or highly compensated individuals. The Plan Administrator each year is responsible for determining whether the Plan is a Topheavy Plan.

If the Plan becomes Topheavy in any year, you may be entitled to certain minimum benefits, and special rules will apply. Among these Topheavy rules are the following:

(a) The Company may be required to provide you with a minimum benefit equal to 2% of your average monthly compensation multiplied by your Years of Service with the Company, limited, however, to a maximum benefit equal to 20% of your average monthly compensation.

(b) In lieu of the vesting schedule set out above, your nonforfeitable right to benefits or contributions derived from Company contributions made to the Plan shall be determined according to the following schedule:

VESTING SCHEDULE

Years of Service	Percentage
2	20%
3	40%
4	60%
5	80%
6	100%

(c) In determining benefits or contributions you are entitled to under the Plan, Covered Compensation shall be limited to $200,000.

(d) If you are a Participant in more than one Plan maintained by the Company, you may not be entitled to minimum benefits under both Plans.

The Plan Administrator will advise you of your rights under the Topheavy Plan rules if the Plan becomes Topheavy.

V
ONE-YEAR BREAK IN SERVICE

(1) *EXPLANATION OF ONE-YEAR BREAK IN SERVICE*

If you work 500 hours or less in any Plan Year, you will incur a "One-Year Break in Service," which may adversely affect your eligibility for benefits under the Plan.

A One-Year Break in Service is a Plan Year during which you have not completed more than 500 Hours of Service with the Company for reasons other than absences described in the following paragraphs. A One-Year Break in Service does not occur for the year in which you enter the Plan or leave the Plan for reasons of death, Total and Permanent Disability, or retirement.

Your status as an employee will not be interrupted or severed because you are transferred from one participating emloyer to another participating employer (if any), or if you are absent from employment due to an authorized leave of absence occasioned by illness, military service, or any other reason established by the Company in a nondiscriminatory manner. Such an authorized leave of absence will not be considered a One-Year Break in Service.

If you are reemployed after a One-Year Break in Service and were vested in any portion of the Company's contributions, you will receive credit for your Years of Service prior to the One-Year Break in Service when you have completed one Year of Service after your reemployment. If you are a nonvested Participant at the time of termination of employment, you will lose credit for your Years of Service prior to a One-Year Break in Service only when your period of absence equals or exceeds your prebreak Years of Service.

VI
NONTRANSFERABLE INTEREST

(1) *ALIENATION OF ACCOUNTS*

Your interests in your accounts, including your "Vested" interests, may not be alienated, that is sold, used as collateral for a loan, given away, or otherwise transferred. Also, your creditors may not attach, garnish, or otherwise interfere with your accounts. However, if at the time you or your Beneficiary are entitled to receive a benefit, and you are indebted to the Plan, the

Administrator may direct the Trustee(s) to first satisfy that debt before paying the benefit over to you or your Beneficiary.

(2) *LOANS*

Upon written application, the Trustee may, based on a uniform nondiscriminatory basis, make a loan to you based solely on the loan's merit. That is, if approved, you must have adequate security. The loan must bear a reasonable rate of interest and have a definite repayment schedule over a reasonable period of time.

Loans that provide for a repayment period extending beyond your Normal Retirement Date shall not be granted to you or your Beneficiary.

Any loans made to you shall be limited to the lesser of

(i) $50,000, or

(ii) one-half (½) of the present value of your vested interest in your Accrued Benefit (but not less than $10,000).

Loans must be repaid over a period not to exceed five (5) years. However, loans used to acquire, construct, reconstruct, or substantially rehabilitate your principal residence or the residence of a member of your family may be repaid over a reasonable period of time that may exceed five (5) years.

If payments under a loan with a repayment period of five (5) years are made so that an amount remains payable at the end of five (5) years, such amount remaining payable shall be treated as a distribution from the Plan and will be taxable income to you.

Loans shall not be made to any Owner-Employee.

(3) *VOLUNTARY CONTRIBUTIONS*

Each Participant in the Plan may voluntarily contribute to the Trust Fund up to 10% of his total annual Covered Compensation for each year he is in the Plan. These contributions will be held in a separate Voluntary Contribution Account.

This contribution is not mandatory or tax deductible. Any investment income and/or gains earned on the monies in your account will not be currently taxable to you, but you will be taxed on the investment interest and gains when you withdraw them from your account.

The money you contribute will be invested by the Trustee in a federally insured savings account, certificate of deposit in a bank or savings and loan association, money market certificate, short-term debt security (bond, note, etc.), or as part of the general trust fund, in the discretion of the Plan Administrator.

You will always be fully Vested in your Voluntary Contribution Account, including any investment gains or minus any investment losses, and your interest cannot be Forfeited for any reason.

You may withdraw your voluntary contributions from your Voluntary Contribution Account, including, with the Administrator's consent, any gain thereon; in such event however, you will be barred from making any additional voluntary contributions for one (1) year.

When you retire or otherwise become eligible for Plan benefits, the value of your Voluntary Contribution Account will be used to provide additional benefits for you or your beneficiaries.

VII
CLAIMS BY PARTICIPANTS OR BENEFICIARIES

(1) *CLAIMS PROCEDURE*

In anticipation of retirement or at termination of employment for any other reason, you or your Beneficiary should make a request for any Plan benefits to which you are entitled. The request may be made orally or in written form and should be made to the Administrator who will act on such request.

Such request shall be considered a claim and shall be subject to a full and fair review. If a claim is wholly or partially denied, the claim may be appealed in accordance with the claims review procedure below.

(2) *CLAIMS REVIEW PROCEDURES*

Claims for benefits under the Plan may be filed with the Administrator on forms supplied by the Employer. Written notice of the disposition of a claim shall be furnished the claimant within 90 days after the application is filed. In the event the claim is denied, the reasons or the provisions of the Plan shall be cited and, where appropriate, an explanation as to how the claimant can perfect the Claim will be provided.

Any Employee, Former Employee, or Beneficiary of either who has been denied a benefit shall be entitled, upon request to the Administrator, to appeal the denial of his claim. If the claimant wishes further consideration of his position, he may obtain a form from the Administrator on which to request a hearing. Such form, together with a written statement of the claimant's position, shall be filed with the Administrator no later than 60 days after receipt of the written notification. The Administrator shall schedule an opportunity for a full and fair hearing of the issue and decide on the appeal within 60 days after receipt of the written notification (unless there has been an extension of 60 days due to special circumstances, provided the delay and the special circumstances occasioning it are communicated to the claimant within the 60-day period). The Administrator's decision shall be communicated in writing to the claimant and shall advise the claimant if he has any right to appeal the decision.

(3) DESIGNATION OF BENEFICIARIES

You may designate the person or persons who are to receive benefits under the Plan in the event of your death. This designation shall be made on a form available from, and to be filed with, the Administrator. You may change your designation at any time.

(4) REQUEST FOR QUALIFICATION

A Determination Letter from the Internal Revenue Service has been or will be requested with respect to Plan qualification.

VIII
STATEMENT OF ERISA RIGHTS

(1) EXPLANATION

As a Participant in this Plan you are entitled to certain rights and protections under the Employee Retirement Income Security Act of 1974. ERISA provides that all Plan Participants shall be entitled to

a) examine, without charge, at the Plan Administrator's office and at other specified locations such as worksites and union halls, all Plan documents, including insurance contracts, collective bargaining agreements, and copies of all documents filed by the Plan with the U.S. Department of Labor, such as detailed annual reports and Plan descriptions;

b) obtain copies of all Plan documents and other Plan information upon written request to the Plan Administrator; the Plan Administrator may make a reasonable charge for the copies;

c) receive a summary of the Plan's annual financial report; the Plan Administrator is required by law to furnish each Participant with a copy of this summary annual report.

d) obtain a statement telling them whether they have a right to receive a pension at normal retirement age (which is specified in the Summary Plan Description) and if so, what their benefits would be at normal retirement age if they stopped working under the Plan now. If they do not have a right to a pension, the statement will tell them how many more years they have to work to get a right to a pension. This statement must be requested in writing and is not required to be given more than once a year. The Plan must provide the statement free of charge.

In addition to creating rights for Plan Participants, ERISA imposes duties upon the people who are responsible for the operation of the employee benefit plan. The people who operate your Plan, called "fiduciaries" of the Plan, have a duty to do so prudently and in the interest of you and other Plan Participants and Beneficiaries. No one, including your employer, your union, or any other person, may fire you or otherwise discriminate against you in any way to prevent you from obtaining a pension benefit or exercising your rights under ERISA. If your claim for a pension benefit is denied in whole or in part, you must receive a written explanation of the reason for the denial. You have the right to have the Plan review and reconsider your claim. Under ERISA, there are steps you can take to enforce the above rights. For instance, if you request materials from the Plan and do not receive them within 30 days, you may file suit in a federal court. In such a case, the court may require the Plan Administrator to provide the materials and pay you up to $100 a day until you receive the materials, unless the materials were not sent because of reasons beyond the control of the Administrator. If you have a claim for benefits which is denied or ignored, in whole or in part, you may file suit in a state or federal court. If it should happen that Plan fiduciaries misuse the Plan's money, or if you are discriminated against for asserting your rights, you may seek assistance from the U.S. Department of Labor, or you may file suit in a federal court. The court will decide who should pay court costs and legal fees. If you are successful the court may order the person you have sued to pay these costs and fees. If you lose, for example, if it finds your claim is frivolous, the court may order you to pay these costs and fees. If you have any questions about your Plan, you should contact the Plan Administrator. If you have any questions about this statement or about your rights under ERISA, you should contact the nearest Area Office of the U.S. Labor-Management Services Administration, Department of Labor.

SAMPLE COMPANY, INC.
DEFINED-BENEFIT PLAN AND TRUST

TABLE OF CONTENTS

ARTICLE I
DEFINITIONS

ARTICLE II
TOPHEAVY AND ADMINISTRATION

ARTICLE III
ELIGIBILITY

ARTICLE IV
CONTRIBUTION AND VALUATION

ARTICLE V
BENEFITS

ARTICLE VI
LIMITATION OF BENEFITS

ARTICLE VII
TRUSTEE

ARTICLE VIII
PLAN AMENDMENT

ARTICLE IX
PLAN TERMINATION

ARTICLE X
MERGER, CONSOLIDATION, OR TRANSFER OF ASSETS

ARTICLE XI
MISCELLANEOUS

ARTICLE XII
PARTICIPATING EMPLOYERS

SAMPLE COMPANY, INC.
DEFINED-BENEFIT PLAN AND TRUST

THIS AGREEMENT, hereby made and entered into this _____ _____ day of _____, 19____, by and between Sample Company, Inc. (herein referred to as the "Employer"), and James Sample (herein referred to as the "Trustee").

W I T N E S S E T H :

WHEREAS, the Employer desires to recognize the contribution made to its successful operation by its employees and to reward such contribution by means of a Pension Plan for those employees who shall qualify as Participants hereunder;

NOW, THEREFORE, effective January 1, 1984 (hereinafter called the "Effective Date"), the Employer hereby establishes a Pension Plan and creates this trust (which plan and trust are hereinafter called the "Plan") for the exclusive benefit of the Participants and their Beneficiaries, and the Trustee hereby accepts the Plan on the following terms:

ARTICLE I
DEFINITIONS

1.1 *Accrued Benefit* shall be the retirement benefit a Participant would receive at his Normal Retirement Date as provided in Section 5.1 of this Agreement, multiplied by a fraction not greater than one (1), the numerator of which is the Participant's total number of Plan Years of Service commencing with the Effective Date of this Agreement, and the denominator of which is the aggregate number of Plan Years of Service the Participant could have accumulated, commencing with the Effective Date of this Agreement, if he continued his employment until his Normal Retirement Date.

Notwithstanding the above, if an Employee resumes participation in the Plan following a One-Year Break in Service, he shall be credited with a Plan Year of Service for the period commencing on his reemployment date and ending at the beginning of the first day of the next Plan Year.

The value of a Participant's Accrued Benefit as of any Anniversary Date shall not be less than the value of his Accrued Benefit at any prior Anniversary Date.

The accrual of benefits provided for by this Section 1.1 shall not become effective until an Employee has completed, from his commencement date of employment, two (2) 12-month periods of employment, during which such Employee has completed at least 1000 Hours of Service in each 12-month period, which are not separated by a One-Year Break in Service. Upon completion of such service requirement, the accrual of benefits shall be retroactive to a Participant's date of participation in the Plan.

A Non-Key Employee's Accrued Benefit for any Topheavy Plan Year shall also be determined subject to the minimum accruals pursuant to Section 5.2.

1.2   *Act* shall mean the Employee Retirement Income Security Act of 1974, as it may be amended from time to time.

1.3   ***Actuarial Equivalent*** shall mean a form of benefit differing in time, period, or manner of payment from a specific benefit provided under the Plan, but having the same value when computed using preretirement, IAM '71, 8%, postretirement, IAM '71, 5%.

In the event this Section is amended, the Actuarial Equivalent of a Participant's Accrued Benefit on or after the date of change shall be determined as the greater of (1) the Actuarial Equivalent of the Accrued Benefit as of the date of change computed on the old basis, or (2) the Actuarial Equivalent of the total Accrued Benefit computed on the new basis.

1.4   ***Administrator*** shall mean the person or persons designated by the Employer pursuant to Section 2.4 to administer the Plan on behalf of the Employer.

1.5   ***Age*** shall mean age at nearest birthday.

1.6   ***Aggregate Account*** shall mean, with respect to each Participant, the value of all accounts maintained on behalf of a Participant, whether attributable to Employer or Employee contributions, used to determine Topheavy Plan status under the provisions of a defined-contribution plan included in any Aggregation Group (as defined in Article II).

1.7 ***Agreement*** or ***Plan*** shall mean this instrument including all amendments thereto.

1.8 ***Anniversary Date*** shall be December 31.

1.9 ***Average Monthly Compensation*** shall mean the monthly Compensation of a Participant averaged over the five consecutive total Years of Service which produce the highest monthly average. If a Participant has less than 60 Months of Service from his date of employment to his date of termination, his Average Monthly Compensation will be based on his monthly Compensation during his Months of Service from his date of employment to his date of termination. Compensation subsequent to termination of participation pursuant to Section 3.5 shall not be recognized.

Compensation shall not be recognized subsequent to the Participant's Normal Retirement date.

1.10 ***Beneficiary*** or ***Beneficiaries*** shall mean the person or persons designated as provided in Section 5.5 to receive the benefits which are payable under the Plan upon or after the death of a Participant.

1.11 ***One-Year Break in Service*** shall mean a Plan Year during which an Employee has not completed more than 500 Hours of Service with the Employer, for reasons other than absences referred to in Section 1.52, except for a Plan Year in which the Employee becomes a Participant or he retires, dies, or suffers Total and Permanent Disability.

1.12 ***Code*** shall mean the Internal Revenue Code of 1954, as amended.

1.13 ***Compensation***, with respect to any Participant, shall mean total compensation paid or accrued by the Employer for a Plan Year, excluding compensation paid for bonuses. Amounts contributed by the Employer under the within Plan and any fringe benefits shall not be considered as Compensation.

Compensation for any Self-Employed Individual shall be equal to his Earned Income.

For any Topheavy Plan Year, Compensation in excess of $200,000 (or such other amount as the Secretary of the Treasury may designate) shall be disregarded.

1.14 ***Contract*** or ***Policy*** shall mean a life insurance policy or annuity contract (group or individual) issued by the insurer as elected.

All Contracts or Policies issued pursuant to Section 5.5 shall be acquired on a uniform and nondiscriminatory basis with respect to the face amount of the death benefit stated in such Contract or Policy.

1.15 ***Determination Date*** shall mean (a) the last day of the preceding Plan Year, or (b) in the case of the first Plan Year, the last day of such Plan Year.

1.16 ***Early Retirement Date*** This Plan does not provide for a retirement date prior to Normal Retirement Date.

1.17 *Earned Income* shall mean, with respect to a Self-Employed Individual, the net earnings from self-employment as defined in Code Section 401(c) (2) (reduced by the Employer's deductible contribution made on behalf of such individual for each year).

1.18 *Eligible Employee* shall mean any Employee who has satisfied the provisions of Section 3.1.

1.19 *Employee* shall mean any person who is employed by the Employer, but shall exclude any person who is employed as an independent contractor.

1.20 *Employer* shall mean Sample Company, Inc., a corporation, with principal offices in the State of Chicago, any Participating Employer (as defined in Section 12.1) which shall adopt this Plan, any successor which shall maintain this Plan, and any predecessor which has maintained this Plan.

1.21 *Fiduciary* shall mean any person who (a) exercises any discretionary authority or discretionary control respecting management of the Plan or exercises any authority or control respecting management or disposition of its assets, (b) renders investment advice for a fee or other compensation, direct or indirect, with respect to any monies or other property of the Plan or has any authority or responsibility to do so, or (c) has any discretionary authority or discretionary responsibility in the administration of the Plan, including, but not limited to, the Trustee, the Employer and its representative body, and the Administrator.

1.22 *Fiscal Year* shall mean the Employer's accounting year of 12 months commencing on January 1 of each year and ending the following December 31.

1.23 *Former Participant* shall mean a person who has been a Participant, but who has ceased to be a Participant for any reason.

1.24 *Hour of Service* shall mean (1) each hour for which an Employee is directly or indirectly compensated or entitled to compensation by the Employer for the performance of duties during the applicable computation period; (2) each hour for which an Employee is directly or indirectly compensated or entitled to compensation by the Employer (irrespective of whether the employment relationship has terminated) for reasons other than performance of duties (such as vacation, holidays, sickness, disability, layoff, military duty or leave of absence) during the applicable computation period; and (3) each hour for back pay awarded or agreed to by the Employer without regard to mitigation of damages.

Notwithstanding (2) above, (i) no more than 501 Hours of Service are required to be credited to an Employee on account of any single continuous period during which the Employee performs no duties (whether or not such period occurs in a single computation period); (ii) an hour for which an Employee is directly or indirectly paid, or entitled to payment, on account of a period during which no duties are performed, is not required to be credited to the Employee if such payment is made or due under a plan maintained solely for the purpose of complying with applicable worker's compensation, or unemployment compensation, or disability insurance laws; and (iii) Hours of Service are not required to be credited for a payment which solely reimburses an Employee for medical or medically related expenses incurred by the Employee.

For purposes of this Section, a payment shall be deemed to be made by, or due from, the Employer regardless of whether such payment is made by, or due from, the Employer directly or indirectly through, among others, a trust, fund, or insurer, to which the Employer contributes or pays premiums and regardless of whether contributions made or due to the trust fund, insurer, or other entity are for the benefit of particular Employees or are on behalf of a group of Employees in the aggregate.

An Hour of Service must be counted for the purpose of determining a Year of Service, a year of participation for purposes of accrued benefits, a One-Year Break in Service, and employment commencement date (or reemployment commencement date). The provisions of Department of Labor regulations 2530.200b-2(b) and (c) are incorporated herein by reference.

1.25   *Investment Manager* shall mean any person, firm, or corporation who is a registered investment adviser under the Investment Advisers Act of 1940, a bank, or an insurance company, and (a) who has the power to manage, acquire, or dispose of Plan assets, and (b) who acknowledges in writing his fiduciary responsibility to the Plan.

1.26   *Key Employee* shall mean any Employee or former employee (and his Beneficiaries) who, at any time during the Plan Year or any of the preceding four (4) Plan Years, is

(a)   An officer of the Employer (as that term is defined within the meaning of the regulations under Code Section 416). Only those Employers which are incorporated shall be considered as having officers.

(b)   One of the ten Employees owning (or considered as owning within the meaning of Code Section 318) the largest interests in all employers required to be aggregated under Code Sections 414(b), (c), and (m). However, an Employee will not be considered a top ten owner for a Plan Year if the Employee earns less than $30,000 (or such other amount adjusted in accordance with Code Section 415(c) (1) (A) as in effect for the calendar year in which the Determination Date falls).

(c)   A "five percent owner" of the Employer. "Five percent owner" means any person who owns (or is considered as owning within the meaning of Code Section 318) more than five percent (5%) of the outstanding stock of the Employer or stock possessing more than five percent (5%) of the total combined voting power of all stock of the Employer or, in the case of an unincorporated business, any person who owns more than 5 percent (5%) of the capital or profits interest in the Employer. In determining percentage ownership hereunder, employers that would otherwise be aggregated under Code Sections 414(b), (c), and (m) shall be treated as separate employers.

(d) A "one percent owner" of the Employer, having an annual Compensation from the Employer of more than $150,000. "One percent owner" means any person who owns (or is considered as owning within the meaning of Code Section 318) more than one percent (1%) of the outstanding stock of the Employer or stock possessing more than one percent (1%) of the total combined voting power of all stock of the Employer or, in the case of an unincorporated business, any person who owns more than 1 percent (1%) of the capital or profits interest in the Employer. In determining percentage ownership hereunder, employers that would otherwise be aggregated under Code Sections 414(b), (c), and (m) shall be treated as separate employers. However, in determining whether an individual has Compensation of more than $150,000, Compensation from each employer required to be aggregated under Code Sections 414(b), (c), and (m) shall be taken into account.

1.27 **Late Retirement Date** shall mean the Anniversary Date coinciding with or next following a Participant's actual Retirement Date after having reached his Normal Retirement Date.

1.28 **Month of Service** shall mean a calendar month during any part of which an Employee completed an Hour of Service. Except that, however, a Participant shall be credited with a Month of Service for any period in which he has not incurred a One-Year Break in Service.

1.29 **Non-Key Employee** shall mean any Employee who is not a Key Employee.

1.30 **Normal Retirement Date** shall be the first day of the month nearest the Participant's Normal Retirement Age (65th birthday). However, a Participant shall become fully Vested in his Normal Retirement Benefit upon attaining his Normal Retirement Age.

1.31 **Owner-Employee** shall mean a sole proprietor who owns the entire interest in the Employer or a partner who owns more than 10% of either the capital interest or the profits interest in the Employer, and who receives income for personal services from the Employer.

1.32 **Participant** shall mean any Eligible Employee who elects to participate in the Plan as provided in Sections 3.2 and 3.3 and has not for any reason become ineligible to participate further in the Plan.

1.33 **Plan Year** shall mean the Plan's accounting year of twelve (12) months commencing on January 1 of each year and ending the following December 31 (also applicable prior to the Effective Date of this Plan).

1.34 **Plan Year of Service** shall mean a Plan Year during which an Employee is a Participant and completes 1000 Hours of Service.

1.35 ***Present Value of Accrued Benefit*** shall mean the value of a Participant's Accrued Benefit at date of valuation determined pursuant to Section 1.3. Except, however, that the Present Value of Accrued Benefit for the determination of Topheavy Plan status shall be made exclusively pursuant to the provisions of Section 2.2.

1.36 ***Retired Participant*** shall mean a person who has been a Participant, but who has become entitled to retirement benefits under the Plan.

1.37 ***Retirement Date*** shall mean the date as of which a Participant retires for reasons other than Total and Permanent Disability, whether such retirement occurs on a Participant's Normal Retirement Date or on a Late Retirement Date (see Section 5.1).

1.38 ***Self-Employed Individual*** shall mean, with respect to an unincorporated business, an individual described in Code Section 401(c) (1). A Self-Employed Individual shall be treated as an Employee.

1.39 ***Super Topheavy Plan*** shall mean, for Plan Years commencing after December 31, 1983, that, as of the Determination Date, (1) the Present Value of Accrued Benefits of Key Employees or (2) the sum of the Aggregate Accounts of Key Employees under this Plan and any plan of an Aggregation Group, exceeds ninety percent (90%) of the Present Value of Accrued Benefits or the Aggregate Accounts of all Participants under this Plan and any plan of an Aggregation Group.

1.40 ***Survivor Annuity*** shall mean an annuity for the life of the Participant's spouse, the payments under which must not be less than the payments which would have been made to the spouse under the qualified joint and survivor annuity (see Reg. 1.401(a)–11(b) (3)).

1.41 ***Taxable Wage Base*** shall mean, with respect to any year, the maximum amount of earnings which may be considered wages for such year under Section 3121(a) (1) of the Code.

1.42 ***Terminated Participant*** shall mean a person who has been a Participant, but whose employment has been terminated other than by death, Total and Permanent Disability, or retirement.

1.43 ***The Value of the Total Prior Contributions*** shall mean the accumulated value of a level annual deposit using the actuarial assumptions stated in Section 1.3. Such level annual deposit shall be computed from date of entry into the Plan to Normal Retirement Date, recalculated each year based on the monthly pension computed using Average Monthly Compensation, and accumulated based on the Participant's Plan Years of Service. In no event shall the accumulated value be less than the accumulated value as of the prior Anniversary Date.

1.44 ***Topheavy Plan*** shall mean, for Plan Years commencing after December 31, 1983, that, as of the Determination Date, (1) the Present Value of Accrued Benefits of Key Employees, or (2) the sum of the Aggregate Accounts of Key Employees under this Plan and any plan of an Aggregation Group, exceeds sixty percent (60%) of the Present Value of Accrued Benefits or the Aggregate Accounts of all Participants under this Plan and any plan of an Aggregation Group.

1.45 ***Topheavy Plan Year*** shall mean that, for a particular Plan Year commencing after December 31, 1983, the Plan is a Topheavy Plan.

1.46 ***Total and Permanent Disability*** shall mean a physical or mental condition of a Participant resulting from bodily injury, disease, or mental disorder which renders him incapable of continuing any gainful occupation, and which condition constitutes total disability under the federal Social Security Acts.

1.47 ***Trustee*** shall mean the person or persons named as trustee herein or in any separate trust forming a part of this Plan, and his, their, or its successors.

1.48 ***Trust Fund*** shall mean the assets of the Plan and Trust as the same shall exist from time to time.

1.49 ***Typical Level Premium Cost Method*** shall mean the calculation of level annual normal costs for benefits from the attained age of the Participant to his Normal Retirement Date, based upon the actuarial assumptions stated in Section 1.3. Changes in Compensation which affect normal cost will be taken into account in the year in which they occur.

1.50 ***Vested*** shall mean the portion of a Participant's Accrued Benefit that is nonforfeitable.

1.51 ***Voluntary Contribution Account*** shall mean the account established and maintained by the Administrator for each Participant with respect to the Participant's total interest in the Plan and Trust resulting from his nondeductible voluntary contributions made pursuant to this Agreement.

1.52 ***Year of Service*** shall mean the computation period of twelve (12) consecutive months, herein set forth, during which an Employee has at least 1000 Hours of Service.

For purposes of eligibility for participation, the initial computation period shall begin with the date on which the Employee first performs an Hour of Service. The participation computation period beginning after a One-Year Break in Service shall be measured from the date on which an Employee again performs an Hour of Service. The participation computation period shall shift to the current Plan Year (which includes the anniversary of the date on which the Employee first performed an Hour of Service) and be known as a "Plan Year of Service," after the initial period.

For vesting purposes a Year of Service shall be a Plan Year in which an Employee completes 1000 Hours of Service.

"Authorized leave of absence" means a temporary cessation from active employment with the Employer pursuant to an established nondiscriminatory policy, whether occasioned by illness, military service, or any other reason. An "authorized leave of absence" shall not cause a One-Year Break in Service.

Years of Service with any corporation, trade, or business which is a member of a controlled group of corporations or under common control (as defined by Section 1563(a) and Section 414(c) of the Code) or is a member of an affiliated service group (as defined by Section 414(m) of the Code) shall be recognized.

The Administrator may, in accordance with a uniform nondiscriminatory policy, elect to credit Hours of Service pursuant to this Agreement using one of the following methods:

(a)   Count actual Hours of Service for which an Employee is paid or entitled to payment.

(b)   Count 190 Hours of Service for each month in which an Employee is paid or entitled to payment for at least one Hour of Service.

(c)   Count 95 Hours of Service for each semimonthly period in which an Employee is paid or entitled to payment for at least one Hour of Service.

(d)   Count 45 Hours of Service for each week in which an Employee is paid or entitled to payment for at least one Hour of Service.

(e)   Count 10 Hours of Service for each day in which an Employee is paid or entitled to payment for at least one Hour of Service.

ARTICLE II
TOPHEAVY AND ADMINISTRATION

2.1   *TOPHEAVY PLAN REQUIREMENTS*

(a)   For any Topheavy Plan Year, the Plan shall provide the following:

(1)   special vesting requirements of Code Section 416(b) pursuant to Section 5.6 of the Plan;

(2)   special minimum benefit requirements of Code Section 416(c) pursuant to Section 5.2 of the Plan;

(3)   special Compensation requirements of Code Section 416(d) pursuant to Section 1.13 of the Plan.

2.2   *DETERMINATION OF TOPHEAVY STATUS*

(a)   This Plan shall be a Topheavy Plan for any Plan Year commencing after December 31, 1983, in which, as of the Determination Date, (1) the

Present Value of Accrued Benefits of Key Employees or (2) the sum of the Aggregate Accounts of Key Employees under this Plan and any plan of an Aggregation Group, exceeds sixty percent (60%) of the Present Value of Accrued Benefits or the Aggregate Accounts of all Participants under this Plan and any plan of an Aggregation Group.

If any Participant is a Non-Key Employee for any Plan Year, but such Participant was a Key Employee for any prior Plan Year, such Participant's Present Value of Accrued Benefit shall not be taken into account for purposes of determining whether this Plan is a Topheavy Plan (or whether any Aggregation Group which includes this Plan is a Topheavy Group).

(b) This Plan shall be a Super Topheavy Plan for any Plan Year commencing after December 31, 1983, in which, as of the Determination Date, (1) the Present Value of Accrued Benefits of Key Employees or (2) the sum of the Aggregate Accounts of Key Employees under this Plan and any plan of an Aggregation Group, exceeds ninety percent (90%) of the Present Value of Accrued Benefits or the Aggregate Accounts of all Participants under this Plan and any plan of an Aggregation Group.

(c) A Participant's Aggregate Account as of the Determination Date shall be determined under applicable provisions of the defined-contribution plan used in determining Topheavy Plan status.

(d) "Aggregation Group" means either a Required Aggregation Group or a Permissive Aggregation Group as hereinafter determined.

   (1) Required Aggregation Group: In determining a Required Aggregation Group hereunder, each plan of the Employer in which a Key Employee is a participant and each other plan of the Employer which enables any plan in which a Key Employee participates to meet the requirements of Code Sections 401(a) (4) or 410 will be required to be aggregated. Such group shall be known as a Required Aggregation Group.

   In the case of a Required Aggregation group, each plan in the group will be considered a Topheavy Plan if the Required Aggregation Group is a Topheavy Group. No plan in the Required Aggregation Group will be considered a Topheavy Plan if the Required Aggregation Group is not a Topheavy Group.

   (2) Permissive Aggregation Group: The Employer may also include any other plan not required to be included in the Required Aggregation Group, provided the resulting group, taken as a whole, would continue to satisfy the provisions of Code Sections 401(a) (4) or 410. Such group shall be known as a Permissive Aggregation Group.

In the case of a Permissive Aggregation Group, only a plan that is part of the Required Aggregation Group will be considered a Topheavy Plan if the Permissive Aggregation Group is a Topheavy Group. No plan in the Permissive Aggregation Group will be considered a Topheavy Plan if the Permissive Aggregation Group is not a Topheavy Group.

(3)   Only those plans of the Employer in which the Determination Dates fall within the same calendar year shall be aggregated in order to determine whether such plans are Topheavy Plans.

(e)   "Determination Date" means (1) the last day of the preceding Plan Year, or (2) in the case of the first Plan Year, the last day of such Plan Year.

(f)   Present Value of Accrued Benefit: In the case of a defined-benefit plan, a Participant's Present Value of Accrued Benefit shall be determined

(1)   as of the most recent "actuarial valuation date," which is the most recent valuation date within a twelve (12) month period ending on the Determination Date;

(2)   for the first plan year, as if (a) the Participant terminated service as of the Determination Date; or (b) the Participant terminated service as of the actuarial valuation date, but taking into account the estimated Present Value of Accrued Benefits as of the Determination Date;

(3)   for any other plan year, as if the Participant terminated service as of the actuarial valuation date. The actuarial valuation date must be the same date used for computing the defined-benefit plan minimum funding costs, regardless of whether a valuation is performed that plan year.

(g)   The calculation of a Participant's Present Value of Accrued Benefit as of a Determination Date shall be the sum of

(1)   the Present Value of Accrued Benefit using the actuarial assumptions of Section 1.3.

(2)   any Plan distributions made within the Plan Year that includes the Determination Date or within the four (4) preceding Plan Years. However, in the case of distributions made after the valuation date and prior to the Determination Date, such distributions are not included as distributions for Topheavy purposes to the extent that such distributions are already included in the Participant's Present Value of Accrued Benefit as of the valuation date. Notwithstanding

anything herein to the contrary, all distributions, including distributions made prior to January 1, 1984, will be counted.

(3) any Employee contributions, whether voluntary or mandatory. However, amounts attributable to tax-deductible Qualified Voluntary Employee Contributions shall not be considered to be a part of the Participant's Present Value of Accrued Benefit.

With respect to unrelated rollovers and plan-to-plan transfers (ones which are both initiated by the Employee and made from a plan maintained by one employer to a plan maintained by another employer), if this Plan provides for rollovers or plan-to-plan transfers, it shall always consider such a rollover or plan-to-plan transfer as a distribution for the purposes of this Section. If this Plan is the plan accepting such rollovers or plan-to-plan transfers, it shall not consider such rollovers or plan-to-plan transfers accepted after December 31, 1983, as part of the Participant's Present Value of Accrued Benefit. However, rollovers or plan-to-plan transfers accepted prior to January 1, 1984, shall be considered as part of the Participant's Present Value of Accrued Benefit.

With respect to related rollovers and plan-to-plan transfers (ones either not initiated by the Employee or made to a plan maintained by the same employer), if this Plan provides the rollover or plan-to-plan transfer, it shall not be counted as a distribution for purposes of this Section. If this Plan is the plan accepting such rollover or plan-to-plan transfer, it shall consider such rollover or plan-to-plan transfer as part of the Participant's Present Value of Accrued Benefit, irrespective of the date on which such rollover or plan-to-plan transfer is accepted.

(h) "Topheavy Group" means an Aggregation Group in which, as of the Determination Date, the sum of

(1) the Present Value of Accrued Benefits of Key Employees under all defined-benefit plans included in the group, and

(2) the Aggregate Accounts of Key Employees under all defined-contribution plans included in the group

exceeds sixty percent (60%) of a similar sum determined for all Participants.

(i) Notwithstanding anything herein to the contrary, the effective date otherwise provided for herein for the application of Code Section 416 to this Plan (Plan Years beginning after December 31, 1983) shall be extended in accordance with any legislative act of Congress.

2.3   *POWERS AND RESPONSIBILITIES OF THE EMPLOYER*

(a)   The Employer shall be empowered to appoint and remove the Trustee and the Administrator from time to time as it deems necessary for the proper administration of the Plan to assure that the Plan is being operated for the exclusive benefit of the Participants and their Beneficiaries in accordance with the terms of this Agreement, the Code, and the Act.

(b)   The Employer shall establish a "funding policy and method," i.e., it shall determine whether the Plan has a short run need for liquidity (e.g., to pay benefits) or whether liquidity is a long run goal and investment growth (and stability of same) is a more current need, or shall appoint a qualified person to do so. The Employer or its delegate shall communicate such needs and goals to the Trustee, who shall coordinate such Plan needs with its investment policy. The communication of such a "funding policy and method" shall not, however, constitute a directive to the Trustee as to investment of the Trust Funds. Such "funding policy and method" shall be consistent with the objectives of this Plan and with the requirements of Title I of the Act.

(c)   The Employer may in its discretion appoint an Investment Manager to manage all or a designated portion of the assets of the Plan. In such event, the Trustee shall follow the directive of the Investment Manager in investing the assets of the Plan managed by the Investment Manager.

(d)   The Employer shall periodically review the performance of any Fiduciary or other person to whom duties have been delegated or allocated by it under the provisions of this Plan or pursuant to procedures established hereunder. This requirement may be satisfied by formal periodic review by the Employer or by a qualified person specifically designated by the Employer, through day-to-day conduct and evaluation, or through other appropriate ways.

2.4   *ASSIGNMENT AND DESIGNATION OF ADMINISTRATIVE AUTHORITY*

The Employer shall appoint one or more Administrators. Any person, including but not limited to the Employees of the Employer, shall be eligible to serve as an Administrator. Any person so appointed shall signify his acceptance by filing written acceptance with the Employer. An Administrator may resign by delivering his written resignation to the Employer or be removed by the Employer by delivery of written notice of removal, to take effect at a date specified therein, or upon delivery to the Administrator if no date is specified.

The Employer, upon the resignation or removal of an Administrator, shall promptly designate in writing a successor to this position. If the Employer does not appoint an Administrator, the Employer will function as the Administrator.

2.5   *ALLOCATION AND DELEGATION OF RESPONSIBILITIES*

If more than one person is appointed as Administrator, the responsibilities of each Administrator may be specified by the Employer and accepted in writing by each Administrator. In the event that no such delegation is made by the Employer, the Administrators may allocate the responsibilities among themselves, in which event the Administrators shall notify the Employer and the Trustee in writing of such action and specify the responsibilities of each Administrator. The Trustee thereafter shall accept and rely upon any documents executed by the appropriate Administrator until such time as the Employer or the Administrators file with the Trustee a written revocation of such designation.

2.6   *POWERS, DUTIES, AND RESPONSIBILITIES*

The primary responsibility of the Administrator is to administer the Plan for the exclusive benefit of the Participants and their Beneficiaries, subject to the specific terms of the Plan. The Administrator shall administer the Plan in accordance with its terms and shall have the power to determine all questions arising in connection with the administration, interpretation, and application of the Plan. Any such determination by the Administrator shall be conclusive and binding upon all persons. The Administrator may establish procedures, correct any defect, supply any information, or reconcile any inconsistency in such manner and to such extent as shall be deemed necessary or advisable to carry out the purpose of this Agreement; provided, however, that any procedure, discretionary act, interpretation or construction shall be done in a non-discriminatory manner based upon uniform principals consistently applied and shall be consistent with the intent that the Plan shall continue to be deemed a qualified plan under the terms of Section 401(a) of the Code as amended from time to time, and shall comply with the terms of the Act and all regulations issued pursuant thereto. The Administrator shall have all powers necessary or appropriate to accomplish his duties under this Plan.

The Administrator shall be charged with the duties of the general administration of the Plan, including, but not limited to, the following:

(a)   to determine all questions relating to the eligibility of Employees to participate or remain a Participant hereunder;

(b)   to compute, certify, and direct the Trustee with respect to the amount and the kind of benefits to which any Participant shall be entitled hereunder;

(c)   to authorize and direct the Trustee with respect to all nondiscretionary or otherwise directed disbursements from the Trust;

(d)   to maintain all necessary records for the administration of the Plan;

(e)   to interpret the provisions of the Plan, and to make and publish such rules for regulation of the Plan as are consistent with the terms hereof;

(f)   to determine the size and type of any Contract to be purchased from any insurer, and to designate the insurer from which such Contract shall be purchased. All Policies shall be issued on a uniform basis as of each Anniversary Date with respect to all Participants under similar circumstances;

(g)   to compute and certify to the Employer and to the Trustee from time to time the sums of money necessary or desirable to be contributed to the Trust Fund;

(h)   to consult with the Employer and the Trustee regarding the short- and long-term liquidity needs of the Plan so that the Trustee can exercise any investment discretion in a manner designed to accomplish specific objectives;

(i)   to assist any Participant regarding his rights, benefits, or elections available under the Plan;

(j)   to prepare and distribute to Employees a procedure for notifying Participants and Beneficiaries of their rights to elect joint and survivor annuities as required by the Act and Regulations thereunder.

2.7   *RECORDS AND REPORTS*

The Administrator shall keep a record of all actions taken and shall keep all other books of account, records, and other data that may be necessary for proper administration of the Plan and shall be responsible for supplying all information and reports to the Internal Revenue Service, Department of Labor, Participants, Beneficiaries and others as required by law.

2.8 *APPOINTMENT OF ADVISORS*

The Administrator, or the Trustee with the consent of the Administrator, may appoint counsel, specialists, and advisors, and other persons as the Administrator or the Trustee deems necessary or desirable in connection with the administration of the Plan.

2.9 *INFORMATION FROM EMPLOYER*

To enable the Administrator to perform his functions, the Employer shall supply full and timely information to the Administrator on all matters relating to the Compensation of all Participants, their Hours of Service, their Years of Service, their retirement, death, disability, or termination of employment, and such other pertinent facts as the Administrator may require; and the Administrator shall advise the Trustee of such of the foregoing facts as may be pertinent to the Trustee's duties under the Plan. The Administrator may rely upon such information as is supplied by the Employer and shall have no duty or responsibility to verify such information.

2.10 *PAYMENT OF EXPENSES*

All expenses of administration may be paid out of the Trust Fund, unless paid by the Employer. Such expenses shall include any expenses incident to the functioning of the Administrator, including but not limited to, fees of accountants, counsel, and other specialists, and other costs of administering the Plan. Until paid, the expenses shall constitute a liability of the Trust Fund. However, the Employer may reimburse the Trust for any administration expense incurred pursuant to the above. Any administration expense paid to the Trust as a reimbursement shall not be considered as an Employer contribution.

2.11 *MAJORITY ACTIONS*

Except where there have been an allocation and delegation of administrative authority pursuant to Section 2.5, if there shall be more than one Administrator, they shall act by a majority of their number but may authorize one or more of them to sign all papers on their behalf.

2.12   *CLAIMS PROCEDURE*

Claims for benefits under the Plan may be filed with the Administrator on forms supplied by the Employer. Written notice of the disposition of a claim shall be furnished to the claimant within 90 days after the application thereof is filed. In the event the claim is denied, the reasons for the denial shall be specifically set forth in the notice in language calculated to be understood by the claimant, pertinent provisions of the Plan shall be cited, and, where appropriate, an explanation as to how the claimant can perfect the claim will be provided. In addition, the claimant shall be furnished with an explanation of the Plan's claims review procedure.

2.13   *CLAIMS REVIEW PROCEDURE*

Any Employee, former Employee, or Beneficiary of either, who has been denied a benefit by a decision of the Administrator pursuant to Section 2.12, shall be entitled to request the Administrator to give further consideration to his claim by filing with the Administrator (on a form which may be obtained from the Administrator) a request for a hearing. Such request, together with a written statement of the reasons why the claimant believes his claim should be allowed, shall be filed with the Administrator no later than 60 days after receipt of the written notification provided for in Section 2.12. The Administrator shall then conduct a hearing within the next 60 days, at which the claimant may be represented by an attorney or any other representative of his choosing and at which the claimant shall have an opportunity to submit written and oral evidence and arguments in support of his claim. At the hearing (or prior thereto upon five business days written notice to the Administrator) the claimant or his representative shall have an opportunity to review all documents in the possession of the Administrator which are pertinent to the claim at issue and its disallowance. Either the claimant or the Administrator may cause a court reporter to attend the hearing and record the proceedings. In such event, a complete written transcript of the proceedings shall be furnished to both parties by the court reporter. The full expense of any such court reporter and such transcripts shall be borne by the party causing the court reporter to attend the hearing. A final decision as to the allowance of the claim shall be made by the Administrator within 60 days of receipt of the appeal (unless there has been an extension of 60 days due to special circumstances, provided the delay and the special circumstances occasioning it are communicated to the claimant within the 60-day period). Such communication shall be written in a manner calculated to be understood by the claimant and shall include specific reasons for the decision and specific references to the pertinent Plan provisions on which the decision is based.

ARTICLE III
ELIGIBILITY

3.1 *CONDITIONS OF ELIGIBILITY*

Any Employee who has completed one (1) Year(s) of Service and has reached his 25th birthday shall be eligible to participate hereunder as of the date he has satisfied such requirements. The Employer shall give each prospective Eligible Employee written notice of his eligibility to participate in the Plan prior to the close of the Plan Year in which he first becomes an Eligible Employee.

However, any Employee who is within five years of his Normal Retirement Age at the date of his employment shall be excluded from participation in the Plan.

3.2 *APPLICATION FOR PARTICIPATION*

In order to become a Participant hereunder, each Eligible Employee must make application to the Employer for participation in the Plan and agree to the terms hereof. In the event any Employee otherwise qualified to become a Participant fails to file such application, the Employer shall file such application on behalf of such Employee on a nondiscriminatory basis. Upon the acceptance of any benefits under this Plan, such Employee shall automatically be bound by the terms and conditions of this Agreement and all amendments thereto.

3.3 *EFFECTIVE DATE OF PARTICIPATION*

An Employee who has become eligible to be a Participant shall become a Participant effective the first day of the Plan Year in which such Employee met the eligibility requirements of Section 3.1.

3.4 *DETERMINATION OF ELIGIBILITY*

The Administrator shall determine the eligibility of each Employee for participation in the Plan based upon information furnished by the Employer. Such determination shall be conclusive and binding upon all persons, as long as the same is made in accordance with this Agreement and the Act, and provided such determination shall be subject to review per Section 2.13.

3.5   *TERMINATION OF ELIGIBILITY*

A Participant shall cease to be eligible to participate in the Plan as of the first day of a Plan Year during which he has a One-Year Break in Service.

In the event a Participant shall go from a classification of Eligible Employee to Noneligible Employee, such Former Participant shall continue to vest in his interest in the Plan until such time as he has a One-Year Break in Service.

3.6   *OMISSION OF ELIGIBLE EMPLOYEE*

If, in any Fiscal Year, any Employee who should be included as a Participant in the Plan is erroneously omitted, and discovery of such omission is not made until after a contribution by his Employer for the year has been made, the appropriate Employer shall make a subsequent contribution with respect to the omitted Employee in the amount which the said Employer would have contributed with respect to him had he not been omitted. Such contribution shall be made by such Employer, regardless of whether or not it is deductible in whole or in part in any taxable year under applicable provisions of the Code.

3.7   *INCLUSION OF INELIGIBLE EMPLOYEE*

If, in any Fiscal Year, any person who should not have been included as a Participant in the Plan is erroneously included and discovery of such incorrect inclusion is not made until after a contribution for the year has been made, the appropriate Employer shall not be entitled to recover the contribution made with respect to the ineligible person regardless of whether or not a deduction is allowable with respect to such contribution. In such event, the amount contributed with respect to the ineligible person shall constitute a Forfeiture for the Fiscal Year in which the discovery is made.

3.8 *ELECTION NOT TO PARTICIPATE*

Notwithstanding Section 3.2, an Employee may, subject to the approval of the Employer, elect voluntarily not to participate in the Plan. The election not to participate must be communicated to the Employer in writing at least thirty (30) days before the beginning of a Plan Year.

A Participant making this election shall have the right to modify or revoke this election during a subsequent Plan Year. However, in no event shall a Participant's Accrued Benefit be reduced. Benefit decreases caused as a result of this election shall be recognized notwithstanding provisions to the contrary in Section 5.1. Benefit increases as a result of the revocation or modification of this election in any Plan Year subsequent to a Plan Year in which benefits have been decreased pursuant to such election shall be treated as benefit increases resulting from a Plan amendment. Accordingly, funding for such increases shall be based upon reasonable actuarial assumptions commonly utilized to fund benefit increases resulting from a Plan amendment. Furthermore, such benefit increases shall be subject to those restrictions imposed upon distribution of benefits upon early termination in Section 9.2.

ARTICLE IV
CONTRIBUTION AND VALUATION

4.1 *PAYMENT OF CONTRIBUTIONS*

No contribution shall be required under the Plan from any Participant. The Employer shall pay to the Trustee from time to time such amounts in cash or property acceptable to the Trustee as the Administrator and Employer shall determine to be necessary to provide the benefits under the Plan determined by the application of accepted actuarial methods and assumptions. The method of funding shall be consistent with Plan objectives.

4.2 *ACTUARIAL METHODS*

In establishing the liabilities under the Plan and contributions thereto, the enrolled actuary will use such methods and assumptions as will reasonably reflect the cost of the benefits. The Plan assets are to be valued on the basis of any reasonable method of valuation that takes into account fair market value pursuant to regulations prescribed by the Secretary of the Treasury. There must be an actuarial valuation of the Plan at least once every three years.

4.3   *TRANSFERS FROM QUALIFIED PLANS*

(a)   With the consent of the Administrator, amounts may be transferred from other qualified corporate and, after December 31, 1983, noncorporate plans, provided that the trust from which such funds are transferred permits the transfer to be made and, in the opinion of legal counsel for the Employer, the transfer will not jeopardize the tax exempt status of the Plan or Trust or create adverse tax consequences for the Employer. The amounts transferred shall be considered an additional Accrued Benefit and set up in a separate account herein referred to as a "Participant's Rollover Account." Such account shall be fully Vested at all times and shall not be subject to Forfeiture for any reason.

(b)   Amounts in a Participant's Rollover Account shall be held by the Trustee pursuant to the provisions of this Plan, and such amounts shall not be subject to Forfeiture for any reason and may not be withdrawn by, or distributed to, the Participant, in whole or in part, except as provided in Paragraph (c) of this Section.

(c)   At Normal Retirement Date, or such other date when the Participant or his Beneficiary shall be entitled to receive benefits, the Accrued Benefit shall be used to provide additional benefits to the Participant pursuant to Section 5.1(d) or such other optional method as the Administrator shall elect pursuant to Section 5.7.

(d)   The Accrued Benefit under this Section shall be the balance of a "Participant's Rollover Account" as of any applicable date. Unless the Administrator directs that the Participant's Rollover Account be segregated into a separate account for each Participant in a federally insured savings account, certificate of deposit in a bank or savings and loan association, money market certificate, or other short-term debt security acceptable to the Trustee, it shall be invested as part of the general Trust Fund and shall share in any income earned thereon, any investment gains and losses attributable thereto, less any expenses, pursuant to the terms of this Agreement.

(e)   The Administrator may direct that employee transfers made after the first month of the Plan Year pursuant to this Section be segregated into a separate account for each Participant in a federally insured savings account, certificate of deposit in a bank or savings and loan association, money market certificate, or other short-term debt security acceptable to the Trustee until such time as the allocations pursuant to this Agreement have been made.

(f)   For purposes of this Section the term "amounts transferred from another qualified corporate and noncorporate plan" shall mean (i) amounts transferred to this Plan directly from another qualified corporate and, after December 31, 1983, qualified noncorporate plan; (ii) lump-sum distributions received by an Employee from another qualified Plan, which are eligible for tax free rollover treatment, and which are transferred by the Employee to this Plan within sixty (60) days following his receipt thereof; (iii) amounts transferred to this Plan from a conduit individual retirement account provided that the conduit individual retirement account has no assets other than assets which were previously distributed to the Employee by another qualified plan (other than an individual retirement account or, if transferred prior to January 1, 1984, an H.R. 10 plan) as a lump-sum distribution, which were eligible for tax free rollover treatment, and which were deposited in such conduit individual retirement account within sixty (60) days of receipt thereof, and other than earnings on said assets; and (iv) amounts distributed to the Employee from a conduit individual retirement account meeting the requirements of clause (iii) above and transferred by the Employee to this Plan within sixty (60) days of his receipt thereof from such conduit individual retirement account. Prior to accepting any transfers to which this Section applies the Administrator may require the Employee to establish that the amounts to be transferred to this Plan meet the requirements of this Section and may also require the Employee to provide an opinion of counsel satisfactory to the Employer that the amounts to be transferred meet the requirements of this Section.

(g) For purposes of this Section, the term "qualified corporate or noncorporate plan" shall mean any tax qualified plan under Code Section 401(a).

4.4 *VOLUNTARY CONTRIBUTIONS*

(a) In order to allow Participants the opportunity to increase their retirement income, each Participant may elect to voluntarily contribute up to 10% of his aggregate compensation earned while a Participant under this Plan. Such contributions shall be paid to the Trustee no later than 30 days after the Plan Year for which it is to be deemed paid. The balance in each Participant's Voluntary Contribution Account shall be fully Vested at all times and shall not be subject to Forfeiture for any reason.

(b) A Participant may elect to withdraw his voluntary contributions from his Voluntary Contribution Account and, with the Administrator's consent, the actual earnings thereon. In the event such a withdrawal is made, a Participant shall be barred from making any additional voluntary contributions to the Trust Fund for a period of one (1) Plan Year.

(c)   The Administrator shall maintain a separate Participant's Voluntary Contribution Account for each Participant's Accrued Benefit derived from any contributions made pursuant to this Section, and the Accrued Benefit shall be fully Vested at all times.

(d)   At Normal Retirement Date, or such other date when the Participant or his Beneficiary shall be entitled to receive benefits, the Accrued Benefit shall be used to provide additional benefits to the Participant pursuant to Section 5.1(d).

(e)   In any case in which an individual is a Participant in two or more qualified plans maintained by the same Employer, the aggregate voluntary contributions to all plans may not exceed 10% of his aggregate compensation earned while a Participant in the respective plans.

(f)   The Administrator may direct that voluntary contributions made after the first month of the Plan Year pursuant to this Section be segregated into a separate account for each Participant in a federally insured savings account, certificate of deposit in a bank or savings and loan association, money market certificate, or other short-term debt security acceptable to the Trustee until such time as the allocations pursuant to this Agreement have been made.

(g)   The Accrued Benefit derived from contributions made under this Section shall mean the balance of a Participant's Voluntary Contribution Account as of any applicable date. Unless the Administrator directs that Voluntary Contributions made pursuant to this Section be segregated into a separate account for each Participant in a federally insured savings account, certificate of deposit in a bank or savings and loan association, money market certificate, or other short-term debt security acceptable to the Trustee, they shall be invested as part of the general Trust Fund.

(h)   Employee contributions made pursuant to this Section shall be considered as a separate defined-contribution plan for the purposes of applying the limitations of Section 415 of the Code.

ARTICLE V
BENEFITS

5.1   *RETIREMENT BENEFITS*

(a)   The amount of monthly retirement benefit to be provided for each Participant who retires on his Normal Retirement Date (which benefit is herein called his Normal Retirement Benefit) shall be equal to 24% of such Participant's monthly Compensation determined as provided in Section 5.1(c), in excess of the amount shown below for the calendar year in which his 65th birthday occurs, computed to the nearest dollar.

Calendar Year of 65th Birthday	Monthly Covered Compensation
1983	$ 1,000
1984	1,050
1985	1,150
1986	1,200
1987	1,250
1988	1,350
1989	1,400
1990	1,450
1991	1,500
1992	1,550
1993	1,550
1994	1,600
1995	1,700
1996	1,750
1997	1,850
1998	1,900
1999	2,000
2000	2,050
2001	2,150
2002	2,200
2003	2,250
2004	2,350
2005	2,400
2006	2,450
2007	2,550
2008	2,600

Calendar Year of 65th Birthday	Monthly Covered Compensation
2009	2,650
2010	2,700
2011	2,750
2012	2,800
2013	2,850
2014	2,900
2015	2,950
2016	2,950
2017	2,950
2018 or later	2,975

Such monthly retirement benefit shall be reduced by one-nineteenth for each Year of Service that such Participant's Years of Service are less than 19.

(b)   This Plan does not provide for a retirement date prior to Normal Retirement Date. In the event a Participant retires prior to his Normal Retirement Date, his benefit shall be the benefit payable per Section 5.6(a).

(c)   The Normal Retirement Benefit shall be based on Average Monthly Compensation as defined in Section 1.9 of this Agreement.

(d)   The Normal Retirement Benefit payable to a Participant pursuant to this Section 5.1 shall be a monthly pension commencing on his Retirement Date and continuing for life. If a Retired Participant dies prior to the completion of 120 monthly payments, such monthly payments shall be continued to the Retired Participant's Beneficiary until the monthly payments made to the Retired Participant and to the Beneficiary shall total 120.

(e)   At the request of a Participant he may be continued in employment beyond his Normal Retirement Date. Except, however, the Participant may not be employed beyond age 70 without the written consent of the Employer. In such event, no retirement benefit will be paid to the Participant until he actually retires, and no further contributions toward current costs on behalf of such an Employee will be made past his Normal Retirement Date. The retirement benefit commencing at his actual Retirement Date shall be the Actuarial Equivalent of the benefit he would have received at his Normal Retirement Date.

(f)   A Participant shall become fully Vested in his Normal Retirement Benefit or his Accrued Benefit if greater, pursuant to Section 1.30.

(g) If a Former Participant again becomes a Participant, such renewed participation shall not result in duplication of benefits. Accordingly, if he has received a distribution of a Vested Accrued Benefit under the Plan by reason of prior participation (and such distribution has not been repaid to the Plan with interest at an annual rate of 5%, compounded annually from the date of distribution to the date of repayment, within the earlier of (1) the end of the two-year period beginning with the Employee's resumption of employment covered by the Plan, or (2) the end of the five-year period beginning with the date of withdrawal), his Normal Retirement Benefit or Accrued Benefit shall be reduced by an amount equal to the value of the Vested Accrued Benefit previously distributed.

5.2 *MINIMUM BENEFIT REQUIREMENT FOR TOPHEAVY PLAN*

(a) For any Topheavy Plan Year, the following minimum annual benefit shall be provided for each Non-Key Employee: The minimum Accrued Benefit at any point in time must equal at least the product of a Non-Key Employee's "average compensation" for the five (5) consecutive years when such Non-Key Employee had the highest aggregate Compensation from the Employer and the lesser of two percent (2%) per Year of Service, or twenty percent (20%). Thus, each Non-Key Employee shall accrue a retirement benefit equal to two percent (2%) of his "average compensation" for each Topheavy Plan Year. The compensation required to be taken into account is the compensation described in Code Section 415. However, compensation received by a Non-Key Employee for non-Topheavy Plan Years shall be disregarded. For purposes of this Plan, the two percent (2%) minimum annual retirement benefit means a benefit payable annually in the form of a single life annuity (with no ancillary benefits) at the Normal Retirement Age under the Plan.

(b) Extra Minimum Benefit Permitted for Topheavy Plans Other Than Super Topheavy Plans: If a Key Employee is a Participant in both a defined-contribution plan and a defined-benefit plan that are both part of a Topheavy Group, the defined-contribution and the defined-benefit fractions set forth in Section 6.1(k) shall remain unchanged, provided each Non-Key Employee who is a Participant receives an extra Accrued Benefit (in addition to the minimum Accrued Benefit set forth above) equal to not less than the lesser of (1) one percent (1%) of the such Non-Key Employee's "average compensation" multiplied by his Year of Service, or (2) ten percent (10%) of his "average compensation." This extra benefit shall be determined in the same manner as the minimum benefit set forth in this Section and shall be provided for each Topheavy Plan Year in which one or more Key Employees is a Participant in both the defined-benefit and defined-contribution plans.

(c)   For any Topheavy Plan Year, the minimum benefits set forth above shall accrue to each Non-Key Employee who has completed a Year of Service, including each Non-Key Employee who has completed a Year of Service but has been excluded from participation or has accrued no benefit because (1) such Non-Key Employee's compensation is less than a stated amount, or (2) such Non-Key Employee declined to make mandatory contributions (if any) to the Plan.

(d)   If a Non-Key Employee participates in both a defined-benefit plan and a defined-contribution plan included in a Topheavy Aggregation Group, the Employer is not required to provide the Non-Key Employee with both the full and separate minimum benefit and the full and separate minimum contribution. Therefore, for Non-Key Employees who are participating in a defined-contribution plan maintained by the Employer, and if the minimum allocations under Code Section 416(c) (2) are being provided to the Non-Key Employees under such Plan, the minimum benefits provided for above may not be applicable if the minimum contributions and/or benefits are being provided for the Non-Key Employees under any one of the safe harbor rules set forth in Regulation 1.416-1(m-10).

5.3   *PAYMENT OF RETIREMENT BENEFITS*

When a Participant retires, the Administrator shall immediately take all necessary steps and execute all required documents to cause the payment to him of the retirement benefit available to him under the Plan or his Accrued Benefit if greater.

5.4   *DISABILITY RETIREMENT BENEFITS*

(a)   If a Participant becomes Totally and Permanently Disabled pursuant to Section 1.46 prior to retirement or separation from service, and such condition continues for a period of six (6) consecutive months and by reason thereof such Participant's status as an Employee ceases, then said disabled Participant shall be entitled to receive his Present Value of Accrued Benefit. As of the Anniversary Date coinciding with or next following the event of a Participant's Total and Permanent Disability, the Administrator shall direct the Trustee to commence payment of the benefits payable hereunder pursuant to the provisions of Sections 5.7 and 5.9.

(b)   The benefit payable pursuant to (a) above shall be computed as of the Anniversary Date subsequent to termination of employment.

5.5   DEATH BENEFITS

(a)   On the Anniversary Date coinciding with or next following a Participant's satisfaction of the eligibility requirements of Section 3.1, the Administrator may instruct the Trustees to purchase a life insurance Contract with a face amount to be determined by the Administrator using a uniform nondiscriminatory policy consistently applied. Additional life insurance Contracts shall be purchased and/or surrendered on subsequent Anniversary Dates as are necessary pursuant to the policy established by the Administrator.

(b)   Insurance Policies shall be purchased only for those Participants who have completed three (3) Plan Years of Service.

(c)   Additional Policies shall not be purchased for any Participant who has attained Age 57.

(d)   No insurance Contracts shall be purchased or surrendered until the change of coverage is at least $10,000.

(e)   Death benefits payable by reason of the death of a Participant or a Retired Participant shall be paid to his Beneficiary in accordance with the following provisions:

  (i)   Upon the death of a Participant prior to his Normal Retirement Date, his Beneficiary shall be entitled to a death benefit in an amount equal to The Value of the Total Prior Contributions, as of the Anniversary Date coinciding with or subsequent to death, and any additional Policy proceeds payable at death in accordance with this Section 5.5.

  (ii)   If life insurance is issued on behalf of a Participant, and less than two-thirds of the Plan's normal cost for the Participant under the Typical Level Premium Cost Method has been invested in life insurance premiums, having cash surrender value on the Participant's life or, if less than one-third of the Plan's normal cost under the Typical Level Premium Cost Method is used to purchase term insurance, the preretirement death benefit for that Participant shall be the insurance in force minus the cash value, plus the reserve calculated under the Typical Level Premium Cost Method using the actuarial assumptions stated in Section 1.3.

If the limitations set forth in this subparagraph are exceeded, then such death benefit shall be equal to the insurance that would have been provided if the premium payments satisfied such limitations, minus the cash value of such Policies attributable to the reduced premiums, plus the reserve calculated under the Typical Level Premium Cost Method using the actuarial assumptions stated in Section 1.3. The additional Policy proceeds shall inure to the Trust Fund and be used to reduce the future contributions of the Employer.

(iii) Upon the death of a Participant subsequent to his Retirement date, but prior to commencement of his retirement benefits, his Beneficiary shall be entitled to a death benefit in an amount equal to the Actuarial Equivalent of the benefit the Participant would have received at his Retirement Date, credited with interest subsequent to such date at the rate determined under Section 411(c)(2)(C) of the Code, if applicable.

(iv) Upon the death of a Participant subsequent to the commencement of his retirement benefits, his Beneficiary shall be entitled to whatever death benefit may be available under the settlement arrangements pursuant to which the Participant's benefit is made payable.

(f) For a Participant who is found by the Administrator to be insurable only at a mortality classification other than standard, the Trustees on a uniform and nondiscriminatory basis shall either (1) purchase a whole life or term insurance Contract, as the case may be, with a face amount that can be purchased at the standard rate for coverage as provided in Section 5.5(a) for such Participant if he could obtain such coverage, (2) purchase such whole life or term insurance Contract, as the case may be, and pay the additional premium attributable to the excess mortality hazards, or (3) allow the Participant the right to pay the additional premium attributable to the excess mortality hazards. If a Participant is determined to be uninsurable, no life insurance Contract shall be required to be purchased on the life of such Participant.

(g) The Administrator may require such proper proof of death and such evidence of the right of any person to receive the death benefit payable as a result of the death of a Participant as the Administrator may deem desirable. The Administrator's determination of death and the right of any person to receive payment shall be conclusive.

(h) Each Employee, upon becoming a Participant, may designate in writing a Beneficiary of his own choosing, and may, in addition, name a contingent Beneficiary. Such designation shall be made in a form satisfactory to the Administrator; however, the designation on the latest application for life insurance purchased in accordance with the terms of this Plan shall apply to all death benefits payable from the Plan. Any Participant may at any time revoke his designation of Beneficiary by filing written notice of such revocation or change with the Administrator. In the event no Beneficiary or contingent Beneficiary is surviving at the time any payment is to be made, such payment shall be made to such Participant's spouse, if living, or if there is no spouse living, to the Participant's issue, per stirpes, or if neither the Participant's spouse nor any of his issue are living, to such Participant's estate.

(i) The benefit payable under this Section shall be paid pursuant to the provisions of Sections 5.8 and 5.9.

(j) Unless he elects otherwise, a Participant, Retired Participant, or Former Participant who was married on his date of death, and who had not begun to receive payments under the Plan on or after he had become eligible for Normal Retirement Benefit, shall have the present value of his death benefit paid to his surviving spouse in the form of a Survivor Annuity.

Any election under this provision shall be in writing and may be changed at any time. The election period shall begin on the later of (1) the 90th day before the Participant attains the "qualified early retirement age" (see Section 5.7(a)), or (2) the date on which any Participant's participation begins, and shall end on the date the Participant terminates employment.

With regard to the election, the Administrator shall provide the Participant with a written explanation including the following:

(i)   a general description of the Survivor Annuity,

(ii) an explanation of the circumstances in which the annuity will be paid, if elected,

(iii) notice of the availability of the election, and

(iv) a general explanation of the relative financial effect the election wil have on the Survivor Annuity or other form of benefit that may be offered.

(k) If a Participant dies before any insurance coverage to which he is entitled under this Agreement is effected, his death benefit from such insurance coverage shall be limited to the standard-rated premium which was or should have been used for such purpose.

5.6   *TERMINATION OF EMPLOYMENT BEFORE RETIREMENT*

(a)   When a Participant has incurred a One-Year Break in Service, his participation in the Plan shall cease. Payment to a Former Participant of the Vested portion of his Accrued Benefit, unless he otherwise elects, shall begin not later than the 60th day after the close of the Plan Year in which the latest of the following events occurs:

(1)   the date on which the Participant attains the earlier of age 65 or the Normal Retirement Age specified herein,

(2)   the 10th anniversary of the year in which the Participant commenced participation in the Plan, or

(3)   the date the Participant terminates his service with the Employer.

In the event of the Terminated Participant's Total and Permanent Disability subsequent to his termination of employment, the Terminated Participant (or his Beneficiary) shall receive the Present Value of his Vested Accrued Benefit as of the Anniversary Date coinciding with, or next following, the date of his Total and Permanent Disability pursuant to Sections 5.7 and 5.9.

In the event of the Terminated Participant's death subsequent to his termination of employment, his Beneficiary shall receive the Present Value of such Participant's Vested Accrued Benefit as of the Anniversary Date coinciding with, or next following, the date of his death pursuant to Sections 5.7, 5.8 and 5.9.

However, the Administrator may, in accordance with a nondiscriminatory policy, direct earlier payment of the Vested portion of the Present Value of Accrued Benefit. If the Vested portion of the Present Value of Accrued Benefit at time of payment exceeds $1,750, the Terminated Participant must give written consent to the Administrator before payment can be made. In no event, however, shall a distribution be made to a Former Participant until such time as he has incurred a One-Year Break in Service.

However, if the Vested portion of the Terminated Participant's Present Value of Accrued Benefit does not exceed $1,750, the Administrator shall direct the Trustee to distribute such amount to such Terminated Participant within a reasonable time after the Anniversary Date coinciding with, or next following, such Terminated Participant's termination of employment. In no event, however, shall a distribution be made to a Terminated Participant until such time as he has incurred a One-Year Break in Service.

If Contracts have been issued under the Plan on the life of a Terminated Participant, the Administrator may (1) surrender such Contracts to the insurer for their cash value, and such cash shall become part of the Trust Fund assets; or (2) in the event that the Vested portion of the Terminated Participant's Present Value of Accrued Benefit equals or exceeds the cash surrender values of any Contracts, the Trustee, when so directed by the Administrator and agreed to by the Terminated Participant, shall assign, transfer, and set over to such Terminated Participant all Contracts on his life in such form or with such endorsements, if any, as the Administrator may, in his discretion, direct, restricting the right of the Terminated Participant to surrender, assign, or otherwise realize cash on the Contract or Contracts prior to Normal Retirement Date. In the event that the Vested portion of the Terminated Participant's Present Value of Accrued Benefit does not at least equal the cash surrender values of the Contracts, if any, the Terminated Participant may, with the approval of the Administrator, pay over to the Trustee the sum needed to make the distribution equal to the value of the Contracts being assigned or transferred, or the Trustee may borrow the cash surrender values of the Contracts from the insurer and then assign the Contracts to the Terminated Participant.

That portion of a Terminated Participant's Accrued Benefit that is not Vested shall be forfeited and used only to reduce future costs of the Plan.

(b) The Vested portion of any Participant's Accrued Benefit shall be a percentage of such Participant's Accrued Benefit, determined on the basis of the Participant's number of Years of Service according to the following schedule:

VESTING SCHEDULE

Years of Service	Percentage
4	40 %
5	45 %
6	50 %
7	60 %
8	70 %
9	80 %
10	90 %
11	100 %

(c) Notwithstanding the vesting schedule in paragraph (b) above, for any Topheavy Plan Year, the Vested portion of any Participant's Accrued

Benefit shall be determined on the basis of the Participant's number of Years of Service according to the following schedule:

VESTING SCHEDULE

Years of Service	Percentage
2	20 %
3	40 %
4	60 %
5	80 %
6	100 %

If in any subsequent Plan Year, the Plan ceases to be a Topheavy Plan, the Administrator may, in his sole discretion, elect to (1) continue to apply this vesting schedule in determining the Vested portion of any Participant's Accrued Benefit, or (2) revert to the vesting schedule in effect before this Plan became a Topheavy Plan. Any such reversion shall be treated as a Plan amendment pursuant to the terms of this Agreement.

(d)   The computation of a Participant's nonforfeitable percentage of his interest in the Plan shall not be reduced as the result of any direct or indirect amendment to this Article. In the event that this Agreement is amended to change or modify Section 5.6(b), a Participant with at least five (5) Years of Service as of the expiration date of the election period may elect to have his nonforfeitable percentage computed under the Plan without regard to such amendment. If a Participant fails to make such election, then such Participant shall be subject to the new vesting schedule. The Participant's election period shall commence on the adoption date of the amendment and shall end 60 days after the latest of

(i)   the adoption date of the amendment,

(ii)   the effective date of the amendment, or

(iii)   the date the Participant receives written notice of the amendment from the Employer or Administrator.

(e)   If any Terminated Participant shall be reemployed by the Employer before a One-Year Break in Service occurs, he shall continue to participate in the Plan in the same manner as if such termination had not occurred.

(f)   If any Former Participant is reemployed after a One-Year Break in Service has occurred, for the purposes of Section 5.6(b) and for calculating Plan Years of Service, the Years of Service and Plan Years of Service shall include Years of Service and Plan Years of Service prior to his One-Year Break in Service subject to the following rules:

(i) If a Former Participant completes a Year of Service (a One-year Break in Service previously occurred, but employment had not terminated), he shall participate in the Plan retroactively from the first day of the Plan Year during which he completes one (1) Year of Service.

(ii) Years of Service and Plan Years of Service prior to a One-Year Break in Service shall not be counted until such time as the Former Participant has been reemployed by the Employer for at least one year, after which time the waiting period shall be counted as a Year of Service.

(iii) If the rehired Former Participant had a Vested Accrued Benefit at the time of his termination, all Years of Service and Plan Years of Service prior to his termination shall be included in the aggregate Years of Service and Plan Years of Service.

(iv) Each nonvested Former Participant shall lose credit for Years of Service and Plan Years of Service otherwise allowable under (i) and (ii) above if his consecutive One-Year Breaks in Service equal or exceed his prebreak Years of Service and Plan Years of Service.

(v) If a Former Participant completes one (1) Year of Service for eligibility purposes following his reemployment with the Employer, he shall participate in the Plan retroactively from his date of reemployment.

5.7 DISTRIBUTION OF BENEFITS

(a) Unless he elects otherwise, a Participant who is married on the annuity starting date, and (1) who begins to receive payments under the Plan on or after his Normal Retirement Age, or (2) who, if the Plan provides for the payment of benefits before the Normal Retirement Date, begins to receive payments under the Plan on or after the date the "qualified early retirement age" (defined below) is attained, shall receive the Actuarial Equivalent of his benefits in the form of a joint and survivor annuity. The joint and survivor annuity shall be the actuarial equivalent of a single life annuity. Such joint and survivor benefits following the Participant's death shall continue to the spouse during the spouse's lifetime at a rate equal to fifty percent (50%) of the rate at which such benefits were payable to the Participant. The Participant may, however, elect to receive a smaller annuity benefit with continuation of payments to the spouse at a rate of seventy-five percent (75%) or one hundred percent (100%) of the rate payable to a Participant during his lifetime. The term "qualified early retirement age" means the latest of

(i)   the earliest date under the Plan on which the Participant could elect (without regard to any requirement that approval of early retirement be obtained) to receive retirement benefits (other than disability benefits),

(ii)   the first day of the 120th month beginning before the Participant reaches Normal Retirement age, or

(iii) the date on which the Participant begins participation.

(b)   In the event a Participant elects not to receive the form of retirement benefit named in subparagraph (a) above (if applicable), the Administrator in his sole discretion may in lieu of the benefit described in Section 5.1(d) elect one of the following methods of payment, which is the Actuarial Equivalent of the monthly retirement benefit provided in Section 5.1(d):

(i)   One lump-sum payment in cash or in property.

(ii)   Payment in equal monthly, quarterly, semiannual, or annual cash installments over a period not exceeding fifteen (15) years. The number of years may not exceed the Participant's life expectancy.

(iii) Purchase of an annuity (other than those provided for in Sections 5.1(d) and 5.7(a)). However, such annuity may not be in any form that will guarantee payments beyond the earlier of twenty (20) years or age 85.

(iv)   Purchase of a joint and survivor option when the joint annuitant is someone other than the spouse of the Participant, in which case the monthly payments to the Participant must be the Actuarial Equivalent of the amount he would have received had he elected a period certain and life thereafter option, as limited by (iii) above.

(c)   Any election under this provision shall be in writing and may be changed at any time. The election period shall begin on the later of (1) the 90th day before the Participant attains the "qualified early retirement age" (as defined in Section 5.7(a)), or (2) the date on which any Participant's participation begins, and shall end 60 days before the commencement of benefits.

With regard to the election, the Administrator shall provide the Participant with a written explanation, including the following:

(i)   a general description or explanation of the joint and survivor annuity,

(ii) an explanation of the circumstances in which the joint and survivor annuity will be provided, unless the Participant elected not to have benefits provided in such form,

(iii) notice of the availability of the election, and

(iv) a general explanation of the relative financial effect the election will have on the Survivor Annuity or other form of benefit that may be offered.

(d)   Any election made by a Participant with regard to a joint and survivor annuity may be revoked in writing and a new election made at any time during the election period.

(e)   Notwithstanding any provision above to the contrary, for Plan Years beginning after December 31, 1983, a Participant's benefits shall be distributed to him not later than the later of (i) the taxable year in which he attains age 70½, or (ii) in the case of an Employee other than a Key Employee who is a Participant in a Topheavy Plan, the taxable year in which he retires. Alternatively, distributions to a Participant must begin no later than such taxable year and must be made over the life of the Participant (or lives of the Participant and the Participant's spouse) or over a period not exceeding the life expectancy of the Participant (or the life expectancies of the Participant and the Participant's spouse). Distributions (as described above) may be made to a Participant and a non-spouse Beneficiary, provided the measuring lives remain those of the Participant and the Participant's spouse.

(f)   The mandatory commencement of distribution to Participants and/or to a named Beneficiary pursuant to this Section shall not apply (i) provided that prior to January 1, 1984, a Participant (including Key Employees) made a written designation providing for the commencement of distributions at a later date, and (ii) further providing for a method of distribution of the benefit which satisfies the provisions of Code Section 401(a) (9) as in effect prior to the enactment of the Tax Equity and Fiscal Responsibility Act of 1982 (including rules relating to incidental death benefits). Any written designation, if made, shall be binding upon the Plan Administrator notwithstanding the provisions of 5.6(b).

5.8   *DISTRIBUTION OF BENEFITS UPON DEATH*

(a)   The death benefit, other than a Survivor Annuity, payable pursuant to Section 5.5, shall be paid to the Participant's Beneficiary by either of the following methods, to be determined in the sole discretion of the Administrator:

   (i)   One lump-sum payment in cash or in property;

   (ii) Payment in monthly, quarterly, semiannual, or annual cash installments over a period to be determined in the sole discretion of the Administrator and in installments as nearly equal as practicable. After periodic installments commence, the Administrator shall have the right, in the Administrator's sole discretion, to direct the Trustee to reduce the period over which such periodic installments shall be made, and the Trustee shall adjust the cash amount of such periodic installments accordingly.

In the event the death benefit payable pursuant to Section 5.5 is payable in installments pursuant to Section 5.8(a) (ii), then, upon the death of the Participant, the Administrator shall direct the Trustee to segregate into a separate Trust Fund(s) the death benefit as provided in Section 5.5(a), and the Trustee shall invest such segregated Trust Funds separately, and the funds accumulated in such Trust Fund(s) shall be used for the payment of the installments hereinabove provided.

(b)   The Administrator, in his sole discretion, shall select the mehtod of distributing the Participant's benefits to his Beneficiary. However, a Participant may request the method by which payment shall be made to his Beneficiary pursuant to Section 5.8(a). The Administrator shall take into consideration, but shall not be bound by, such request. A Participant may at any time revoke such request by filing written notice of such revocation with the Administrator, and after such revocation, the Participant may again request an alternate method of payment.

(c)   The Administrator, in his sole discretion, may direct the Trustee, as provided under Section 5.8(a), to (1) accelerate any installment payment to a Participant's Beneficiary for any reason the Administrator in his discretion deems sufficient, or (2) at any time, purchase for the benefit of the Participant's Beneficiary, an annuity with all monies or property held in the segregated Trust Fund(s).

For purposes of Sections 5.7 and 5.8, in the event a Trustee or Administrator is also a Participant's Beneficiary (including, if any trust is named a Beneficiary, the beneficiaries of such trust), he shall abstain from participation in the exercise of such discretion provided herein.

(d)   Notwithstanding any provision in this Agreement to the contrary, for Plan Years beginning after December 31, 1983, if a Participant

   (i)   dies before his entire interest has been distributed to him, or

(ii)   distributions have commenced to his surviving spouse, and such surviving spouse dies before his entire interest has been distributed to such surviving spouse,

his entire interest (or the remaining part of such interest if distribution thereof has commenced) will be distributed within five (5) years after his death (or the death of his surviving spouse). The preceding sentence shall not apply if distribution has commenced and is payable over a term certain which does not exceed the Participant's life expectancy or the life expectancy of the Participant and the Participant's spouse. In addition, the five (5) year distribution rule shall not apply if the Participant has, prior to January 1, 1984, made a written designation to have his death benefits paid in an alternative method acceptable under Section 401(a) of the Code as in effect prior to the enactment of the Tax Equity and Fiscal Responsibility Act of 1982. Any written designation, if made, shall be binding upon the Plan Administrator notwithstanding the provision of 5.8(a).

5.9   TIME OF SEGREGATION OR DISTRIBUTION

Notwithstanding any other provision of this Agreement to the contrary, whenever the Trustee is to make a distribution or to commence a series of payments on or as of an Anniversary Date, the distribution or series of payments may be made or begun on such date or as soon thereafter as is practicable, but in no event later than 180 days after the Anniversary Date. However, unless otherwise elected in writing by the Former Participant (such election may not result in a death benefit that is more than incidental), a distribution as the result of Normal or Late Retirement shall begin not later than the 60th day after the close of the Plan Year in which the latest of the following events occurs:

(1)   the date on which the Participant attains the earlier of age 65 or the Normal Retirement Age specified herein,

(2)   the 10th anniversary of the year in which the Participant commenced participation in the Plan, or

(3)   the date the Participant terminates his service with the Employer.

5.10   DISTRIBUTION FOR MINOR BENEFICIARY

In the event a distribution is to be made to a minor, then the Administrator may, in the Administrator's sole discretion, direct that such distribution be paid to the legal guardian, or if none, to a parent of such Beneficiary or a responsible adult with whom the Beneficiary maintains his residence, or to the custodian for such Beneficiary under the Uniform Gift to Minors Act or Gift to Minors Act, if such is permitted by the laws of the state in which said Beneficiary resides. Such a payment to the legal guardian or parent of a minor Beneficiary shall fully discharge the Trustee, Employer, and Plan from further liability on account thereof.

5.11   *MINIMUM BENEFITS PAYABLE*

Notwithstanding the provisions of Sections 5.1(b) and 5.4, the benefits payable to a Participant or a Beneficiary pursuant to such Sections shall not be less than a Participant's Present Value of Vested Accrued Benefit as of the date of distribution.

5.12   *LOCATION OF PARTICIPANT OR BENEFICIARY UNKNOWN*

In the event that all, or any portion, of the distribution payable to a Participant or his Beneficiary hereunder shall, at the expiration of five (5) years after it shall become payable, remain unpaid solely by reason of the inability of the Administrator, after sending a registered letter, return receipt requested, to the last known address, and after further diligent effort, to ascertain the whereabouts of such Participant or his Beneficiary, the amount so distributable shall be forfeited and shall be used to reduce the cost of the Plan. In the event a Participant or Beneficiary is located subsequent to his benefit being forfeited, such benefit shall be restored.

5.13   *EFFECT OF SOCIAL SECURITY ACT*

Benefits being paid to a Participant or Beneficiary under the terms of this Agreement may not be decreased by reason of any postseparation Social Security benefit increases or by the increase of the Social Security wage base under Title II of the Social Security Act. Benefits to which a Former Participant has a Vested interest may not be decreased by reason of an increase in a benefit level or wage base under Title II of the Social Security Act.

5.14 *LIMITATION ON DISTRIBUTIONS*

In the event a Participant receives a distribution of his Vested Accrued Benefit prior to his Normal Retirement Date, the amount of the distribution shall be limited to his Vested Accrued Benefit reduced by one-fifteenth for each of the first five (5) years and one-thirtieth for each of the next five (5) years and reduced actuarially for each additional year thereafter that the Anniversary Date on which he commenced to receive his benefit precedes his Normal Retirement Date.

ARTICLE VI
LIMITATION OF BENEFITS

6.1 *ANNUAL BENEFIT*

(a) Maximum Annual Benefit: Subject to exceptions below, the "annual benefit" payable under this Plan shall not exceed the lesser of (1) $90,000 or (2) 100% of the Participant's compensation for the period of three consecutive years during which the Employee had the greatest aggregate compensation from the Employer. In determining an Employee's high three years, any 12-month period may be used, provided that it is uniformly and consistently applied.

(b) For purposes of this Article, "annual benefit" means the benefit under the Plan expressed on an annualized basis (exclusive of any benefit not required to be considered for purposes of applying the limitations of Section 415 of the Code to the Plan) payable in the form of a straight life annuity with no ancillary benefit. If a benefit is payable in any other form, the "annual benefit" limitation shall be applied by adjusting the benefit to the equivalent of a straight life annuity in accordance with the regulations of the Secretary of the Treasury. For purposes of such adjustment, actuarial equivalence shall be determined in accordance with the provisions of Section 1.3, unless otherwise specifically provided herein or in the Regulations under Section 415 of the Code.

(c) For the purpose of the maximum limitation of this Article all defined-benefit plans maintained by the Employer shall be viewed as a single plan.

(d) If the "annual benefit" begins before age 62, the $90,000 limitation (but not the 100% of compensation limitation) shall be actuarially reduced so that it is the equivalent of an "annual benefit" beginning at age 62. However, the limitation shall not be actuarially reduced to less than (1) $75,000, if the "annual benefit" commences on or after age 55, or (2) the amount which is the actuarial equivalent of $75,000 at age 55, if the "annual benefit" commences prior to age 55.

(e) If the "annual benefit" begins after age 65, the $90,000 limitation shall be increased so that it is the actuarial equivalent of the maximum "annual benefit" at age 65.

(f) For purposes of adjusting any "annual benefit" payable prior to age 62 or in a form other than a straight life annuity, the interest rate assumption shall be the greater of five percent (5%) or the rate specified in Section 1.3 for preretirement interest.

(g) For purposes of adjusting any "annual benefit" payable after age 65, the interest assumption shall be the greater of five percent (5%) or the rate specified in Section 1.3 for postretirement interest.

(h) For purposes of adjusting any "annual benefit" under subparagraph (b), (d), and/or (e), no adjustments shall be taken into account before the year for which such adjustment first takes effect.

(i) Secondary Maximum Annual Benefit: If a Retired Participant has less than 10 Years of Service with the Employer, the maximum "annual benefit" payable to the Retired Participant shall be reduced by multiplying such maximum "annual benefit" by the fraction, the numerator of which is the number of Years of Service, or part thereof, with the Employer, and the denominator of which is ten (10).

(j) Exception Benefit: Subject to the limitations of Section 6.1(i) above, this Plan may pay an "annual benefit" to any Retired Participant which shall exceed 100% of such Participant's average compensation (6.1(a) above), provided the "annual benefit" shall not be in excess of $10,000 for the current Plan Year and for all other prior Plan Years, and provided the Participant shall not be or have been at any time considered as an active Participant in any defined-contribution plan maintained by the Employer.

(k) Multiple Plan Reduction: If an Employee is a Participant in one or more defined-benefit plans and one or more defined-contribution plans maintained by the Employer, the sum of the defined-benefit plan fraction and the defined-contribution plan fraction for any year may not exceed 1.0. The defined-benefit plan fraction for any year is a fraction, the numerator of which is the projected "annual benefit" of the Participant under the Plan (determined as of the close of the Plan Year), and the denominator of which is the lesser of (1) the product of 1.25 mutiplied by the maximum dollar limitation in effect under Section 415(b)

(1) (A) of the Code for such year, or (2) the product of 1.4 multiplied by the amount which may be taken into account under Section 415(b) (1) (B) of the Code for such year. The defined-contribution plan fraction for any year is a fraction, the numerator of which is the sum of the "annual additions" to the Participant's Account as of the close of the Plan Year, and the denominator of which is the sum of the lesser of the following amounts determined for such year and each prior year of service with the Employer: (1) the product of 1.25 multiplied by the dollar limitation in effect under Section 415(c) (1) (A) of the Code for such year (determined without regard to Section 415(c) (6) of the Code), or (2) the product of 1.4 multiplied by the amount which may be taken into account under Section 415(c) (1) (B) of the Code for such year.

Notwithstanding the foregoing, for any Topheavy Plan Year, 1.0 shall be substituted for 1.25 unless the extra minimum benefit is being provided pursuant to Section 5.2. However, for any Plan Year in which this Plan is a Super Topheavy Plan, 1.0 shall be substituted for 1.25 in any event.

For the purposes of this paragraph, the term "Participant's Account" shall mean the account established and maintained by the Administrator for each Participant with respect to his total interest in the defined-contribution plan maintained by the Employer resulting from the Employer's contribution.

(l) Special Rule for Defined-Contribution fraction: At the election of the Administrator, in applying the provisions of Section 6.1(k) with respect to the defined-contribution plan fraction for any Plan Year ending after December 31, 1982, the amount taken into account for the denominator for each Participant for all Plan Years ending before January 1, 1983, shall be an amount equal to the product of (a) the amount of the denominator determined under Section 6.1(k) (as in effect for the Plan Year ending in 1982) for Plan Years ending in 1982, multiplied by (b) the "transition fraction."

For purposes of the preceding paragraph, the term "transition fraction" shall mean a fraction, the numerator of which is the lesser of (1) $51,875 or (2) 1.4 multiplied by twenty-five percent (25%) of the Participant's compensation for the Plan Year ending in 1981, and the denominator of which is the lesser of (1) $41,500 or (2) twenty-five percent (25%) of the Participant's compensation for the Plan Year ending in 1981.

Notwithstanding the foregoing, for any Topheavy Plan Year, $41,500 shall be substituted for $51,875 in determining the "transition fraction," unless the extra minimum benefit is being provided under Section 5.2.

(m)   Excessive Benefit: If the sum of the defined-benefit plan fraction and the defined-contribution plan fraction shall exceed 1.0 in any year for any Participant in this Plan, the Employer shall adjust the numerator of the defined-contribution plan fraction so that the sum of both fractions shall not exceed 1.0 in any year for such Participant.

(n)   "Annual benefit" as used in this Article shall mean the benefit payable from the Plan for retirement purposes on an annualized basis.

(o)   Limitation Year: For purposes of determining "annual benefits," the limitation year shall be the Plan Year.

(p)   In the case of a group of employers which constitutes either a controlled group of corporations, trades, or businesses under common control (as defined in Section 1563(a) or Section 414(b) as modified by Section 415(h) and Section 414(c) of the Code), or an affiliated service group (as defined by Section 414(m) of the Code), all such employers shall be considered a single employer for purposes of applying the limitation of section 415 of the Code.

(q)   The maximum benefit stated in paragraph (a) above shall be adjusted annually as provided by Section 415(d) of the Code to take into account increases in cost of living as allowed by TEFRA in accordance with the regulations prescribed by the Secretary of the Treasury. The adjusted dollar limitation is effective as of January 1 of each calendar year and applies with respect to the limitation year ending with or within that calendar year.

(r)   Except as specifically permitted in the Regulations of the Secretary of the Treasury under Section 415 of the Code, the benefits paid or payable at any time shall not exceed the limitations of subparagraph (a) above.

ARTICLE VII
TRUSTEE

7.1   *BASIC RESPONSIBILITIES OF THE TRUSTEE*

The Trustee shall have the following categories of responsibilities:

(a)   Consistent with the "funding policy and method" determined by the Employer, to invest, manage, and control the Plan assets subject, however, to the direction of an Investment Manager if the Employer should appoint such manager as to all or a portion of the assets of the Plan in accordance with the provisions of Section 2.3(c);

(b) At the direction of the Administrator, to pay benefits required under the Plan to be paid to Participants, or, in the event of their death, to their Beneficiaries;

(c) To maintain records of receipts and disbursements, and furnish to the Employer and/or Administrator for each Fiscal Year a written annual report per Section 7.7.

If there shall be more than one Trustee, they shall act by a majority of their number but may authorize one or more of them to sign papers on their behalf.

7.2 INVESTMENT POWERS AND DUTIES OF THE TRUSTEE

(a) The Trustee shall invest and reinvest the Trust Fund to keep the Trust Fund invested without distinction between principal and income and in such securities or property, real or personal, wherever situated, as the Trustee shall deem advisable, including, but not limited to, stocks, common or preferred, bonds and other evidences of indebtedness or ownership, and real estate or any interest therein. The Trustee shall at all times in making investments of the Trust Fund consider, among other factors, the short- and long-term financial needs of the Plan on the basis of information furnished by the Employer. In making such investments, the Trustee shall not be restricted to securities or other property of the character expressly authorized by the applicable law for trust investments; however, the Trustee shall give due regard to any limitations imposed by the Code or the Act so that at all times this Plan may qualify as a qualified Pension Plan and Trust.

(b) The Trustee may employ a bank or trust company pursuant to the terms of its usual and customary bank agency agreement, under which the duties of such bank or trust company shall be of a custodial, clerical, and recordkeeping nature.

(c) The Trustee may from time to time with the consent of the Employer transfer to a common, collective, or pooled trust fund maintained by any corporate Trustee hereunder, all or such part of the Trust Fund as the Trustee may deem advisable, and such part or all of the Trust Fund so transferred shall be subject to all the terms and provisions of the common, collective, or pooled trust fund, which contemplate the commingling for investment purposes of such trust assets with trust assets of other trusts. The Trustee may, from time to time with the consent of the Employer, withdraw from such common, collective, or pooled trust fund all or such part of the Trust Fund as the Trustee may deem advisable.

(d)   If life insurance policies have been issued under the Plan to insure the death benefits provided hereunder, the Trustee, at the direction of the Administrator, shall apply for, own, and pay premiums on such life insurance policies. Life insurance policies shall, at the direction of the Administrator, be surrendered to the insurer for their cash value or transferred to the Former Participant under the terms of this Agreement. The Trustee must convert the entire value of life insurance policies at retirement into cash or provide for a periodic income (under the terms of this Agreement) so that no portion of such value may be used to continue life insurance protection.

7.3   *OTHER POWERS OF THE TRUSTEE*

The Trustee, in addition to all powers and authorities under common law, statutory authority including the Act, and other provisions of this Agreement, shall have the following powers and authorities, to be exercised in the Trustee's sole discretion:

(a)   To purchase, or subscribe for, any securities or other property, and to retain the same. In conjunction with the purchase of securities, margin accounts may be opened and maintained;

(b)   To sell, exchange, convey, transfer, grant options to purchase, or otherwise dispose of any securities or other property held by the Trustee, by private contract or at public auction. No person dealing with the Trustee shall be bound to see to the application of the purchase money or to inquire into the validity, expediency, or propriety of any such sale or other disposition, with or without advertisement;

(c)   to vote upon any stocks, bonds, or other securities; to give general or special proxies or powers of attorney with or without power of substitution; to exercise any conversion privileges, subscription rights, or other options, and to make any payments incidental thereto; to oppose or to consent to, or otherwise participate in, corporate reorganizations or other changes affecting corporate securities, to delegate discretionary powers, and to pay any assessments or charges in connection therewith; and generally to exercise any of the powers of an owner with respect to stocks, bonds, securities, or other property;

(d) To cause any securities or other property to be registered in the Trustee's own name or in the name of one or more of the Trustee's nominees, and to hold any investments in bearer form; but the books and records of the Trustee shall at all times show that all such investments are part of the Trust Fund;

(e) To borrow or raise money for the purposes of the Plan in such amount and upon such terms and conditions, as the Trustee shall deem advisable; and for any sum so borrowed, to issue a promissory note as Trustee, and to secure the repayment thereof by pledging all, or any part, of the Trust Fund; and no person lending money to the Trustee shall be bound to see to the application of the money lent or to inquire into the validity, expediency, or propriety of any borrowing;

(f) To keep such portion of the Trust Fund in cash or cash balances as the Trustee may, from time to time, deem to be in the best interests of the Plan, without liability for interest thereon;

(g) To accept and retain for such time as the Trustee may deem advisable any securities or other property received or acquired as Trustee hereunder, whether or not such securities or other property would normally be purchased as investments hereunder;

(h) To make, execute, acknowledge, and deliver any and all documents of transfer and conveyance and any and all other instruments that may be necessary or appropriate to carry out the powers herein granted;

(i) To settle, compromise, or submit to arbitration any claims, debts, or damages due or owing to or from the Plan, to commence or defend suits or legal or administrative proceedings, and to represent the Plan in all suits and legal and administrative proceedings;

(j) To employ suitable agents and counsel, and to pay their reasonable expenses and compensation (such agent or counsel may or may not be agent or counsel for the Employer);

(k) To apply for and procure from responsible insurance companies, to be selected by the Administrator, as an investment of the Trust Fund, such annuity or other Contracts (on the life of any Participant) as the Administrator shall deem proper; to exercise, at any time or from time to time, whatever rights and privileges may be granted under such annuity or other Contracts; to collect, receive, and settle for the proceeds of all such annuity or other Contracts as and when entitled to do so under the provisions thereof;

(l) To invest funds of the Trust in time deposits or savings accounts bearing a reasonable rate of interest in the Trustee's bank;

(m)   To invest in Treasury Bills and other forms of United States government obligations;

(n)   Except as hereinafter expressly authorized, the Trustee is prohibited from selling or purchasing stock options. The Trustee is expressly authorized to write and sell call options under which the holder of the option has the right to purchase shares of stock held by the Trustee as a part of the assets of this Trust, if such options are traded on and sold through a national securities exchange registered under the Securities Exchange Act of 1934, as amended, which exchange has been authorized to provide a market for option contracts pursuant to Rule 9B-1 promulgated under such Act, and as long as the Trustee at all times, up to and including the time of exercise or expiration of any such option, holds sufficient stock in the assets of this Trust to meet the obligations under such option if exercised. In addition, the Trustee is expressly authorized to purchase and acquire call options for the purchase of shares of stock covered by such options if the options are traded on and purchased through a national securities exchange as described in the immediately preceding sentence, and as long as any such option is purchased solely in a closing purchase transaction, meaning the purchase of an exchange traded call option, the effect of which is to reduce or eliminate the obligations of the Trustee with respect to a stock option contract or contracts which it has previously written and sold in a transaction authorized under the immediately preceding sentence;

(o)   To deposit monies in federally insured savings accounts or certificates of deposit in banks or savings and loan associations;

(p)   To pool all or any of the Trust Fund, from time to time, with assets belonging to any other qualified employee pension benefit trust created by the Employer or an affiliated company of the Employer, and to commingle such assets and make joint or common investments and carry joint accounts on behalf of this Plan and such other trust or trusts, allocating undivided shares or interests in such investments or accounts or any pooled assets of the two or more trusts in accordance with their respective interests;

(q)   To do all such acts and exercise all such rights and privileges, although not specifically mentioned herein, as the Trustee may deem necessary to carry out the purposes of the Plan.

7.4   *LOANS TO PARTICIPANTS*

(a)   The Trustee may, in the Trustee's sole discretion, make loans to the Participants and Beneficiaries under the following circumstances:

    (1) Loans shall be made available to all Participants and Beneficiaries on a reasonably equivalent basis;

    (2) Loans shall not be made available to highly compensated Employees, officers, or shareholders in an amount greater than the amount made available to other Participants and Beneficiaries;

    (3) Loans shall bear a reasonable rate of interest;

    (4) Loans shall be adequately secured; and

    (5) Loans shall provide for periodic repayment over a reasonable period of time.

(b) Loans shall not be made to any Owner-Employee.

(c) Loans shall not be granted to any Participant or his Beneficiary, that provide for a repayment period extending beyond such Participant's Normal Retirement Date.

(d) Loans made pursuant to this Section shall be limited to the lesser of

    (i) $50,000, or

    (ii) one-half (½) of the present value of the Vested interest of such Participant's Accrued Benefit (but not less than $10,000).

(e) Loans shall provide for periodic repayment over a period not to exceed five (5) years.

(f) However, loans used to acquire, construct, reconstruct, or substantially rehabilitate any dwelling unit which, within a reasonable time, is to be used (determined at the time the loan is made) as a principal residence of the Participant or a member of his family (within the meaning of Section 267(c) (4) of the Code), shall provide for periodic repayment over a reasonable period of time that may exceed five (5) years.

7.5 DUTIES OF THE TRUSTEE REGARDING PAYMENTS

At the direction of the Administrator, the Trustee shall from time to time, in accordance with the terms of the Plan, make payments out of the Trust Fund. The Trustee shall not be responsible in any way for the application of such payments.

7.6 TRUSTEE'S COMPENSATION, EXPENSES, AND TAXES

The Trustee shall be paid such reasonable compensation as shall from time to time be agreed upon in writing by the Employer and the Trustee. An individual serving as Trustee who already receives full-time pay from the Employer shall not receive compensation from this Plan. In addition, the Trustee shall be reimbursed for any reasonable expenses, including reasonable counsel fees incurred by it as Trustee. Such compensation and expenses shall be paid from the Trust Fund, unless paid or advanced by the Employer. All taxes of any kind that may be levied or assessed under existing or future laws upon, or in respect of, the Trust Fund or the income thereof, shall be paid from the Trust Fund.

7.7 *ANNUAL REPORT OF THE TRUSTEE*

Within sixty (60) days after the later of the Anniversary Date or receipt of the Employer's contribution for each Fiscal Year, the Trustee shall furnish to the Employer and Administrator a written statement of account with respect to the Fiscal Year for which such contribution was made setting forth the following:

(a) the net income, or loss, of the Trust Fund;

(b) the gains, or losses, realized by the Trust Fund upon sales or other disposition of the assets;

(c) the increase, or decrease, in the value of the Trust Fund;

(d) all payments and distributions made from the Trust Fund; and

(e) such further information as the Trustee and/or Administrator deems appropriate.

The Employer, forthwith upon its receipt of each such statement of account, shall acknowledge receipt thereof in writing and advise the Trustee and/or Administrator of its approval or disapproval thereof. Failure by the Employer to disapprove any such statement of account within thirty (30) days after its receipt thereof shall be deemed an approval thereof. The approval by the Employer of any statement of account shall be binding as to all matters embraced therein as between the Employer and the Trustee, to the same extent as if the account of the Trustee had been settled by judgment or decree in an action for a judicial settlement of its account in a court of competent jurisdiction in which the Trustee, the Employer, and all persons having or claiming an interest in the Plan were parties; provided, however, that nothing herein contained shall deprive the Trustee of its right to have its accounts judicially settled if the Trustee so desires.

7.8 *AUDIT*

(a) If an audit of the Plan's records shall be required by the Act and the regulations thereunder for any Plan Year, the Administrator shall direct the Trustee to engage on behalf of all Participants an independent qualified public accountant for that purpose. Such accountant shall, after an audit of the books and records of the Plan in accordance with generally accepted auditing standards, within a reasonable period after the close of the Plan Year, furnish to the Administrator and the Trustee a report of his audit setting forth his opinion as to whether each of the following statements, schedules or lists, or any others that are required by Section 103 of the Act or the Secretary of Labor to be filed with the Plan's annual report, are presented fairly in conformity with generally accepted accounting principles applied consistently:

   (i) Statement of the assets and liabilities of the Plan;

   (ii) Statement of changes in net assets available to the Plan;

   (iii) Statement of receipts and disbursements, a schedule of all assets held for investment purposes, a schedule of all loans or fixed income obligations in default at the close of the Plan Year;

   (iv) A list of all leases in default or uncollectible during the Plan Year;

   (v) The most recent annual statement of assets and liabilities of any bank common or collective trust fund in which Plan assets are invested or such information regarding separate accounts or trusts with a bank or insurance company as the Trustee and Administrator deem necessary; and

   (vi) A schedule of each transaction or series of transactions involving an amount in excess of three percent (3%) of Plan assets.

   All auditing and accounting fees shall be an expense of the Trust Fund and may, at the election of the Administrator, be paid from it.

(b) If some or all of the information necessary to enable the Administrator to comply with Section 103 of the Act is maintained by a bank, insurance company, or similar institution, and regulated and supervised and subject to periodic examination by a state or federal agency, the bank, insurance company, or other institution shall transmit and certify the accuracy of that information to the Administrator as provided in Section 103(b) of the Act within one hundred twenty (120) days after the end of the Plan Year or such other date as may be prescribed under regulations of the Secretary of Labor.

7.9 *RESIGNATION, REMOVAL, AND SUCCESSION OF TRUSTEE*

(a) The Trustee may resign at any time by delivering to the Employer, at least thirty (30) days before its effective date, a written notice of his resignation.

(b) The Employer may remove theTrustee by mailing by registered or certified mail, addressed to such Trustee at his last known address, at least thirty (30) days before its effective date, a written notice of his removal.

(c) Upon the death, resignation, incapacity, or removal of any Trustee, a successor may be appointed by the Employer; and such successor, upon accepting such appointment in writing and delivering same to the Employer, shall, without further act, become vested with all the estate, rights, powers, discretions, and duties of his predecessor with like respect as if he were originally named as a Trustee herein. Until such a successor is appointed, the remaining Trustee or Trustees shall have full authority to act under the terms of this Agreement.

(d) The Employer may designate one or more successors prior to the death, resignation, incapacity, or removal of a Trustee. In the event a successor is so designated by the Employer and accepts such designation, the successor shall, without further act, become vested with all the estate, rights, powers, discretions, and duties of his predecessor with the like effect as if he were originally named as Trustee, herein immediately upon the death, resignation, incapacity, or removal of his predecessor.

(e) Whenever any Trustee hereunder ceases to serve as such, he shall furnish to the Employer and Administrator a written statement of account with respect to the portion of the Fiscal Year during which he served as Trustee. This statement shall be either (i) included as part of the annual statement of account for the Fiscal Year required under Section 7.7 or (ii) set forth in a special statement. Any such special statement of account should be rendered to the Employer no later than the due date of the annual statement of account for the Fiscal Year. The procedures set forth in Section 7.7 for the approval by the Employer of annual statements of account shall apply to any special statement of account rendered hereunder, and approval by the Employer of any such special statement in the manner provided in Section 7.7 shall have the same effect upon the statement as the Employer's approval of an annual statement of account. No successor to the Trustee shall have any duty or responsibility to investigate the acts or transactions of any predecessor who has rendered all statements of account required by Section 7.7 and this subparagraph.

7.10 TRANSFER OF INTEREST

Notwithstanding any other provision contained in this Plan, the Trustee at the direction of the Administrator shall transfer, upon a One-Year Break in Service of a Participant, the Vested interest, if any, of such Participant in the Present Value of his Accrued Benefit to another trust forming part of a pension, profit-sharing, or stock bonus plan maintained by such Participant's new employer and represented by said employer in writing as meeting the requirements of Code Section 401(a), provided that the trust to which such transfers are made permits the transfer to be made.

The Trustee may accept funds transferred from such trusts or a "conduit" Individual Retirement Account for the account of a Participant under this Plan, provided the conditions precedent to such transfer set forth in Section 4.3 are satisfied. In the event of such a transfer to a Participant's Account under this Plan, the Trustee shall maintain a separate, nonforfeitable "Participant's Rollover Account" for the amount transferred. The Trustee may act upon the direction of the Administrator without determining the facts concerning a transfer.

ARTICLE VIII
PLAN AMENDMENT

8.1 AMENDMENT

The Employer shall have the right at any time and from time to time to amend, in whole or in part, any or all of the provisions of this Agreement. However, no such amendment shall authorize or permit any part of the Trust Fund (other than such part as is required to pay taxes and administration expenses) to be used for or diverted to purposes other than for the exclusive benefit of the Participants or their Beneficiaries or estates; no such amendment shall cause any reduction in the Accrued Benefit of any Participant theretofore, or cause or permit any portion of the Trust Fund to revert to or become the property of the Employer; and no such amendment which affects the rights, duties, or responsibilities of the Trustee and Administrator may be made without the Trustee's and Administrator's written consent. Any such amendment shall become effective upon delivery of a duly executed instrument, provided that the Trustee shall in writing consent to the terms of such amendment, if the Trust provisions contained herein are a part of this Agreement.

ARTICLE IX
PLAN TERMINATION

9.1   *TERMINATION*

The Employer shall have the right at any time to terminate the Plan by delivering to the Trustee and Administrator written notice of such termination. Upon any termination (full or partial), all unallocated amounts shall be allocated in accordance with the provisions hereof, and the Accrued Benefit of each affected Participant shall become fully Vested and shall not thereafter be subject to Forfeiture. Upon termination of the Plan, the Employer, by written notice to the Trustee, may direct either

(a)   continuation of the Trust created by this Agreement and the distribution of benefits at such time and in such manner as though the Plan had not been terminated; or

(b)   subject to the following paragraphs of this Section, complete distribution of the assets in the Trust Fund to the Participants, in cash or in kind, in one lump-sum payment, or in the form of a deferred annuity payable at Normal Retirement Date, as soon as the Trustee deems it in the best interest of the Participants (no later than three (3) years after such termination).

Plan Termination Procedure

(a)   The Employer must first notify the Pension Benefit Guaranty Corporation at least ten (10) days prior to the date of the proposed termination.

(b)   No termination distribution shall be made pending notification from the Pension Benefit Guaranty Corporation as to whether the Trust Assets are sufficient to discharge all insured benefit obligations. Notification that Assets are not sufficient shall be treated as a termination by the Pension Benefit Guaranty Corporation as of the date of notification.

Priority of Benefits

Upon approval from the Pension Benefit Guaranty Corporation of the Plan termination, the Administrator shall allocate the assets of the Plan among Participants and Beneficiaries in the following order of priority and subject in any event to the provisions of the Act:

(a) first to that portion of each Participant's Accrued Benefit which is derived from his Voluntary Contributions;

(b) equally among individuals in the following two categories:

(1) Benefits to Retired Participants and their Beneficiaries to whom payment commenced at least three (3) years prior to the termination date, based on Plan provisions in effect during the five (5) year period ending on such date; the lowest benefit in any pay status during the most recent three (3) year period shall be considered the benefit in pay status for such period.

(2) Benefits as respects a Participant wherein payment would have commenced at least three (3) years prior to the termination date if the Participant had actually retired, based on the lowest benefit determined under the Plan provisions in effect during the five (5) year period ending on such date.

(c) All other benefits guaranteed (insured under the Act determined without regard to Section 4022 (b) (5)) thereof; and additional benefits, if any, under this subparagraph if Section 4022(b) (6) of the Act did not apply.

(d) All other (uninsured) Vested benefits.

(e) All other benefits under the Plan.

(f) Return of any excess funds to the Employer or reallocated to the Participants on the basis of their Present Value of Accrued Benefit, if authorized by the Employer, only after satisfaction of all liabilities, fixed and contingent.

9.2 *LIMITATION OF BENEFITS ON EARLY TERMINATION*

In the event the Plan is terminated for any reason other than the failure to obtain Internal Revenue Service approval pursuant to Section 11.14, then notwithstanding any provision in this Plan to the contrary, during the first ten (10) years after the Effective Date hereof, and thereafter until full current costs are met, the benefits provided by the Employer's contributions for the Participants whose anticipated annual retirement benefit at Normal Retirement Date exceeds $1,500 and who at the Effective Date of the Plan were among the twenty-five (25) highest paid Employees of the Employer will be subject to the conditions set forth in the following paragraphs:

(a) Such benefits payable to any such Participant or his Beneficiary shall not exceed those purchasable by the greater of (1) $20,000 or (2) an amount equal to 20% of the first $50,000 of the Participant's annual Compensation multiplied by the number of years from the Effective Date of this Agreement to (i) the date of termination of the Plan, (ii) in the case of an Employee described in the first paragraph of this Section, the date the benefit of the Employee becomes payable, if before the date of the termination of the Plan, or (iii) in the case of an Employee described in the first paragraph of this Section, the date of the failure to meet the full current costs of the Plan.

(b) If the Plan is terminated or the full current costs thereof have not been met at any time within ten (10) years after the Effective Date, the benefits which any of the Participants described in this Section may receive from the Employer's contribution shall not exceed the benefits set forth in Section 9.2(a). If at the end of the first ten (10) years the full current costs are not met, the restrictions will continue to apply until the full current costs are funded for the first time.

(c) If a Participant described in this Section leaves the employ of the Employer or withdraws from participation in the Plan when the full current costs have been met, the benefits which he may receive from the Employer contributions shall not at any time within the first ten (10) years after the Effective Date exceed the benefits set forth in Section 9.2(a), except as provided in Section 9.2(i).

(d) These conditions shall not restrict the full payment of any survivor's benefits on behalf of a Participant who dies while in the Plan and for whom the full current costs have been met.

(e) These conditions shall not restrict the current payment of full retirement benefits called for by the Plan for any Retired Participant while the Plan is in full effect and its full current costs have been met, provided an agreement, adequately secured, guarantees the repayment of any part of the distribution that is or may become restricted.

(f) If the benefits of, or with respect to, any Participant shall have been suspended or limited in accordance with the limitations of Section 9.2(a), (b), and (c) above because the full current costs of the Plan shall not then have been met, and if such full current costs shall thereafter be met, then the full amount of the benefits payable to such Participant shall be resumed and the parts of such benefits which have been suspended shall then be paid in full.

(g) Notwithstanding anything in Section 9.2(a), (b), and (c) above, if on the termination of the Plan within the first ten (10) years after the Effective Date, the funds, Contracts, or other property under the Plan are more than sufficient to provide Accrued Benefits as defined in Section 1.1 for Participants and their Beneficiaries including full benefits for all

Participants other than such of the twenty-five (25) highest paid Employees as are still in the service of the Employer and also including Accrued Benefits as limited by this Section for such twenty-five (25) highest paid Employees, then any excess of such funds, Contracts, and property shall be used to provide Accrued Benefits for the twenty-five (25) highest paid Employees in excess of such limitations of this Section up to the benefits to which such Employees would be entitled under Section 1.1 without such limitations.

(h) In the event that Congress should provide by statute, or the Treasury Department or the Internal Revenue Service should provide by regulation or ruling, that the limitations provided for in this Article are no longer necessary in order to meet the requirements for a qualified pension plan under the Internal Revenue Code as then in effect, the limitations in this Article shall become void and shall no longer apply without the necessity of amendment to this Plan.

(i) In the event a lump-sum distribution is made to an Employee, subject to the above restrictions, in an amount in excess of that amount otherwise permitted under this Article, an agreement shall be made, with adequate security guaranteeing repayment of any amount of the distribution that is restricted. Adequate security shall mean property having a fair market value of at least 125% of the amount which would be repayable if the Plan had terminated on the date of distribution of such lump sum. If the fair market value of the property falls below 110% of the amount which would then be repayable if the Plan were then to terminate, the distributee shall deposit additional property to bring the value of the property to 125% of such amount.

ARTICLE X
MERGER, CONSOLIDATION, OR TRANSFER OF ASSETS

10.1 REQUIREMENTS

Before this Plan can be merged or consolidated with any other qualified plan or its assets or liabilities transferred to any other qualified plan, the Administrator must secure (and file with the Secretary of Treasury at least 30 days beforehand) a certification from a government-enrolled actuary that the benefits which would be received by a Participant of this Plan, in the event of a termination of the Plan immediately after such transfer, merger, or consolidation, are at least equal to the benefits the Participant would have received if the Plan had terminated immediately before the transfer, merger, or consolidation.

ARTICLE XI
MISCELLANEOUS

11.1   *PARTICIPANT'S RIGHTS*

This Plan shall not be deemed to constitute a contract between the Employer and any Participant or to be a consideration or an inducement for the employment of any Participant or Employee. Nothing contained in this Plan shall be deemed to give any Participant or Employee the right to be retained in the service of the Employer or to interfere with the right of the Employer to discharge any Participant or Employee at any time regardless of the effect which such discharge shall have upon him as a Participant of this Plan.

11.2   *ALIENATION*

No benefit which shall be payable out of the Trust Fund to any person (including a Participant or his Beneficiary) shall be subject in any manner to anticipation, alienation, sale, transfer, assignment, pledge, encumbrance, or charge, and any attempt to anticipate, alienate, sell, transfer, assign, pledge, encumber, or charge the same shall be void; and no such benefit shall in any manner be liable for, or subject to, the debts, contracts, liabilities, engagements, or torts of any such person, nor shall it be subject to attachment or legal process for or against such person, and the same shall not be recognized by the Trustee, except to such extent as may be required by law. However, this provision shall not apply to the extent a Participant or Beneficiary is indebted to the Plan, for any reason, under any provision of this Agreement. At the time a distribution is to be made to or for a Participant's or Beneficiary's benefit, such proportion of the amount distributed as shall equal such indebtedness shall be paid by the Trustee to the Trustee or the Administrator, at the direction of the Administrator, to apply against or discharge such indebtedness. Prior to making a payment, however, the Participant or Beneficiary must be given written notice by the Administrator that such indebtedness is to be deducted in whole or part from his Participant's Accrued Benefit. If the Participant or Beneficiary does not agree that the indebtedness is a valid claim against his Vested Participant's Accrued Benefit, he shall be entitled to a review of the validity of the claim in accordance with procedures provided in Sections 2.12 and 2.13.

In the event a Participant's benefits are garnisheed or attached by order of any court, the Administrator may bring an action for a declaratory judgment in a court of competent jurisdiction to determine the proper recipient of the benefits to be paid by the Plan. During the pendency of said action, any benefits that become payable shall be paid into the court as they become payable, to be distributed by the court to the recipient it deems proper at the close of said action.

11.3 CONSTRUCTION OF AGREEMENT

This Plan and Trust shall be construed and enforced according to the Act and the laws of the State of Chicago, other than its laws respecting choice of law, and to the extent not pre-empted by the Act.

11.4 GENDER AND NUMBER

Wherever any words are used herein in the masculine, feminine, or neuter gender, they shall be construed as though they were also used in another gender in all cases where they would so apply, and whenever any words are used herein in the singular or plural form, they shall be construed as though they were also used in the other form in all cases where they would so apply.

11.5 LEGAL ACTION

In the event any claim, suit, or proceeding is brought regarding the Trust and/or Plan established hereunder to which the Trustee or the Administrator may be a party, and such claim, suit, or proceeding is resolved in favor of the Trustee or Administrator, they shall be entitled to be reimbursed from the Trust Fund for any and all costs, attorney's fees, and other expenses pertaining thereto incurred by them for which they shall have become liable.

11.6 PROHIBITION AGAINST DIVERSION OF FUNDS

It shall be impossible by operation of the Plan or of the Trust, by termination of either, by power of revocation or amendment, by the happening of any contingency, by collateral arrangement, or by any other means, for any part of the corpus or income of any trust fund maintained pursuant to the Plan or any funds contributed thereto to be used for, or diverted to, purposes other than the exclusive benefit of Participants, Retired Participants, or their Beneficiaries.

11.7 *BONDING*

Every Fiduciary, except a bank or an insurance company, unless exempted by the Act and regulations thereunder, shall be bonded in an amount not less than 10% of the amount of the funds such Fiduciary handles, provided, however, that the minimum bond shall be $1,000 and the maximum bond, $500,000. The amount of funds handled shall be determined at the beginning of each Plan Year by the amount of funds handled by such person, group, or class to be covered and their predecessors, if any, during the preceding Plan Year, or if there is no preceding Plan Year, then by the amount of the funds to be handled during the then current year. The bond shall provide protection to the Plan against any loss by reason of acts of fraud or dishonesty by the Fiduciary alone or in connivance with others. The surety shall be a corporate surety company (as such term is used in Section 412(a) (2) of the Act), and the bond shall be in a form approved by the Secretary of Labor. Notwithstanding anything in this Agreement to the contrary, the cost of such bonds shall be an expense of and may be paid from, at the election of the Administrator, the Trust Fund or by the Employer.

11.8 *EMPLOYER'S AND TRUSTEE'S PROTECTIVE CLAUSE*

Neither the Employer nor the Trustee, nor their successors, shall be responsible for the validity of any Contract issued hereunder, for the failure on the part of the insurer to make payments provided by any such Contract, or for the action of any person which may delay payment or render a Contract null and void or unenforceable in whole or in part.

11.9 *INSURER'S PROTECTIVE CLAUSE*

Any insurer who shall issue Contracts hereunder shall not have any responsibility for the validity of this Plan or for the tax or legal aspects of this Plan. The insurer shall be protected and held harmless in acting in accordance with any written direction of the Trustee and shall have no duty to see to the application of any funds paid to the Trustee nor be required to question any actions directed by the Trustee. Regardless of any provision of this Plan, the insurer shall not be required to take or permit any action or allow any benefit or privilege contrary to the terms of any Contract which it issues hereunder or to the rules of the insurer.

11.10   *RECEIPT AND RELEASE FOR PAYMENTS*

Any payment to any Participant, his legal representative, Beneficiary, or to any guardian or committee appointed for such Participant or Beneficiary in accordance with the provisions of this Agreement, shall, to the extent thereof, be in full satisfaction of all claims hereunder against the Trustee and the Employer, either of whom may require such Participant, legal representative, Beneficiary, guardian or committee, as a condition precedent to such payment, to execute a receipt and release thereof in such form as shall be determined by the Trustee or Employer.

11.11   *ACTION BY THE EMPLOYER*

Whenever the Employer under the terms of this Agreement is permitted or required to do or perform any act or matter or thing, it shall be done and performed by a person duly authorized by its legally constituted authority.

11.12   *NAMED FIDUCIARIES AND ALLOCATION OF RESPONSIBILITY*

The "named Fiduciaries" of this Plan are (1) the Employer, (2) the Administrator, (3) the Trustee, and (4) any Investment Manager appointed hereunder. The named Fiduciaries shall have only those specific powers, duties, responsibilities, and obligations as are specifically given them under this Agreement. In general, the Employer shall have the sole responsibility for making the contributions provided for under Section 4.1 and shall have the sole authority to appoint and remove the Trustee, the Administrator, and any Investment Manager which may be provided for under this Agreement; for formulating the Plan's "funding policy and method;" and for amending or terminating, in whole or in part, this Agreement. The Administrator shall have the sole responsibility for the administration of this Agreement, which responsibility is specifically described in this Agreement. The Trustee shall have the sole responsibility of management of the assets held under the Trust, except those assets the management of which has been assigned to an Investment Manager, who shall be solely responsible for the management of the assets assigned to it, all as specifically provided in this Agreement. Each named Fiduciary warrants that any directions given, information furnished, or action taken by it shall be in accordance with the provisions of this Agreement, authorizing or providing for such direction, information or action. Furthermore, each named Fiduciary may rely upon any such direction, information, or action of another named Fiduciary as being proper under this Agreement, and is not required under this Agreement to inquire into the propriety of any such direction, information, or action. It is intended under this Agreement that each named Fiduciary shall be responsible for the proper exercise of its own powers, duties, responsibilities, and obligations under this Agreement. No named Fiduciary guarantees the Trust Fund in any manner against investment loss or depreciation in asset value. Any person or group may serve in more than one Fiduciary capacity.

11.13   *HEADINGS*

The headings and subheadings of this Agreement have been inserted for convenience of reference and are to be ignored in any construction of the provisions hereof.

11.14   *APPROVAL BY INTERNAL REVENUE SERVICE*

(a) Notwithstanding anything herein to the contrary, if, pursuant to an application filed by or on behalf of the Plan, the Commissioner of the Internal Revenue Service or his delegate should determine that the Plan does not initially qualify as a tax-exempt plan and trust under Sections 401 and 501 of the Code, and such determination is not contested, or if contested, is finally upheld, then the Plan shall be void ab initio, all amounts contributed to the Plan by the Employer, less expenses paid, shall be returned within one year, the Plan shall terminate, and the Trustee shall be discharged from all further obligations.

(b) In the case of a contribution which is made by a mistake of fact, such contribution shall be returned to the Employer within one year after the payment of the contribution.

(c) Notwithstanding any provisions to the contrary, except Sections 3.6 and 3.7, any contribution by the Employer to the Trust Fund is conditioned upon the deductibility of the contribution by the Employer under the Code, and, to the extent any such deduction is disallowed, the Employer may within one (1) year following a final determination of the disallowance, whether by agreement with the Internal Revenue Service or by final decision of a court of competent jurisdiction, demand repayment of such disallowed contribution, and the Trustee shall return such contribution within one (1) year following the disallowance.

11.15   *UNIFORMITY*

All provisions of this Plan shall be interpreted and applied in a uniform, nondiscriminatory manner.

ARTICLE XII
PARTICIPATING EMLOYERS

12.1   *ADOPTION BY OTHER EMPLOYERS*

Notwithstanding anything herein to the contrary, with the consent of the Employer and Trustee, any other corporation or entity (provided an Owner-Employee of such entity does not participate in the Plan for Plan Years beginning before January 1, 1984), whether an affiliate or subsidiary or not, may adopt this Plan and all of the provisions hereof and participate herein and be known as a Participating Employer, by a properly executed document evidencing said intent and will of such Participating Employer.

12.2   *REQUIREMENTS OF PARTICIPATING EMPLOYERS*

(a)   Each such Participating Employer shall be required to use the same Trustee as provided in this Plan.

(b)   The Trustee may, but shall not be required to, commingle, hold, and invest as one Trust Fund all contributions made by Participating Employers as well as all increments thereof.

(c)   The transfer of an Employer from or to a company participating in this Plan, whether he be an Employee of the Employer or a Participating Employer, shall not affect such Participant's rights under the Plan, and the Participant's Present Value of Accrued Benefit, his accumulated service time with the transferor or predecessor, and his length of participation in the Plan shall continue to his credit.

(d)   Any contributions made by a Participating Employer, as provided for in this Plan, shall be paid to and held by the Trustee for the exclusive benefit of the Employees of such Participating Employer and the Beneficiaries of such Employees, subject to all the terms and conditions of this Plan. On the basis of information furnished by the Administrator, the Trustee shall keep separate books and records concerning the affairs of each Participating Employer hereunder and as to the Accrued

Benefits of the Participants of each Participating Employer. The Trustee may, but need not, register Contracts so as to evidence that a particular Participating Employer is the interested Employer hereunder, but in any event of Employee transfer from one Participating Employer to another, the employing Employer shall immediately notify the Trustee thereof.

(e) In the event of termination of employment of any transferred Employee, any portion of the Accrued Benefit of such Employee which has not been Vested under the provisions of this Plan shall be allocated by the Trustee at the direction of the Administrator to the respective equities of the Participating Employers for whom such Employee has rendered service, in the proportion that each Participating Employer has contributed toward the benefits of such Employee. The amount so allocated shall be retained by the Trustee and shall be used to reduce the contribution by the respective Participating Employer, for the next succeeding year or years.

(f) Any expenses of the Trust which are to be paid by the Employer or borne by the Trust Fund shall be paid by each Participating Employer in the same proportion that the total amount standing to the credit of all Participants employed by such Employer bears to the total standing to the credit of all Participants.

12.3 *DESIGNATION OF AGENT*

Each Participating Employer shall be deemed to be a part of this Plan provided, however, that with respect to all of its relations with the Trustee and Administrator for the purpose of this Plan, each Participating Employer shall be deemed to have designated irrevocably the Employer as its agent. Unless the context of the Plan clearly indicates the contrary, the word "Employer" shall be deemed to include each Participating Employer as related to its adoption of the Plan.

12.4 *EMPLOYEE TRANSFERS*

It is anticipated that an Employee may be transferred between Participating Employers, and in the event of any such transfer, the Employee involved shall carry with him his accumulated service and eligibility. No such transfer shall effect a termination of employment hereunder, and the Participating Employer to which the Employee is transferred shall thereupon become obligated hereunder with respect to such Employee in the same manner as was the Participating Employer from whom the Employee was transferred.

12.5 *AMENDMENT*

Amendment of this Plan by the Employer at any time when there shall be a Participating Employer hereunder shall only be by the written action of each and every Participating Employer and with the consent of the Trustee where such consent is necessary in accordance with the terms of this Plan.

12.6 *DISCONTINUANCE OF PARTICIPATION*

Any Participating Employer shall be permitted to discontinue or revoke its participation in the Plan. At the time of any such discontinuance or revocation, satisfactory evidence thereof and of any applicable conditions imposed shall be delivered to the Trustee. The Trustee shall thereafter transfer, deliver, and assign Contracts and other Trust Fund assets allocable to the Participants of such Participating Employer to such new Trustee as shall have been designated by such Participating Employer, in the event that it has established a separate pension plan for its Employees. If no successor is designated, the Trustee shall retain such assets for the Employees of said Participating Employer pursuant to the provisions of Article VII hereof. In no such event shall any part of the corpus or income of the Trust as it relates to such Participating Employer be used for or diverted for purposes other than for the exclusive benefit of the Employees of such Participating Employer.

12.7 *ADMINISTRATOR'S AUTHORITY*

The Administrator shall have authority to make any and all necessary rules or regulations, binding upon all Participating Employers and all Participants, to effectuate the purpose of this Article.

IN WITNESS WHEREOF, this Agreement has been executed the day and year first above written.

Sample Company, Inc.

By _____
EMPLOYER

_____
TRUSTEE

(INTEG) DEFINED BENEFIT 001

No. _____	Atty. _____

FYE December 31
PYE December 31

Sample Company, Inc.
ANV December 31
1234 West Forsythe
INC 01-01-1980
Chicago, Illinois 60601
BUS CODE 1001
(312) 555-9876 CONTACT: _____
CO   ID   59-1234567

SAMPLE COMPANY, INC. DEFINED-BENEFIT PLAN AND TRUST
TRUSTEES: James Sample
EFF. DATE OF PLAN: January 1, 1984
EFF. DATE OF AMND:
NO: 1. _____   2. _____   3. _____   4. _____   5. _____

PLAN SPECIFICATIONS		SEC/PG
ACCRUED BENEFIT	Fractional, Plan Years of Service to NRD	1.1p374
	No accruals for 2 years	
ACTUARIAL EQUIV	Means amounts of equal value using preretirement, IAM	
	'71, 8%, postretirement, IAM '71	1.3p375
BENEFITS	24% of Compensation over Table	5.1p397
	Ben red one-nineteenth for ea yr under 19	5.1p397
—Minimum Benefits for Topheavy Plan		
	2% times Years of Service	5.2p399
—Disability	100% of present value of Accrued Benefit	5.4p400
—Death	Ins plus The Value of the Total Prior Contributions ...	5.5p401
	If less than ⅔ for ins; plcy plus side fund	5.5p401
—Early	None, treated as a terminated Participant	5.1(b)p398
—Late	Act. equiv of ben he wld hv received at NRD	5.1(d)p398
—Normal	Life and 120 mo certain or Act. Equiv.	5.1(d)p398
COMPENSATION	Total Plan Yr Comp paid or accrued excl Bonuses	1.13p376
	based on highest 5 total Years of Service	1.9p376
ELIGIBILITY	All Employees with;	1.18p377
	one (yr) & age 25	3.1p391
	Emp hired within 5 yrs of NRD are EXCLUDED	3.1p391
ENTRY DATE	First day of Plan Year	3.3p391
DISABILITY	Determined by S.S. benefits	1.46p381
INVESTMENTS		
—Loans	Participant loans allowed	7.4p420
PBGC	Plan is covered under PBGC	
RETIREMENT		
—Early	None	1.16p376
—Normal	First day of the month nearest 65th birthday	1.30p379
ROLLOVERS	Permitted	4.3p394
—Voluntary	10%	4.4p395

(INTEG) DEFINED BENEFIT 001 (continued)

PLAN SPECIFICATIONS	SEC/PG

TOPHEAVY PROVISIONS

Administration and Determination 2.1p382
Minimum Benefit Requirement 5.2p399
Topheavy Vesting Schedule 5.6p404

VESTING
—Include Svc Only with employer 1.52p381
—Schedule 4–40; 5–45; 6–50; 7–60; 8–70; 9–80; 10–90; 11–100% .... 5.6(b)p405
—Alternative Topheavy Vesting 5.6p404
—Schedule 2–20; 3–40; 4–60; 5–80; 6–100 .... 5.6p404

————————————— NOTES —————————————

An application is to be made to the Internal Revenue Service for a determination on the qualification of the following employee retirement plan:

Name of Plan: SAMPLE COMPANY, INC.
                                 DEFINED-BENEFIT PLAN AND TRUST

Name of Applicant: Sample Company, Inc.
                                        1234 West Forsythe
                                        Chicago, Illinois 60601

Applicant's I. D. Number: 59-1234567

Name of Plan Administrator: Sample Company, Inc.
                                        1234 West Forsythe
                                        Chicago, Illinois 60601

The application will be submitted on _____ to the District Director of the Internal Revenue at the below address for an advance determination as to whether the Plan qualifies under Section 401, 403(a), and 405(a) of the Internal Revenue Code of 1954, with respect to initial qualification.

A determination letter for the Plan has not previously been issued.

All Employees will be eligible to participate when age and service requirements, if applicable, are satisfied.

You have the right to submit, either individually or jointly with other interested parties, or request the Department of Labor to submit, to the District Director described above, your comment as to whether this Plan meets the qualification requirements of the Internal Revenue Code. If such a person or persons requests the Department of Labor to submit a comment, and that department declines to do so in respect of one or more matters raised in the request, the person or persons so requesting may submit a comment to the District Director in respect of the matters on which the Department of Labor declines to comment. A comment submitted to the District Director must be received on or before _____, the 45th day after the application is received by the IRS. A comment submitted to the District Director on a matter about which the Department of Labor refused to comment must be received by the later of _____, the 45th day after the application is received by the IRS, or the 15th day after the Department of Labor notified the interested party that it (the Department of Labor) refused to comment; but in no event can this type of comment be received later than _____, the 60th day after the original application was received by the Internal Revenue Service. The Department of Labor must receive a request to comment on the application no later than _____, the 25th day after the IRS receives the application; or, on or before _____, the 15th day after the application is received by the Internal Revenue Service, if the person or persons making the request wish to preserve their right to submit a comment to the District Director in the event the Department of Labor declines to comment.

The Department of Labor may not comment on behalf of interested parties unless requested to do so by the lesser of 10 employees or 10 percent of the employees who qualify as interested parties. If you request the Department to comment, your comment must be in writing, must specify the matters upon which comments are requested, and must include

(1) the name of the plan and plan number;

(2) the name and address of the company;

(3) the number of persons needed for the Department to comment.

A request to the Department to comment should be addressed as follows:

Administrator of Pension and Welfare Benefit Programs
U.S. Department of Labor
200 Constitution Avenue, N.W.
Washington, D.C. 20216
ATTN: 3001 Comment Request

Detailed instructions regarding the requirements for notification of interested parties may be found in Sections 6, 7, and 8 of Revenue Procedure 80-30. Additional information concerning this application (including, where applicable, an updated copy of the plan and related trust; the application for determination; any additional documents dealing with the application that have been submitted to the IRS; and copies of Section 6 of Revenue Procedure 80-30) is available at the company's principal and/or local office during the hours of 10:00 AM to 3:00 PM for inspection and copying. (There is a nominal charge for copying and/or mailing.)

INTERNAL REVENUE SERVICE, EP/EO DIVISION
230 S. Dearborn Street
Chicago, Illinois 60604

CERTIFICATE OF CORPORATE RESOLUTIONS

The undersigned Secretary of Sample Company, Inc. (the Corporation), hereby certifies that the following resolutions were duly adopted by the board of directors of the Corporation on _____, and that such resolutions have not been modified or rescinded as of the date hereof:

RESOLVED, that the form of Pension Plan and Trust effective January 1, 1984, presented to this meeting is hereby approved and adopted, and that the proper officers of the Corporation are hereby authorized and directed to execute and deliver to the Trustee of the Plan one or more counterparts of the Plan.

RESOLVED, that for purposes of the limitations on contributions and benefits under the Plan, prescribed by Section 415 of the Internal Revenue Code, the "limitation year" shall be a 12-month period ending on December 31, which is the Plan Year of the Plan.

RESOLVED, that prior to the due date (including extensions hereof) of the Corporation's federal income tax return for each of its fiscal years hereafter, the Corporation shall contribute to the Plan for each such fiscal year not less than such amount as shall be required to meet minimum funding standards, and that the Treasurer of the Corporation is authorized and directed to pay such contribution to the Trustee of the Plan in cash or property and to designate to the Trustee the fiscal year for which such contribution is made.

RESOLVED, that the proper officers of the Corporation shall act as soon as possible to notify the employees of the Corporation of the adoption of the Pension Plan by delivering to each employee a copy of the summary description of the Plan in the form of the Summary Plan Description presented to this meeting, which form is hereby approved.

The undersigned further certifies that attached hereto as Exhibits A, B, and C, respectively, are true copies of Sample Company, Inc. Defined-Benefit Plan and Trust, Summary Plan Description, and Funding Policy and Method, approved and adopted in the foregoing resolutions.

_____
Secretary

Date: _____

SAMPLE COMPANY, INC.
DEFINED-BENEFIT PLAN AND TRUST

FUNDING POLICY AND METHOD

A pension benefit plan (as defined in the Employee Retirement Income Security Act of 1974) has been adopted by the company for the purpose of rewarding long and loyal service to the company by providing to employees additional financial security at retirement. Incidental benefits are provided in the case of disability, death, or other termination of employment.

Since the principal purpose of the plan is to provide benefits at normal retirement age, the principal goal of the investment of the funds in the plan should be both security and long-term stability with moderate growth commensurate with the anticipated retirement dates of participants. Investments other than "fixed dollar" investments should be included among the plan's investments to prevent erosion by inflation. However, investments should be sufficiently liquid to enable the plan, on short notice, to make some distributions in the event of the death or disability of a participant.

431

Index

A

Actuarial assumptions:
  benefit costs, 161, 164–65
  interest, 161
  salary scales, 161, 163–64
  turnover, 161–62
Actuarial method, 30
  comparing methods, 34
  employer flexibility, 32–34
  frozen initial past service liability, 33–34
  individual level premium, 32–33
Administrative functions:
  chronological checklist, 279–84
Affiliated service organization, 247–48
Age and service requirements, 20
Annual additions, 57–61
  adjustment of, 59
  client's benefit, 59–60
  components of, 58
  limitations, 58–59
  trap, 131–32
Annual pension expense, 172–73

Annuity contracts, 292–93
Attained age level funding, 154–56
  real-life situations, 156–58
Avoiding income taxes, 3–4

B

Benefit approach, 48–49
Benefit-oriented pension plans, 42–43
  integration of, 43–45
Book value withdrawals, 291–92
Business maturity, 3

C

Calculating plan deposits, 30
Cash plans, 98–99
"Catch-up tier," 46
Census analysis, 17–18
Choosing investments, 286–87
  actuarial method, 286–87

433